MARRIAGE AND THE FAMILY

COLLEGE OUTLINE SERIES

MARRIAGE
and the
FAMILY

Second Edition

ALFRED McCLUNG LEE
and ELIZABETH BRIANT LEE

BARNES & NOBLE, INC. NEW YORK

Publishers . Booksellers . Since 1873

To

Leslie, Alfred, Guinevere, and Andrew

©

Printed in the United States of America

ABOUT THE AUTHORS

ALFRED MCCLUNG LEE received his B.A. and M.A. degrees from the University of Pittsburgh and his Ph.D. degree from Yale University. He has been on the faculties of Yale University, the University of Kansas, New York University, Wayne University, the University of Michigan, and Brooklyn College of the City University of New York, where he is Professor of Sociology. He has also served as UNESCO Professor of Sociology in Milan, as Senior Fulbright Lecturer in Sociology at the University of Rome, and as American Specialist Lecturer in universities in the Far and Middle East and in Europe and Iceland. Professor Lee organized and served as second president of the Society for the Study of Social Problems. He has also been president of the Michigan and the Eastern Sociological Societies. In addition to numerous articles in professional journals and symposiums here and abroad, his published works include *The Daily Newspaper in America, The Fine Art of Propaganda* (coauthor), *Race Riot* (coauthor), *Social Problems in America* (coauthor), *How to Understand Propaganda, Public Opinion and Propaganda* (co-editor, coauthor), *Fraternities Without Brotherhood, La Sociologia delle Comunicazioni* (Italian), *Che Cos'è la Propaganda* (Italian), *Multivalent Man,* and two companion College Outlines, *Principles of Sociology* (editor, coauthor) and *Readings in Sociology* (editor, co-author). Translations of his works have appeared in Arabic, Chinese, French, German, Hebrew, Hindi, Italian, Portuguese, and Spanish.

ELIZABETH BRIANT LEE received her B.A. and M.A. degrees from the University of Pittsburgh and her Ph.D. degree from Yale University. She has been on the faculties of Wayne University, Brooklyn College, the Hartford Seminary Foundation, Connecticut College for Women, and Fairleigh Dickinson University. She has also lectured in eleven Far and Middle Eastern and European countries and conducted special research in Ireland and Italy. In addition to many articles published in journals and magazines here and abroad, her works include: *Personnel Aspects of Social Work in Pittsburgh, Eminent Women: A Cultural Study, The Fine Art of Propaganda* (coauthor), *Social Problems in America* (coauthor), and *Mental Health and Mental Disorder: A Sociological Approach* (coeditor).

FOREWORD

Social scientists and social practitioners have produced a wealth of books, pamphlets, and articles on courtship, mate-selection, marriage, and family life. In this book, we summarize and interpret what we regard as the most useful among their findings. In doing so, we go beyond a mere synthesis. We include the results of our own research, and we try to present an integrated and helpful treatment. We want this book to be of service to students, to social workers and counselors, to social scientists, and to concerned parents and other general readers.

In preparing this work we both benefited from the experiences and suggestions given to us by our friends and associates. We especially wish to thank our colleagues and students at Brooklyn College of the City University of New York. The College administration was most considerate in providing facilities and in releasing time for research.

In this as in our other books in the College Outline Series, we have had the sympathetic aid, counsel, and keen suggestions of Dr. Samuel Smith, Editor-in-Chief, and, especially with this volume, the helpful assistance of Miss Nancy Cone and of Mr. Harvey Graveline of the Editorial Department, Barnes & Noble, Inc.

A. McC. L.
E. B. L.

TABLE OF CONTENTS

Part One: The Changing Family

Part Two: Childhood and Adolescence

Part Three: Courtship and Marriage

TABULATED BIBLIOGRAPHY
OF STANDARD TEXTBOOKS

The following list gives author, title, publisher, and date of the standard textbooks and books of readings referred to in the tables on pages xvi–xxi.

Bell, Norman W., and Ezra F. Vogel, eds., *A Modern Introduction to the Family*, rev. ed., 1968, Free Press.

Bell, Robert R., *Marriage and Family Interaction*, rev. ed., 1967, Dorsey Press.

Blood, Robert O., Jr., *Marriage*, 2nd ed., 1969, Free Press.

Bowman, Henry A., *Marriage for Moderns*, 5th ed., 1965, McGraw-Hill.

Burgess, Ernest W.; Locke, Harvey J.; and Thomas, Mary Margaret, *The Family: From Institution to Companionship*, 3rd ed., 1963, American Book.

Cavan, Ruth Shonle, *The American Family*, 4th ed., 1969, Thom. Y. Crowell.

Cavan, Ruth Shonle, ed., *Marriage and Family in the Modern World: A Book of Readings*, 2nd ed., 1965, Thom. Y. Crowell.

Christensen, Harold T., ed., *Handbook of Marriage and the Family*, 1964, Rand McNally.

Clemens, Alphonse H., *Design for Successful Marriage* (formerly *Marriage and the Family: An Integrated Approach for Catholics*), 2nd ed., 1964, Prentice-Hall.

Duvall, Evelyn Millis, *Family Development*, 3rd ed., 1967, Lippincott.

Farber, Bernard, *Family: Organization and Interaction*, 1964, Chandler.

Kenkel, William F., *The Family in Perspective*, 2nd ed., 1966, Appleton-Century-Crofts.

Kephart, William M., *The Family, Society, and the Individual*, 2nd ed., 1966, Houghton Mifflin.

Kirkpatrick, Clifford, *The Family: As Process and Institution*, 2nd ed., 1963, Ronald Press.

Landis, Paul H., *Making the Most of Marriage*, 3rd ed., 1965, Appleton-Century-Crofts.

Lantz, Herman R., and Snyder, Eloise C., *Marriage*, 2nd ed., 1969, Wiley.

Magoun, F. Alexander, *Love and Marriage,* rev. ed., 1956, Harper.

Merrill, Francis E., *Courtship and Marriage,* rev. ed., 1959, Holt.

Mihanovich, Clement Simon; Schnepp, Gerald J.; and Thomas, John L.; *A Guide to Catholic Marriage,* 1963, Bruce.

Peterson, James A., *Education for Marriage,* 2nd ed., 1964, Scribner's.

Saxton, Lloyd, *The Individual, Marriage, and the Family,* 1968, Wadsworth.

Stephens, William N., ed., *Reflections on Marriage,* 1968, Thom. Y. Crowell.

Stroup, Atlee L., *Marriage and Family: A Developmental Approach,* 1966, Appleton-Century-Crofts.

Sussman, Marvin B., ed., *Sourcebook in Marriage and the Family,* 3rd ed., 1968, Houghton Mifflin.

Udry, J. Richard, *The Social Context of Marriage,* 1966, Lippincott.

Waller, Willard, *The Family: A Dynamic Interpretation,* revised by Reuben Hill, 1951, Holt, Rinehart & Winston.

Williamson, Robert C., *Marriage and Family Relations,* 1966, Wiley.

Winch, Robert F., *The Modern Family,* rev. ed., 1963, Holt, Rinehart & Winston.

Winch, Robert F., and Louis W. Goodman, eds., *Selected Studies in Marriage and the Family,* 3rd ed., 1968, Holt, Rinehart & Winston.

Womble, Dale L., *Foundations for Marriage and Family Relations,* 1966, Macmillan.

QUICK REFERENCE TABLE TO STANDARD TEXTBOOKS AND READERS

All numbers refer to chapters or to numbered articles in books of readings.

Chapter in Outline	Topic	(1) N. Bell & Vogel	(2) R. Bell	(3) Blood	(4) Bowman	(5) Burgess et al.	(6) Cavan, Am. Fam.	(7) Cavan, ed. Readings	(8) Christensen, ed.	(9) Clemens	(10) Duvall
Introd.	The Study of Marriage and the Family	Introd., 1–5	1	Introd.	1	1	2	1	24	1, 3	Preface
I	Varieties of Family Life	7, 19, 21, 24, 28, 34	1, 10	3	10–12	1, 2, 7	1	4	2–4, 12	2, 3	1
II	America's Family Heritage	6, 11, 38	2	3		3–6	4, 8	3	5, 11	2	3
III	Is an American Pattern Emerging?	8	3	3	2	16	8, 10	3	5, 13	3	3
IV	Socioeconomic Aspects of the Family	10, 12–14, 16	1, 3	10, 11	10–12	23	3–7, 9	2, 12–13	14	17	4
V	Welfare Roles of the Family	17–18, 29, 32	10, 11	22	14	23		16, 21	20	16	4
VI	Population Characteristics and Problems	9	12	19		16	App.	1	9		3
VII	The Child in the Family	15, 26, 30–31, 43–45	14	12, 21, 22	15–16	8–10	19	11, 14, 20	17–18	14	1, 2, 9
VIII	The Child in Group Process	22–23, 39–40	14	21, 22	15–16	10, 13	19	14	17–18	15–16	6
IX	The Child in the Community	20	14	13, 23	4, 15–16	13	19	14	13	15	2, 5, 10, 12
X	Love and Identity	33	5	2, 4–5, 14	4, 13	11	16	5, 7	15–16	4–5, 12	6, 11

xvii

QUICK REFERENCE TABLE TO STANDARD TEXTBOOKS AND READERS (continued)

All numbers refer to chapters or to numbered articles in books of readings.

Chapter in Outline	Topic	(11) Farber	(12) Kenkel	(13) Kephart	(14) Kirk-patrick	(15) Landis	(16) Lantz, Snyder	(17) Magoun	(18) Merrill	(19) Mihano-vich et al.	(20) Peterson
Introd.	The Study of Marriage and the Family	1	Preface	1, 23	1	Introd.	1	Preface	5, 26	1	1
I	Varieties of Family Life	1–2	1–2, 9	3	3–4		2	2	2	1	2
II	America's Family Heritage	8, 11	3–8	4–7	3, 5		2		2	7	18
III	Is an American Pattern Emerging?	4		8	6	15–16	10	13	2	7	18, App. 1
IV	Socioeconomic Aspects of the Family	4		8	7, 17	6–7, 26–27	3, 13, Apps. B&D		15–16	5	17
V	Welfare Roles of the Family			23	8		3, 13, 19		25	13	19
VI	Population Characteristics and Problems	7			8, 10						14
VII	The Child in the Family	7, 11	10, 16, 18	18	8–10	4–5, 29–30	17	11	1–2, 12	9	5
VIII	The Child in Group Process	7, 11	11, 19	18	8, 10	6–8, 30–31	17	11	1–2, 12	9	5–6
IX	The Child in the Community	11	11	18	11	8	17	11, 13	21	9	5–6
X	Love and Identity	3	12	11	2, 12	9–10	4–6	1, 10	3–4, 13	2–4	3

xix

Chapter in Outline	Topic	(21) Saxton	(22) Stephens	(23) Stroup	(24) Sussman	(25) Udry	(26) Waller	(27) Williamson	(28) Winch	(29) Winch & Goodman	(30) Womble
Introd.	The Study of Marriage and the Family	1	8	1, 4	1	1, 19	1	1	1	1	1
I	Varieties of Family Life	7, 10	8	2	1–2	2	2, 25	4	1–3	2	3
II	America's Family Heritage	7		2	4	2	25	2	11	4	
III	Is an American Pattern Emerging?	7, 9	16	3	5–6, 8, 13, 15	2		3	11	3, 5, 15	
IV	Socioeconomic Aspects of the Family	10		12, 16	7, 12, 19–22, 32–33		25	15	4, 6, 12	17	13
V	Welfare Roles of the Family	10		27	19–22, 50	19	6, 24	21	5, 12	11	11, 20
VI	Population Characteristics and Problems	4			14		18		7		
VII	The Child in the Family	1, 12	13	12, 20–21	11, 18, 30–31, 37–38, 41–42	4–5, 11, 13	2–5, 19	16–18	9, 15	5–6, 9–11	18
VIII	The Child in Group Process	1, 12	13	22	9–10, 34–36	4–5	3–5, 20	17–18	15–16	9–11	15, 18
IX	The Child in the Community	12	13	13, 23	3, 9–10, 43	14	20	17–18	8, 16	9–12	
X	Love and Identity	2	1–6	7	29	3–4, 7, 9	6–7	5–6, 9	18–19	14, 16	6–7, 12, 15

	(21)	(22)	(23)	(24)	(25)	(26)	(27)	(28)	(29)	(30)
XI	Courtship and Mate-Selection	2, 5-6	1-5	5-6, 8	16, 23-25	6	6, 8-11	7-8	10, 20	14-16	4, 6
XII	Engagement: Planning for Marriage	2	1-5	9-11	26-27	6, 10	12	11-12	20	14-16	9-10
XIII	Will the Marriage Work Out?	8	7, 14-15		17, 28	8-9, 12	13-17	13-14	21	5	3-5
XIV	Marriage Customs and Laws	10	8	11	59	8	25	11, 20	12, 21		2
XV	Children in Prospect	3, 11	9-10	14-15	52	3-4, 11, 15-16	18	16-17	12	7-8	8, 16
XVI	Childbirth and Care of the Newborn	4		18-19	38-40, 52	17	18	16	13-15	7-8	17
XVII	Adoption			25							
XVIII	The Single Parent			26	60		24	20	8	18-19	19
XIX	The Post-Child Family			25	43-46		20	15	17	13	
XX	Illness, Disability, Unemployment, War Service	9		25	45-46, 50, 53		21	19		18	19
XXI	Separation, Annulment, Desertion, Divorce, Bereavement	8	11-12	26	47-49	18	14-15, 22-24	19-20	22-23	18-19	19
XXII	Scientific Research	App. 2	7	27	51, 54-58, 62	1				1	21
XXIII	The Happy Family	1		18	62	11, 13	25	13	24	11, 14	11, 14

Introduction

THE STUDY OF MARRIAGE
AND THE FAMILY

Marriage practices and family arrangements are so often taken for granted that objective study of them is rare. Only during periods of rapid social change and intellectual unrest, when moral controls appear to be either too rigid or too lax, do we turn critical eyes upon anything so intimate and important as the family. We are now in such a period, an especially complicated and difficult one, and as a consequence the scientific study of marriage and the family is attracting widespread attention and substantial support.

The perpetuation of all societies is tied up with marriage, however it might be defined. Marriage is regarded as crucial for the proper reproduction and rearing of a society's personnel and thus for the transmission of its culture, its common and typical ways of thinking, feeling, and acting. In other words, men identify marriage with their concern for the continuance of their society, not only biologically but also in terms of society's basic values or root ideas concerning government, property, work, and religion.

All tribes have specified the form and nature of marriage and have regulated family relationships. These specifications are rarely along novel lines. They almost always continue traditional usages. Efforts at radical experimentation, such as those made during the early years of the Soviet Union, seldom persist, and in Soviet Russia they were short-lived. Change in this social area usually consists of modest adaptation to altered conditions of life. For this reason, a change in patterns of family relationship may not be recognized until long after it has gradually taken place.

Concern with the family's functions appears in our earliest ethical documents. For example, one of the Ten Commandments enjoins us to "Honour thy father and thy mother," and four others deal, in part, with family obligations. The second Commandment warns: "I the Lord thy God am a jealous God, visiting the iniquity of the fathers upon the children unto the third and fourth generation of them that hate me." The fourth Commandment asks that no one in a household—"thou, nor thy son, nor thy daughter"—shall work on "the sabbath day." The seventh and the tenth forbid, respectively, marital infidelity and the coveting of "thy neighbour's wife."

PROPOSALS FOR CHANGE

Periods of dislocation and stress bring forth criticisms of the existing social order. Proposals are advanced for the modification, abolition, replacement, restoration, or reinforcement of various or all social institutions. Each plan has its group of advocates, and the groups war among themselves. Because all aspects of a society are interrelated, and the family serves basically to maintain a society's customary character and organization, these criticisms and proposals often concern the family as a principal point of attack.

Radical proposals for reform of the family have often been influenced, directly or indirectly, by those Plato set forth in his *Republic* some twenty-three centuries ago. His ideal city-state was to be a complete and harmonious unity dedicated to the nurturing of order and virtue. It was to function like a large family. He specified equality of educational opportunity for all, regardless of parentage or sex. For those who attained the highest status, through success in meeting educational criteria, there was to be a kind of group marriage in a regulated community of mates and children, and this elite would control the property of the republic and the services of the less privileged classes. This program included, among other things, state supervision of breeding, new forms of mating and cohabitation, the putting to death of sickly infants by exposure, and compulsory state regulation of all aspects of training and education. In his ideal aristocratic-socialistic society, Plato granted supreme power to specialists in ideas—in other words, to the philosophers—and his proposals have therefore often appealed to the philosophically-minded.

Plato apparently constructed his plan for a republic out of ideas which he had seen applied in places other than Athens or which he had developed in hopes of remedying the injustices and other disharmonies he had witnessed in the Athenian city-state. Often mentioned as examples of the application of certain Platonic ideas in social reorganization, especially of his assignment of supreme authority to an elite selected in a training process, are the Roman Catholic rule of Christendom during the Middle Ages and the Communist party rule of Russia in the twentieth century. Thomas More, in his *Utopia* (1516), and many "utopian" thinkers since have been inspired by Platonic ideas to put forth radical proposals for social reorganization, including, as a rule, drastic changes in sex and family relationships.

THE RENAISSANCE AND THE INDUSTRIAL REVOLUTION

In medieval society there was officially a rigid hierarchy of authority which extended from pope and emperor or king down to the serf. Within the families of freemen, the authority of the father represented church and state and could not formally be challenged. The serfs had only limited personal and family rights. A system involving so much inequity and oppression could not maintain its grasp upon society indefinitely.

Stirrings against tyranny and injustice appeared century after century from remote antiquity in many parts of Europe, and they gradually became more insistent from the thirteenth century onward. Nobles fought to limit the authority of kings. Merchants struggled for greater freedom from the aristocracy. By the fourteenth century, there were peasant uprisings of significance, and religious reformers and heretical religious sects were insistently questioning the authority of the Roman Catholic Church.

For more than six centuries, tides of change have been rising in the Western world which have made for personal freedom and social equality. They resulted not only from resentment of social injustice but from new learning and new freedom to think that came with the Renaissance. Beginning in Italy in the fourteenth century, the Renaissance was inspired by the rediscovery of Greek classical literature and was furthered by the invention of movable type for printing, which resulted in the greater production and wider dissemination of books, and by expanding commerce. The discovery and exploration of the American continents stimulated imagination and unsettled old patterns of thought and information. Technological developments and the improvement of communication and transportation stimulated industrialization. All these changes extended human horizons and led toward the integration as well as the urbanization of all human society.

Especially in the first half of the eighteenth century these broad

changes swept Europe and then America and brought with them dislocations, needs, hopes, and opportunities. These stimuli led to social agitation and to fundamental modifications of culture. They
fostered and still foster the rapid growth of population, vast migrations, rises in living standards, the growth of cities, the urbanization
of those outside of cities, the questioning of traditional ways, and the
struggle for power among nations around the world. From their
outset, these adaptive processes have been accompanied by a flowering of new social doctrines, many of them utopian or revolutionary.

Industrialization siphoned off more and more of the activities which
traditionally took place in the home, whether on the farm, in the
village, or even in the city. On the farm, family members ceased to
gather, raise, and process all their food; they came to specialize more
and more. Wherever people lived, they no longer did such things as
weave wool into finished cloth solely for themselves to wear. They
did not have to entertain and educate themselves. They no longer
mastered the folk arts of medical care. Increasingly, these and other
functions were taken over, were replaced, or were provided with substitutes by factories and other organizations and by specialists.

The Industrial Revolution continues unabated. Research and invention constantly add to our technical and human-relations novelties
and complexities. The directions in which such changes may lead us
in the modification of our family patterns is far from apparent. We
do, however, have a great deal of information about our experiences
in adapting the family to changing conditions. We also know a great
deal about our current needs and problems. This book attempts to
outline and to digest in a systematic manner as much as possible of
that fund of knowledge.

MODERN ATTACKS ON THE FAMILY

The utopian socialistic ideas of Saint-Simon, Fourier, Owen, Cabet,
and others in the late eighteenth and early nineteenth centuries stimulated social experimentation. These reformers inspired the formation
of small socialistic communities in the United States. All these
experiments failed, often because of dissatisfaction with their impractical marital forms. Consequently, the impact of these ideas and experiments upon society at large was limited; they influenced intellectual speculation but aroused little popular interest.

Karl Marx's revolutionary theories for the reorganization of society were a different matter. They sprang from and took root in the rising unrest of the industrial workers. The Marxists organized the workers and sought to change the existing power structure of society, Marx's proposals thus posed a threat to established institutions. Marx set out to prove that the capitalistic economic and social system could not provide continuing social stability.

Marx's program of change is one which he and his followers did not merely advocate but also brashly predicted to be inevitable. Marxists demanded a redistribution of social power through a dictatorship of the proletariat (the working class) and looked forward to the eventual creation of a classless society. As part of their critique of the *status quo,* they characterized the middle-class family as a bulwark of an unjust and decaying social order. They insisted upon its replacement by a contractual relationship between husband and wife readily dissolvable by either partner. They wanted the state to be given responsibility for much of the care and all of the training and education of children. In the Soviet Union—the first government which attempted to reorganize society on Marxist principles—there was an attempt to put easy divorce into practice, but this effort became an early casualty to the realities of interpersonal relations and to the persistence of older ideals. Nevertheless, Soviet ideals of marriage and the family remain in some respects colored by Marxist ideas.

During the past century, spokesmen for established society have been forced to re-examine and to rethink more and more fundamentally the nature of human relationships. They have been compelled to do so not only by the reawakening of men's minds through the expansion of industry, trade, and communication but also by the related rise of popular democracy, which brought a demand for equal rights for women. They also have had to face the implications of the work of modern biologists, psychologists, cultural anthropologists, and sociologists, such as Darwin, Freud, Cooley, and Sumner. Darwin presented dramatic evidence of how man the animal evolved from other animal forms. Furthermore, the conception of organic evolution led to investigations of the evolving nature of man's social institutions and to a realization that institutions change in response to changed life conditions. Freud and Cooley probed the life histories of individuals to find unsuspected motivations and new dimensions. Freud's investigations forced the recognition of early biological and interpersonal experiences as lifelong ingredients of personality. Cooley broadened our conceptions of the processes of human socialization and helped to clarify their nature. Sumner demonstrated the changing and relative character of morality.

The defenders of established social institutions have sometimes reacted to these unsettling discoveries and ideas with reinterpretations of religious and ethical principles. Often these revisions have been in vague or confused terms, but some of them have met the challenge of changed conditions and knowledge and have thus become useful and influential. Even some of the most defensive spokesmen for the preservation of institutional forms have shown an increasing appreciation of the value of scientific attitudes and methods in the study of the intimacies of family life.

THE FAMILY–STUDY MOVEMENT

As a result of all the foregoing developments, the twentieth century has seen—especially in the United States—a very rapid growth of interest in the scientific study of marriage and the family. Until the turn of the century, the family had been discussed, if at all, in vague and syrupy generalities, and the intimate problems of marriage and family life were "unmentionables." It was frequently asserted that traditional common sense is the best guide to dealing with the apparent simplicities and practicalities of family living and hence that those who had "trouble" did not have "common sense." Sentimentality and false modesty, old wives' tales, oversimplified one-root explanations of trouble, panaceas, and shallow preachments—all these persisted and, for that matter, still persist. But now many conscientious scientists and counselors are at work on the discovery, interpretation, and application of knowledge which can help us to understand and perhaps to ease or solve the problems of our many maladjusted families. There remain areas of ignorance, pseudoknowledge, and fads; but dependable understanding and effective techniques are becoming available. This is certainly not to say that all traditional ideas about marriage and the family are outworn, but it is to contend that scientific investigation and critical reappraisal are necessary ways of meeting drastically changed conditions of life.

Classes and discussion groups on sex and family problems now flourish in a great many high schools and colleges, churches and Y's, and other organizations. Certain religious groups have fought bitterly against the provision of opportunities for the young to obtain accurate and dependable sex education unavailable to them in their homes. Despite obstacles, the need for classes in the problems of dating, mating, homemaking, and family living is becoming more and more recognized. Classes and discussion groups are also benefiting married persons who are disturbed or bewildered by their family problems. Though these activities and services vary widely in quality, with some of them damaging or futile rather than helpful, they are improving. They are often effective in imparting useful facts and in providing the benefits of group therapy.

In the family-study movement, three groups of specialists are facilitating the development of new approaches and techniques: (1) the *researchers*—notably sociologists, cultural anthropologists, and psychologists, who study the experiences of specialists in counseling as well as many other types of data; (2) the *general counselors*—clergymen, lawyers, physicians, and, especially, psychiatrists and psychoanalysts, who deal with family problems as an important part of their work; and (3) the *specialized counselors*—marriage counselors, social caseworkers, family-study group leaders, and family-study teachers and lecturers for elementary, high school, college, graduate school, and less formal classes. The chief contributions of researchers are summarized in succeeding chapters. Chapters 5, 11 to 14, and 17—particularly 13—touch upon the functions of counselors. Chapter 22 outlines the history of scientific research in this field and the current opportunities existing in it.

ORGANIZATION OF THIS BOOK

This book describes and analyzes information about marriage and the family. Part One outlines many facets of family change—historical, geographic, economic, political, and social. It asks: Is a single American pattern of family life now emerging? Will the existing variety of patterns persist in the foreseeable future? Parts Two, Three, and Four discuss, respectively, childhood and adolescence, courtship and marriage, and parenthood. Attention is given to such problems as the struggle toward maturity, tests for the prediction of marital success, childbirth, adoption, the single parent, the post-child family, parents-in-law, and grandparents. Part Five is concerned with crises and with the use of specialists in coping with them; these crises include illness, disablement, unemployment, war service, separation, annulment, desertion, divorce, and bereavement. The concluding Part Six attempts to outline the development of scientific research and to formulate briefly some characteristics of the happy family.

PART ONE

THE CHANGING FAMILY

Chapter I

VARIETIES OF FAMILY LIFE

In common usage *marriage* means both "wedding" and "wedlock." It refers to the public and sanctioned act of pledging or joining for the purposes of sexual relations and cohabitation. This is the "saying of vows" or, as it has also been put, the "public confession of a private intention." In addition, marriage means the continuing matrimonial relationship.

Marriage in any particular society is an accumulation of customs and, in literate societies, laws with regard to the sexual association of adults for the purpose of reproduction. It differs from other relationships which may involve sexual intercourse through being societally prescribed and regulated as the proper status for those who wish to reproduce themselves and thus to help reproduce their society. Certain societies permit concubinage and even casual sex relations, but the children of such unions do not regularly have status equivalent to that of the children of married couples.

Custom or law specifies for a given group and society the persons who are permitted to marry and the proper ways to conduct courtship, to become betrothed, to wed, to fulfill marriage obligations, and to deal with the termination of a marriage by separation, annulment, divorce, or death. Such custom or law differs from one society to another, and custom even varies from group to group within a society. In any given group the prevailing custom has great prestige and influence and is not violated with impunity.

The word *wedding* usually signifies the public events immediately connected with becoming married. It often takes place with solemn ritual and is accompanied by happy festivities. The word *nuptials* refers to both the marriage rites and the private fulfillment of public vows. The expressions "nuptial mass" and "nuptial bed" are both used.

So much for marriage as a term. What is the nature of the social situation of marriage into which young people enter? The sociolo-

3

gist Willard Waller * concludes that marriage should be considered both as a form which is socially defined and also as a relatively unde-fined sort of tentative process: "Not with the words 'I now pronounce you,' but early in the functioning engagement did the dyadic proc-esses begin which will go on 'till death us do part.'" For better or for worse, the partners in a marriage have their separate life histories and are also constantly adapting or failing to adapt themselves to each other. Such a tentative process of adjustment takes place within the customary patterns specified for family living by any given culture or subculture. The patterns become both mediums and limits for such interpersonal relationships.

WHAT IS A "FAMILY"?

Only in the broadest sense can one give a single meaning to the term *family* throughout the world. Everyone thinks he knows what a family is, but each person's definition is likely to deal only with the kind of family he has experienced in his ethnic group, social class, and society. The precise denotation of the term varies widely among groups and societies.

That the one term family can be applied so widely is a fact of so-cial significance. Even in our own society it means a great many dif-ferent things. For example, in its 1940 reports the United States Bureau of the Census defined a family as "the head of the household and all other persons in the household related to the head; heads of households living alone, as well as those living with relatives, were counted as families." In its 1950 reports, however, the Bureau refers to a family as "a group of two or more persons related by blood, mar-riage, or adoption and residing together; all such persons are consid-ered as members of one family." In the latter reports, therefore, some four million "one-person families" are no longer tabulated as families. In certain regions of the world, too, a "family" may include several wives and one husband or several husbands and one wife.

Is there a common denominator among human families? In other words, can we find a basic definition which applies reasonably well to at least the most salient aspects of all human families? The an-thropologist Ralph Linton † concludes that even the simplest known

* *The Family* (rev. by Reuben Hill; New York: Dryden Press, 1951), p. 254. Reprinted by permission of the publisher.

† *The Cultural Background of Personality* (New York: Appleton-Century-Crofts, 1945), pp. 61–62.

societies "include within their organization smaller, internally organized units of two sorts: (1) family groups, membership in which is established on the basis of biological relationships, real or assumed, and (2) association groups, membership in which is established on the basis of congeniality and/or common interest." Linton's "family group" might be either small or large. It might be something which could be called a basic family unit. It might be a combination of such units, joined by ties of polygamy or blood. Unfortunately, his "family group" is not sufficiently different from his "association group" to permit adequate discrimination between the two types. His definition is useful and accurate enough as far as it goes, but we need to go further.

In common American usage, a "family" is: (1) the group which lives in a house under a single head; (2) a group of immediate kinsmen, especially of parents and children, whether living together or not; and (3) the descendants of a common forebear, whether immediate or remote. These three meanings are also found in other societies, but they are not accepted universally.

It will be serviceable to define the "basic family unit" and then to consider the various combinations of that unit linked together by ties of marriage and blood. In this way, a more adequate conception of the family will emerge.

THE BASIC FAMILY UNIT

It is necessary to avoid confusion between the biological phenomenon, the "basic reproductive unit," and the societal phenomenon, the "basic family unit." A basic family unit may or may not be biologically reproductive. A basic reproductive unit may or may not become a family.

The *basic reproductive unit* is composed of a man and a woman who have a fertile sexual relationship and whatever offspring they may have. The term refers only to a biological relationship as such. It does not allude to the cultural, subcultural, and other social elaborations, modifications, and substitutions which are typical of families.

The *basic family unit,* on the other hand, is a culturally specified relationship which those constituting it down through many generations have elaborated and adapted. It is a group of two or more persons, bound together by marriage, blood, or adoption, who are socially distinguished as making up a single household or subhousehold. Such a unit need not include more than one person serving actively in the principal maternal or paternal role. It may lack either. It rarely lacks both. If a single parent or parent-substitute does not head the unit, it may consist only of siblings. Usually a basic family unit is initiated by marriage. It may eventually include children; grandchildren would usually be members of other basic family units. A basic family unit set apart as a section of a household, as for example a son's family, in other words as a subhousehold, is often called a *subfamily*.

A basic family unit may at a given time consist of only one generation or of any of the other types of membership mentioned, but it has certain similarities wherever it is found. It is publicly recognized and sanctioned as an arrangement for dwelling together in relatively intimate face-to-face association, and it has the ability to assimilate new members, especially the young, into it and thus into society.

A basic family unit is usually launched by a process of the differentiation of two individuals from their own parental family units. The new social entity thus created becomes the scene of the same sort of tentative processes—of ever changing adjustments in living together —mentioned in connection with engagement and marriage. The members of the unit interact with one another in terms of their life histories and sex and age roles. They tend to modify their ways of behaving, thinking, and feeling, and thus their personalities, in response to such continuing interaction whether it be characterized by accommodation, competition, or conflict. The members of the family group gradually develop a set of subcultural patterns typical of that group and somewhat different from those typical of other family groups in the same culture. These patterns are special ways of joking, eating, greeting one another, and much else. Members of a family group thus acquire a sense of cohesiveness that reinforces the basic bonds of marriage, blood, or adoption.

The type of household most commonly found in the United States today is the single basic family unit with ethnic, class, and regional variations. However, some multi-unit or extended families are still to be found, and even polygamous families are occasionally discovered.

As a rule, each person is, during his lifetime, a member of at least two basic family units: the family into which he is born or adopted, and the family which he helps by marriage to form and in which he may become a parent. These two types are called, respectively, the *family of orientation* and the *family of procreation*.

TYPES OF MARRIAGE AND FAMILY

The basic family unit might be associated with any form of monogamy or polygamy. In the United States and most other countries, monogamy is the only moral and legal form of marriage.

Monogamy. Under monogamy, a man or woman may have a marriage in force at one time with only one member of the other sex. That marriage must be terminated by annulment, divorce, or death before it can be followed by another. In our society, we tend to romanticize the exclusive form of monogamy called *pair-marriage,* a mutually monopolistic union which is based upon a footing of equality. It is a union "forever." The sociologist A. G. Keller * calls it "a tendency or ideal; existing in the case of individual pairs, it has never formed a general working system."

In places where monogamous marriages may be relatively easy to terminate by divorce, and remarriage is common, the situation is sometimes facetiously labeled "tandem polygamy." But ordinarily divorce is a nerve-racking experience for both individuals and their associates. Hence few people contract marriage with the intention of breaking it off. Societies place formidable obstacles in the way of divorce, even when they permit it as a means of correcting the individual's errors in judgment or of coping with problems unforeseen or unforeseeable at the time of marriage. The most effective restraints against divorce are those personal attachments which culture and the processes of living together build within persons themselves.

Polygamy. The various forms of multiple marriage, or polygamy, are ways of combining basic family units into more complex structures. Types of polygamy are monandry, polygyny, monogyny, polyandry, group marriage, and sexual communism.

Monandry is a term sometimes used to describe the relatively amorphous and unregulated type of marriage found among certain simple peoples. It is "a more or less durable informal monopoly of a woman by one husband (at a time)."† An uncommon type of arrangement, it may be an incipient or a decadent form of polygyny, and it does not exclude polygyny.

* *Man's Rough Road* (New York: Stokes, 1932), p. 400.
† W. G. Sumner and A. G. Keller, *The Science of Society* (New Haven, Conn.: Yale University Press, 1927), III, 1559.

Polygyny involves the marriage of one husband with more than one wife of full (approximately equal) status. It is a more permanent and highly developed arrangement than monandry. Where polygyny is practiced, the sex ratio is rarely unbalanced enough to make it universally possible. To those for whom a second wife—or perhaps even a first wife—is not available, polygyny remains an enticing possibility. It is frequently only the older and wealthier men who can practice it.

Among the American Mormons in 1843–1890 (the period in which they practiced polygyny), the relaxed societal controls of the frontier made a polygynous system temporarily workable for a small minority. For that minority, said to have been less than one in twenty of the Mormons, each wife and her offspring constituted a separate family unit with a separate household, or subhousehold, and the units were linked chiefly through having a husband in common.* After federal pressure resulted in the official abolition of polygyny in 1890, a fundamentalist group unsanctioned by the Church of Jesus Christ of Latter Day Saints (the Mormon Church) continued to practice polygyny at least until 1960 in isolated parts of Utah, Arizona, and Idaho.

Whether polygyny is rare or common depends upon how one uses terms. For many anthropologists polygyny includes much of what will be described below as "monogyny." At any rate, one finds few instances in which multiple wives have relatively equal status.

Monogyny is the commonest form of polygamy. It may be defined as the marriage of one husband with one full-status wife and with one or more other mates of lesser status, possibly concubines. Monogyny may be sororal; that is, the husband may be permitted or obliged to take as mates one or more younger sisters of his full-status wife. This type is sometimes called a *sororate*. Monogyny may also be associated with the *levirate* (from "levir," Latin for "husband's brother"). Under the levirate, as it existed,among the ancient Jews, a deceased husband was replaced for the purposes of procreation by his brother or by another close male relative, whether or not the latter might already be married. Deuteronomy (25:5–6) rules that "the wife of the dead shall not marry without unto a stranger: her husband's brother shall go in unto her, and take her to him to wife, and perform the duty of an husband's brother unto her." The firstborn

* For a description of the Mormon family system, see Kimball Young, *Isn't One Wife Enough?* (New York: Henry Holt and Co., 1954).

of such a union "shall succeed in the name of his brother which is dead, that his name be not put out of Israel." This was a special aspect of Jewish monogyny.

As we have indicated, sometimes the marriage form labeled "monogyny" is not used, and the phenomena discussed are divided between "polygyny" and "monogamy." This classification does not, however, appear to us to be precise enough. One can bring together a series of examples which exhibit variations beginning with a type of polygyny such as that of the Mormons and continuing through monogyny and monogamy to pair-marriage. This gradually varying series would include such modifications as the following. In polygyny, one commonly finds a difference in status between the "primary marriage" and the one or more "secondary marriages." In either polygyny or monogyny, a man may be permitted to accumulate one or more "concubines," in other words women who are his socially recognized sex partners but without the rights of a wife. Concubinage is also found in places where monogamy is the official rule. The persistence of extramarital relations in our society has been used as evidence by cultural evolutionists that monogyny was a pre-existing form and a more realistic and stable one than monogamy. At any rate, the known history of mankind shows a trend from monogyny towards monogamy. There is no evidence of an antecedent stage of polygyny prior to monogyny. The series of variations ranging from polygyny to pair-marriage is merely an arbitrary classification of cases. It is not an evolutionary sequence in which one form would necessarily develop into the next one.

In *polyandry,* a woman has more than one husband at a time. It is quite rare. Among the South Pacific Marquesans a woman of high status may take a number of unrelated husbands. In western Tibet, the husbands are usually brothers. Husbands of relatively equal status usually live separately. When one husband outranks others, as may be the case in fraternal polyandry if the older brother commands higher status than his brothers, they may all live together. The Todas, a tribe in India, maintain an unequal sex ratio through female infanticide and thus create a situation facilitating polyandry. The practice is often associated with economic deprivation or with certain types of occupation, such as herding, which require men to be away from home much of the time.

Group marriage is also rare. In this form of polygamy, two or more men are married to two or more women at the same time. It is found only mixed with other types of marriage. It does not occur as the dominant type in any society. In certain cases, it appears to result from the addition of a second wife to a polyandrous union.

Sexual communism (also called "sexual pluralism" or "communal marriage") may be exemplified by the Community Perfectionists (1848–1876) of Oneida, New York. Each adult member of this community was given the right to have sexual relations with any adult member of the opposite sex. Here the basic family unit consisted of the mother, her children, and her current sexual companion. Such experiments never last long. They fail because the day-to-day life experiences—especially interpersonal rivalries—wear away the experimental enthusiasm of participants.*

The Extended Family. In a polygamous family, the basic family units are linked by conjugal ties. In the monogamous extended family, they are bound together by ties of consanguinity. The extending ties in monogamy are those which exist among parents and their children and grandchildren and among siblings. In American history, the extended family has been common among immigrant, rural, and frontier groups. Examples are still found today among such diverse segments of the population as groups of individuals with great inherited wealth, successful farmers, and certain recent immigrants.

Trial Marriage. Among nonliterate people, there are many illustrations of marriages on an experimental basis or for a specific trial period. Such trial marriages are usually for the purpose of testing the wife's qualities, especially her fecundity. The couple may be permitted to live together as man and wife until the union appears to be a success or a failure. If the woman becomes pregnant or perhaps after she has borne a child, the couple is regarded as joined in a lasting union. If a specific period of trial is customary, the expression *marriage of term* is used. The rather general acceptance of sterility as grounds for the end of a trial marriage or for the annulment or termination with divorce of all other types of marriage reflects the societal concern with procreation in marriage.

Adaptations of the trial marriage idea have had advocates in the United States during this century. These proposals recognized and sought a way to regularize the widespread use of modern contraceptive devices by the unmarried as well as the married, and they were

* R. A. Parker, *A Yankee Saint: John Humphrey Noyes and the Oneida Community* (New York: G. P. Putnam's Sons, 1935).

put forward as a means of counteracting our high divorce rate. The proponents of trial marriage believed that a formal relationship should be established in which a couple might live together and enjoy sex relations without involving themselves in the permanent bonds of regular marriage. These efforts were to make acceptable socially what appeared possible physiologically and psychologically—an arrangement that might separate considerations of heterosexual companionship from those of reproduction and of raising children.

Before World War I, Elsie Clews Parsons * shocked society by contending that trial marriage with easy divorce would be a way of making possible earlier and more stable marriages. She contended that such trial marriages should be "entered into with a view of permanency." If there were no children, they could be terminated easily.

Melvin M. Knight † suggested in 1924 that a childless marriage be called a "companionate" and that only a married couple with a child be called a "family." He recommended that a "companionate" should be dissolvable upon mutual consent after nine months of separation. He argued that, because of societal interest in child-rearing, the dissolution of "family" ties by divorce should continue to be difficult. Judge Ben B. Lindsey ‡ of Denver did not differentiate between a "companionate" and a "marriage"; he gave the term "companionate marriage" a vogue for a short time in the late 1920's. On the basis of his extensive experience with young men and women in his court, he advocated trial marriage as an alternative to widespread illicit sexual relations. Commenting on Lindsey's work, the sociologist Willystine Goodsell § concluded: "The honest realism of Judge Lindsey has met with a storm of hostile criticism, indicating that society is not yet ready to face with frankness the actual sexual laxity that exists in its midst. In course of time, when public opinion is more soundly informed, it may be brought to sanction companionate marriage and divorce by mutual consent *in the interest of a finer sexual morality.*"

Proposals to institute trial marriage have never been widely ac-

* *The Family* (New York: G. P. Putnam's Sons, 1906), pp. 348–349.

† "The Companionate and the Family," *Journal of Social Hygiene,* X (1924), 257–267.

‡ Ben B. Lindsey and Wainright Evans, *Companionate Marriage* (New York: Boni and Liveright, 1927), Chapters 7–9.

§ *Problems of the Family* (rev. ed.; New York: Appleton-Century, 1936), p. 505.

cepted or supported in this country, but a voluntary period of child-lessness has become common among young married couples as they strive for a firmer financial basis. The termination of intolerable marriages, whether childless or not, must still go through the usual channels.

Other Significant Variations. Other kinds of marital and familial patterns include those having to do with (1) kinship or relationship, (2) location of home, and (3) relative rights and powers of members. As regards kinship, descent may be traced through (*a*) the male side, (*b*) the female side, or (*c*) both the male and the female sides of the family. As regards location, the home may be in or near that of (*a*) the father, (*b*) the mother, (*c*) the mother's brother, (*d*) the father and the mother, (*e*) either the father or the mother, or (*f*) neither the father nor the mother (a new location selected for other considerations). The focus of formal control among family members may be indicated by the terms: (*a*) *patriarchal*, with formal authority vested principally in the father; (*b*) *matriarchal*, with authority vested in the mother; (*c*) *avuncular*, with authority vested in the mother's brother, (*d*) *child-centered*, or perhaps child-dominated, and (*e*) *relatively balanced*, with the rights of each member understood and respected and his powers held in restraint. In an extended family, paternal or other power may be exercised over children even after they are adults with children of their own, and over grandchildren.

The preceding terms for marriage forms may appear to be categories, but they are not so intended. They label certain cultural *types* and suggest the variety of families to be found in societies around the world, but the family forms of a given society often vary from the types listed. The fact of variation is the important thing to bring out here.

DOES VARIATION JUSTIFY EXPERIMENTATION?

The United States has a rich variety of family life even though our "melting pots" tend to smooth out our differences. Drawn from all the world, American patterns in this field comprise a vast collection of ethnic and class types which will be discussed in the next three chapters.

Do the many varieties of marriage justify an experimental attitude toward this institution? Let us discuss this question in terms of the differences between the social catch phrase "cultural relativ*ism*" and the scientific conception "cultural relativ*ity*."

Social propagandists use the term cultural relativism both positively and negatively. Positively, it is employed to justify proposed experiments of a casual and irresponsible sort with novel ideas concerning marriage and other social institutions. Negatively, it becomes an effort to cry down those who would adapt a custom or law to changed conditions.

Both terms recognize the relatedness of the culture of a tribe or people to its background and its life conditions. A culture is the product of the traditions, historical influences, and economic and geographic factors which have formed it. When certain writers observe the fact of cultural differences and the dependence of such differences upon background factors, rather than upon absolute and unchanging bases, they then assert that the relativity of culture to background justifies a social doctrine of cultural relativism. By this they mean the treatment of culture as rational and contractual, subject to modification in response to purely logical appeals. They contend that this doctrine justifies what in our society would be considered immoral experimentation. These are conclusions which neglect the irrational factors pervading culture, the ability of cultural forms to persist, and the intimate involvement of all human personalities in their cultural background. Our marital beliefs and practices are deeply rooted in all aspects of our society, both religious and secular, and in the habits of thought, emotion, and behavior of its members.

When we cast aside the catch phrase cultural relativism and the various social doctrines associated with it, we can learn certain important things from what social scientists call "cultural relativity" or just "cultural variability." We can learn that cultural patterns and especially the morals and mores of a given society have great stability; they resist change, but they change. They are likely to remain much the same in a society as long as life conditions do not change, but that is not for long because society is constantly changing. As change comes, such overt forms as symbols may continue to appear the same while the associated conceptions—the significance of the symbols—can be modifying all the while. Sweeping alterations of life conditions change values and even symbols; these alterations arise from migrations, mechanical inventions, discoveries of new resources, the development of cities, and the growth of vast industries. It was a long time, for example, before people would accept the words "love, honor, and cherish" in place of "love, honor, and obey" in the marriage service. But the change in the nonsymbolic aspects of the cultural form had already taken place before the words were changed to conform with the social modification.

Cultural relativity is a scientific conception which points to the continuity, complexity, and nonrationality of the processes of cultural specification and respecification. To understand how culture influences individual thinking, feeling, and acting and is influenced by personal and group experiences, we have to examine the factors to which culture-and-personality is relative, that is, from which it arose and to which it is responding. Just as social scientists integrate the conception of culture-and-personality, so also in cultural relativity they integrate culture-and-personality with a conception of continuing variability and adaptation. If we ignore the name-calling use of cultural relativ*ism*, we can learn from cultural relativ*ity* how to help patterns of family living to adapt to changed conditions.

INSTITUTION, ASSOCIATION, PROCESS

As we have seen, in spite of its many manifestations, the family is roughly threefold in character: (1) a cultural form, (2) an organized group of two or more persons, and (3) a continuing process of interpersonal behavior and adjustment.

The family is often called an *institution*. By this is meant that in any given time, society, ethnic group, social class, and region there is a complicated pattern of customary ideas, feelings, and behavior in connection with the family. This configuration is in part based upon law but to a far greater extent upon the oral and written traditions of the people concerned.

Each family is an *association* of two or more individuals who conform to—and also modify—the institutional form as it is found in their society, class, ethnic tradition, and region or neighborhood. It is an organized group with many characteristics similar to other face-to-face human groups of a comparable size. As each adult enters the family group, he brings into it within himself the consequences of his own life history, together with his understanding of his roles in the family and of those of other members. As the processes of living together within the family group go on, and experience and age exert their influences, the social personalities of the adults gradually modify and those of the children take form, mature, and adjust. At times members try to accommodate themselves to one another; at other times they are competitive or in conflict. At any rate, each person changes and continues to change in the association and effects changes in the others.

A processual viewpoint concerning the family brings institution, association, persons, and activities into an integrated perspective which is both dynamic and historically adequate. The philosophers John Dewey and Arthur F. Bentley * offer a similar way of thinking about human behavior which they call "transactional," a conception which they propose in place of the older conceptions of "self-action" and "interaction." They reject self-action because it views individuals as entities who act under their own powers. Dewey and Bentley recognize the gains which came from the more careful applications of a broad conception of interaction, but they regard this term as confusing and inconsistent. They observe that it often leads to a consideration of a social interaction as somehow detachable from the persons who participate in it, from the more general social situation to which it is related, and from its physical environment.

The idea of transaction is a more inclusive one. In order to embrace considerations of the interrelatedness of all things in a social situation, a *transaction* is defined as a doing, proceeding, or dealing in which persons, things, precedents (including those in culture), and all else are viewed as its aspects. It involves no detachable or independent "elements," "entities," "essences," "realities," or "relations" because detachment of any aspect of a transaction immediately changes both the "aspect" and the "transaction" into something different.

We prefer to call our viewpoint "processual" rather than "transactional" because the latter term appears to imply the division of the continuing tentative process of human behavior into sections. When viewed processually, the living present is seen in a sense fully related to all its past, its current ramifications, and its future possibilities. With this processual perspective on society, we see more clearly that a cultural pattern is not a model for a type of action which occurs between individuals; no cultural pattern can accurately be separated out from its contexts. A cultural pattern influences a recurring aspect of group and personal processes, not solely a single type of act. When we look upon family behavior as a process, we no longer depend upon oversimplified theories of cause and effect. Even a recog-

---

* *Knowing and the Known* (Boston: Beacon Press, 1949), esp. Chapters 4 and 5.

nition that one event may have a complicated array of causes and multiple consequences appears inadequate in comparison with the more fluid and dynamic implications of seeing personal and interpersonal behavior as a continuous process.

CONCLUSION

Human beings have tried out many—perhaps all possible—institutional forms of marriage and the family. In spite of all this variability, we see that the marriage form in any given society, class, ethnic group, and region is very durable. The values associated with an established pattern of family life, even though it may be outmoded, are deeply ingrained in childhood and are constantly reinforced during maturation. Only under the pressure of the urgent needs of individuals and of society can modifications of family values and behavior take place. Even then, changes may become evident in superficial rationalizations or rituals rather than in daily routines of behavior. On the other hand, the superficialities may remain the same long after popular routines and attitudes have modified. When one adopts a processual viewpoint, one can acquire a more adequate understanding of stability and change in family life.

Chapter II

AMERICA'S FAMILY HERITAGE

As with all other aspects of our social life, we Americans owe our marriage and family patterns to all the rest of the world and to our own ability to adapt "foreign" ways of life to our own changing conditions and needs. This mixed heritage has given our marriage and family life refreshing variety. At the same time, pressures toward conformity have generated amazing tendencies toward similarity in spite of the great size and heterogeneity of our population.

The quantity written about the New England Puritans and the Virginia Cavaliers tends to obscure the many other aspects of our heritage. English control of the American colonies and the early predominance of immigrants from the British Isles gave American society a British cast and an English language. Four-fifths of our population in 1790 are assigned British origin, but the largest "British" segment consisted of the anti-English Ulster Irish and other Irish Dissenters. The Irish Roman Catholics did not come in any appreciable numbers until the next century. The British also included such diverse groups as Scottish Highlanders and Lowlanders, Welsh Quakers and other Dissenters, impoverished English gentry, and London Cockneys. Among the non-British, the largest groups to come to America in colonial times were the African Negroes, the Palatinate Germans (mostly absorbed into the "Pennsylvania Dutch"), and the French Huguenots. Smaller early immigrations involved the Dutch, Swedes, Swiss, and others. The native American Indian tribesmen were culturally influential even though they were shamefully abused and slaughtered. As early as the eighteenth century, we were already attracting immigrants from other parts of the Americas.

These streams of population brought with them the conceptions of the Hebrew patriarchal family as set forth in the Old Testament and of St. Paul's ascetic morality for Christian family life. They varied these ancient ideas in terms of their own ethnic traditions and of

17

other doctrines drawn from Jewish, Roman Catholic, and Protestant sources.

European immigrants came very largely from the deprived and exploited masses of their countries. In general, they shared a rebelliousness against political, economic, and religious authority. Politically, they favored greater power for themselves, the masses, through democratic reforms. Economically, they wished greater freedom to become small enterprisers; they wanted to limit the power of government to grant special monopolistic privileges. Religiously, they tended to be purists, in revolt against what they regarded as aristocratic or royalist corruptions of church and clergy. Their attitudes toward marriage and the family were a part of their popular, purist revolt. But they often combined strict traditional principles with a sense of ways to meet the practical needs of new colonial towns and the advancing frontier.

Since 1820, more than six million immigrants have come from Germany. Italy, Ireland, Great Britain, and Austria-Hungary have each furnished between four and five millions, and Russia more than three. Canada and Sweden have each supplied more than one million. A total of about five millions have immigrated from the other Americas. Smaller numbers have come from Norway, Greece, Poland, Denmark, and other countries. In all, we are, or are descended from, some forty-one million immigrants, plus the small aboriginal population.

These figures do not give an accurate estimate of ethnic composition. To illustrate, Irish immigrants, and especially those who were not Roman Catholics, often identified themselves as Scots, or even English. It is estimated that more than seven million Irish (and possibly eight) came to the United States, about one-half of them Dissenters and Anglican Catholics and the other half Roman Catholics. The Poles who landed before 1919 are listed as being from Austria-Hungary, Germany, and Russia. Just how many Poles immigrated is not known, but it is estimated that by 1950 there were between four and five million people of Polish background in this country. The situation with regard to the Jews is even more complicated. They migrated to the United States from a great many countries and reflect the ethnic and, to a degree, the racial characteristics of such countries as well as certain common ethnic patterns of their own Jewish communities and Hebrew tradition.

The nineteenth- and twentieth-century streams of people gave us more of an all-European character. These people fled from famines, poverty, pogroms, militarism, wars, and postwar collapses. They sought the promise and security beyond the "golden door." Only a few left fairly good opportunities in the old country in order to find better ones here. A very few were distinguished refugees.

EXAMPLES OF CULTURAL INFLUENCES ON FAMILY LIFE

In the following brief descriptions, we try to suggest something of the range of marriage and family customs in these many rich traditions. The examples selected are: (1) the Hebrew patriarchal family, (2) St. Paul's ideas of family morality, (3) the Puritans of Massachusetts Bay, (4) the Irish Dissenters, (5) the plantation aristocrats of Virginia, (6) the Negro freedmen, (7) the South Italians, and (8) the Eastern European Jews. A few of the more important experiments in family forms were mentioned in the previous chapter. Here we wish to deal only with examples of major cultural influences.

1. *The Hebrew Patriarchal Family.* The "Old Testament Christians," who were so numerous among our pre-Revolution immigrants, were strongly influenced by the Hebrew patriarchal family as they understood it. These Protestants overlooked the Old Testament legitimation of more than one wife and its sanctioning of one or more concubines. They accepted as an ideal the tendency for the Old Testament family to be predominantly monogamous and made this a generality so far as their own cultural patterns were concerned. They liked the dignity and the power of the authoritarian father and the way in which he was permitted to control his extended family organization of children, grandchildren, and servants. Such ideas on family organization were about as well adapted to rural needs on a new frontier as they were to the needs of Asiatic nomads.

By Israelite custom, the suitor gave a valuable present to his bride's family; this was called a *mohar*. The marriage ceremony was a simple one, at the end of which a rabbi, or some elderly male, would pronounce the benediction. Then all would partake of a wedding breakfast. The Hebrews developed an elaborate marriage code which even set forth how the child of a concubine or a slave might achieve a degree of status as a legitimate offspring.

2. *St. Paul's Ideas of Family Morality.* The ideas of St. Paul deeply influenced both Roman Catholic and Protestant precepts. The apostle

regarded the marital state as second best to celibacy. He advised the unmarried and widows to remain unmarried, but "if they cannot contain, let them marry: for it is better to marry than to burn. . . . Let not the wife depart from her husband: But and if she depart, let her remain unmarried, or be reconciled to her husband: and let not the husband put away his wife." * Only after a spouse died might a husband or wife marry again.

3. *Puritans of Massachusetts Bay (before 1650).* Men needed housekeepers and children. Women required a family setting in which to live and work. Therefore widows and widowers remarried almost immediately after the death of their mates. Public opinion was intolerant of unmarried adults. A Massachusetts law of 1636 specified "that all townes shall take care to order and dispose of all single persons and inmates within their towne, to service, or otherwise." Women were supposed to follow the advice of parent or guardian on choice of mate, and in marriage they had to bow in most matters of policy to their husband's decision. Formal education for girls was considered wasteful. Women's chief rights were those to life, to remarriage after the death of a husband, and to some freedom from chaperonage prior to marriage.

These Puritans betrothed themselves on much the same terms as the ancient Hebrews. Prior to marriage, the clergyman proclaimed the banns three times to determine if anyone knew of any reason why the two should not be joined. Betrothal dated from the first proclamation. The Puritans found nothing in the Bible giving marriage the status of a sacrament, and they therefore required magistrates rather than clergymen to officiate. As among the ancient Hebrews, a clergyman might merely pronounce a benediction or a "word of exhortation." Following the ceremony, the Puritans—again like the Israelites—feasted, drank, danced, and generally made merry. Marriage could terminate only through annulment, legal separation, or the death of a partner. Annulment could be obtained for such reasons as bigamy and consanguinity in degrees prohibited by the Levitical laws. The Court of Assistants had the right to grant divorce without the right of remarriage for such causes as adultery, extreme cruelty, desertion, sterility, and failure to provide. Very few cases were heard. Most mates apparently preferred to bear and forbear.

4. *Irish Dissenters.* These people streamed to the colonies and es-

* I Corinthians 7:9–11.

pecially to the expanding frontier before and after the American Revolution. In established towns, they were rapidly assimilated, but on the frontier they settled in small communities and were often held together by ties of blood and marriage. Although religiously similar to the Puritans, they had lived under conditions of extreme danger as well as oppression on another frontier in Ireland, and they were therefore freer, more individualistic, less somber, and more aggressive. Their simple matrimonial customs included the reading of banns on two successive Sundays after the church service. The girl had undergone training in homemaking and her hope chest was in preparation for her marriage almost from her birth. The marriage was in the bride's home. After a feast and great merrymaking, the couple would be conducted to their new home. They appeared ceremonially together at church the next Sunday. Family loyalty was extreme, and sacrifice for the education of children was a rule. In their large families, this sometimes meant that daughters were deprived of almost all opportunities in order that sons might get ahead. Wherever they went, the Irish Dissenters tried to take with them their teachers as well as their clergymen, or to have their clergymen double as educators. They regarded divorce as unthinkable and exerted strong pressures against separation.

5. *Plantation Aristocrats of Virginia.* In spite of the mixed class and ethnic backgrounds of early Virginians of all ranks, those who achieved wealth and power in the colony based their way of life on that of the English manorial estate as they thought it to be. That many of these "aristocratic" families came from modest or obscure backgrounds probably spurred their aspirations and pretensions. Their relatively easy wealth and the control they could exert over slaves and indentured servants made it possible for them to re-create a pattern of life that was disappearing in England. Many plantations were nearly complete economic and social units; their trade could be limited to the exchange of farm products for special items such as often could come only from abroad. The male head of the extended family attempted to become a "gentleman" devoted to leisure and to public responsibilities. His wife gave her attention, within a protective framework, to the management of her household and eventually to the advantageous marrying off of her children. In contrast with wealthy people in the North, who stressed entrepreneural virtues of hard work and business acumen, Virginia aristocrats trained their children in upper-class graces and pleasures. A double stand-

ard of morality was learned early. Girls had lower status, limitations on their freedom, and enforced chastity. Boys had greater personal freedom, including liberty to experiment sexually with a selected servant or slave.

6. *Negro Freedmen.* The Civil War and Emancipation disrupted both the slave system and Negro family life. Many freed Negroes wandered aimlessly, and it was only gradually that they recognized the merits of a more settled existence. Families of Negroes freed before the war and families permitted to remain together under slavery helped to stabilize post-Emancipation Negro family and community life. Such families had the bonds of affection which were sufficient to give their members a sense of belonging in a chaotic period. Free Negro husbands who became tenants or landowners in rural areas were able to reinforce sentimental and habitual family ties with economic ones. These farmers often tried to assume formal responsibilities resembling the modified Hebrew patriarchal model, but the mother-centered family was the most common pattern and continues in importance among Negroes. It was a heritage of slavery, of post-slavery confusion, of opportunities of work for women which were often more stable or attractive than those for men, and of the frequent need for men to follow work wherever they could find it. Since a similar matricentrism among Irish Roman Catholics is also accompanied by a similarly high frequency of alcoholism, social scientists suggest that matricentrism may be related to certain types of alcoholism, but it is possible that class or other factors may have a more significant bearing on alcoholism. Among Negro families seeking to take on middle-class patterns from the white community, premarital chastity for women and the acceptance of marital responsibilities by both men and women took on pressing importance. In commenting on the consequences of twentieth-century migrations of Negroes to our cities, the sociologist E. Franklin Frazier * concludes that urban living "has not resulted simply in the disorganization of the family, . . . but in the reorganization [of it] according to middleclass patterns, thus reflecting the new class structure in urban communities."

7. *South Italians.* A great many of our Italian immigrants were born in the southern provinces of the Italian peninsula or in Sicily. To them, "family" meant an extended and very cohesive group of grandparents, aunts, uncles, cousins, and godparents as well as fa-

* *The Negro in the United States* (rev. ed.; New York: Macmillan Co., 1957), p. 333.

ther, mother, and children. Thus the family provided a high degree of personal, social, and economic security. It made separation of husband and wife difficult and rare.

The South-Italian extended family fitted into a system of attachments to neighbors and to fellow villagers and of interfamily antagonisms, some of long standing. As a result, when family surnames first came into official use during the Napoleonic period, family networks gave them a similarity in a given area which made nicknames and informal occupational and place identifications more common in popular usage.

The father commanded deep respect, and the mother ruled formally as the interpreter of her husband's wishes. Her chief joys were to give "her man some food every day and a child every year," as a folk saying puts it. The mother held the family purse and chose wives for her sons, but the males were much more privileged than the females. Sons often earned their own marriage "gifts" from their parents, but father and brothers jointly shared the responsibility for dowries for the girls as well as the protection of their reputation.

The elder son usually brought his wife home to live, and upon his father's death he became head of the family. A child had a pair of godparents for each of two occasions—baptism and confirmation; the two sets might or might not be the same persons. These spiritual relatives had great significance in a child's development and social acceptance. From an early age, the sexes were segregated in education. Girls over six or seven were kept busy and seldom permitted to play games. Their chastity was a family concern, but boys were encouraged to have premarital sexual experiences. Girls were married as young as fourteen to boys only a year or two their elder.

In spite of religious differences, the family life of the southern Italians, when brought into the American environment, appears to have more in common with that of the Eastern European Jews than with that of the Irish Roman Catholics. South-Italian immigrants were almost all at least nominally Roman Catholics, but their anticlericalism and their superstitious belief in the "evil eye" (the ability of certain people to exert a magical evil influence) are traditional.

8. *Eastern European Jews*. The Jewish family, as it existed in the Old World, was large not merely because many children were valued but also because parents, grandparents, brothers, sisters, uncles, aunts, cousins (that is, the extended and the consanguine families, the "gantze mishpokheh") were regarded as family members. Indeed, the entire community could be included under the category, "family

group." A joint household of three generations living under the same roof was common. The head of this family was the senior male, whose status grew more elevated as his years increased. The aged were regarded as repositories of wisdom. Much of Jewish life focused on the maintenance and strengthening of family solidarity. The customs which reinforced family identification included having the entire kinship group come together during the holidays and for family celebrations such as weddings and "bar mitzvahs." Jewish marriage arrangements were primarily the responsibility of the heads of the two extended families concerned. This meant that marriage was not entrusted to the young man and woman who were to be mated. Marriage for love was a privilege of the very poor. In the Old World, and sometimes in the New, the specific job of bringing two people together was often given to a professional matchmaker, the "shadkhan" with his "little dog-eared book and umbrella." Underlying the custom of the arranged marriage was the conception of marriage as a relationship with rules under which any normal couple from the same background could be happily joined. There was pressure on both men and women to get married, and the unmarried girl was a pitiful figure. The Jewish housewife-mother, although hardly the social equal of her husband, nevertheless suffered no feelings of inferiority. Keeping a "kosher" house and rearing children were important services, and the Jewish wife who played this role well won high praise and respect. The large, cohesive, intimate Jewish family is rapidly becoming a thing of the past. It is being divided into smaller units by the same influences transforming other ethnic traditions in the United States.*

CONCLUSION

These patterns of marriage and family life are all prominent parts of America's past, but they are now changed into something different. What is happening to the marriage and family patterns of these and a great many other immigrant and aboriginal ethnic groups in the United States? What are they becoming? How are our "melting pots" functioning? These are major questions discussed in the next chapter.

* Digested by permission from Sidney Aronson, "Jewish Family Life in America," *Jewish Digest*, IV, No. 4 (January, 1959), 1–7. (*Jewish Digest* is a monthly magazine published in Houston, Texas.)

Chapter III

IS AN AMERICAN PATTERN EMERGING?

Millions of immigrants brought the United States the marriage and family traditions of the world. These forms have gradually been modified in the American environment. Currently they appear to be taking three major directions of development: (1) toward ethnoid patterns; (2) toward class patterns; and (3) toward over-all conformity. We shall discuss each of these tendencies in the following pages.

TOWARD ETHNOID PATTERNS

Our many and diverse ethnic groups are rapidly being assimilated into four major ethnic-like, or "ethnoid," segments of our population. These segments are set aside from one another through two prominent types of social labeling: religious identification and apparent skin color. These segments are, in order of their size, the "white Protestant," "Roman Catholic," "colored," and "Jewish." The religious terms are used here strictly for social designation and should not be thought to imply any specific degree of orthodoxy or of adherence. A great many persons under each of the religious labels rarely attend, and are not members in good standing of, a religious organization, but they continue to identify themselves, or at least to be identified by others, as "Protestant," "Roman Catholic," or "Jewish." Each of the four terms should be taken to refer to a general ethnic background which is growing into a new amalgam in the American environment and not to a strictly religious or racial group. Each of the four segments tends to be a semidetached subsociety within our society concerned especially with its separate social persistence through such techniques as banning or discouraging the marriage of members to outsiders. This concern with *endogamy* (in-marriage) within the segment helps to erect social dikes against over-all American conformity in detailed aspects of marriage and family life and to preserve the peculiar subcultural patterns and special organizations of the ethnoid segments. It does not completely prevent *exogamy* (out-marriage), marriage outside the ethnoid segment.

The social label of being nonwhite rather than actual skin pigmentation determines the membership of a great many Americans in the colored segment. For example, some people of European descent are darker than some who are part Negro, but the former are usually labeled "white" and the latter "colored." Some persons with colored skin—for example, some Japanese-Americans and American Indians—under certain circumstances can move, through intermarriage, into one of the "white" social segments from the colored segment. While a great many of the colored are Protestants, some are Roman Catholics, and a few are Jews (notably the Abyssinian Jews). Possibly the colored who are Spanish-speaking and Roman Catholic, especially nonwhites of Puerto Rican and Mexican-Indian origin, will come to constitute a second colored segment, but social pressures tend to push these groups into the more general colored segment, with its largely Protestant cultural orientation.

The Roman Catholic segment brings together the disappearing ethnic groups which originally came from such countries as Ireland, Italy, France, Germany, and Belgium.

Even though certain Jewish groups have tried hard to maintain their separateness from the rest of the Jewish segment (aided by Jewish religious denominationalism and special schools), their gradual assimilation into the Jewish composite proceeds steadily. The movement of Jewish families to the suburbs is seen as speeding up this integrative tendency.

In many ways the "white Protestant" social segment is a vague and loosely linked social entity. Its members constitute roughly two-thirds of the American population, and they feel and behave like a dominant group. They consider general American traditions and behavior norms as largely their own and hence give little attention to the preservation of their special ethnic and ethnoid patterns. They do, however, try to maintain endogamy within the white Protestant segment, and they look upon the other social segments as "minorities," which are to be kept differentiated and detached from their own majority. At the same time, the white Protestants are so divided into denominational, class, and other social groups that each white Protestant has in some degree the sense common in the United States of belonging to a minority. Certainly the National Council of the Churches of Christ in the United States, even though it is the principal federation of Protestant churches, does not represent all the religious organizations of the social segment. There are other federations of Protestant churches, and a great many white "Protestants" do not adhere to any particular Protestant church or even to the idea of a church or of institutionalized religion at all.

TOWARD CLASS PATTERNS

The chief limitation placed upon the integration of ethnic groups into ethnoid segments is this: Ethnic groups figure differentially in the formation of social classes. To illustrate, those who immigrated earliest often succeeded in giving their traditions and behavior patterns a disproportionate share in shaping the subculture of their segment's upper classes. They accomplished this by founding religious, educational, economic, and political organizations to which they gave their ethnic stamp and over which they were able, for a time, to maintain control. In so democratic a society as ours, with the possibility presumably open to all to achieve "success" and to move upward on a ladder of social recognition, it is paradoxical that the influence of the prestige symbols entrenched by early-arrivers remains powerful. Such symbols include family names and pedigrees, memberships in ancient and exclusive organizations, and inherited ownership of early pieces of Americana. The ability to relate oneself to tradition and to function "naturally" in terms of accepted behavior patterns becomes a device through which more recent immigrants attempt to legitimize their success. In this social legitimation, family names have often been modified to resemble those of the dominant ethnic group, as a measure of "Americanization." A single ancestor of conveniently early immigration is permitted to overshadow many others who arrived more recently. However, the success of people with "foreign-sounding" names in many prominent activities has offset the tendency to change patronymics.

The next chapter treats the conception of "social class" more fully, and we therefore touch upon it here merely in an introductory manner. The term *social class* refers to the way in which we customarily divide society into horizontal social categories. These categories are based on criteria as to who are (1) our social equals, (2) our social inferiors, and (3) our social superiors. Through the efforts of succeeding generations to stratify people, our society has evolved a customary system of social-class categories which gradually change but which influence an individual's associations, aspirations, thoughts, emotions, and actions. Class criteria involve, it is well to note, factors other than the wealth or dollar income of a family.

Social classes crosshatch, as it were, our ethnoid segments. Since an ethnoid segment includes a number of social classes, it is a "vertical" social category. A notable generalization regarding social classes within an ethnoid segment is that the subculture—the folkways and mores—of one class in one ethnoid segment has much·more in common with that of a comparable class in another segment than it has with other class subcultures in the same segment. For example, white Protestant skilled mechanics have social personalities more similar to those of colored or Roman Catholic skilled mechanics than to those of white Protestant lawyers or physicians. Interesting social contradictions also occur. For example, colored public school teachers are given higher prestige among the colored than white Protestants give their own public school teachers. Society in general tends to place public school teachers of all segments in the same social class, and the training and experience of such teachers place them in much the same class subculture. But in spite of these considerations, in many communities colored public school teachers are assigned lower prestige by white groups than their counterparts among the whites.

TOWARD OVER-ALL CONFORMITY

Because of the pervasive influence of the press, cinema, radio, and television, the four emerging segmental subcultures and the many social-class subcultures are under strong pressure to conform to an over-all American ethos (the sum of characteristic culture traits). Especially do our advertisements and retail displays present compelling patterns of family values and behavior models that foster at least a superficial similarity among a great many Americans. Thus Roman Catholic and Jewish family patterns in the United States exhibit strong intermixtures of things and actions typically and generally American as well as ideas drawn from Old World Roman Catholic and Jewish traditions. Practical child-care manuals are also influential in promoting this conformist trend. Whether a child is expected in the family of a captain of industry or of a trade-union member (in any ethnoid segment), the child's mother may accept the guidance of the very popular booklets developed by the United States Children's Bureau, Washington, D.C. Like millions of other mothers around the world, she may also read Dr. Benjamin Spock's *Baby and Child Care.*

As a result of the kinds of social pressures described above, we have probably achieved a higher degree of over-all social conformity in this huge country than more coercive methods ever produced in the smaller and more compact countries of the Old World. At the same time, beneath superficial resemblances, we continue to be divided by skin color, religious affiliation, and social class. We reinforce these divisions through organized group life oriented along ethnoid and social-class lines; the reference is to churches, special periodicals and books, residential neighborhoods, schools, and social clubs. Thus our ethnoid segments as well as social classes are likely to continue to crosshatch our society and to differentiate our social behavior, thoughts, and emotions during the foreseeable future. They will continue to change, but they will continue in our minds and in our social environment.

Most significant in the over-all changes to be found among American families is that fewer and fewer extended families now dwell together. In all classes and segments, families consisting of one basic family unit are becoming more common. In Europe and among the early Americans, the closely-knit extended family was common and practical. But our family life has now become so compressed into small urban dwelling units and the units are so scattered that grandparents are forced to live in special institutions or special dwelling arrangements; married children have to find their own habitations.

WHAT ABOUT INTERMARRIAGE?

To what extent does intermarriage break down interclass, interreligious, and interracial barriers and differences? Will America become even more homogeneous? Probably not. At least, not without the appearance of unforeseeable changes in life conditions. Why not? Interclass, interreligious, and interracial marriages take place, but the participants in these marriages must surmount difficult social obstacles. When a couple marries across such a barrier, the resulting family is usually assimilated into one of the two ethnoid segments or into one of the two social classes even though a degree of double identification will persist. The full assimilation of a mixed family typically requires at least a generation. For no less than that period are they likely to remain somewhat marginal among their fellow segment or class members. But the mate who crosses the barrier often has the fervor of a convert, whether because of pride or because of self-justification. Rather than making for greater general conformity, intermarriage may help strengthen class and segment differences.

Let us look at each of these types of intermarriage a little more closely.

Interracial Marriage. Three out of five American states, chiefly in the South and West, have had laws against interracial marriage. Six went so far as to place this prohibition in the state constitution. One-half of the states still bar Negro-white marriages, and about one-fourth forbid Mongolian-white marriages. The Fourteenth Amendment to the federal Constitution would appear to cancel such legislation, but the United States Supreme Court has not yet ruled on the question.

Marriages between Japanese citizens and white personnel in the American armed forces in Japan during and after World War II were common enough to result in some ten thousand Oriental spouses, mostly brides. Such intermarriages have also been common of Japanese-Americans, and it is possible that this group will merge more and more into the white ethnoid segments.

Studies of the rate of interracial marriage in selected urban areas indicate a little more than one in two hundred marriages. For the country as a whole, it would be a fraction of that. The couples frequently consist of a male from the less privileged racial group and a female from the more privileged. The commonest interracial marriages are across the lines of nonwhite groups, for example Negro-Indian.

Interreligious Marriage. A number of the larger religious organizations flatly forbid marriage outside of their faith or permit it only after substantial concessions from the outsider. The would-be spouse from outside is often given the choice of conversion or of promising to permit offspring of the union to be reared in the mate's religion.

The Orthodox, Conservative, and Reformed Jewish rabbis all oppose intermarriage. Their policy is to officiate at a marriage only after the outsider has become a Jew.

The Roman Catholic rule "has always been one of severely forbidding marriages of Catholics and non-Catholics; she [the Church] has from time to time merely tolerated such marriages by granting dispensation when guarantees were given that conditions designed to protect the faith of the Catholic party and the offspring would be fulfilled." * To this needs to be added, *"Even after she grants a dis-*

---

* G. J. Schnepp, "Mixed and Interracial Marriages," Chapter 7 in C. S. Mihanovich, G. J. Schnepp, and J. L. Thomas, *A Guide to Catholic Marriage* (Milwaukee, Wisc.: Bruce Publishing Co., 1963), p. 158.

pensation the Church withholds her approval. This is evident from her refusal to permit the marriage to occur at Mass and her refusal to impart the nuptial blessing upon the couple." * Such a dispensation is granted only for "just and grave" reasons.

Protestant churches in general do not favor interdenominational marriages, but they especially oppose unions with persons outside of the Protestant segment. Since individual Protestant congregations tend to draw their members largely from one social class, their religious pressures against marriage across Protestant denominational lines are reinforced by social-class pressures. In general, Protestant clergymen have taken a less rigid attitude than Jewish or Roman Catholic clerics toward religious intermarriage for these three reasons: "(1) the feeling that religion is essentially a personal matter and that the rights of individual consciences must be respected; (2) a sense on the part of Protestant ministers that in officiating at a marriage ceremony they are civil as well as religious authorities; and (3) the conviction that on an occasion which ought to [have] . . . sanction . . . religious ceremony should not be withheld." †

Several factors have stimulated in many Protestants a spirit of religious toleration which extends to a degree to marriage with a Roman Catholic of similar class and not too different ethnic characteristics. One of these factors has been the ecumenical movement, so popular among Protestants, which looks to a reunion of all Christian churches throughout the world. Another is the sense of strength given the Protestants by their being a kind of federative "majority" religious group. In spite of this general spirit of tolerance, formal opposition to religious exogamy continues to be strong. Lack of informal opposition to marriage with a Roman Catholic usually depends upon the degree of conviction that the outsider will become a convert. Ethnoid opposition to Jews and other non-Christians of a similar or lesser social class and degree of assimilation is considerably greater. Here as elsewhere in human relationships, such emergency problems as premarital pregnancy can make a great difference.

* Alphonse H. Clemens, *Marriage and the Family: An Integrated Approach for Catholics.* (C) 1957. Prentice-Hall, Inc., U.S.A. (P. 135.) See also Roman Catholic Canon 1061, and 1062.

† M. L. Barron, "Race, Religion, and Nationality in Mate Selection," Chapter 4 in Morris Fishbein and R. J. R. Kennedy, eds., *Modern Marriage and Family Living* (New York: Oxford University Press, 1957), p. 64. Reprinted by permission of the publisher.

To sum up, interreligious marriages meet little opposition so long as they are within an ethnoid segment and do not involve too great class difference.

Interclass Marriage. Romantic novels of earlier generations glorified interclass marriage. The poor-but-beautiful girl who married the wealthy young man was the female equivalent of the Horatio Alger who escaped from penury through thrift and hard work. Only the adaptations of these formulas were American; their prototypes dealt with peasants, folk heroes, princes, princesses, gods, and goddesses. In societies and periods in which the wife had little choice but to adjust herself to her husband as her lord and master, inequality in social background may not have mattered; it may even have strengthened male authority and made marital inequality seem more just. In the rags-marrying-riches novels, the story fortunately stopped at engagement or marriage and seldom faced the intricate processes of adaptation of two persons with contrasting values, emotional-conditioning, habits, and friends. A doctrine of equal rights in the family for husband and wife tends to make marriages more problematic among those who consider themselves socially unequal. The more psychological and sociological "romances" of recent years, when optimistic, have frequently portrayed a couple with similar backgrounds struggling toward "success" together.

In studies of mating, sociologists find a tendency for husbands to be drawn from the same general occupational group as their fathers-in-law. Where this is not the case, women are more likely than men to marry into a higher social-class group. In the case of marriages which are both interethnoid and interclass, women usually offset a loss in ethnoid prestige by a gain in class rank.

HOW MANY "MELTING POTS"?

On the basis of her studies of marriage license records in New Haven from 1870 to 1950, the sociologist Ruby Jo Reeves Kennedy raises the question, "Single or Triple Melting Pot?" * The term "melting pot" refers to how immigrant groups are "melted down" and fused together in this country. In response to her question, Kennedy interprets her evidence as pointing to three religiously labeled

* *American Journal of Sociology*, XLIX (1943–44), 331–339 and LVIII (1952–53), 56–59. Israel Zangwill popularized the term in his famous play *The Melting Pot* (1908).

"melting pots" in the United States—Jewish, Roman Catholic, and Protestant—rather than the one traditionally assumed to exist. On the contrary, careful studies of Jewish and Roman Catholic data indicate high and apparently still rising rates of intermarriage by members of the three major faiths.

The Jewish community, as the sociologist Erich Rosenthal * judges from data for Greater Washington (D.C.) and the state of Iowa, appears to be moving "from the stage of acculturation into the last phase of the . . . cycle, assimilation and amalgamation." In Washington, for example, "the intermarriage rate rises from about 1 per cent among the first generation—the foreign-born immigrants—to 10.2 per cent for the native-born of foreign parentage and to 17.9 per cent for the native-born of native parentage (third and subsequent generations)." He therefore concludes that "the ethnic and religious bonds that welded the immigrant generation into a highly organized community are becoming progressively weaker." His data "cast doubt on the doctrine of the persistence of religious endogamy in American life and on the idea of the 'return of the third generation.'"

In summarizing data on exogamy by Roman Catholics, the sociologist G. J. Schnepp † concludes that "valid mixed marriages" (*i.e.*, Roman Catholic marriages in which one spouse is Catholic) have held steadily at about 25 to 30 per cent of all Roman Catholic marriages between 1930 and 1960. He underscores, however, "that invalid [*i.e.*, non-Church] mixed marriages are not included in these statistics; their extent is unknown, nor do we know whether they are increasing or decreasing." He found the following influences those chiefly operative: (1) In large Catholic communities, there was less intermarriage; in small communities, there was more. (2) Catholics with higher socioeconomic status are more likely to find non-Catholic mates. (3) Mixed marriages are also more frequent on lower social status levels. (4) They are more often among those marrying younger. (5) "Mixed marriage rates seem to be lower in areas occupied by cohesive ethnic groups. . . . However, with the flight to the suburbs, such parishes have become fewer and fewer, and such traditions consequently weaker and weaker."

Do such high rates of intermarriage mean serious "leakage" from

---

* "Studies of Jewish Intermarriage in the United States," *American Jewish Year Book*, LXIV (1963), 3–53; pp. 52–53 quoted.

† *Op. cit.*, pp. 166–167.

the Jewish and Roman Catholic communities? Do they suggest eventual amalgamation in a single "melting pot"? Are they better interpreted as suggesting the evolution of new bases for ethnoid identity and cohesiveness? They may well suggest something of all these points. The Jewish and Roman Catholic communities as they have been are "leaking" members. Their members are thus probably amalgamating into somewhat different types of social status groups. In our multivalent society, social status groups of cohesive and contrasting sorts most likely will continue to exist, and ethnoid identification would appear to be one of their continuing characteristics. The mate who changes from one ethnoid segment to another often defensively takes on an anxious overadherence, and the children of such a marriage frequently make a similar overcompensation.

The chief claim that our ethnoid segments, other than the colored, have upon continuity appears to be their organizational vested interests. Immigrant ethnic groups fail to persist through their lack of a durable and exclusively controlled "American" organizational structure. Ethnoid groups, on the other hand, are "American" and control religious, residential, political, economic, and social organizations formally or informally. They are likely to contribute for many years to the pluralistic character of our society.

With regard to the future of our ethnoid segments, two predictions are often made. These are:

1. *The segments will become more segregated geographically.* Because of the tendency of the ethnoid segments to segregate themselves and to be segregated, large areas of our cities are becoming colored, and other areas which are urban, suburban, or exurban are coming to be known as typically Roman Catholic, Jewish, or Protestant. As new residential areas develop, their religious and other organizational centers are notably ethnoid rather than ethnic. Private elementary and secondary schools help to carry segregation even further in public school districts which overlap several ethnoid areas, but public school districts are often gerrymandered to coincide with ethnoid areas. The increasing financial benefits being obtained for the pupils in private schools, as well as the parochialization of public schools in segregated ethnoid areas, further facilitate the segregative tendency.

2. *The segments may eventually,* some social scientists contend, *become more classlike.* This possibility is related to the limited number of social classes represented in the schools and other social organizations that emerge in our segregated ethnoid residential areas.

The prediction is that we may eventually have social classes each of which is overwhelmingly colored or Jewish or Roman Catholic or Protestant. This would imply a degree of curtailment of vertical mobility and a degree of freezing of inherited status which would, we trust, be intolerable to Americans. Before World War I, especially in the older parts of the United States, certain ethnic groups had succeeded in perpetuating, from generation to generation, their control of high-status positions in finance, industry, selected professions, and "society." As other groups have challenged the dominance of the white Protestants, their monopoly is gradually being broken.

Rather than ethnoid monopolies of certain social classes or ethnoid mergers along class lines, experience appears to indicate that interethnoid tensions develop at the class levels where a preponderance of one ethnoid group appears. Thus middle-class white Protestants have relatively little antagonism toward Negroes and other members of the evolving colored segment, but they exhibit relatively strong anti-Jewish sentiments. Lower-class white Protestants are not nearly as concerned with Jews as with the competing colored segment. The size, strength, and organization of the Roman Catholic ethnoid segment, especially in the large cities, have brought about a resurgence of militant anti-Catholicism. This resistance to the upward mobility of the members of the Roman Catholic segment takes different forms in each of the non-Roman-Catholic social-class groups. When Roman Catholics set up their own special organizations of trade unionists, public employees, and professional men and women, the other ethnoid groups tend to organize or to use existing organizations to compete.*

CONCLUSION

As national and international events influence American social life, the ethnocentrism of our ethnoid segments and of our social classes rises and falls. We can see an American pattern of marriage and family life taking form in the sense that the subcultures of all American groups influence one another and also share common influences. Popular education and mass communications exert powerful pres-

* A. McC. Lee, "Sociological Insights into American Culture and Personality," *Journal of Social Issues,* VII, No. 4 (1951), 7–14; and his "The Impact of Segregated Housing on Public Schools," *School and Society,"* LXXXVIII (1960), 241–243.

sures toward conformity. In a rather vague and general way, all Americans tend thus to share certain cultural patterns, a kind of general over-all American culture. But we also have ethnoid and class subcultures which are likely to persist and to enrich our social life with their folkways and mores for a great many years to come.

Chapter IV

SOCIOECONOMIC ASPECTS OF THE FAMILY

The terms "standard of living," "mode of living," "division of labor," "occupation," "social status," and "social class" deal with basic aspects of individual and family life which are both economic and more broadly social. They lead directly into discussions of changing class differences and changing roles within the family. They are related to the movement of individuals and families upward and downward in the social scale ("vertical mobility"). They are modified by the increasing ease and greater frequency with which Americans change their places of work and of habitation ("horizontal mobility"). Permeating all such conceptions, too, are the possible consequences of booms and depressions, "good times" and recessions, natural catastrophes, and wars, cold wars, and sometimes peace. In other words, such terms help to confront us with the more general and overall socioeconomic changes which constantly influence families.

In the following discussion, we take up these complicated and interrelated aspects of marriage and the family.

STANDARD OF LIVING

A useful brief definition for *standard of living* is that it consists of "all those things which one insists upon having." It is a folk conception. It is an integration of habitual and traditional patterns of thought, emotion, and behavior. It is "something more than the sum of its parts, something different from any one of them, a power to which we defer unconsciously in every choice we make, and which we frequently invoke to sustain arguments or justify general policies" * In the definition given, "all those things" enter into a configuration of values dealing with economic needs and desires. It is both a positive and a negative pattern; it is important both for what it includes and for what it omits or rejects. It is a composite of in-

* E. T. Devine, *The Normal Life* (2nd rev. ed.; New York: Macmillan Co., 1917), pp. 1, 129.

sistences upon economic "having" as stimulated by example, formal education, news, fiction, advertising, informal social pressures, and opportunity.

Whose Standard of Living? The current conceptions of a standard of living for a society at large are vague and general but, within the limits typical of that society, they are compelling. A societal standard is never seen and understood in the same way by all of a society's members. As a standard of living is typically found in a given time, place, and society, it is subject to definition in the over-all conventions and morals (culture) of the society. For a social group —a class, ethnoid segment, or family—a more specific conception of this standard also exists, and it is much more mandatory than the societal standard. It is more specific and is defined by each group's folkways and mores (its subculture). For an individual, decisions with respect to standards of living depend upon the social situation in which he at the moment of decision finds himself. His values have been shaped by his life experiences, and those experiences include his having assimilated the often contradictory standards of his society and his groups.

Multiple Standards of Living. There are thus in a society a great many standards of living, each typical of some part of the population when functioning as members of that part. Each configuration or standard is a mosaic, as it were, of social artifacts. Each is a gradual human creation out of tradition and experience and life conditions. It is real and influential because people try to live by it and find it, for the time, worth living by. It may be restricted to a modest selection of items concerned chiefly with subsistence; it may include a great many alleged needs for goods, facilities, and services which may be sought for the most part to heighten social prestige, status, or power. Items desired and used solely to raise or maintain status are cited by the social economist Thorstein B. Veblen * as instances of "conspicuous consumption" or even of "conspicuous waste."

Those who hold and try to implement a given standard of living are usually able to make its nature clear enough either to interviewers or to those observing socioeconomic behavior. Policy-makers who try, with the aid of social researchers, to set forth "minimum" or "adequate" standards of living sometimes perform useful educational or social-welfare services. In any discussion, however, it is necessary

* *The Theory of the Leisure Class* (1899; New York: Modern Library, 1934), esp. Chapter 4.

to know and remember whether a mentioned standard is one held popularly and by which people try to live or is one being advocated or to which people aspire.

MODE OF LIVING

In contrast to a standard of living, a *mode of living* is a matter not of insistence or aspiration but of actual behavior or ·accomplishment. It is the pattern apparent in the processes of family economic activity typical of a society or of a group within a society. It involves more than the mere amount of energy or number of dollars available, used, and reserved. No single numerical index can suggest it. Six families making similar expenditures of energy can have six different modes of living. Even if they have similar monetary incomes, they can still have six different modes of living. The terms "plane of living" and "contour of living" are also used, but "mode of living" more adequately labels the social behavior in question. Like a standard of living, a mode is also "something more than the sum of its parts." It is an interrelated pattern of behavior. It is the result at a given time and in the light of existing circumstances of the efforts by individuals and groups to implement their standard of living. It includes acquisitions of a great many kinds. It also includes the diverse use of similar items. As we have seen, the goods and services acquired may be essential in a very narrow sense to the sustenance of life, or they may be primarily for conspicuous exhibition or consumption. Their acquisition and the manner of their use by a given family depend chiefly upon the degree of the family's assimilation into its ethnoid segment and its social class.

DIVISION OF LABOR

Unless one insists upon some special definition of "profession," the world's oldest profession is obviously that of motherhood. The woman's tie to this age-old calling, the helpless dependence of relatively recent offspring, and the greater freedom of the adult male to cope with problem situations external to the family are the three basic and continuing factors running historically through the division of labor among family members. Beyond the implications of those constants, vast variation has been possible and is still to be found.

Except for childbearing, men typically concern themselves with all the activities of a society which are its major public preoccupations. Thus men have been free to give their energies to, and even to specialize in, war, the hunt, herding, politics, religion, agriculture, manufacture, distribution, education, or finance. Women, on the other hand, have had to be unspecialized Jills-of-many-trades. This arises from the responsibility of women for children and often also for food-preparation and the maintenance of shelter. Their chief vocation has kept all but relatively few women from specializing in anything but child-rearing and homemaking.

Women retained substantial control of each of a great many practical arts until the art entered importantly into trade and commerce. Then males, with their greater freedom to specialize, gave it their concentrated attention, far more attention than women could take from their endless domestic tasks and concerns. When individual women find themselves in circumstances where they must assume public responsibilities, a number of them achieve distinction.* Relatively few women in any society find themselves in such a position. Almost always it had to be men rather than women, therefore, who developed industrial arts technologically for systematic and large-scale exploitation. "Down through the ages," concludes the social economist Hazel Kyrk,† "men's work has been the honorific, women's the nonhonorific. It has been considered a disgrace for a man to do a woman's work and an exceptional honor for a woman to be permitted to do men's work."

Recent Changes in the Division of Labor. The traditional division of labor was well exemplified by our early rural American immigrants. The husband did the fighting, hunting, house-building, furniture-making, large-scale farming, principal trading, and managing of assistants available to him in the extended family. The wife did the vegetable-gardening, spinning, weaving, knitting, sewing, child-rearing, cooking, preserving, washing, ironing, and all the rest, including educating the young and even helping to fight the Indians. The wife could use children and other family members as assistants when she and they were not needed "in the fields." Everyone had a share in the family enterprise. For example, we know a great deal

---

* See the study of 628 American women by Elizabeth Briant Lee in her *Eminent Women: A Cultural Study* (Ph.D. dissertation, Yale University, 1937).

† *The Family in the American Economy* (Chicago: University of Chicago Press, 1953), p. 273.

about the frontier exploits of Daniel Boone but little about the work of his wife, Rebecca Briant Boone, whose contributions included writing much of Daniel's "autobiography."

The family situation evolving today in the United States is in sharp contrast with the foregoing and is without precedent. As our homes become more and more mechanized, with a larger and larger share of preparatory work on food, clothing, and other materials done outside of the home, and as a large part of the care of children and other dependents becomes institutionalized, women are being presented with the possibility of social freedom approaching that of men. As long as there is a national situation of approximately full employment, women will have considerable freedom in the choice of career; they will also continue to have little incentive for concentration upon a vocation other than homemaking.

Women ordinarily work outside the home when they feel they have to do so. They do it to support themselves or dependents, to help their husband get established, or to maintain a desired mode of living. Even though such employment may continue throughout a large part of their adult lives, the traditional association of women with the roles of wife and mother still gives their vocational activities something of a temporary flavor. This is so despite the fact that the employed women may often long defer or even reject the function of childbearing. A man is conceded to have a primary concern with his public career, but a woman still has to do a great deal of proving to be given a similar concession.

Life Phases of Modern Women. Modern men have so many possible choices of career in any social class that they often have difficulty in selecting a pursuit and in focusing their interests upon it. This selection is further complicated by the fact that too many young men can see little connection between earlier phases of their lives and their career interests. For a modern woman, the choice of a principal vocation is usually simple enough, but the sequence of life phases for which she should prepare is likely to be even more complex than that of a man. Women now face the practical necessity of preparing for homemaking and at least one other vocation. Perhaps they no longer need to be "Jills" of as many trades as were their ancestresses, but they still often must cope with difficult problems of adjustment during five periods of their life span: (1) at the parental home, (2) in commercial employment before marriage, (3) in commercial employment after marriage, (4) during active motherhood, and (5) in commercial employment after children are no longer in need of constant attention. Often little of her experience in any one of these periods prepares the woman for the next, and she may not wish to plan realistically for the next phase of her life. For instance, she may not care to think of employment immediately following marriage, and she may not wish to get ready for a return to commercial work within ten or twenty years after marriage. Let us look briefly at other aspects of these life phases that may be troublesome for many American women.

During informal and formal education at home and in school, a girl finds it difficult to plan definitely for a possible commercial career when she feels the problems of the "marriage market" are more pressing, speculative though that market might be. A husband is not a certainty for every woman; granted a husband, a woman's future in marriage depends upon many unpredictable factors. Girls try to be ready to "make some money" which they may need before marriage. At the same time, they try to develop personality traits that will be useful in the rating, dating, and mating procedures of their groups. This period terminates when they pass the age for compulsory education or when they finish the additional schooling considered appropriate or desirable. It may end at the time of marriage.

The trend toward younger marriages during and following World War II has been accompanied by an increase in the number of young wives who continue in commercial employment until their first pregnancy. The combination of commercial employment with wifehood is complicated by anxieties about pregnancy and finance. In addition, the wife may be poorly equipped for the detailed demands of childbearing and child-rearing, even for the routine tasks of housekeeping. The operation of needed household gadgets may tax the combined skills of wife and husband.

Perhaps the fifth period of a woman's life span is the most difficult, even though it might become a pleasant and useful one. When it is necessary or desirable for a middle-aged woman to find a commercial position, she may discover that the skills of her youth have either been forgotten or are no longer saleable. Fortunately, the increasing public awareness of the new pattern for the life histories of women in our society is encouraging them to plan their lives ahead more realistically. Girls now discuss the need for preparing for their probable changes in role. Mothers of young children study and look forward to the time when they may again seek the challenge and financial rewards of a career outside the home. This new pattern is not restricted to certain social classes. "It is shared by many, many women who have received little or no higher education, who have had rather routine, unglamorous jobs before their children were born. For women of all types and temperaments have been stimulated by the sights and sounds of our civilization, by our political, social, and economic issues as well as by our sports and our entertainments. They have begun to wonder whether marriage and motherhood are all-consuming." *

OCCUPATION

Occupation is a concept which is closely related not only to the division of labor in the family and in society but also to "social status" and "social class" (see page 27). Perhaps the best definition of occupation is that of the psychologist Anne Roe,† namely, "whatever an adult spends most of his time doing." To this she adds, "That may be what he does to earn a living or it may not." The individual's principal activity may be a hobby; it may or may not be remunerative. In this sense, being a homemaker or a mother is most frequently regarded as an occupation. Being a father is rarely so regarded, for it almost never absorbs the major part of a man's time or attention. An occupation becomes the major focus of a person's behavior, usually also of his thoughts, and possibly even of his emotions. The general question, "What do you do?" or even "What are you?" usually is taken to refer to occupation.

Occupational status can be spoken of as a separable aspect of occupation. Like occupation, this term also refers to a job or anything else upon which an adult spends most of his time, but occupational status denotes the position or pursuit without concern (*a*) for the person who may be involved in it, (*b*) for the role or roles it may require that person to perform, or (*c*) for the manner in which he may exemplify such an aggregation of behavior patterns. In a society and its appropriate groups, such a status is accorded a degree of prestige, of privilege, and of control over others, and usually also a degree of rejection, of deprivation, and of control by others. When one defines a person's occupation, it is clear that status, role, and performance are all necessarily relevant.

* Sidonie M. Gruenberg and Hilda S. Krech, "The Modern Mother's Dilemma," *Public Affairs Pamphlet* No. 247 (New York, 1957), p. 1.

† *The Psychology of Occupations* (New York: John Wiley, 1956), p. 3.

Occupational status ladders each contain a series of steps with rising prestige, privilege, and control. Society develops status ladders in each principal area of human activity. In industry, for example, a status ladder extends from the unskilled laborer through the ranks of the skilled and the minor bosses to the managers who control vast enterprises. In a refined classification of industrial statuses, one might point to an entrepreneural status ladder, a technical status ladder, and a bureaucratic status ladder. The first of these three ladders has a similarity to those of labor and political organizers and manipulators. The bureaucratic one resembles the status ladders of the army and of government. Then there are the status ladders of the educational, religious, legal, medical, and research professions and those of the creative arts. Some call status ladders "pecking orders" from an analogy to the way in which chickens in a flock work out among themselves an order of priority as to the privilege of pecking one another. The most favored or aggressive hen can peck at all the others, and the least favored can be pecked at by all the others. The rest fall into a series between the two extremes.

A society gains much of its special character from the occupational status ladder or ladders to which it gives most prominence. Sometimes there is a differentiation among the ladders to which a society gives greatest prestige, privilege, or control; but there is also a constant tendency for such differentiations to be eliminated and for one status ladder to assume a greater share of all three attributes. For example, in certain of the early American colonies the clergy enjoyed the greatest prestige, privilege, and control. Then they were stripped of much of their control by secular politicians and businessmen, and they saw their claims on popular prestige diminished by competing secular counselors, writers, and speakers. Soon the special privileges of the clergy started to slip from them as well. Our earliest secular occupational status ladders of great prestige were ones associated with government. Governmental spokesmen still are accorded high prestige, but in peacetime top business leaders have greater and more independent power over others, and they now press harder and harder for matching prestige. As the interchange of skilled persons among business, education, government, and the military becomes more possible and common, the values associated with our status ladders in occupations come more and more to resemble those of the "big-time gravy train," those of business. Even the "old-fashioned" values of the arts and professions tend to conform to those of business and especially of the absorbing status ladder of the enterprisers to whom bureaucrats in industry, commerce, finance, and government are sub-servient.

SOCIAL STATUS

Social status is a more general term than occupational status. It in-cludes the many statuses which persons, families, and other groups may possess. To illustrate, there are religious, marital, legal, and edu-cational statuses. Each status is a recognized position or relationship to society or a group without reference to the specific person who may possess the status. For any given time and place, a social status is defined in the current conventions and morals of a society and in the folkways and mores of its appropriate groups. Each status tends to open and to close doorways to privilege, to grant and to limit con-trol over others and by others, and to yield and to deny social pres-tige. Associated with each social status is a social role or several roles, and the person holding the status interprets and adapts the roles within limits prescribed socially, but the term status refers to the po-sition and not to the role or its adaptation. For instance, there are many ways in which a woman can perform as mother and still earn social approval; the social status of motherhood carries with it for any mother a pattern of privilege, control, and prestige.

In societies which emphasize more than ours the inheritance of privileges, social statuses are commonly *assigned* to a person as a re-sult of his birth into a given family, sex, color, ethnoid group, social class, and place and of his reaching a given age. The "cake of cus-tom" of the society protects and maintains the traditional assignment of social statuses. As the "cake" breaks up under the impact of chang-ing conditions, more equalitarian societies with more freedom to *achieve* statuses come into being at least for the time. In all societies, regardless of the rigidity or "staleness" of the "cake of custom," a great many statuses are open to persons who are adroit and aggres-sive enough to recognize and use means available to circumvent tra-ditional assignments of status. Such means are especially open in times of emergency.

Social status ladders take on a coloration from occupational status ladders, but they also provide alternative or supplementary pathways to distinction, privilege, and control. For example, a church board of trustees is likely to consist of the holders of esteemed occupational statuses, especially businessmen, but it frequently also includes at least a few to whom their church status is their most prestigious ac-tivity. Similarly, university professors advance through the academic ranks on the basis of various qualifications, some academic (a record of effective teaching, research, publication, or administration) but others based on status outside the academic world (experience in commercial or governmental consultation, access to men of power or wealth). University boards of control consist overwhelmingly of high-ranking businessmen, rarely of specialists in education or research.

Prestige, privilege, and control gained by a person in one social status are, when handled with care, useful in his efforts to achieve comparable statuses on other social status ladders. To a considerable degree, individuals making up families tend to have places on social status ladders which are complementary. In our relatively free and open society, occupational statuses are most often *achieved,* albeit often with family assistance, but many other social statuses are *assigned* as a result of occupational achievement, birth, sex, and age. A child is born into a family with a collection of social statuses which he may or may not be able to assume. He may wish to escape them. At least he starts life with the advantages and disadvantages of given ethnic, ethnoid, and class statuses.

SOCIAL STRATIFICATION

Social stratification enables most people to simplify their thinking about the relative status of others. They accept popular judgments of *stratum,* that is of social level or layer, which sum up general estimates of social status. Few members of a community bother to ascertain their community's whole structure of social classes, which includes both strata and class groups. Most of them are satisfied with identifying the persons they and others consider to be "as good as," "better than," or "not so good as" themselves. Some may use additional categories, perhaps designating "those at the top," "ne'er-do-wells," and people who are merely "different." Class assignments are based to some extent upon unique personal characteristics, but to a larger measure upon categorical estimates of where others stand in relation to oneself on the social status ladders of the community. These categories are customary and social.

A social stratum consists of the persons and groups who are placed by common usage on the same general level and who above all share a similar class subculture. A class group is a subdivision of a stratum, and it is more limited. It is the part of a social stratum within an ethnoid segment or one possessing other common, specialized, and segregating interests. To illustrate, what is ordinarily called the "middle class" consists of one or more social strata depending upon the size of the community. Each stratum consists of persons roughly equivalent socially. Then, as the previous chapter brought out in the discussion of multiple "melting pots," the white Protestants, Roman Catholics, Jews, and colored divide each stratum into social class groups.

In addition to simplifying the social landscape, as it were, social strata and class groups also have these characteristics: They are somewhat endogamous; marriage outside of a stratum, especially "downward," is frowned upon and deemed inexpedient or irresponsible. Strata develop their own subcultures, and so do class groups. Class groups have cultural patterns drawn from both a stratum subculture and an ethnoid subculture. Whether highly or lowly privileged, strata and class groups develop and use organizations, neighborhoods, and other social facilities to perpetuate and strengthen their moretic values and the welfare of their personnel. The boundary lines among social strata and class groups are not drawn precisely; but, except for marginal cases, a community makes its members aware of its stratification as well as of its further class subdivisions.

Under American frontier conditions, social classes as social categories were at least in theory minimized. The status ladders built around the church, land-ownership, and government were presumably open equally to all members of the dominant ethnic or ethnoid stock. Such terms as "hereditary aristocracy," "proletariat," and "peasantry" were not popular and did not fit social realities. The distinction common in England between the "gentry" and others persisted for a while in some older American centers at least until the Revolution; then it lost its Old World meaning of hereditary rank. At the same time, cultural differences among individuals and families gradually became more obvious as social conditions settled, numbers increased, population centers took on urban characteristics, the different parts of the country developed their own types of economy, and ethnic, racial, and religious segments became large enough to constitute recognizable and continuing variants in social organization and structure.

How Many Social Classes Are There? The European threefold pattern of social strata (upper, middle, and lower) has had some general applicability in the United States throughout our history, but it is actually oversimple. In our smaller communities, there might be as few as one or two social strata, and in our large centers there may well be a great many more than three strata. The social anthropologist W. Lloyd Warner,* preoccupied with a unidimensional conception of social classes, has identified himself with the six-strata system he found in a number of his community studies in the United States. These levels are: (1) the upper upper class of old-family aristocrats, people with inherited wealth and station, (2) the lower upper class of newly successful families, (3) the upper middle class of managers, leading professional people, enterprisers with moderate-sized businesses, and civic leaders, (4) the lower middle class of small business enterprisers, white-collar workers, and highly skilled workmen, the upper part of the Common Man level, (5) the upper lower class of semiskilled workers, small tradesmen, the "honest workmen," who constitute the lower part of the Common Man level, and (6) those who are somehow outside of the "system" and yet dependent upon it, the "worthless," the not respectable, the pitied unfortunates, the ne'er-do-wells, and the new "greenhorn" immigrants.

This sort of vertical stratification of social classes fails to account adequately for (1) certain highly significant *qualitative differences* among social class groups on the same general status level and in the same ethnoid segment, (2) *ethnoid differences,* and (3) the operation of *geographical factors.* We shall outline the significance of these three elements in the following paragraphs.

1. *Qualitative differences* among social class groups on the same general level arise from the contrasting values associated with the four principal groups of occupational status ladders in our society. These are: (*a*) the entrepreneural, (*b*) the bureaucratic, (*c*) the professional, and (*d*) the inventive. The speculative and exploitative values associated with the entrepreneural status ladders pervade their families. Such values differ markedly from those of the more conservative, appeasing, and maneuvering bureaucrats and their families. The identification of bureaucrats with the goals of the institutions they represent drives a wedge between them and the more intellectually autonomous professionals whose concentration is upon techniques. The values of the more inventive—those of creative craftsmen, artists, inventors, writers, and researchers—many times are as upsetting and alienating to the bureaucrats and professionals as are

* *American Life: Dream and Reality* (Chicago: University of Chicago Press, 1953), pp. 55–60.

those of the entrepreneurs. The entrepreneural and the inventive status ladders, as the less stable and less controllable ones, are more open to invasion on a mixed basis by people from a variety of eth-noid segments. The arts have been especially hospitable to talented aspirants from the less favored ethnoid segments and social classes.

In small communities, where the limited number of possible associates helps to breed a greater tolerance for value differences, these four groups of occupational ladders do not splinter the social strata; but in our large centers such qualitative differences develop within the horizontal divisions (strata). These more specialized social class groups, many of them further divided along ethnoid lines, are common, and they are relatively isolated from one another. They even seek specialized areas in our cities, suburbs, and exurbs in which to live and work, or at least in which to center their activities and interests.

2. *Ethnoid differences* within classes have been discussed in connection with the American patterns of family life. Here their effect upon stratification should be noted. A member of a social stratum in our society has similar class folkways and mores reflected in his thoughts, emotions, and behavior regardless of his ethnoid segment; but the prestige, privileges, and relation to social control accorded him depend upon whether he is inside or outside of his ethnoid segment and reflect the general status of that segment as well as of his social stratum.

3. *Geographical factors* profoundly modify the character of strata and of class groups within them. American cities, towns, and rural areas have always had one or another form of local class-patterning. This local process reflects, reinforces, and helps to preserve existing over-all class arrangements. In addition, there has long been a tendency toward increasing regional and national socializing among our wealthy old families, our newly rich, the managers of similar businesses, and the members of similar professions. As modern means of communication and transportation bring geographic areas (whether they be parts of city, state, or nation) closer together, a partial national structure of social classes is evolving through a generalization or merging of certain local class groups. The sociologist C. Wright Mills * concludes: "The strivings of the new upper class and the example of the managerial elite of the national corporation cause local

* *The Power Elite* (New York: Oxford University Press, 1956), p. 46.

societies everywhere to become satellites of status and class and power systems that extend beyond their social horizon." Vast and integrated corporations, labor unions, professions, governmental departments, trades, and political parties are giving all activities and values an increasingly national orientation. On many a university campus, for example, it is often noted that a specialist will know his fellow specialists across the country better than he does a specialist in another field in the next office. The new upper-class groups center about prestigious clubs in our most important cities and in our most expensive estate areas. These groups subject their children to the initiatory and standardizing procedures in vogue in a few exclusive preparatory schools and colleges. The managerial elite, the top "hired men" for the new upper-class groups, are similarly national but, as the perceptive journalist William H. Whyte, Jr.,* notes, are in a great many ways the creatures of "the organization."

What About "Class Consciousness"? Usage gives "class consciousness" the sense "of both a feeling of membership in a class and the possession of certain attitudes, interests, ideas, etc. typical of some class." † When asked for the name of the social class to which they belong, Americans are quite vague and often mention the traditionally respectable and modest "middle class." Our class consciousness is not appreciably a matter of class-labeling. If one defines "a feeling of membership" as a reciprocated sense of identification with certain groups of people as being social equals and "like us" and not with others, then both conditions of the definition given of class consciousness have prevailed for a long time and are abundantly met now in the United States. Lacking precise labels and publicly discussed ideologies, however, our class consciousness is only generally of a kind to which competing propagandists may appeal. Because of the related openness of our social classes, if not of our ethnoid segments, class cleavage is invidious but rarely acrimonious. In the politico-economic area, according to social psychologist Richard Centers,‡ class cleavage "as yet exists only as a sort of non-support and dissent of a class, and as an organized protest and struggle for mainly immediate and tangible goals by a militant minority of that class." In our

* *The Organization Man* (New York: Simon and Schuster, 1956), esp. Chapter 11.

† Richard Centers, *The Psychology of Social Classes* (Princeton, N.J.: Princeton University Press, 1949), p. 33 note.

‡ *Ibid.,* pp. 218–219.

social clubs, public, parochial, and private schools, churches, marriages, and other such organizations and activities, class cleavage is marked, effective, and growing.

Horizontal Mobility. The increased ease and frequency with which we change our places of work and habitation is modifying a great many aspects of American family life in addition to stimulating the regionalization and nationalization of certain of our social class groups. Three of the most obvious evidences of the change are (1) the "explosion" of our cities into suburbs, into satellite centers and satellite cities, and beyond into the exurbs; (2) the appearance of a "floating" population, many of them housed in trailers; and (3) the constant insertion of employment advertisements from other parts of the country in local newspapers. We are less tied to one locality than ever before, and this fact increases our sense of rootlessness. We have gained an exhilarating feeling of freedom as the result of being able to leave a home or job of which we are tired and to start "in a fresh place" elsewhere, but we are losing the values of disciplining ourselves to make the best of the "old town" and of relishing long-time human associations.

Vertical and Intergroup Mobility. In our multidimensional conception of social-class groups, movement from one class group to another is not necessarily a matter of going "up" or "down" in some social scale. When the son of a prominent lawyer in private practice becomes a sculptor or perhaps a salesman of relatively equal prominence, there is no "vertical" mobility, but there has been a shift from one class group to another with strikingly different folkways and mores and with strikingly different types of prestige, control, and privilege. The two groups may have equivalent prestige, for example, but it is scarcely the same kind of prestige. It would seem best, therefore, to reserve the term "vertical mobility" for changes in horizontal strata, a going "up" or "down," as judged socially, and to speak of "intergroup mobility" as a more inclusive and accurate label for movement between any two of our many social-class groups.

The ethnoid and qualitative divisions of our social strata are the relatively recent consequences of upward mobility by ethnoid minorities other than the Protestant. These divisions also arise from the increasing socializing in urban areas among people who belong to the same occupational group rather than among those who happen to live within the same neighborhood. Another outstanding change is the relatively greater ability of unionized workers to up-grade themselves socially as well as economically. They thus now appear in a different relative position than they did previously to the largely nonunionized workers in such white-collar jobs as school-teaching, clerical work, and selling behind the counter in a store. We thus have a tendency for whole social class groups as well as in-dividuals to be mobile in relation to the general class situation. It takes far more than equal income, however, to make the families of highly skilled factory or railroad workers and school principals re-gard each other as being "our kind of people."

Over-all changes in socioeconomic conditions are the modifying situation in terms of which all social events take place. Sooner or later they modify all frames of reference with regard to the nature of our society and of the human situation. They include changes in our general economic and technological prospects, the impacts upon our daily lives of the current varieties of war, cold war, hot peace, and peace, the implications of atomic fission and rocketry, and the opera-tion of such catastrophes as crop failures, floods, disease epidemics, atomic-fission-induced genetic abnormalities, and atomic mishaps. These considerations will be discussed in several later chapters; they are mentioned here as part of the economic influences so determina-tive in marriage and family life.

CONCLUSION

In modern education, it has been a practical convenience to organ-ize university departments of economics, political science, history, an-thropology, psychology, and sociology, but such divisions do not occur in life. One cannot study marriage and the family "purely" as an economist or a sociologist. When one tries to simplify the task a little by concentrating upon an economic or a political or an historical *approach* to marriage and the family, one is drawn on and on. If one is really curious, a single approach is not satisfying. All ap-proaches are not only relevant but necessary in order to provide the synthesis we need.

This interrelatedness of many social sciences has been emphasized in the present chapter. Family standards and modes of living can be seen at the outset as economic considerations, but the economic approach does not take us far enough. Social class has a strong rela-tionship to the occupational status or statuses held in a family, but it becomes the basis of the formation of subcultures which define how individuals will typically relate themselves to the other sex, to standards of consumption, and to dreams about this and the next world. Only this chapter is entitled "socioeconomic," but all chapters in this book touch upon matters which are socioeconomic as well as political, technological, historical, and, in a more general sense, social.

Chapter V

WELFARE ROLES OF THE FAMILY *

Recent American family life presents this paradox: The family appears to be declining in size and to be turning many of its services over to other agencies; at the same time, what a family can contribute to personal stability and welfare in our complex society has never been more important.

One commonly hears a great deal today about the contraction of the American family, the transfer of its functions, the disappearance of the extended family, and the increasing separateness of small family units. The contemporary period is one of high divorce rates, anonymity, and mobility. Symbols of the time are the moving van, house trailer, rented room, and hotel apartment. It is a day of vast urban and suburban housing developments without community character, in which the populations are constantly changing.

Factories, schools, service industries, hospitals, and other social service agencies have taken over a great many functions once carried on by the extended rural family. Beginning in their early years, children frequently find playmates, parent substitutes, guidance, education, and entertainment outside of the home. When children and adults have marked physical or mental problems, they are often placed in hospitals or other special-care centers. Aged parents, whether dependent or not, usually live elsewhere than in the home of one of their children. With so much of the population rootless in their current environment, the control of welfare activities is surrendered to those who make a business or profession of social management.

In the face of the diminishing self-sufficiency of families, the welfare paradox forces us to realize the irreplaceability of the family in basic welfare roles. What is more, we are beginning to make our social policies reflect this realization. In the past, our extended fami-

* Richard H. P. Mendes of Brooklyn College read a draft of this chapter and made useful suggestions.

lies apparently took care of the financial and emotional problems of their members, but actually those and other difficulties were often ignored, tolerated, or hidden away. Such problems are now being handled much more satisfactorily by our small family units with the aid of public and private social service agencies.

RE-EMPHASIS ON THE FAMILY

Compared with the family, no other arrangement succeeds so well in rearing children and in giving adults a modicum of stability and psychological security. As a consequence, in spite of the decrease in family functions during the past few decades, the proportion of men and women married and living together has steadily risen. A high remarriage rate offsets some of the effects of the high divorce rate. We now realize that healthy conditions of family living offer the best environment in which to avoid or to cope with some of the maladjustments that require the services of pediatricians, family physicians, psychiatrists, special teachers, clergymen, social caseworkers, policemen, and lawyers.

Viewed in a practical way rather than nostalgically, the modern family is probably more useful in many respects than was its more complicated and less intimate predecessor. Rather than replace family functions with other arrangements, our more intelligently operated social agencies now do all they can to help families carry on their basic activities more effectively as well as to meet emergency situations. Whenever a broken family unit finally appears to be irreparable, resourceful efforts are made by the better agencies to place the members in new family units.

HISTORICAL BACKGROUNDS OF WELFARE AGENCIES

Faced with the mounting personal and family problems of our urbanizing society during the past century, leaders in the field of social welfare services utilized two traditional procedures: (1) the development of special facilities for the segregation and treatment of maladjusted persons; and (2) the subsidizing of individuals and families. Hospitals and prisons of many sorts had become well established. Charitable handouts for beggars were common practice throughout recorded history, but the inadequacy of alms is reflected in the words of the old German proverb: "Charity sees the need, not the cause."

From crude beginnings at *substitutional* services mentioned under (1), we went on to develop presumably more effective reformatories and prisons, hospitals for the physically or mentally ill, special facilities for the retarded and the maimed, and children's and old people's "homes." Many of these organizations still continue to grow and to specialize. Some are perhaps the best means now available to provide the special equipment and services that can economically be furnished for problem people only in large, well-financed, and well-staffed centers. But these centers all too often achieved principally the impoundment of problem people; they merely kept them out of sight and did not solve their problems or alleviate their conditions.

From (2) gradually evolved the modern *supportive* or supplemental social services which try to go beyond need and attempt to treat causes. They focus upon helping families to continue as working units. This is an objective to which social security and insurance schemes contribute substantially through helping families to cope with the more predictable periods of financial emergency. Other social services, both public and private, offer types of guidance and aid other than financial that may be far more important than money in meeting specific problem situations. Above all, they help confused and disturbed individuals and families to find their ways toward independence.

FAMILY SERVICE MOVEMENT

Problem investigation is a principal characteristic of agencies supportive of family life. It grew out of an organizational tradition which goes back to the London Charity Organisation Society founded in 1869. Its introduction into the United States in 1877 with the formation of the Buffalo Charity Organization Society marked the beginning of the family service movement. The social work educator Philip Klein * describes the viewpoint toward which these organizations were groping in the latter part of the nineteenth century as follows: "The manifold causes of poverty and distress were recog-

---

* "Social Case Work," *Encyclopaedia of the Social Sciences*, XIV (New York: Macmillan Co., 1934), 173–183; pp. 173–174 quoted.

nized; assistance other than monetary was emphasized; the study of all social and psychological factors in the life of the client was urged; and the full resources of the community, both private and public, were marshaled and coordinated." In other words, they were seeking to remove the causes of poverty as they saw them and to replace indiscriminate giving with an ordered and purposeful program that included attention to such problems as ill health and the poor planning of expenditures. Notions of the "causes of poverty and distress" tend to be influenced by the personal views of donors to agencies and to change with social conditions and social knowledge.

To accomplish their goals, these and other comparable organizations had to create and manage local social service exchanges. These exchanges, later often brought under councils of social agencies, now function in more than two hundred cities to minimize the duplication of efforts and to help promote the co-ordination of facilities. As far back as 1882 the charity societies established bureaus which furnished facts to donors about the nature of family service agencies and other organizations appealing for contributions. Regular professional training for family service and for other types of social casework began in a New York City summer school during the year 1898, an effort that led to the founding of the New York School of Philanthropy, later the New York School of Social Work, now a part of Columbia University. There are more than sixty of these advanced professional schools, most of them connected with a college or university. Influential in this professionalization was a text and guide written by the pioneer Mary E. Richmond; called *Social Diagnosis*,* this book was the first authoritative formulation of the principles and practices of social casework.

The National Conference of Charities and Correction, later known as the National Conference of Social Work, was organized in 1874 and helped to stimulate professional development in the whole field of which family service is a part. At least from 1905, the family service agencies themselves began to work out their own organizational arrangements for the national sharing of experiences and methods. Following preliminary conferences and correspondence and with the encouragement of the Russell Sage Foundation, the Family Service Association of America was formed in 1911; it now includes more than 342 member agencies and is helping other agencies to estab-

* New York: Russell Sage Foundation, 1917. (Free Press, 1965.)

lish standards of service satisfactory to qualify for membership. According to specialists in this area, these agencies devote a considerable share of their staff time to work with family members on their marital adjustment problems. These Family Service agencies are providing the bulk of professional marriage counseling in the United States. In 1921, the social work field established its principal professional society, the American (now National) Association of Social Workers; this society has since provided important leadership in professional planning and expansion.

SECTARIAN INTERESTS IN FAMILY CASEWORK

To a large extent, community social services of a private nature sprang up in this country under Jewish, Roman Catholic, and Protestant auspices, and this has made for a considerable variation in practices and in receptivity to modern psychological and psychiatric views and techniques. Roman Catholic social work "is basically religious in character, drawing its inspiration and its special social objectives directly from the Christian virtue of charity and other Catholic teachings." † In contrast, Protestant agencies have in a great many cases become nonsectarian. What specifically Protestant social work remains is chiefly of the sort carried on directly by individual congregations and missions; Protestants generally support the nonsectarian agencies. Jewish agencies maintain close ties with other Jewish community organizations. Both the nonsectarian and the Jewish agencies adapt their programs to local needs and opportunities as they view them. The activities of private agencies appear to be spread unevenly, but data on their extent and degree of coverage are not nearly so complete as those for the public organizations.

THE SPHERES OF PUBLIC AND PRIVATE AGENCIES

From their beginnings, state governments exercised social welfare functions. State boards of charities and of health date from the Civil War decade. During the last quarter of the nineteenth century, the National Conference of Charities and Correction often sponsored discussions of the proper roles in social welfare of the state and of state

† J. T. McDonnell, "Catholic Social Work," *Social Work Year Book: 1949* (New York: Russell Sage Foundation, 1949), p. 85.

boards. During the period 1900–1930, many states started to assist local governmental bodies in meeting the financial needs of certain dependent groups, especially the orphaned, the aged, and the blind; but the local units often failed to draw on available funds, and state appropriations in any event were inadequate. By 1929, state and local governmental units already provided some three-fourths of all relief funds in the country, and they operated a great many of the substitutive centers.

The impact of the depression of the 1930's overwhelmed both private and public agencies of all sorts and forced them to make clearer their respective responsibilities and procedures. In spite of heroic efforts by private agencies to care for unemployed persons and their families in the early 1930's, the emergency situation required the more precise recognition of the responsibility of public agencies for the basic financing of families in need. Only after crisis conditions had swept away the lifetime savings of many did New Deal legislation firmly establish the federal government as crucial in social welfare.

With the public agencies strengthened to deal with financial needs, the private agencies returned more exclusively to programs oriented about social-psychiatric casework. The public supportive agencies were also improved in such specific areas as employment, housing, nursing, and child day-care.

Social Security. The recent expansion of financial aid has centered largely on the further development of the federal social security program. This has been built chiefly upon the Social Security Act of 1935 as amended thereafter. This legislation set up the federal system of old-age and survivors' insurance, helped the individual states to organize unemployment insurance systems financed by the federal payroll tax, and assisted states with aid to the aged, the blind, the disabled, and dependent children, maternal and child welfare, public health services, vocational rehabilitation, and, beginning in 1966, Medicare for those 65 and older. Medicare pays a substantial portion of hospital costs and 40 to 60 per cent of medical expenses and is now available to a wide range of categories.

Compulsory and Voluntary Insurance. In states with compulsory insurance for industrial accidents, occupational diseases, disability and death benefits, and sickness, the necessarily complicated provisions are specified in a variety of state laws. Enlightened public opinion, employer policies, and union pressures combined with insurance sales-manship have helped to make the insurance schemes of private and quasi-public corporations very important factors in this area of per-sonal and family protection. Whether compulsory or voluntary, these insurance plans may include medical, hospital, accident, and dis-ability insurance as well as life-insurance provisions; the cost may be paid by the employer, jointly by the employer and the employee, jointly by the employer and the union, or by the individual. Medical clinics and even medical services administered by the employer, the union, or a quasi-public corporation are now in operation. In 1963, three-quarters of all Americans had some form of voluntary health insurance, and one-quarter had major medical insurance. Insurance then took care of 27 per cent of all private health service costs; 69 per cent of all bills for hospital services; 58 per cent of the costs of surgical operations; and 32 per cent of the costs of obstetrical services.

Veterans of Armed Services. In addition to such general public and private supportive and security provisions, veterans of the armed forces are granted other protection for themselves and their families under a variety of federal, state, and local acts. The assistance bestowed through these acts has included cash grants, business credits, housing credits, special privileges in qualifying for govern-mental positions, life insurance, medical and hospital care, education, and other services.

Fee Social Casework. Family service agencies were developed to help problem families, chiefly the underprivileged. As we have seen, they grew out of efforts to go beyond mere stopgap charity and at-tempted to deal with certain types of causes. Their services were traditionally available gratis. In consequence, many specialists pointed out how unfortunate it was that middle-class families with similar needs for social-psychiatric aid either did not wish to accept such "charity" or were not eligible for it. Often the alternative available was either too expensive or too uncertain. In response to this unfilled need, more and more family service agencies have accepted clients who undertake to pay fees for the aid they receive in their efforts to solve their marital and other family problems. Almost all members of the Family Service Association of America (more than 342 agencies) now provide counsel for fees as well as without charge. To an extent, a variety of other nonprofit agencies as well as psychiatrists, clergymen, and lawyers also offer professional marriage and family counseling for a fee.

Family Allowances. Cash payments may be made by a government for each child or for a specified number of children. They may go to all families or only to underprivileged ones. While family allowances have not found favor in the United States, they are now established policy in at least 27 countries, but their nature varies widely. In this country, a growing sentiment during the 1930's for family allowances was reversed during the 1940's by the "baby boom" in soldiers' families. The "boom" came as an unplanned and unexpected consequence of our enlarged military forces; wartime conditions stimulated earlier marriages and more children. This "baby boom" occurred chiefly among young families in better physical and mental health and with better educational advantages than a cross section of the whole population. The usual program of family allowances, however, subsidizes the birth and rearing of babies in families which are relatively needier, with more problems of physical and mental health, and with less education than the average. Whether allowances would encourage such families to have more children or to provide better for their existing children is a controversial issue. In the United States, the theory most often held on this matter is that procreation is a private privilege and responsibility; parents should expect to have to support their own children. We tend to oppose any program that would set up outright subsidies for breeding and child-rearing. Such a program is associated in the minds of Americans with European militarism and dictatorship, even though it is in operation in practically all European countries and in a great many of the other English-speaking lands. Some of our own family relief practices are often criticized for providing increased funds following a birth in a needy family.

SPECIAL AGENCIES

Special agencies include agencies for children, agencies for adults, agencies for socializing and recreation, and agencies dealing with community problems.

Agencies for Children. When a problem family with children does not respond adequately to such supportive aids as marital counseling, child guidance, public assistance, or day care, then some substitutive arrangement becomes necessary. If a good foster family is available, it is the best type of substitute. It is essential for children under six who have been deprived of their own parents; it is highly desirable for older children. As Mrs. Kathleen Cassidy Doyle * observes, "Today, foster care is looked upon as a treatment for a temporarily disturbed parent-child relationship, and ideally is available to any child, regardless of economic circumstances, whose family cannot give him a satisfactory home." To achieve the desired goals of such placement, the child must "feel just as 'chosen' as the youngster who is adopted." He and the family must be mutually acceptable to one another so that they can both develop the warm affection he needs.

Professional social workers regard the placement of a child in living arrangements other than a foster family as a last resort. Permanent adoption and temporary foster care are the most desirable substitutes for his own family. Less desirable are family-like group homes, chiefly for adolescents, the more old-fashioned and less commendable children's "homes," junior republics, boarding schools, and reformatories, and the residential hospitals and schools for the disturbed, maimed, and retarded.

As social workers learn better the ways to locate, motivate, instruct, and supervise foster families, we shall probably be able to make more constructive and extensive use of them. In doing so, we should not overlook the added advantage that an increasing number of families will thus be led to benefit from the experience of providing a foster relationship. Possibly only a residue consisting of the most unfortunate children will eventually need to be placed in large centers. Even in such centers, family-like conditions yield promising results. For example, mental hospitals are learning to use mentally defective young women patients as "big sisters" for seriously disturbed children. Under the supervision of nurses, these big sisters work wonders by cuddling their charges, aged two to twelve; the gains from this process are both for the defective young women and the disturbed children. In all problem areas, the children affected are concentrated in a relatively small percentage of the total families. These same families often include other problem members. This situation has long suggested that such families require and would benefit from

* "Homes for Foster Children," *Public Affairs Pamphlet* No. 223 (New York, 1955), pp. 7, 8.

careful case-by-case approaches with the use of adequate facilities.

Agencies for Adults. Adults are less adaptable than children, and more of them appear to be incurable. They thus are more often than children conceded to need substitutive services, and this is likely to continue to be the case. Among adults as well as among children, however, the love and identifications available within a family, a foster family, or a family-like group home are most helpful to unwed expectant mothers, the aged, the mentally retarded or disturbed, the criminal, the physically sick, and the maimed.

The treatment problems of people with chronic diseases illustrate the welfare roles of both families and agencies in helping adults with difficulties of a personal nature. One in each six Americans has a chronic illness. If hospitals for tuberculosis and the mentally ill are included, three out of every four hospital patients have long-term illnesses. These include cerebral palsy, rheumatic fever, polio, epilepsy, rheumatoid arthritis, diabetes, diseases of the heart and the arteries, cancer, tuberculosis, and mental afflictions. Chairman Leonard W. Mayo * of the Commission on Chronic Illness sums up the whole problematic situation briefly as follows: "Many of these patients are chronically ill because they did not seek the attention of doctors early enough. Some are crowding hospitals who would be better off at home, if professional supplementary home care were available. And still others are incapacitated who could learn to take care of themselves and lead useful lives with proper rehabilitation. As a result, the chronically ill are taking a disproportionate amount of time of doctors, nurses, and welfare workers, and are overloading hospitals and other medical facilities."

What is being done to cope with this situation? Medical and surgical treatment is first and basic. The vocational rehabilitation program of the Federal Security Agency in co-operation with the states then does much to give the chronically ill new opportunities for independence and a normal life. A new trend in medical care was initiated at Montefiore Hospital (New York City) which shortened the period of hospitalization by expanding its program of outpatient care and enlisting the co-operation of the patient's family in such care. The hospital tries to make available for the patients adequate care and equipment at their homes while assuring them that

* Introductory note in Herbert Yahraes, "Something Can Be Done about Chronic Illness," *Public Affairs Pamphlet* No. 176 (New York, 1951).

they will be readmitted to the hospital if necessary. It also furnishes a social worker to aid each family in adapting to the presence of a person with a continuing illness, seldom an easy thing to do. Hospitals in Chicago, San Francisco, Washington, and elsewhere have also inaugurated such programs, and the movement is likely to spread. As Herbert Yahraes * states, "Besides saving money and stretching institutional services, it offers an even greater advantage: it puts the patient home, where he wants to be and where he can have personal medical service."

The aged constitute the most rapidly growing problem group among adults. By 1950 there were some 14 million Americans over 65 years of age, more than a fourfold increase in a half-century. It is estimated that by 1975 there will be 21 million elderly people in this country, of whom three in five will probably be women. Many aspects of this group's problems will be discussed elsewhere in this book, especially in the chapters dealing with the post-child family and bereavement. At this point it is worth noting that the best substitute home for the aged parent who cannot live with his own son or daughter is not some large center organized for the elderly; it is a well-selected foster family. Even though a child or in-law may get along well with an aged parent, often a foster home may be a welcome means whereby an aged person can retain or re-establish his independence.

Agencies for Socializing and Recreation. Special recreational facilities are most often developed for teen-agers. It is in that tense age-period that many contemporary homes fail to furnish sufficiently absorbing activities or to guide children to helpful community facilities. Unfortunately the families whose children need community recreational facilities most are those that do the poorest job of encouraging them to use such programs. The distracting influence of excessive television-viewing, especially among the more disorganized families, is scarcely improving the situation. No recreational or other useful facilities are panaceas for juvenile delinquency or for any other such problem, but they can help to promote family and personal welfare. Social workers or educators have to have patience, understanding, and enthusiasm to lead members of problem families to accept new friends and opportunities for socializing in new groups.

Agencies helpful in socializing and recreation include those operating athletic fields and parks, the Scouts, the Y's, others serving youth,

* *Ibid.*, p. 21.

and clubs for unmarried adults, for young couples, and for the aged. The latter clubs may devote themselves to card-playing, art, dramatics, dancing, or hiking. Golden-age clubs and other organized groups in community centers and churches can make vast differences in the lives of today's urban dwellers, and they are growing in number, in richness of program, and in membership.

Agencies Dealing with Community Problems. These are among the more satisfying agencies for adult participation. Such agencies help groups to work constructively on the problems of other people or of their neighborhood. In doing so, the agencies influence people to help both themselves and others. In addition to contributing to the welfare of others, they may solve their own problems of loneliness, of a need for activity, or of lacking a sense of purpose. To illustrate, one of the most effective of such organizations is Alcoholics Anonymous, a voluntary association of abstaining alcoholics which has as its purpose the giving of aid, friendship, and moral support to alcoholics who wish to give up drinking. In helping other alcoholics, the members do even more to help themselves. A great many individuals have found a new sense of personal meaning and direction in such organizations. Even couples with long-standing domestic irritations have found new satisfaction in living with one another after they have turned their energies into one or several community organizations.

To be active in an organization dealing with community problems does not necessarily require either great tactical ability or personal wealth. There are many opportunities for service already in existence; organizations often need voluntary assistance of a variety of types. Once one starts to do helpful things in a community, other opportunities are likely to present themselves.

Such agencies deal with the whole gamut of community problems. They range from Friends of the Library to locals of the League of Women Voters and the American Civil Liberties Union, from a hospital or health association to backers of the youngsters' baseball league or of a community center, from the women's club to the Rotary Club or a trade union or a chamber of commerce, and a great many more. One interesting guide to such work in the welfare field is Elizabeth Ogg's pamphlet, "Good Neighbors: The Rise of Community Welfare Councils." * Any clergyman, social worker, or neighborhood newspaper editor can make numerous practical suggestions.

* *Public Affairs Pamphlet* No. 277 (New York, 1959).

HOW MANY ARE INVOLVED IN WELFARE PROGRAMS?

A four-year study of *Community Planning for Human Services** (1952) in St. Paul, Minnesota gives an over-all view of the relation of welfare agencies to that city's families. In the month of November, 1948 some two-fifths (41,000) of the more than 100,000 families in St. Paul benefited from the efforts of one or more of the city's 109 public and private health and welfare agencies. One-sixth (17,000) of the total had members who participated only in the recreational programs of the Public Recreation Department, Boy Scouts, Girl Scouts, YMCA, YWCA, and other youth-serving organizations. An additional one-fourth (25,000 families) of the total had members involved in the three other major welfare fields (dependency, ill-health, and maladjustment); in other words, one family in four had one or more disabilities that impaired domestic relations, income-producing efforts, or some other aspect of its happiness or efficiency. But 6 per cent of all St. Paul families (roughly 6,500) required more than one-half of all the services of the city's welfare agencies. As a result, about one-half of all the funds—contributions and taxes—handled by the agencies of the city were used to deal with the health, dependency, and adjustment problems of this unfortunate core group. The organization making the study concludes that a co-ordinated effort by the St. Paul social agencies would gradually reduce the size of that core considerably below 6 per cent of the city's total families. It calls for a more synthetic, a more whole-family, approach. It would end the practice of classifying people with problems into rigid categories, such as those of dependency, physical health, mental health, child care, the aged, and the rest, with each category often handled by one or more types of specialized agency. The techniques for community teamwork to meet such extreme family problem situations are gradually emerging.

THE TWO APPROACHES TO WELFARE WORK TODAY

The supportive and the substitutive approaches to family welfare problems are now growing toward one another. As we have seen,

* Bradley Buell and associates, Community Research Associates, Inc. (New York: Columbia University Press).

hospitals are developing programs to expand out-patient services and to furnish the counsel and aid of social workers who specialize in personal problems in family settings. These and other agencies are also making it possible for problem children, physical and mental patients of all ages, and the aged to live in their own homes or in foster families. In field after field, the re-emphasis upon family living and upon treatment of individuals in relation to their family setting rather than merely upon individuals as such is growing rapidly and is yielding impressive results. Even the family-like conditions of certain substitutive centers fall short of the values to be found in reasonably healthy family environments. There is no substitute for the personal affection and identification possible in a family environment.

The stress on the family as the basic welfare unit is not new. At the beginning of this century, Richard Cabot developed such a viewpoint in his medical social work program at Massachusetts General Hospital. From more recent researches in internal medicine, Henry B. Richardson * came to similar conclusions: "The individual is a part of the family in illness as well as in health. . . . The idea of disease as an entity which is limited to one person . . . fades into the background, and disease becomes an integral part of the continuous process of living." Two analysts † of public health problems recall, "Before the era of specialization, the family doctor had a more intimate knowledge of all the family members, of their incomes and ambitions, of the subtle ways in which each reacted to the other. In treating each of his families, he could call on a store of firsthand social, economic, and cultural data, mostly unrecorded on the medical history, and apply this knowledge both to diagnosis and therapy." They also note that the "wide spectrum" of public health problems involve "not only tuberculosis, poliomyelitis, and other infectious diseases but also many noninfectious ailments such as obesity, alcoholism, asthma, and essential hypertension, all of which are influenced usually by the family situation."

In closing, several comments on this family emphasis in social welfare are necessary: The problems of individuals and families have community settings. The community pressures exerted upon fathers, mothers, and children can create situations within the family which

---

* *Patients Have Families* (New York: Commonwealth Fund, 1945), p. 76.

† H. L. Dunn and Mort Gilbert, "Public Health Begins in the Family," *Public Health Reports*, LXXI (1956), 1002–1010; pp. 1006–1007 quoted.

are not at all healthy and which are not susceptible to casework or family service methods. Thus we are asking for a great deal when we call for the development of families which are more healthy and for a society conducive to healthy families.

Chapter VI

POPULATION CHARACTERISTICS
AND PROBLEMS

Millions shudder at the possibility of atomic warfare or emotionally repress such a fearful thought. The same millions of people around the world thrill to predictions in the press, on the radio, and on television that men will soon travel to the moon and beyond. At the same time, however, the peoples of the earth pay scant attention to their most explosive and important problem—the vast world-wide expansion of population—to which they are quite literally giving birth. Few concern themselves with that. Few appear to understand that they share responsibility for anything so frightening. This threat to world peace, to national welfare, and to domestic security should be considered in all serious discussions of world politics, national planning, and family life, but most often it is not.

Few of us are likely to travel to the moon. Our mounting population pressures can scarcely be solved by interplanetary migration. Almost all of us will have to face here on earth the consequences of an increasing population. These consequences will compel us to choose public policies in the light of the different rates of increase among social classes, ethnic groups, regions, and countries. Throughout history, public policies have been determined largely on the basis of the size and power of the groups sponsoring them; the "fast breeders" become numerous and through organization may become powerful enough to make their ideas dominant. In the future, most of us may escape the dangers of atomic bombs and fall-out; or, on the other hand, these monstrous forces may decimate, cripple, or biologically distort the race. In either event, those who remain alive will have to cope with the same old problems of population in all their intricacies. Let us sketch briefly the principal consequences of the falling death rate and of the relatively high birth rate of recent times.

World Population Tendencies. Currently the population of the world is increasing by about 70 million a year, a figure equal to the present population of France, Belgium, and Holland. Red China alone—with a growth rate in large areas estimated to be up to 3.5 per cent annually—is accounting for some 15 to 18 million a year.

Prior to 1500, world population mounted gradually, with the rate of increase rising slightly during the course of thousands of years. The rate of growth varied among the different regions. It responded to changes in the productivity and distribution of goods and to such events as wars, plagues, and famines. The rate rose only from 0.04 to 0.07 per cent per year during some thirty thousand years. Then the growth rate shot up to an average of 0.2 per cent per year during the period 1500–1800, to 0.6 per cent per year during the 1800's, to 0.75 in 1900–1950, and recently to at least 1.2 and maybe as much as 1.8 per cent annually. Growth at an annual rate of about 1.0 per cent doubles a population in less than 70 years.

Stated in terms of population rather than of rates of growth, world population had reached an estimated 0.5 billion by 1650, and the explosion was under way. Within only two centuries thereafter, by 1850, the total had reached 1.2 billion, and by 1950 had doubled again, with 2.5 billions in all. It is estimated that the figure reached 3.0 billions by 1960 and will climb to 4.0 by 1975. In the same three centuries and as a part of the general trend of civilization, life expectancy for the average person in the more advanced Western countries increased from about 33 years in 1650 to 47 in 1900 and again to 70 in the 1950's.

Population Developments in Selected Areas. From 1650 to 1950, the total population of the world multiplied five times; at the same time the British peoples multiplied 26.5 times as they spread to many parts of the world, a rise from 6 to 159 million in only three centuries. This tremendous growth of the British was made possible largely through the colonization of relatively underdeveloped areas such as those which now constitute the United States, Canada, and Australia. A similar development is under way within the Soviet Union. While the population of the world doubled in 1850–1950, that of the area now constituting the Soviet Union more than tripled; it went up from 62 million to 200 million, with a substantial part of the increase east of the Urals. Other national groups, including many people on a very low standard of living and possessing scant resources immediately available, are similarly expanding as a result of a decline in the death rate, attributed mainly to the introduction of modern health measures. Mention has been made above of the high annual rate of increase—about 3.5 per cent—in parts of Red China. The annual rate of increase in India, now about 2.0 per cent, may shortly be expected to reach the figure of 3.0 per cent. Both countries have programs of birth-control education, but as yet these programs are neither extensive nor effective. Taiwan, Mexico, Ceylon, and the Philippines already have rates of from 2.8 to 3.5 per cent.

Population Trend in the United States. As a consequence of a high rate of immigration, a low rate of emigration, and an excess of births over deaths, continental United States has experienced its own population explosion. From a total of 30 million on the eve of the Civil War in 1858, our population was increased by increments of 30 millions, as follows: the total reached 60 million by 1888, 90 million by 1908, 120 million by 1928, 150 million by 1949, and 180 million by 1960. There is a strong possibility that the figure will be 210 million by 1970 or 1975. In 1960, the population was four and one-half times the total of the number of immigrants plus the original primitive stock. In 1960, more than three out of every five Americans lived in the 212 metropolitan areas of the country, and the overflow of urban residents into surrounding suburbs and rural districts formed an important aspect of the general population change.

Within the United States, differentials in the birth rates of certain groups have been traditional. Larger than average families have been found historically in groups with little education, low incomes, rural backgrounds, and unskilled occupations, including many recent immigrants. Differences in the birth rate attributed to religious affiliations often appear upon investigation to depend more upon one or several other types of difference, not connected with religious mandates; only thus can one explain the great variations in fertility among class groups within the same major religious segment. The "baby boom" of the 1940's and 1950's tended to reduce the differences in birth rate among the various social-class groups; families with more education and higher incomes increased appreciably in size. An extensive survey * made in 1955 indicated that such trends might be expected to continue. The largest differential reported in this survey was one indicated by married women in the 18–24 age group as to their *hopes* and *plans* for offspring. Roman Catholic women planned for 3.8 children, and Protestant women for 2.9, but such anticipations do not necessarily point to future eventualities. The same publication

* P. K. Whelpton, A. A. Campbell, and Ronald Freedman, *Family Planning, Sterility, and Population Growth* (New York: McGraw-Hill Book Co., 1959).

sharply contrasts the actual sizes of the families of older women with the higher numbers of children such women assert to be ideal.

The Struggle for Subsistence. An English clergyman of the eighteenth century, the Rev. Thomas Robert Malthus, in 1798 wrote a famous *Essay on the Principle of Population* which oversimplified the complex problem of providing subsistence for the ever growing population. He attempted to arrive at a mathematical formula that would clarify the problem. He noted that populations tend to increase faster (in a geometric ratio) than do their means of subsistence (which increase more slowly, in an arithmetic ratio). He contended that this "natural inequality" in rates of growth may provide an obstacle that is "insurmountable in the way to the perfectibility of society." This unequal expansion of population and subsistence, he maintained, could be counteracted only through such "positive checks" as disease, famine, and war or through such more or less voluntary "preventive checks" as delayed marriages, abstinence from sexual relations, and celibacy. The former raise the death rate, and the latter, to which should be added modern techniques of contraception, lower the birth rate. The only alternative to these remedial measures is human misery resulting from overpopulation.

The basic problem that concerned Malthus may be stated in terms of contemporary society: How can humanity find resources with which to solve the current undernourishment among two-thirds of the world's population and at the same time discover means of obtaining food for an additional 10 to 12 per cent or more added to the population every decade? Each such increment is about equal to the entire population of the Americas. Under these population pressures, how good a society can any nation maintain over an extended period of time? What will happen to the modes of living of even the favored one-third of mankind?

Two Harvard University scientists disagree sharply on the outcome. Geologist Kirtley F. Mather optimistically contends in his book *Enough and to Spare* (1944) that the prediction of Malthus does not apply and, on the basis of current trends, never will apply to man. Botanist Karl Sax, in his *Standing Room Only,** concludes: "A survey of world history provides ample proof that the Malthusian checks have always controlled the growth of human populations. Man can now choose which of the two checks he desires—high death rates or low birth rates."

* Boston: Beacon Press, 1955, p. 27.

A few brief quotations by thoughtful leaders highlight the situation. Director-General H. L. Keenleyside * of the United Nations Technical Assistance Administration concludes: "It would be impossible for anyone who has been in touch with conditions in the less highly developed parts of the world to be unimpressed by the rapidly increasing dangers that are arising from the almost unrestricted growth in population. This may very well become, if, indeed, it has not already, the greatest problem with which humanity will be faced. I can think of no field in which scientific research is more badly needed, or in which greater dividends in human welfare will attend success." Arnold J. Zurcher,† executive director of the Alfred P. Sloan Foundation notes: "Unless we can do something definitive about this problem, all of our economic benevolence, our technological advances and the great progress that has been made in medicine are not going to do civilization much good."

In contrast with the foregoing, the Russian Soviet political leader Nikita S. Khrushchev ‡ asserted to a Communist youth gathering in Moscow in 1954: "Bourgeois ideologists have invented cannibalistic theories, including the theory of overpopulation. They are thinking about how to reduce the birth rate, how to slow down the growth of population. It is different with us, comrades. . . . The more people we have, the stronger our country will be."

The Man/Land Ratio. The social scientist Albert Galloway Keller § gives a more adequately sociological formulation than Malthus to a "law of population" that he made basic to his theory of societal change. He concludes that "population tends to increase up to the limit of the supporting power of the environment (meaning, above all, land), on a given stage of the arts, and for a given standard of living—that is, for a given stage of civilization." He thus provides a formula in which there are four complicated variables: (1) population; (2) environment in the sense of physical resources; (3) stage or general level of the arts of production and distribution—the arts we use in making our physical resources available to meet human needs and desires; and (4) the standard of living viewed in an average sense but with the implication that it varies from group to group

* Quoted in *The Population Bomb* (New York: Hugh Moore Fund, n.d.), p. 19.
† Quoted, *ibid.*, p. 2.
‡ Quoted in Karl Sax, *Standing Room Only* (Boston: Beacon Press, 1955), p. 190.
§ *Societal Evolution* (rev. ed.; New York: Macmillan Co., 1931), p. 31. See also W. G. Sumner and A. G. Keller, *The Science of Society* (New Haven: Yale University Press, 1927), I, 4–6 and Chapter 2.

within a society. As a society's population increases, it can be sustained by bringing more resources into production and distribution, by improving the arts, or by lowering the level of living. Population increases through lowering the death rate or raising the birth rate. A sudden increase in available resources (such as followed the opening of the Americas to colonization by peoples with advanced arts) or marked improvement in the arts (such as the modern technological revolutions) can at least temporarily raise the mode of living before population again catches up and begins to depress it.

This situation is further complicated by differences in standards and modes of living and in fertility among the various social-class groups within a society. Among middle-class groups in which the members strain to maintain or improve their mode of living, the practice of limiting births is typical. Thus the application of the man/land ratio within each such group is more specific than and varies from the average of society as a whole.

Population Explosion as Transition. When modern medicine is applied to improve health conditions in any country, the rate of live births in relation to pregnancies rises sharply and the death rate goes down. Then, unless the birth rate decreases and the use of physical resources improves rapidly enough to support a larger population, either the mode of living will start to decline or detrimental influences may again begin to raise the death rate. In this way, the recent population explosion can be viewed as transitional. Some of the peoples in the Western world were beginning about 1800 to go through a "transition from a high-birth-rate, high-death-rate culture (with low living standards) to a low-birth-rate, low-death-rate culture (with relatively high living standards)." * Perhaps one-fifth of mankind has now gone through that demographic transition and has established relatively high modes of living somewhat protected by the application of rational preventive checks upon fertility. Two-thirds of the world's people have yet to enter upon such a transition or are just beginning to do so. Before the transition is over in any given country, its population may skyrocket. The Swedes went through the transition during the period 1800–1950 with an accompanying multiplication of their domestic population by three and of their total international population by five. On the other hand, the French population did not increase more than twofold during a comparable transition. For most peoples, the interval between a decline in death rate

* Sax, *op. cit.*, p. 4.

and a subsequent decline in the birth rate is some 75 to 100 years, to judge from experience with this recent societal adaptation in Europe and America. In spite of the recent "baby boom," the population specialist Pascal K. Whelpton * concludes that we have passed this transitional period in the United States and after 1965 or 1975 our "rate of population growth will start down." Since the levels of living among the depressed two-thirds of the world are so different from those among the more privileged one-third, further population increases among the less developed nations are likely to have grave world-wide consequences. They could contribute to a continuing and dangerous explosion rather than a transition. For that matter, we are not at all sure that the recent population increases among the favored one-third are demographic transitions which are completed or even completable.

Birth-Control Measures. How can the current and forthcoming demographic transitions or population explosions be short-circuited, as it were, in order to minimize further overcrowding of the globe? How can birth rates be brought into line with falling death rates? The usual alternatives advanced are either famine, pestilence, and war, on the one hand, or some form of birth control, on the other. A great many Western peoples practice birth control in one or another of the many forms available, but even among those practicing it there is no agreement on the moral issues involved. The various religious groups cannot arrive at a consensus even about the merits of abstinence, delayed marriage, and celibacy. Forms of birth control which appear highly desirable and practical—a pill and an intrauterine device ("the loop") either of which renders a woman temporarily and harmlessly sterile—have now been developed and are gaining more and more acceptance. Other available methods require a degree of intelligent co-operation and emotional acceptance; they are either complicated or expensive. They include the "safe period" or "rhythm" technique approved by the Roman Catholic church but opposed by others as too unreliable and the more common mechanical and chemical contraceptive procedures that are unacceptable to Roman Catholics and certain other religious groups.

The problem is further complicated by the fact that the individuals reproducing most rapidly and irresponsibly are most frequently lack-

* "A Generation of Demographic Change," in R. G. Francis, ed., *The Population Ahead* (Minneapolis: University of Minnesota Press, 1958).

ing in education, funds, foresight, or interest necessary for voluntary birth-control procedures. Compulsion in such an intimate phase of life is neither practical nor allowable.

Certain governments have ordered, encouraged, or permitted sterilization, especially of persons thought to be genetically undesirable. Where it has been merely encouraged or available, sterilization has been a useful limited check on reproduction. Where the practice has been ordered, it has too often been used as a means of oppression. Thus, in Nazi Germany it became a vicious genocidal device. An arbitrary government might contemplate the use of abortion, infanticide, or other violent methods of limiting reproduction, but such measures are virtually impossible as governmental policies in advanced societies. In the present stage of our knowledge and techniques, however, deliberate governmental action to reduce the birth rate is becoming more and more likely in any modern country. In his inaugural address in 1965, President Lyndon B. Johnson stated: "I will seek new ways to use our knowledge to help deal with the explosion in world population." As John D. Rockefeller III has noted, "Today, men and governments, deeply concerned, are working desperately to avert the world's nuclear suicide—and these efforts must of course continue, undaunted by difficulty. Yet it is unbelievable that we do not apply comparable attention to the control of population. Both problems threaten the well-being of humanity: one threatens mankind as an act of violence threatens, the other with the erosive quality of a wasting illness." *

Our greatest hopes for birth limitation lie in research having to do with the physical, emotional, intellectual, and social aspects of the human reproductive processes. Public concern and free public discussion of this important subject would help to bring about the needed revolution in our thinking about it and might result in solutions more enlightened than those heretofore put forward. An effective campaign to educate the masses of the less fortunate peoples constituting two-thirds of the world population would probably be our most helpful immediate step—provided that the information imparted is made definite and precise. But time for action is short; the world population "clock" ticks faster and faster.

Implications for American Families. Americans find the following aspects of the world-wide population boom most immediate and apparent: suburbs and country districts are being covered with real-

* Quoted in *The Population Bomb* (New York: Hugh Moore Fund), p. 22.

estate developments, and central cities are suffering more and more from slum blight. Consequently, costs of additional public services— for example, for roads, schools, hospitals, police, fire protection—necessitate higher tax rates both in rural and in urban areas. Mass transportation in our burgeoning metropolises is becoming prohibitively expensive, unprofitable, and unwieldly. Automobiles, trucks, and buses are choking even our newest highways, bridges, and tunnels. The families with no children, or only one child, are being replaced by those with two, three, and four children. In large families, the parents' attention becomes more divided, and sibling relationships present difficult problems. The increased life span has been modifying our patterns of family life. From association with three, four, and even five generations living at the same time in a single family connection, individuals derive a sense of family continuity. This involves, on the one hand, new responsibility for the aged and, on the other hand, enlarged opportunities for children to know their grandparents and great-grandparents.

Thus, while the global aspects of the population explosion tend to be ignored, the changes in family size and organization, the increased life span, and new conditions of urban living are well known because they affect most people directly. These new factors demand new perspectives of family planning and community planning. We have seen that many forces have modified American family patterns, and it appears certain that change will continue to be our lot in this as in other aspects of human society.

PART TWO

CHILDHOOD AND ADOLESCENCE

Chapter VII

THE CHILD IN THE FAMILY

Each new family has its roots in its predecessors. Its social processes continue those of the parental families of the mates. We should therefore consider the experiences of childhood and adolescence in the family of orientation before discussing problems of courtship and marriage. It is useful to ask: What is being done to prepare children for courtship, marriage, and parenthood?

In fact, customs drawn from folk experience through endless generations provide us with methods of preparing children from their earliest years so that they will eventually undertake the tasks of parenthood and thus ensure the perpetuation of society. Ancient customs also provide patterns of emotional response and behavior directed at stimulating sexual maturation and at eradicating remnants of infantilism (such as sexual deviation) in the adolescent and the adult.

In this section we shall outline the typical methods whereby the modern family serves as a matrix for the physical and personal maturation of children. Tradition rather than rational planning furnishes the chief norms for family influences upon children. It is tradition that gives parents a sense of security in following the norms of their culture—a sense of rightness sanctioned by "our own kind of people" in following such norms with their children. But in a period such as our own these norms are changing more rapidly than before. Many people are confused, doubtful about the validity of traditional norms, and the norms appear to be less certain, less sanctioned, than they were only a generation or two ago. Accepted standards do not always seem to meet new conditions of family life.

In consequence, there arise certain critical problems. Will the patterns of thinking, feeling, and behaving among modern family members change rapidly and securely enough to meet new social conditions and thus maintain the health of society? Will changes in the patterns continue to be based on such dubious influences as popular fads, the pronouncements of "authorities" (who may or may not have wisdom that matches the plausibility of their assertions), commercial advertisements, and trial-and-error procedures? Can guidance for new patterns of family life come rather from more dependable scientific sources? Can this guidance come in time? The situation is not hopeless; in fact, some of the scientific findings already available can help us to understand and meet these challenges.

The succeeding paragraphs discuss factors making for high or low family morale and describe ways in which the individual attempts to fit into group patterns and processes. Then quite briefly they outline pertinent data concerning physical and personal maturation. There is special emphasis upon processes which prepare children for subsequent sexual and parental roles, such as the channeling of sexuality, the significance of male and female models and of incest and other tabooed sex relations, and the coloration of individual character by striking events and by family-drama patterns. Clinical suggestions for the handling of children's problems are summarized.

A FAMILY'S MORALE HAS MANY ROOTS

The sources of a family's relatively high or low morale may be traced to a great many influences, among the most important of which are the early childhood experiences of each parent and grandparent. As the poet William Wordsworth phrases it, "The child is father of the man"; but in our context the implications of even this statement scarcely go far enough. To borrow another passage from the same poet, it is the "little, nameless, unremembered acts of kindness and of love" involved through many years in the life processes of the family that do so much to determine the basic core of character for the person and of morale for the family in which that person may become a parent. Conversely, other "little, nameless, unremembered acts" of bitterness, rejection, and hate can have helped produce instability and basic unhappiness. Almost always there are to be considered both the acts of love and those of hate.

More specifically, what are the forces which tend to make a family basically happy or unhappy? We do not refer to temporary elations and sorrows. Deaths, separations, accidents, and other misfortunes are parts of life just as are the joys of marriages, births, and vocational accomplishments; but persons and families react to such events differently. Booms and depressions, wars, and pestilences have a pervasive effect upon personal adjustment and family morale, but these historical influences elicit diverse reactions from individuals. The environmental conditions to be found in urban and rural slums and in privileged neighborhoods profoundly affect adjustment and morale, but not in the same ways for all families.

We know that within any given neighborhood at any given time and under like circumstances there are wide variations in the ways families meet quite similar crises. Incidents and conditions that come to one family as a challenge may tear another apart. Behavior such as drunkenness may reveal disastrous tensions in one family and be nonexistent, even unthinkable, in another. The children in one slum family struggle their way through education to higher class status; the children in a family next door launch themselves upon a variety of illicit careers.

A family's morale arises from the physical and mental health of its members, from its recognition of opportunities, from ethnic and class backgrounds, from the relation of those backgrounds to the family's current situation, and from family acceptance of bases for adaptation to life conditions and to society. A family's morale is thus primarily its group sense of vitality and direction. The family of a banker, clergyman, or thief may have high or low morale. A family's class or ethnic beliefs may prompt it or permit it, in certain circumstances, to behave in ways called immoral by society at large and contrary to the mores of other groups. Family morale reflects to some extent society's acceptance or rejection of the family.

A family with relatively high morale is one with a developed ability to meet the blows of life and to work out adaptations to life conditions which are fairly satisfying to its members. It is a family that gives evidence of being basically happy. A family with low morale, on the other hand, is one which fails to meet the challenges open to it in terms of its class and ethnic standards. It is basically unhappy.

Factors that make for such differences in family morale are very numerous and quite complex. To understand them, we must be far more historical in our approaches to family study than is so often the case. We need to realize that the apparent and the present are only small phases of what we have to learn about any family or family-member. We can never have too much of a time-perspective on a given situation or family. Much more would become known about family life if we were to have reasonably detailed studies of typical families over several succeeding generations. Ideally this would mean studies of at least the four grandparental and two parental families which a given couple's family of procreation may number as precursors.

THE GAP BETWEEN GENERATIONS

Family processes are continuous, but human life starts and stops. Much of the energy of a family goes into coping with the problems raised by reproduction and by death. Much of family drama is built directly or indirectly around these terminal events. Their anticipation is so preoccupying that sometimes their actuality appears anticlimactic.

Biological attraction helps to bring a couple together and makes a substantial contribution to marital tranquillity and continuity, but the mates often find biological reproduction to be relatively uncomplicated in contrast with the worrisome ramifications of cultural reproduction—of developing within children what are called "satisfactory" social personalities. These complexities have increased during recent decades when the conditions of life have been rapidly changing. Each generation must be different in order to meet the changed conditions of its time, but many families continue to follow established customs and appear bewildered by the pressures upon them to decide upon necessary or desirable changes in their life patterns.

Adults in a family do much positively and negatively to shape the personalities of children. At the same time adult models often appear too remote and too complete, as well as too anachronistic, for easy and satisfying emulation. How can a boy find his way from what he thinks he sees himself to be to what his father appears to be? In particular, how can he do this when, as is so often the case, he has few contacts with his father and these reveal only the social personality the father shows to his son in family situations? This is only one of a number of social personalities the father probably has developed to meet the various facets of his life. How might a more up-to-date man, such a man as will belong to the son's own generation, really behave with a "boss," with workaday associates, with a girl friend, with male friends? It is easier for a girl to make adjustments, even in our urbanized and rather abstract society, but how can she discern enough of the road from herself to her mother or to another female ideal to be hopeful of emulating or surpassing that model? The increasing multitudes of mothers who are employed outside the home are making the girl's problem of maturation more like her brother's.* Stating the question more from the parent's standpoint, how quickly is it "safe" or "wise" to initiate a child into one or another aspect of the practical affairs of life? For example, what does one do about information concerning sex?

PHYSICAL–SELF–PERSONAL MATURATION

We link these three adjectives together in relation to maturation because the aspects of growth to which they refer cannot meaningfully be considered as entities which are entirely separate one from another. The child grows in body, intellect, and behavior under the influences of his physical, interpersonal, and cultural environment. Food is important to physical growth, but physical growth also reflects psychosomatic gains and disorders brought on by the character of the child's interpersonal relations and cultural norms. As the psychiatrist Erik H. Erikson † observes, "We . . . retain at least the semantic assumption that the mind is a 'thing' separate from the body, and a society a 'thing' outside the individual." This assumption may be an obstacle to accurate thinking. Erikson speaks of a psychoneurosis as "psycho- *and* somatic, psycho- *and* social, and *inter*-personal." The same sort of thing should also be said of other aspects of individual thought, feeling, and behavior. The sociologist Charles Horton Cooley ‡ calls a separate individual "an abstraction unknown to experience, and so likewise is society when regarded as something apart from individuals." The difference between individual and society "is rather in our point of view than in the object we are looking at; when we speak of society, or use any other collective term, we fix our minds upon some general view of the people concerned, while when we speak of individuals we disregard the general aspect and think of them as if they were separate."

The groups and the society to which we belong, into which we grow as we mature, are intimate parts of us and we, of them. Groups and societies are their members and something more, the something which the functioning of an aggregate adds to its parts. Thinking is

* See A. McC. Lee, "Attitudinal Multivalence in Relation to Culture and Personality," *American Journal of Sociology,* LX (1954–55), 294–299, and *Multivalent Man* (New York: George Braziller, 1966), esp. chaps. 11–13.

† *Childhood and Society,* 2nd ed. (New York: W. W. Norton & Co., 1963), p. 23. Reprinted by permission of the publisher.

‡ *Human Nature and the Social Order* rev. ed. (1922; reissued, Glencoe, Ill.: Free Press, 1956), pp. 36–37.

certainly a most private and personal experience, but we even think with the symbols and conceptions that our parents and other associates relayed to us from their groups and from society. When we decide to marry a person for reasons of physical attraction and romantic love, we are usually following accepted mental, emotional, and behavioral norms.

"Original Nature." Psychologists and physiologists tell us that, irrespective of the society, social class, and neighborhood into which children are born, they ordinarily start life with much the same array of physical needs and responses. From birth onward, there are innumerable gross and subtle differences in the ways of satisfying and shaping an infant's needs; these differences in experience combine with a wide range of biological heredities to supply the diversity of personalities needed in each new generation. The differences in physical and social environment often vary along national, class, and regional lines; they help lay the deep roots of contrast among such groups. There are also, however, the individual divergences that enrich life within all sorts of groups.

Like all other newborn organisms, an infant requires food, warmth, and protection. We humans differ from other animals in these respects: our infancy lasts longer, and our instinctive patterns are of much less significance. We depend more upon learned ways of doing things. During the first few days, weeks, or even months of life, we cannot look after ourselves instinctively. Someone must continue for a long time to bring us nourishment, provide us with clothing and shelter, and shield us from such hazards as falling or being fallen upon, excessive exposure, and unsanitary conditions.

The infant devotes himself to breathing, sleeping, digesting, growing, eliminating waste, and making random muscular movements. At birth he reacts with a few simple reflexes such as sneezing, coughing, swallowing, eye-blinking, and inward curling of the fingers and toes in response to a touch on his palm or sole. Most mothers are certain that their babies also smile, though physicians may attribute such facial contortions to gas in the stomach. When an infant's needs are not met or some part of him does not function to his satisfaction, he cries. If held too tightly or made fearful through the sudden withdrawal of physical support, he screams.

The foregoing responses are but a few of the simplest behavior patterns of the neonate. Psychologists have made detailed studies of maturation among children in different American social classes and ethnic groups. They have concluded that the infant is not merely the social product of his parents but also the social product of his time and place, of many groups, and of society. In any society, and in this our society is certainly no exception, he is very likely to become a conformist to what he thinks are proper group and societal norms. Certain experiences during maturation make for conformity and help to determine the maturing individual's heterosexual and familial adjustments. Before discussing these aspects of maturation, however, it is necessary to dispose of two general problems: (1) the erroneous notion of prenatal influences upon child development, and (2) the excessive anxieties of young parents about the task of providing effective and wise guidance.

Prenatal Influences. Discussion of the "original nature" of the child at birth always brings up the persistent superstitions about prenatal influences. Thus, the old wives' tales trace birthmarks to the frightening of the mother during pregnancy. They give assurance as to the piety of any child whose mother does enough praying during pregnancy. They also offer a wealth of irrelevant ways to control or at least to predict the sex of the child before birth. Even a well-educated woman can be heard to say, in confidence, with regard to some alleged prenatal influence, "I know there is nothing to it; it is probably just a coincidence, but . . ." So far as modern science can discover, such matters are just that: merely coincidences and nothing more.

Anxieties of Young Parents. To most young parents our statements about the social development of children will seem at times like oversimplifications. For many such parents, experience in handling the problems of early childhood has been limited to occasional baby-sitting for neighbors during adolescent years. Young mothers and fathers often feel overwhelmed by responsibilities to their children. They worry about doing "the right thing" without having any clear guide as to what "the right thing" in any given situation might be.

Because the family problems they face seem unique, young parents are often emotionally blocked from depending upon useful general rules as guides to solutions. This is particularly true of those who were brought up in small families. The tasks of child guidance in large families are so numerous, so continuous, and so apparent to all members that guidance problems lose much of their mystery and complexity.

Although many of them have studied problems of guidance in special courses, college-trained middle-class Americans are especially disturbed about the emotional and intellectual consequences for their children of almost everything they may or may not do in caring for or associating with them. They fail to realize that much more can be accomplished through taking a concerned but relaxed and confident attitude toward the complexities of child-rearing than through "trying too hard." To repeat the quotation from Wordsworth, children thrive on "little, nameless, unremembered acts of kindness and of love." Tenseness often has a way of begetting tenseness, and confidence, confidence. Parents cannot always be right, but they can be loving and supportive. They can have and show respect for the integrity and autonomy of their children.

In the work cited above, E. H. Erikson * contributes these pertinent comments: "Parents who are faced with the development of a number of children must constantly live up to a challenge. They must develop with them. We distort the situation if we abstract it in such a way that we consider the parent as 'having' such and such a personality when the child is born and then, remaining static, impinging upon a poor little thing. For this weak and changing little being moves the whole family along. Babies control and bring up their families as much as they are controlled by them; in fact, we may say that the family brings up a baby by being brought up by him." Thus, to reiterate, the family is a process, and the arrival of each new member extends the range of experience involved in that process.

The "Self" Is Social. What we eventually call the "I" and "me" and "self" is only vaguely present in us at birth. All is then apparently a blur. Our eyes and our minds cannot focus. Both we ourselves and the world appear as generalized rather than specific objects. Only slowly do we sort things out somewhat. We gradually and then more rapidly explore and experiment; eventually we begin to comprehend the nature of stimuli that come to us, identify our needs, and determine potential forms of self-expression. But we have to be stimulated to sort out our consciousness of self, and this consciousness gradually takes shape and strengthens as a product of the processes of physical-self-personal maturation.

Charles Horton Cooley calls the self a "looking-glass self" because the self evolves largely in response to the reactions made by the child's

---

* *Op. cit.,* p. 68. Reprinted by permission of the publisher.

mother and other associates. The behavior of others is the looking glass in which the child first detects his self and then watches that self grow. We perceive from the reactions of our face-to-face associates what and who we are. In their evaluations, we learn how to evaluate ourselves. They tell us directly and indirectly what we might become. They give us models of appropriate social roles which we learn to perform in given types of social situation. They supply us with words and other patterns of action, emotion, and even thought which we know to be accepted, understood, and used in our society and in the groups which are becoming ours. Before these intimate mirrors, provided by those who evaluate and inspire us, we try out, adapt, and then adopt such patterns until they become integral parts of our self.

In Freudian terminology, the "self" is nearly identical with the "ego," which is said to arise as a mediator among the contradictions and conflicts within and from outside the individual. Internally, the "ego" lives with the "id" (an unruly reservoir of psychic energy related to somatic processes) and with the "superego" (the internalization within the individual of the moral controls of society and of our groups). Externally, there impinge upon the ego the complicated demands of the social and physical environments; with them, the self works out its constantly modifying relationships. The "ego" evolves as a conscious mediator; the "id" is a bully which is never wholly socialized; the "superego" is a gradually built-in monitor. Aided by the "looking-glass" processes mentioned above (the processes of primary or face-to-face interaction), the "self" or "ego" gradually gains some autonomy, enough grasp of social patterns, and sufficient experience to serve as the agent for mediation and consciousness.

Both Cooley and Freud recognize the imperiousness and the largely unconscious character of biological drives. Both indicate that environmental influences help to shape the unconscious as well as the conscious aspects of the self or ego and that the unconscious aspects, even though they are unrecognized, constantly do much to determine behavior. Cooley and Freud analyzed human nature from entirely different points of view and were apparently unacquainted with each other's work, but they reached many similar conclusions and many others which are complementary.

Sex and the Self. Sigmund Freud contributed the first comprehensive theory to clarify somewhat complex problems—attended by tragedies, tensions, and comedies—which people encounter in relation to the apertures of the body. Freud created formulations that he apparently knew to be oversimplifications or even caricatures of the complexities of human nature. He called his evolving conceptions his "mythology." He regarded his theories as steps toward knowledge of behavior that had been cloaked in prudery and in coarse humor. His theories greatly aid understanding, but Freud himself should be understood as having been too much the scientist to have been a "Freudian" in any cultist sense. As efforts to summarize his specific cases and the findings of others, his theories could scarcely appear as qualified and as tentative to enthusiastic Freudians as they apparently did to him. He made it clear that he was aware, as none of his followers apparently can be, of the connotations his wealth of observations and readings gave to his statement in his own thoughts. When read in the order in which they were written, his contributions indicate how he tried to press on to more and more satisfactory observations and explanations of hitherto obscure phenomena. As he stated, "If we cannot see things clearly, we will at least see clearly what the obscurities are."

The following paragraphs outline briefly some crucial points in the theories of Freud and his successors about the individual's psychosexual maturation. The summary is necessarily a rapid, capsular overview, in some respects an oversimplification, and more extensive reference works must be consulted for fuller and more adequate treatment.*

As noted above, the development of a child is physical-self-personal; all three aspects are inseparably intertwined. The sex function, in its broadest sense, arises from interrelated somatic, intellectual, group, and physical-environmental factors. Freud reports many interconnections among a child's pleasurable and painful experiences centered about his mouth, the sphincters controlling his anal and urethral passages, and his genitals. Such experiences have these apertures as focal points, but they involve much else—emotions, unconscious and conscious thoughts, other parts of the body, other people, and impressions of the accompanying situation.

Freud notes the order in which such experiences ordinarily take place among the kinds of people with whom he was acquainted. He points to apparent consequences of deviations (deprivations, exaggerations, traumata) in such experiences. Other students of depth psy-

* See George Simpson, *People in Families: Sociology, Psychoanalysis, and the American Family* (Cleveland: Meridian Books, World Publ. Co., 1966).

chology and dynamic sociology have found that for each society and each social class there is a different "normal" patterned sequence of stages in psycho-sexual development. When the society is relatively settled and bound by tradition, one of these patterned sequences helps set the emotional and intellectual bases for each child's assimilation into society and into groups represented by his parents. In a society that is changing, as is our own, the socially prescribed sequence may maladapt and confuse the child instead of preparing him for the available adult roles. For this reason much study and experimentation are needed to explore such patterned sequences in our society with all their obvious and also unsuspected differences.

Breast-feeding introduces the sucking period of child development. Some infants are deprived of this experience; for others, it may be either very brief or extensive. Sucking activities are apparently satisfying and, in fact, necessary for healthy growth. Parents should be aware of the fact that "demand feeding" and "feeding by the clock" have markedly different effects upon the child's maturation. Too often parents fail to consider how too little or too much sucking activity may influence the child's personality; they do not understand in any event the importance of the circumstances surrounding such childhood experiences as sucking. They may permit the infant to suck only the breast and other objects associated with food. They often assume that through deprivation they can keep the child from forming such a "naughty habit" as thumb-sucking or using the tongue as an extra finger.

As he begins to experience the painful eruption of teeth, the child progresses from the sucking to the biting stage. Now, especially if he is still being breast-fed, he may confront new maternal pressures which teach him that no one likes to be bitten even though biting may be pleasurable and even necessary. He thus starts to learn the merits of reciprocity. In some societies, breast-feeding continues until the biting activity ends it abruptly; in our society, weaning from breast or bottle usually occurs prior to the biting stage.

The stages of sucking and biting are closely related to later stages of development. This association is suggested by the frequency with which the oral excitation of feeding from breast or bottle is accompanied by a bowel movement, urination, and erection of the penis or clitoris. The stimulation of one erogenous zone, especially in the very young, carries over quite easily to others.

Before pressures come to bear upon a child to control his sphincters, he apparently enjoys releasing urine or stools whenever enough are present. He is under no compulsion other than physical pressure from within or without to retain or expel waste products. Then, at an early age in the child's development, parents in our society begin to demand and to reward sphincter-control. Persistent repetition of such demands and rewards affects the child's personality; they induce him to associate the entire zone with ideas of coercion and of frustration. In societies in which people wear little or no clothing, with no problem of keeping the child's clothing clean, control may be permitted to develop slowly and with little guidance. But Americans want their Johnny to get on with "growing up." Mothers even compete in such training, just as they compete in pushing their children on toward other goals. An early first tooth, a first step, the ability to walk, an absence of bed-wetting, weaning, or control of stools can figure in the contest for prestige in many kinds of neighborhoods. Parents may allude to these minor achievements to bolster maternal or family prestige until Johnny can make some high grades in school or, better still, score heavily in football.

Actually, the experts are not sure about the precise influence of experiences in these pregenital stages upon the individual's future personality. Maturation cannot be understood in terms of cause-and-effect sequences or even of multiple causation and multiple consequences. Maturation is an adaptive process in which the significance of any event or factor depends upon its whole processual context and thus cannot be precisely separated out, delineated, and assessed. There is now emerging an important tendency to forego child-rearing fads and to return to intelligent adaptations of traditional methods. Thus we now hear more and more about "natural" childbirth, breast-feeding (with the breast available "on demand"), gradual weaning (to be accepted by the child rather than being imposed as an abrupt change), and other means of reducing the pressures toward aperture-control.

The child's experiences with his apertures can easily be oversimplified and overstated, but it must be granted that they have profoundly formative influences upon his development. When a type of experience is pleasurable and then is blocked, the frustrated child finds other ways, permissible or surreptitious, in which to express or to sublimate his urges. In other words, the child discovers alternative activities or fantasies with which to offset deprivation, limitation, or trauma. What happens during the pregenital stages of maturation lends color to the individual's self and to his subsequent social personalities. Pregenital and genital experiences help to provide him with ways of thinking, with symbolism, with emotional attachments, and with a variety of basic themes to re-enact many times during the rest of his life. But this is a complex problem, and the reader must beware of simplified generalizations; the detailed handling of such a problem requires intensive investigation of each specific case by professionally competent counselors.

What Is Psycho-Sexual Maturity? Freud concludes that the mature person is one who goes through his pregenital stages of maturation in a manner that leaves behind no distortions or unresolved problems. This is an ideal, seldom if ever attained, and it leans too heavily upon a kind of instinctivism or biological determinism. It lacks sociological orientation. It does not recognize the existence of societal roles which require many different kinds of mature or "normal" persons.

Let us summarize briefly the findings of depth psychologists as well as those of dynamic sociologists. The mature person is one who has had the kinds of maturational experiences which have accorded him the optimum physical-self-personal conditioning for membership in his society and the particular groups within his society in which he is to live. Much of this conditioning takes place before the child reaches the end of his third year. By then, in our society, he has usually been weaned, he can walk with some confidence, he has gained control of his sphincters, he knows how to communicate somewhat on a nonverbal level and with simple words, and he has attained his first genital stage.

The first genital stage is one of rudimentary genitality. At this stage, the individual usually gains firm identification as male or female and discerns and relates himself to basic family-drama routines to the extent that they interest and involve him. The stage shortly leads into a prolonged latency period of apparent quiescence in all matters relating to sexual interests and sex development. During the stage of infantile genitality, the individual becomes much more conscious of himself, and his self becomes much more defined and autonomous. This consciousness reflects his greater security in movement, inspection, and experimentation with himself and his environment and especially his growing ability to use verbal symbols; his "looking-glass" processes are becoming more and more operative and productive.

According to Freud, the production of artistic works (such as fine paintings, symphonies, and novels), creative accomplishments in science (ranging from astronomy to sociology), and unusual managerial and entrepreneural achievements often are attributable to sublimations of unresolved early problems in psycho-sexual maturation. Conversely, the individual's reactions to such problems may turn his long-term development toward listlessness, alcoholism, or crime.

The terms "sublimations" and "unresolved problems" are objectionable because they imply that biological factors overwhelmingly determine personal characteristics. As used, these terms have the further implication that, in order to become mature, all human beings would have to follow one basic, patterned sequence in their psycho-sexual development and that deviation from this sequence occasions "unresolved problems." These are dubious generalizations. Instead of attributing differences in personality orientation so largely to biological factors, we should investigate the influences of societal cultures, class and ethnic subcultures, and unique personal and family situations upon the development of the self.

Rather than the Freudian term "sublimations," we would prefer to speak of alternatives or substitutes for repressed expressions of deeply entrenched patterns of thought, emotion, and behavior. These alternatives or substitutes become basic themes to which persons recur time after time throughout life. They are related to organic development, but they are significantly psychic and social in their nature. They condition the functioning of the covert self and of the overt person. They recall enjoyable or disturbing events, situations, and human inconsistencies in our earliest years that we re-enact in one context after another. We may often express these themes in new symbols and with new persons to take the places of the old. To illustrate, many a wife unwittingly triggers an old family drama theme in the mind of her husband; she finds it difficult to comprehend his apparently irrational reactions as he sees her standing in a theme situation his mother originated for him in a tense event thirty years earlier. Long ago the origins of such a theme may have been repressed in his subconscious. He rehearses it symbolically in dreams and fantasies or unconsciously in daily life because, without special psychotherapy, he is often unable to think about it consciously. Mixed up in such a deep-set theme are biological deprivation, family-drama patterns, a special incident, and many other factors which go far beyond being either an unresolved psycho-sexual problem or the sublimation of a biological drive.

THE FAMILY IS A MICROCOSM OF SOCIETY

The child sees his family willingly or unwillingly as an epitome of society, even though it is always a distorted epitome. It is distorted by the group memberships and unique experiences of the family as a whole and of his individual family associates. The family matrix exemplifies to the child his family's habitual social-class and ethnic view of society's cultural and human organization.

As he grows, the child emulates and tries to act out his conceptions of adult roles as he sees them in his family and as he learns about them by hearsay. Girls emulate their mothers and older girl associates; they play with dolls and imitate adult activities such as cooking, entertaining other "women," teaching, and acting on television. Boys more frequently depend upon their imaginations rather than direct observation to decide the kinds of behavior typical of maleness and maturity. Their play activities involve more fantasy than realism. In the struggle of boys against femininity and female controls to achieve maleness and autonomy, they try to emulate mythical male symbols of the virile, venturesome, and independent. They thus often devote their playtime to imaginary or actual violence in the guise of military exploits, fights between "cops and robbers" or between Indians and cowboys, and struggles in "interstellar space." American Indians live in the games of boys all over Europe, not merely in their native habitat. As the sociologist Barrington Moore, Jr.* observes, "Radio and television heroes . . . now play a vital part in the socialization process. Parents have an uphill and none too successful struggle against these sources. Like adult mobs, children's groups readily adopt the sensational, the cruel, and the most easily understood for their models and standards. These influences then corrupt and lower adult standards, as parents become increasingly afraid to assert their own authority for fear of turning out 'maladjusted' children."

Social scientists are disturbed by the fact that toy manufacturers cater to these militant attitudes instead of making toys which depict constructively and realistically the peaceful pursuits for which the boys

* *Political Power and Social Theory: Seven Studies* (New York: Harper Torchbooks, 1965), p. 166.

are likely to prepare themselves. Too many parents also fail to consider sufficiently the consequences of such militaristic training both for the education of the individual and the safety, even perhaps the survival, of society. Too many people of all ages think of international conflict in this H-bomb age as somehow merely an enlargement of the game of "Indians and cowboys" they played as a child.*

Our family introduces us to society, and it also goes with us as we go forth into society and colors our characterization of what we find there. For example, the middle-class mother often becomes for her son the source not only of food and loving care but also of morality. She is idealized as representative of "what is good" in society. When she speaks, society is speaking. On the other hand, the father as the prime representative of the male world is many times for the boy a remote ideal, tantalizingly unrealistic, only imperfectly perceived. He comes from and returns to the world of practical affairs that lies beyond the annoying restraints of the maternal sphere. The boy also lives with and prepares for the future through his contacts with three other types of people—his siblings and sibling-substitutes, his peers other than siblings (his gang), and the nebulous world of other people, of strangers. Each of these groups becomes a prototype in childhood of a series of other groups with which the boy associates during the rest of his life. He projects into the subsequent groups the same values and patterns he has learned in his early years in his prototypical groups.

In the middle-class strata of our society, the girl tends to view matters rather differently than the boy in several significant respects. For her, the mother is also the source of food and loving care, but she shortly becomes not an unattainable ideal and a representative of societal morality but a practical model for the future and a competitor for the father's attentions in the present. On the other hand, the father becomes not only a paragon of the male, of the possible mate, but also the representative of morality and of society. The other associates of a girl's childhood—siblings, peers, and strangers—are similar in some respects and dissimilar in others to those of the boy. Thus, for her, nonsibling peer groups do not have the significance in the quest for autonomy which they have for the boy.

Special studies of depth psychology can provide the materials and theories with which to understand the significance of sexual avoid-

* See Elizabeth Briant Lee, "As the Twig is Bent," *Fellowship*, XXV, No. 5 (March 1, 1959), 21–24.

ance patterns, including incest taboos, between mother and son, father and daughter, and brother and sister. The training in these patterns, largely of an informal sort, helps stimulate the child's drive to find in maturity permissible substitutes for parent or sibling as a love object. This drive is reinforced and stimulated by the accompanying sense of guilt at finding the forbidden so enticing.

SOME GUIDES AND SUGGESTIONS

A half-century ago, the problems of family life were just as serious as they are today though perhaps they appeared simpler. Our parents or grandparents tried to solve them chiefly with the aid of a "doctor book." That volume consisted mainly of information about first aid and lists of symptoms of common contagious diseases. It paid scant attention to problems of mental health; there was no mention of psychoneuroses. At that time, every person not confined to an "insane asylum" or an upstairs room was regarded as "sane," even though he might be a bit peculiar in speech or behavior. With an occasional assist from the "doctor book," or rarely from a family physician, mothers were supposed to know instinctively how best to care for their children. What they did know, they had learned as pat formulas from mothers and grandmothers. The consequences were reflected in the tragic statistics of early deaths.

With a vast increase in the college-trained population, better medical knowledge, and mass education through popular mediums of communication, people no longer have recourse to a single "doctor book" of health information. Instead, they purchase a variety of books which deal with all sorts of problems of the modern family—from weaning and cleanliness training to personal adjustment in nursery schools. In health matters they no longer depend even upon one family physician but demand the services of numerous medical specialists, each of whom is an expert in one life-period or in one aspect of human physiology and its ills.

All this has its beneficial aspects, but we might just be overdoing it all somewhat. We may as well realize that we have not always been too well served by our specialists. Let us illustrate. The free-wheeling "doctor book" was supplemented in 1914 by a bulletin, *Infant Care,* published by the United States Children's Bureau. That publication, in the form in which it was very widely used for two decades thereafter, stressed absolute precision in scheduling for infants. In doing so, it reflected the views of a distinguished committee of child specialists. Note this example of some of the advice offered: "Feeding from the second or third day of life must be given with great regularity, by the clock. If this is done the tiny baby will wake at feeding time and sleep between times." Toilet-training (and all else) was fitted into this time-bound mold: "The first essential in bowel training is absolute regularity." Such disciplining "may be begun as early as the end of the first month. It should always be begun by the end of the third month and may be completed during the eighth month. . . . Almost any baby can be so trained that there are no more soiled diapers to wash after he is 6 to 8 months." *

Whereas infants had formerly been pacified in one way or another, the crying baby of the 1920's was permitted to scream and thus exercise his lungs. Mothers were often and sagely warned against picking up, coddling, or rocking their babies. That was thought to "spoil" them and to make them too demanding of attention. Many a young mother in that period held her infant on a pot every hour on the hour.

By the mid-1930's, the country was beginning to be flooded with conflicting advice from child-training experts, pediatricians, psychologists, and all manner of other authorities. The fashion gradually shifted again. No longer was the baby fitted loosely into a mother's life as in the generations before World War I. No longer was "life with baby" to be a stop-watch business regardless of a particular infant's needs and of personality consequences. Now came the period of extreme permissiveness for baby; in some cases, mother became a rightless and opinionless subordinate. Cartoonists of the time jibed that to refuse alcohol to a child of three might give him a sense of rejection. By the late 1940's and the 1950's, fashion veered again. "Naturalism" again emerged to the relief of sociologists and cultural anthropologists. In some respects we went back to where we had been at the turn of the century, but we had gained a great deal of understanding from the findings of psychologists, sociologists, and anthropologists. Mothering the baby, breast-feeding on demand, delayed and permissive toilet-training (with modern technology taking a lot of the work out of diapers), and in general "self-regulation" of a sensible sort in conformity with a baby's own needs and personal routine—these approaches characterize the present mode. Each of

* U.S. Children's Bureau, *Infant Care* (Bureau Publication No. 8; Washington, D.C.: Government Printing Office, 1931), pp. 57–58.

these four waves of fashion—the old-time common sense, the clock-watching of the 1920's, the permissiveness of the 1930's and early 1940's, and the naturalism of recent years—had behind it the weight of respected expert approval.

Even though so-called "experts" have too often misled public opinion, sensible respect for expert opinion is of course necessary. In the field of child development, the findings of scientists came upon our health practitioners and counselors too quickly to be absorbed gradually and without swings to extremes. Contemporary psychologists and sociologists are working out a synthesis of modern scientific findings with what is useful in folk wisdom. They are discarding practices, such as hasty sphincter training, that often serve maternal convenience but may help produce a maladjusted child. They are trying to help parents and children to work out their interrelationships to greater mutual satisfaction.

After World War II, the vade mecum of a great many mothers has been (as noted above) Dr. Benjamin Spock's *Baby and Child Care* of which, within a decade, more than 3.5 million copies were distributed. Spock calls his book "a substitute for grandmother," and he urges parents to view without guilt their own imperfections as parents and the lack of a perfect world for their children, to develop a degree of self-reliance instead of running constantly to specialists, and not to labor too hard over their children.

Major problems of child development center about sex education. As their child develops, parents often appear to feel they are playing with fire every time they have to meet the child's probing questions and experimental behavior in this area. Probably as good a general statement as any about how to handle children in this regard is one by the educator James L. Hymes, Jr.* The statement also expresses attitudes that may well be applied to many other problems of child development. Here are excerpts:

It is easy to worry needlessly. Whenever you read in the paper or hear of some youngster who is in a sex difficulty, you wonder: Doesn't this happen because children are 'wise beyond their years?' This can frighten you and make you want to clamp down and not answer so openly. Or it can make you anxious over everything you do. Suppose you say the wrong thing? Suppose you don't do everything the book

* "How to Tell Your Child about Sex," *Public Affairs Pamphlet* No. 149 (New York, 1949), p. 27. Reprinted by permission of the publisher.

says you should? You begin to feel tight inside, and sex education becomes something Special.

But think: Children don't get into trouble suddenly. No one fact or incident upsets their applecart. All children want so deeply to be good that a great many things in a great many areas over a great period of time must go wrong before real trouble comes. You have a good relationship with your children. You have it through the years. You have had it in all areas of education; you have it now in sex education. You can count on your youngsters. . . .

You may want, as an added safeguard, to put an extra stress on mothers and fathers loving each other, before they have a baby. And it may make it easier for you to talk to children about sex if you give added weight to its love aspects.

CONCLUSION

On the one hand, it is useful to have a grasp of the importance to the child of his family experiences and to give him an environment in which he can grow and thrive. On the other hand, it is essential to give the child at every age a sense that he is taking his place among other people in a healthy family in which he can learn to participate but which has many interests besides himself. Love is something about which parents can talk with their children, but above all it is something that parents can best exemplify in the details of their daily routines of living.

Chapter VIII

THE CHILD IN GROUP PROCESSES

During his most impressionable years, the child observes human relations chiefly as they develop within the circle of his own family and friends. By comparison with their behavior, he evaluates the conduct of persons outside this group. He accepts the patterns of thought, feeling, and behavior customary in his family as a blueprint or a set of criteria for judging the proper ways of family living. As that blueprint enlarges to include his experiences in relations with other children, it becomes for him a microcosm of all human relationships. He may hate and fight what he sees in his family or among his young friends, but even these negative reactions cumulatively become entrenched as his dominant frame of reference. Conversely, he may love his family and try to find its equivalent in his own family of procreation and the fulfilment of its promise in society more generally.

A child's microcosm of society is distorted by the fact that the affiliations and experiences of his family are not precisely typical of those of other families in his social stratum or in society. In addition, no two children perceive the same family in the same way. Thus whenever a child goes outside his family, he takes with him his own caricature of his close associates and tries to understand other people, other groups, and society as a whole in terms of it.

Thus the individual emerges as a socialized person out of processes which have two principal and intimately related emphases. (1) His self gradually emerges and grows as his body and its functions respond to nurture and stimulation from his physical and social environment. Significant in this more individual emphasis is the timing of such basic events in maturation as nursing, weaning, and cleanliness training as well as the interpersonal atmosphere in which the child lives. (2) The child's social competence and assimilation proceed apace with the development of his self. This might be called a more social or group emphasis. The child gradually assumes patterned relationships and finds identities in association with his mother, father, siblings, other peers, and other adults. The individual is thus covertly a self in whom the influences of social interaction are internalized, and he is overtly a person, an individual functioning as a part of social groups. The self is a social self, a "looking-glass self," a product of physical, biological, psychic, and social factors. It gains much of its definition as the child sees and interprets the reactions of relatives and friends to his behavior.

PROTOTYPICAL GROUPS

How does a child come to picture the human interrelations of his parental family as a microcosm of interrelations in society in general? Perhaps we can best explain this complex social-psychological tendency by considering those segments of family experience which become prototypical of later group experiences. In doing so, we shall use as our principal source of examples that portion of the middle class which acquires joint identity through the derivation of income largely from employment as hired professionals and technicians and from membership in the so-called majority, the Protestant-like ethnoid segment of American society. (For purposes of contrast, however, we shall also give some illustrations drawn from several other class groups.)

We shall cite the effects upon the child's looking-glass self of relationships within the following prototypical groups: (1a) maternal: son and mother; (1b) maternal: daughter and mother; (2a) paternal: son and father; (2b) paternal: daughter and father; (3) sibling; (4) nonsibling peer; and (5) stranger.*

With each of his prototypical groups the child works out one or several kinds of identification. He also learns to adjust to other people and to society at large in ways that he later discovers to be similar to the customary ways of successor groups, *i.e.*, of groups which he joins when, in due time, he outgrows the early protypical groups.

1a. *Son and Mother As a Prototypical Group.* As he matures, the

---

* This is not an exhaustive list. For example, it would be more precise to include separate discussions of significant child identifications with other parent-type groups, such as the child and both parents, but for our purposes here such further refinement is not necessary. We wish to give the most salient aspects of this life-history approach to the processes of identification, group participation, and adaptation to the cultural contradictions of society. See A. McC. Lee, "Attitudinal Multivalence in Relation to Culture and Personality," *American Journal of Sociology*, LX (1954–55), 294–299. For more details, see A. McC. Lee *Multivalent Man* (New York: George Braziller, 1966), esp. chaps. 12–13.

child can be said to emerge from the social womb of the mother, just as he had earlier emerged from her physical womb. During the first days after birth, the child is little more than an appendage to the mother and scarcely identifiable as the other member in this group of two persons. From her come food, warmth, and fondling. She may have helpers, but it is doubtful that a child makes much of a distinction for some time between mother and her assistant or substitute. To him she typifies all that is good, supportive, and proper. A little later come weaning and cleanliness training, introducing notions of reciprocity and guilt, and the child learns he is dealing with an entity who can withhold, take away, and discipline as well as give, cuddle, and support. Nurture and love do not continue to come as freely as at the outset. They get involved with pressures for "payment" for them. The child must pay through "being good" and through "becoming a big boy"; he must eat from a spoon and control his bowels. When he is older, he will have to win games, reach goals in schooling, and earn money to demonstrate his worthiness for affection.

Thus the basic, intimate, and erotic relationship with the mother gives the boy two principal kinds of identity. First, the son-mother relationship is the prototype of permitted interpersonal love, tinged with senses of obligation and of guilt. Eventually, in the usual course of a life history, the patterns of thought, of feeling, and even, to a degree, of behavior developed in this relationship are projected into one or more adult heterosexual relationships. Second, the tie with his mother in this earliest group also forms the principal basis for the more abstract tie at a subsequent time with society and society's morality. Even though the mother usually thinks of morality in terms of her own identifications (as personified in its ideal sense by her father, rendered more restrictive and practical by her mother), for the son his mother more directly personifies what later becomes abstracted and elaborated into an ideal definition of society. She is his principal surrogate of societal morality, later reinforced by such mother-substitutes as female schoolteachers. As the social anthropologist Geoffrey Gorer * notes, in speaking of the projection of this sort of identity into adult male life in the United States, "In all the spheres where moral considerations are meant to operate . . . men act as though they were being guided by (or rebelling against) rules and prohibitions enunciated by a moral mother." This "encapsulated

* *The American People* (New York: W. W. Norton & Co., 1948), p. 56.

mother," in Gorer's expression, this feminine nucleus of conscience, gives men a strained attitude toward morality and toward idealism in general; it tends to set masculinity against morality.

Gorer's conclusions would have been more acceptable if he had restricted his characterization to certain middle-class groups. For diverse reasons, mothers in upper- and lower-class groups are not so intimately and imperiously identified with societal morality as he indicates. In upper-class groups, the weakened role of the mother is due to the common employment of mother-substitutes of lower prestige and derived authority whose influence does not often become "encapsulated." In lower-class groups, the mother is more likely to identify herself with the protective mores of her depressed class group. She may claim a morality higher than that of those who call themselves her betters, and she may assert that societal morality is a distortion of "real" morality at the hands of other groups. American leaders in social action—whether in business enterprise or politics or labor—thus often come from either the "bottom" or "top" of the social scale, rarely from the broad "middle." The "bottom" or "top" may have less effective moral inhibitions; their class values also point to what may be gained from the exploitation of opportunities.

1b. *Daughter and Mother As a Prototypical Group.* In part this relationship resembles that between son and mother but only to the point where the daughter starts to see her mother as another female in competition for the affection of another kind of person, a male. For the daughter, the mother is both a competitor and a practical guide in the form of a working model to be observed, criticized, and perhaps improved upon. The mother gives her son both the rudiments of heterosexual love and a feminine definition of societal morality. The mother gives her daughter an enveloping, reassuring, and realistic sense of femininity as well as a working model. It is the emergence of the mother as competitor and the girl's relationship with her father which help the daughter to escape excessive identification with another female.

In a mother-centered family such as one finds in certain underprivileged groups in our society, the daughter's identification with her mother remains absorbing. Through it, the daughter learns usually both to value and to detest the pretensions of a higher morality and the other protective mores of her class group. Women are the more self-sufficient and permanent members of such families and are more likely than men to head them. Arrangements with men often have more of temporary sentimentality than of practicality about them. When heterosexual experience comes to such a daughter, the man is often crudely exploitative.

2a. *Son and Father As a Prototypical Group.* To the degree that he is visible, the father may serve to some extent as a model for rebellion against an overwhelmingly female world. In middle-class groups, the father frequently presents to his son no more than one or two social personalities, one or two aspects of his social person. One aspect is the way he behaves as a father, and the other may be a different way he behaves as a husband—to the extent that the difference is apparent to the son. The father is thus abstract and unsatisfying. He resembles a character in a public school history text. At too many significant places in what would be a well-rounded portrayal, there are plaster and paint, as it were, instead of flesh and blood. How does the father behave when he enters one or another area of the enticing world of men? How should the son play-act such behavior and thus give himself a sense of identity with that important world? In many ways (see page 108), the boy's friends of his own age and their realistic-sounding but imaginative gossip fill in the detail the father fails to give his son. Thus the son has little choice but to substitute fantasy for observation.

A boy on a small farm may be repelled and even sickened by the grinding work he has to do, but there is little time left in the day for him to speculate about how his father behaved as a boy or the way his father and others in the family group grew up to maturity. On the other hand, the intimate association of family members on a farm usually leaves relatively little in maturation about which to speculate. In that type of situation, the idealism and ambition of the mother may help the boy to escape into, instead of rebel against, a world of masculine accomplishment.

2b. *Daughter and Father As a Prototypical Group.* John Levy and Ruth Munroe Levy start their famous book, *The Happy Family,** with a story characteristic of this prototypical group in a middle-class family. Their four-year-old daughter brushed aside a proposal of her father that she aspire to join the chorus of the Follies. " 'I'm going to be a plain lady like mother. . . . I'm going to have five little children.' " In response to an inquiry from her father as to who will be the male parent of the babies, the daughter replied, " 'Why, you, daddy.' "

* New York: Alfred A. Knopf, 1938, p. 3.

Even though a father shortly becomes known to be clearly unattainable as a husband, this basic, intimate, and erotic relationship does much to help the daughter to break any continuing and excessive attachment to her mother. From the relationship with her father, the daughter develops two principal senses of identity: first, the relationship becomes the prototype of permitted interpersonal love, tinged with a sense of guilt; second, it also evolves into the personification of the idealism of society, of morality, in terms of the father's masculine image. The idealized father thus, rather than the actual husband, often becomes the woman's masculine ideal for her own son.

In the first prototypical relationship, that of permitted interpersonal love, the guilt is associated with the competitive nature of the identification and with the fact that incest taboos stop it far short of the little girl's fantasy. In the middle-class groups in our society which we are using as our principal examples, the unselfish generosity and supportiveness of the father toward the daughter—the spoiling of the daughter by the father—ill condition her for the egalitarian anticipations of many young men in dating. At the same time, the daughter has not gone through any such deep-set relationship as the son does with his mother; the middle-class father is almost as abstract for the daughter as he is for the son. Our reference to the more egalitarian anticipations of young men is to their playful dating behavior before they become "serious." Only when young men do become "serious" do they regard girls less as the successors to childhood playmates and more as the heiresses to the patterns of love, guilt, and anxiety formed in the son-mother prototypical group.

In entrenched upper-class groups, the father looks upon his role with his daughter as one of co-operating with his wife in passing the girl along to another well-entrenched male after helping to equip her to play the games of power and amusement common to such a set. His contributions are likely to consist largely of finance and adoration. He considers it amusing to let his daughter exploit him in ways and to degrees he would not permit others. She is likely to have learned more about maleness from father-substitutes (male servants and instructors) than from her father or brothers; toward such substitutes she could look more instrumentally and less identifiably than toward a middle-class father who might perform similar services. Exploitation is thus likely to be a dominant tone in her heterosexual relations—as it is in quite deprived groups—but the upper-class daughter does the exploiting; the lower-class daughter is more likely to be exploited.

3. *Siblings As a Prototypical Group.* The intense interpersonal competitiveness that characterizes the middle-class stratum in our society begins among children at a very early age. Then it is constantly reinforced and stimulated in the numerous formal groups which are instituted to educate and entertain them.

Where there are two or more children in a family, each usually works out for himself a somewhat unique social personality or system of behavior as the basis for self-expression and for competition with his siblings. This social personality which he shows to the family as a whole is not necessarily the same as the personalities he shows separately to his mother, his father, and his siblings; to each of these, he is likely to display a somewhat different social personality. Each audience accepts his inconsistencies as understandable or expedient. The various social personalities of one person have aspects in common; these similarities derive from the fact that the same person, with the same physical, mental, and emotional equipment, acts in terms of each of the social personalities. At the same time, each of a person's social personalities differs from his others; each is keyed to the social group in which he habitually uses it and which expects him so to behave within its own context. Thus siblings "put each other up to things" collectively that a mother would not think possible of her darlings as she knows them separately. Siblings work out bases of co-operation to handle common problems of dealing with their parents, but at the same time they realize that they cannot hope for the others to show a united front very far because of profits to be derived from competing in the big family struggle for parental love and nurture. Their bases of co-operation and of non-co-operation later become characteristic mores of their sibling-group substitutes.

Where there are three or more siblings who are all boys or all girls, the terms of interpersonal rivalry are such as to produce a statistically greater chance of one adopting a homosexual pattern as the most tenable way to gain recognition in the sibling situation. Reference is not to overt homosexuality but to personal conditioning that makes at least for a latently homosexual adjustment to interpersonal relations.

Even though rewards for rivalry may be anxiously stressed by their parents, mixed siblings do much to fill out for each other the details of the other sex's image. In other words, the presence of siblings of

both sexes in a family tends to stimulate the more adequate establishment of sex identifications by each of the children along the lines
which are traditional in the family's social-class group.

The other groups for which the sibling group is the basic prototype are those in which an authoritarian figure (like the middle-
class parent) is in control of discipline and rewards individually
examples of success in interpersonal rivalry. Such groups include
those of the school classroom and the Boy and Girl Scouts when in
formal operation. Adults working in bureaucratic employment form
similar types of organization with quite similar mores. The rivalrous
sibling-type employment groups of the salaried middle class explain
in part the perennial failure among these people of programs of collective action such as trade unions. One can anticipate, for example,
a substantial degree of self-righteous informing on one another to
authority in the sibling-type group that one finds in middle-class
circles. The individualistic practice of peaching disastrous to many
types of collective effort is less likely to appear among fellow members of a peer-type group than of a sibling-type group.

With smaller homes and a tradition of group rather than individualistic action, lower-class families less often stress sibling competitiveness. Both boys and girls, but especially boys, are turned more
toward nonsibling peer groups in the streets and playgrounds.

4. *Nonsibling Peers As a Prototypical Group.* This type of group
is outside the family or on its fringe. As has already been suggested,
it often plays a more pressing and significant role in the lives of boys
than of girls. The prototypical peer group is unsupervised in any
direct and effective sense by an older person. In all classes, it gives
children opportunities to strive for autonomy and expression among
relative equals, away from scolding, driving, and paying court to entrenched authority. Among small children, such groups may be bisexual, but later and until the teens are reached, they are largely or
exclusively male or female.

For boy or girl, prototypical peer-group experience begins casually
as a matter of simple playful activity. More system, imagery, and
games gradually evolve. The conversation of children from ages two
to six has been described by the Swiss psychologist Jean Piaget * as a
kind of "pseudo-conversation" or "collective monologue"; and their
other play is just as self-expressive. Other children serve chiefly as

* *The Moral Judgment of the Child* (London: Kegan Paul, Trench, Trubner &
Co., 1932).

permissive and reactive audiences and sources of stimulation. By age seven the language and other behavior of children become more truly reciprocal. Unstructured play gives way to participation in games. As the social psychologist George Herbert Mead * puts it, in the game "the child must have the attitude of all the others involved in the game."

The foregoing characteristics are discernible both in sibling and in nonsibling peer groups. The basic difference between the two types of groups is in the structuring of authority. In the sibling-type group the societal surrogate (parent or parent-substitute) in effect calls the tune (with or without a candy-coated hand); in the peer-type group the children can play with greater freedom, can experience greater self-control and reciprocal control, can assume adult roles, and can get some sense of adult responsibilities. As the social psychologist Hubert Bonner † observes, "The need to withdraw or rebel, in our society, is not only directed against the family but against any group or institution whose norms the young person finds it difficult to accept and endure. . . . Since the adolescent has little or nothing to say regarding those school policies which directly touch his emotional needs, he becomes either indifferent, negative, or aggressive."

The rule that only one sex may be represented in a peer group is a general middle-class pattern. This is the class in which boys feel themselves so much engulfed in femininity. It is with regard to the boys of that stratum that Geoffrey Gorer ‡ speaks when he reports their "constant necessity to prove to their fellows, and to themselves, that they are not sissies, not homosexuals." He mentions how this anxiety bounds their lives and "drastically" curtails their interests. For example, the dread of being labeled effeminate often undermines budding masculine enthusiasm for sibling-type group activities (such as doing work in school for a female teacher) and even discourages participation in athletic games, excepting only the most strenuous sports such as football. "Indeed," Gorer notes, "all intellectual pursuits and interests are somewhat tainted; and when American intellectuals meet together, an enormous amount of time is wasted in proving boisterously to each other that they are just regular fellows."

---

* *Mind, Self and Society,* ed. C. W. Morris (Chicago: University of Chicago Press, 1934), p. 152.

† Hubert Bonner, *Group Dynamics: Principles and Applications.* Copyright 1959, The Ronald Press Company. (P. 135.)

‡ *Op. cit.,* p. 129.

The chasm between the anti-intellectual athletes and their followers, on the one hand, and the "grinds" and academic faculty of a college, on the other, is a common and traditional campus phenomenon.

The female peer group typically develops into something quite different from the male. Teen-age girls who have a great need for female peer-group activity and great involvement in it are looked upon as having somehow fallen short in their ability to compete with other girls for male attention. Female peer-groups are practical expedients, not too different from sibling-type groups and often about as competitive for rewards from outside the group. Especially from the early teens, girls find themselves increasingly absorbed in meeting and testing out the reactions of boys, and this precludes much collective female activity. In finding a husband, association with competitors has only limited advantages.

The contrasts between college social fraternities and sororities illustrate the situation in middle-class groups. Women copied fraternity forms from men. They may have coveted the men's relative independence but not to the extent of giving themselves the reputation of being independent. Sororities fulfill rather different functions than do men's fraternities. A sorority house has been accurately described as the equivalent of a "home" filled with "sisters"; conversely, the earlier prototype of a men's fraternity house would be a children's shack in a vacant lot. A women's lodge is more like a home in which the daughters have replaced the mother in control, with little change in policies. A men's house often has about it the air of a living arrangement without parents or parent-substitutes, the headquarters of a middle-class boys' gang. The girls use a sorority chiefly for personal advertisement of a snobbish sort; they value its certification of their social rating. The boys find that their fraternity has similar utility for labeling them, but that it is also a useful offensive and defensive alliance against the rigidities of the academic and female worlds.*

The teen-age groups of underprivileged adolescents are often denoted by the term "gangs," a term which has become a rejective misnomer. The "invidious coloration" of this word is given by middle-class sociologists "to what they consider to be a uniquely lower-class phenomenon. Rarely in sociological literature are middle-class adolescent groups referred to as gangs, irrespective of their similarity

* Summarized from A. McC. Lee, *Fraternities Without Brotherhood* (Boston: Beacon Press, 1955), Chapter 6.

to their lower economic-class counterparts." * The hostility of lower-class peer groups to middle-class parent substitutes is a compound of adolescent (in this case both male and female) striving for autonomy in an inhospitable world. These adolescents react against both the inadequacies of their own parents and the efforts of teachers, social workers, and police to make them become middle-class in orientation, to make them follow careers and ways of life that seem too hard, alien, and closed for them. In contrast, the relaxed atmosphere of their homes, the antagonism of their parents toward middle-class parent substitutes, and the exciting activities of their peer groups make their lives interesting and, within their narrow horizons, important.

5. *Strangers As a Prototypical Group.* This is a prototypical group in which the individual does not actually participate. It has been called a "reference group," that is, a group which is external to his own but which the individual takes into consideration in his thinking and associates with a certain scale of values. It becomes a point of reference in his thinking. Actually such a group is more a creature of a family's customary patterns of talk and action than of anything objectively attributable to an existing aggregate of people. Unlike other prototypical groups, the "strangers" are usually not known as persons.

The "strangers" begin as the general outgroup, the people to be avoided, the children with whom one does not or should not play, the adults whose candy must not be accepted. In their anxiety to build a shield against harm into their children's minds and to bind their children to themselves and to their own kind, parents project many fantasies of evil into the "strangers." Later, as children grow older, "strangers" are differentiated into "foreigners," the "ne'er-do-well," the "would-be's," the "queer," and more specific ethnic, racial, and class groups. As symbols of vaguely specified hazards, they are rarely or only accidentally subject to firsthand acquaintanceship. Such labeling helps to create barriers of "social distance," of social ignoring, among groups of people. From such practices grow sentiments which become ready tools for irrational political manipulation. In extreme cases, these sentiments become bases for "Red" scares and for adherence to extremist movements such as the Communist, Nazi, or Fascist.

* H. A. Bloch and Arthur Niederhoffer, *The Gang* (New York: Philosophical Library, 1958), p. 7.

PROTOTYPICAL GROUPS NURTURE MULTIVALENCE

The various prototypical groups require of their participants different attitudes and practices. As children are assimilated and develop within these crucial socializing groups, they literally become of "many minds." They become "multivalent" * in the sense that they learn to operate in terms of several different systems of value and of behavior. They acquire different social personalities for each of their basic prototypical groups. This splitting of our self starts, as Charles Horton Cooley † concludes, when we begin "to be different things to different people." It is then that we set forth "to apprehend personality and . . . its operation." Citing illustrations of this multivalent process, he mentions the fact that "children often behave worse with their mother than with other and less sympathetic people."

The reader may recall the development of multivalence in his own experience. He may try to date his first awareness that his parents had a different community of interest with each other or a different type of identification with other adults than with him. He may recollect his first discovery that he could discuss some things more readily and freely with other children, with members of a play group, than with parent or sibling. He may remember when his mother or father first showed surprise at reports of how differently he acted with some of his peers than he did in the presence of his parents. It is not easy to recall consciously such events of early life experience. Much of our ease as adults in slipping from one role (one set of attitudinal valences, one social personality) into another comes from our long habituation to the etiquette of group identities, to behavior keyed to group referents. This "division of man into several selves," as the psychologist William James ‡ discerns, "may be a discordant splitting, as where one is afraid to let one set of his acquaintances know him as he is elsewhere; or it may be a perfectly harmonious division of labor, as where one tender to his children is stern to the soldiers or prisoners under his command."

* A term coined by A. McC. Lee in his "A Sociological Discussion of Consistency and Inconsistency in Intergroup Relations," *Journal of Social Issues,* V, No. 3 (1949), 12–18. See also his "Attitudinal Multivalence in Relation to Culture and Personality," *American Journal of Sociology,* LX (1954–55), 294–299.

† *Human Nature and the Social Order* (rev. ed., 1922, reissued, Glencoe, Ill.: Free Press, 1956), p. 197.

‡ *The Principles of Psychology* (New York: Henry Holt & Co., 1890), I, 294.

IMPLICATIONS FOR GROUP EXPERIENCE

As indicated above, groups are not at all simple matters in the life of a child. A child's groups are his looking glasses in which he sees his social personalities in operation. As children gain experience and mature, they join groups which meet their changing needs and interests. Parents should try to understand their children's needs for protection and adventure, for secure and dependable models, and also for patterns of deviation, criticism, and even revolt. Wise parents do a certain amount of stage-managing in order to make it possible for their child to join desirable groups of peers, but they avoid giving the impression of direct manipulation or interference. For example, they refrain from negative criticism of the child's friend or group of friends.

The problem of parental control recurs in the routine of everyday living. Thus, school-age children may appear to their parents to spend too much time with their peer groups. The following comment points up this type of disciplinary problem: "Parents . . . are in the background now, for, increasingly, home and family are taken for granted. The important thing is that the school-age child knows that he can count on his parents. Meanwhile, he has to make his way in the new, bewildering, and sometimes upsetting world of boys and girls. And so, in a way, home and family are more important than ever. Home is a refuge when things go wrong in school and when Billy or Barbara has problems with friends. . . . Mothers and fathers would be able to relax more if they recognized that one child's 'influence' on another is not necessarily *what the parents see,* nor is it usually as strong as they imagine. Influencing, after all, works both ways." *

The ways of a child with his family, with mother, father, siblings, and friends, are intricate, to say the least, and he becomes a very complex product of all such associations through the years. If the child has had a reasonable chance for assimilation into the basic prototypical groups, he is not likely to exhibit deprivations in socialization that may drive him to strange or dangerous associates.

* S. M. Gruenberg and H. S. Krech, "Your Child's Friends," *Public Affairs Pamphlet* No. 285 (New York, 1959), p. 9. Reprinted by permission of the publisher.

Chapter IX

THE CHILD IN THE COMMUNITY

As a child goes forth into neighborhood play groups, religious classes and clubs, and school activities, both parents and community functionaries worry about these problems: Will he be like us—only, we trust, better? In our efforts to provide the child with opportunities for growth and development, are we doing the things that will help make him a "credit" to family and community? Will he avoid being much of a "problem"; will be become "useful" or "constructive"? In other words, adults hope for what they take to be the best for the child, but above all they want him to conform. When the desirability of creativeness is mentioned, it is so defined that there is no contradiction between "real" creativity and conformity. The "creative person" is the better mechanic, clergyman, mayor, or merchant. He may be inventive in a modest way, in the way of embroidering what exists, but surely he will not be disturbing or odd.

Society has come to know that it owes a great deal to its minority of creative artists and scientists. Popular discussions and scientific investigations concerning creativity are becoming more urgent and realistic. Conformity, nonconformity, and creativity—respectability, resistance to social controls, and innovation—present three principal themes of personal adjustment to community life. Let us look first at the most controversial and least understood of them, creativity.

Creativity is scarcely a routine function which follows a fixed pattern. We need both types of activity—the spontaneous, unsettling type and the ordinary, repetitious type. Considered as a problem with which we have to deal, creativity reveals certain characteristics similar to weather. Both creativity and weather come in many guises, and we need both. In studying them, we have made some progress in description and prediction, but, in both cases, our predictions are not very dependable. We all talk about the weather and do little about it. For all the "salting" of clouds with "dry ice" and chemicals and other experimentation, weather is largely beyond human influence. We also talk a lot about the need the country has for creative people and then we do what we can to suppress those who might create something really novel. Creativity is a fine thing, considered from the standpoint of its more useful products already contributed to science, the arts, and technology; but people ask why should they have to pay the price of having annoyingly "different" individuals around? Can't the artist or scientist, for example, be creative without being different? Above all, why should *their* child be permitted or encouraged to launch himself upon a speculative and disturbing career?

Perhaps this attitude toward creative talent is changing. In 1959, the federal government's National Science Foundation sponsored a conference of twenty-six psychologists, educators, industrialists, and military men to consider creativity. In reporting on this event, *Time* * newsmagazine noted that even though creativity is "one of man's highest qualities, [it] is one of the least understood. It is not sheer volume of work or novelty of expression; it is not always virtuous." The article in *Time* goes on to comment as follows:

Creativity is what Feodor Dostoevsky had: a tremendous capacity for sustained, self-motivated work—despite an untidy outer life that included epilepsy, compulsive gambling and enough hardships to stun Job. But few teachers can recognize creativity in children or tolerate it when they do. The child who paints pretty pictures or whizzes through the IQ test is called 'gifted.' The one who plants an ingenious stink bomb in the teachers' smoke room is a case for the cops. Or is he?

The twenty-six experts whom the National Science Foundation got together agreed, as *Time* put it, with

. . . surprising unanimity, . . . that 1) success in the scientific age is not simply a matter of intellect; 2) U.S. education is distressingly geared to uncovering the 'bright boy' who can dutifully find the right answer to a problem; 3) schools ignore the rebellious 'inner-directed' child who scores low on IQ tests because they bore him; 4) teachers not only make no effort to nurture the creative rebel but usually dislike him. More than 70% of the 'most creative,' reported Educational Psychologist Jacob W. Getzels of the University of Chicago in a startling guesstimate, are never recognized, and so never have their talents developed.

Getzels and Philip W. Jackson told the group that creative youngsters enjoy "the risk and uncertainty of the unknown . . . tend to

* June 29, 1959, p. 66. Courtesy *Time;* copyright Time Inc., 1959.

diverge from stereotyped meanings, to perceive personal success by unconventional standards, to seek out careers that do not conform to what is expected of them." Most tragically it requires a world-wide power struggle, fraught with the possibilities of atomic war, to bring "respectable" American society—as represented by a federal agency and a major news periodical—to report such sensible views and apparently to endorse them.

The social psychologist A. H. Maslow * defines creativity as "a kind of intellectual play, . . . a kind of permission to be ourselves, to fantasy, to let loose, and to be crazy, privately." Maslow contrasts with the creative person the kind whom society ordinarily regards as making "a good adjustment." This sort of person "gives up his primary creativeness. He gives up the possibilities of being artistic . . . his poetry . . . his imagination. He drowns all his healthy childishness." This suppression is part of putting ourselves into "the right harness" and getting on well in the world. Thus we become realistic and mature, take on responsibilities, and have common sense. We may even be rated as being well-rounded. In other words, we succeed in becoming indistinguishable aspects of society—not especially good or bad, useful or disastrous.

In other words, as Maslow † notes elsewhere, "all people were once spontaneous, and perhaps in their deepest roots still are," but we usually offset our "deep spontaneity [with] a superficial but powerful set of inhibitions." We apparently feel that "this spontaneity must be checked so as not to appear very often." Maslow contends that, lacking "choking-off forces, we might expect that every human being would show this special type of creativeness." Enculturation, absorption into the ways of society, makes all but a few fail "to retain this fresh and naïve, direct way of looking at life." Even of those who "have lost it, as most people do, [a few] . . . later in life recover it." The creative are not necessarily great writers or composers or researchers; they "may be much more humble." Among those with more limited talents, "creativeness, being an expression of healthy personality, is projected out upon the world or touches whatever activity the person is engaged in. In this sense there can be creative

* "Emotional Blocks to Creativity," MS. lecture before "Creative Engineering Seminar," U.S. Army Engineers, Ft. Belvoir, Va., April 24, 1957, 18 pp., pp. 6–7. See also H. H. Anderson, ed., *Creativity and Its Cultivation* (New York: Harper & Bros., 1959).

† *Motivation and Personality* (New York: Harper & Bros., 1954), pp. 223–224.

shoemakers or carpenters or clerks." This is rather different from calling an impressive conformist "creative," the sort of thing we referred to at the outset.

CONFORMISTS, NONCONFORMISTS, AND THE CREATIVE

Social pressures and individual drives for and against the development of creativity often intrigue sociologists, psychologists, and other social scientists. In their stimulating consideration of life-history materials, the sociologists W. I. Thomas and Florian Znaniecki * conclude there are factors in individual and society that make for three "typical lines of genesis," three "types" of personality. "None of these forms is ever completely and absolutely realized by a human individual in all lines of activity." The three types also ignore or vaguely include "an indefinite number of variations." Thomas and Znaniecki call one of these types "philistine." Such a person is "always a conformist, usually accepting social tradition in its most stable elements." Like many other students, they then run into difficulties when they try to distinguish between their other two types, which they call the "bohemian" and the "creative."

For the philistine, the "only possibilities of evolution . . . remaining open . . . are the slow changes brought by age in himself and by time in his social milieu, or a change of conditions so radical as to destroy at once the values to whose influence he was adapted and presumably his own character." For the bohemian or nonconformist, the "possibilities of evolution are not closed, simply because his character remains unformed. Some of his temperamental attitudes are in their primary form, others may have become intellectualized but remain unrelated to each other, do not constitute a stable and systematized set, and do not exclude any new attitude, so that the individual remains open to any and all influences." In discussing the "possibilities of evolution" for their third, idealized, "creative" type, Thomas and Znaniecki try hard to keep their model domesticated and respectable. They define the creative individual as one "whose character is settled and organized but involves the possibility and even the necessity of evolution, because the reflective attitudes constituting it include a tendency to change, regulated by plans of productive ac-

* *The Polish Peasant in Europe and America* (New York: Alfred A. Knopf, 1927), II, 1831–1907.

tivity, and the individual remains open to such influences as will be in line of his preconceived development." * Such actual cases of outstanding creativity as appear (for example, in the Nobel prize lists of scientists and artists) contain many individuals who are far from being so socialized. These lists miss many whose contributions become evident only after their death.

The understanding of conformity is neither very difficult nor very important in the fast-moving world of today. The pressures of society and of the individual family are largely directed toward the assurance of as accurate cultural and personal reproduction as possible. In such a categorizing process, little flexibility is provided for adaptation to change; even modest deviations by children are often resented and repressed. If anything, especially in the United States with its elaborate educational system, the institutions for cultural reproduction are so efficient as to make people overconform. In that direction lies the hardening of societal arteries. What we need to understand most are both nonconformity and creativity.

Let us consider how multivalence operates as the child enters the community, then turn to a further examination of nonconformity and creativity, and estimate to what extent the creativity achieved in the United States is due to social and cultural "marginality" provided largely by immigration. We shall also comment briefly on the nature of "bridges" available to the child in going from the family to the community and the possible services and disservices of child-guidance counselors. We shall conclude with a section on maturity as something for which a child has to struggle. In these discussions, we shall bring into relationship a number of points with regard to social classes, ethnoid differences, family differences, and prototypical groups which we have described in previous chapters.

MULTIVALENCE IN PERSONAL ADAPTATION TO COMMUNITY GROUPS

As the preceding chapter has shown, a child develops a group of orientations of his values concerning and behavior toward other people. Each orientation differs and is keyed in the child's mind at first to a specific group which then becomes the prototype of succeeding

* *Social Behavior and Personality: Contributions of W. I. Thomas to Theory and Social Research,* ed. E. H. Volkart (New York: Social Science Research Council, 1951), pp. 159–161.

groups of the same sort. These orientations thus evolve into social personalities, each of which specifies his patterns of thought, feeling, and behavior in relation to a type of group. He develops these social personalities at first in his family and play groups, and then he takes this equipment with him into the community as his basic means of assimilating himself into the successors to his prototypical groups.

The child finds in the community, as his circles within it gradually widen, persons and groups who rather directly succeed his maternal and paternal identifications and his sibling and peer groups. These successors have mores similar to the more pressing patterns of thinking, feeling, and behaving which he learned in the original groups in his earlier years.

The child is thus prepared to enter into sibling-type groups in which individuals compete for recognition and preferment from persons in positions of societal authority, in other words from parent-substitutes. Attempts to gain such prestige take the form of scrambles for grades, ratings, and certificates in school, or in some cases, of trying to short-circuit competition by becoming "teacher's pets." These caterers to authority may become the teacher's assistants or even informers.

The child is also prepared for the kind of behavior he finds in peer-type groups. Like his playmates in their first shack, such groups are more egalitarian than sibling groups. Except in fiction, they rarely have a fixed leader; they have different leaders or specialists in getting things done, with the selection keyed to the kind of problem most pressingly at hand. The child knows, if he has had typical early peer-group experiences, that such a group demands and gets a higher degree of group loyalty than any sibling-type group. In many ways, a peer-type group is an offensive and defensive alliance on any age level against other groups and, to a degree, against societal morality. In this type of group would be a trade-union local when controlled by its members, a women's sewing circle, a group of salesmen who informally but habitually co-operate, and a group of independent businessmen who regularly play poker together. As we have stated, the forms of such groups vary widely from class to class and from one ethnic or ethnoid segment to another.

Rarely is an individual's assimilation into all his prototypical groups similarly complete and satisfying. Special problems may develop with mother or father or both. He may be deprived of sibling-

or peer-group experiences until a relatively advanced age and never be as conditioned to one or the other type as are others of his age, place, social class, and ethnoid background. In consequence, he may be a conformist in politico-economic affairs and a nonconformist in religion or in family affairs. Like Charles Darwin, he may be a religious conformist and a conformist in many other ways but a radical and a rebel in biological investigation. Not only do types of personal adaptation vary beyond any possible list of three, but each individual is likely to exhibit types of adaptation which differ from one major social personality to another.

TYPES OF NONCONFORMITY

In a country founded by heretics and political rebels, nonconformity is a proud part of our heritage. Ralph Waldo Emerson,* as a leading spokesman for that tradition, apparently identified nonconformity and self-reliance with creativity, for he said, "Whoso would be a man, must be a nonconformist. He who would gather immortal palms must not be hindered by the name of goodness, but must explore if it be goodness. Nothing is at last sacred but the integrity of your own mind." But there are many types of nonconformity besides nonconformity to patterns of thought and behavior. Let us look at a few.

When a person does not conform in some way, the community is immediately curious if not agitated. When no ready reason is available for the nonconformity, there is speculation; it is presumed that only conformity is normal and praiseworthy. If the nonconformist is a member of a minority ethnic group or of a family of nonconformists, this is often thought to be an adequate explanation even though not to justify the deviation.

Nonconformity may thus be accounted for in terms of background in an ethnic or social class outgroup or of an individual—possibly "black-sheep"—revolt against the controls of an otherwise respectable family. On the other hand, there are families in American society with a nonconformist tradition in which family conformity means nonconformity to community standards. In the nineteenth century, when the "village atheist" was a respected personage in many American towns, this latter type of family was more common. It is now

* "Self-Reliance," pp. 138–152, Vol. I, in *The Complete Writings* (New York: W. H. Wise & Co., 1929), p. 139.

more restricted to college towns and neighborhoods and to the anonymous downtown apartment-house areas of large cities.

Nonconformity also varies in what it is against. Some nonconformists refuse to conform, for a variety of reasons, to sexual, religious, economic, and political standards ostensibly sanctioned by the general community. They may refuse to conform to one or all such groups of standards as they understand them. In each case, they quite probably are not individualistic deviants but rather are or become members of deviant groups. If a homosexual or shoplifter starts as an individual deviant, he often finds it expedient and comforting to be assimilated into a like-minded group. The same can also be said of the individual intellectual deviant; he too may find it more nearly possible to remain deviant in a like-minded group such as one might find in a university center or among those employed in creative tasks in a city. Some nonconformists by societal standards may be delinquents or criminals, but among their friends and relatives of similar social-class background their behavior may be sanctioned or admired. Successful gangsters and prostitution madams may have high prestige in their home neighborhoods, as do taxdodging and account-juggling businessmen.

Some of the more extreme nonconformists of all sorts gather together in low-rent areas near the downtown business districts of large cities and call themselves "bohemians," "beatniks," or whatever the current label might be. In the summer, country theaters and other art centers give them alternative focal points. The bohemians who are talented and creative furnish a justification and a protective glamor for those who are merely rebellious or disturbed; but without such areas of nonconformity all Americans would be the losers.

In discussing so many kinds of nonconformity at the same time, we do not wish to give the impression that nonconformists have anything more in common than nonconformity of some sort or other. We can, with wisdom, protect ourselves reasonably well against deviants who require special treatment or impoundment, but we need to be very careful not to throw too many nonconformists into such categories as delinquent, criminal, and mentally disturbed. As the newspaper editorial writer Alan Barth * wisely contends, the "test of a free society is its tolerance of what is deplored or despised by a majority of its members." He is aware that "opinions challenging fundamental values and corroding mutual trust present a threat to

* *The Loyalty of Free Men* (New York: Pocket Books, 1951), pp. 240–241, 248.

social stability," and in this connection he points to the twin dangers of Communism and of the McCarthy type of repression. Then he adds, "But, paradoxically, loyalty in a free society depends upon the toleration of disloyalty. The loyalty of free men must be freely given." He calls tolerance "the genius of American growth."

As their children go forth into the community and especially into the children's own important informal peer groups, parents require great patience, tolerance, and faith in the basic integrity of their offspring. Many times efforts to combat community influences upon children do more to augment than to diminish their consequences. Parents need to concentrate upon making their home as much what the child needs for maturation as possible. Outside the home, they would do well to realize that they can be supportive, can do a little circumspect stage-management, and that that is about the limit of their positive effectiveness.

NONCONFORMITY AND CREATIVITY

It is difficult to distinguish between nonconformity and creativity. The chief thing we can say is that the creative are, to some degree at least, nonconformist. As stated above, all of us might become creative within the limits of our abilities and in some aspect at least of our activities. If we are not creative, this is largely because we are inhibited by enculturation, by enmeshment in our society's culture and the subcultures of our groups—in other words by conformity to social standards as we understand them. In our struggle to "get along," we make ourselves cogs in the complicated machinery of society and its groups. Even at that and it may be later in life, changes in circumstances, environment, and acquaintanceship might help us to break through some aspect of our social adjustment and succeed in doing something different and perhaps original.

For the stability of society, to the extent that stability is desirable and does not become so rigid as to prevent nonconformity, there is some utility in the fact that many people willingly become functionaries of existing institutions. But only in nonconformity do individuals achieve the intellectual playfulness, the freeing of emotions, the disrespect for established forms in some area or generally, which characterize the person sufficiently heedless and imaginative to break with the past, to shatter old forms, and to create new, perhaps even outrageous, behavior models and proposals.

NONCONFORMITY AND CREATIVITY AMONG WOMEN

Creativity is most often discussed in relation to men, but data concerning creative women are at least as interesting and significant. One of the authors * of the present book finds abundant evidence of the relation of creativity to nonconformity among American women in her study of the lives of the 628 eminent women whose biographies appear in the *Dictionary of American Biography*,† a work produced by leading scholars. Eminence and creativity are not equivalents, but an inspection of the cases reveals that a great many of the 628 were creative by any reasonable definition as writers, artists, reformers, educators, religious functionaries, business leaders, philanthropists, and other professionals and pioneers. Here is a brief summary of some of the conditions which, over the whole period of the history of the American colonies and the United States, stimulated women who became eminent in a wide range of callings and who died prior to the publication of the *Dictionary*. Note the extent to which such women came from untypically stimulating homes and were nonconformist:

Among the 628 women, a great many were born into small families and spent their childhood in or very near a large urban center. In spite of the largely rural character of the country during most of our history, 31.8 per cent of the women were born in places with a population of 8,000 and more; 55.1 per cent more, in other places referred to as towns. Such circumstances evidently familiarized the child early with a stimulating variety of social conditions, gave her early an intimate impression of the tastes, interests, and accomplishments of her parents, and permitted the parents to concentrate their means and attention upon the rearing and educating of their one or few children. The parents were most often a professional father and an active mother who had adequate means but not what would be called wealth. Such conditions helped encourage self-reliance and economic independence in a daughter, but at the same time the parents could provide formal schooling and other stimulations. Many of these families had outstanding people among their members, rela-

---

* Elizabeth Briant Lee, *Eminent Women: A Cultural Study: The Societal Relationships of 628 Eminent American Women* (Ph.D. Dissertation, Yale University, 1937).

† Ed. Dumas Malone (New York: Charles Scribner's Sons, 1928–36), 20 vols.

tives, or circles of friends. Such contacts are provocative and encouraging both to the young and the mature. One-fourth of the women (155) had a total of 250 relatives who were also subjects of biographies in the *Dictionary*. The religious connections of only 305 of the 628 women are known, but these are suggestive, as is the fact that 323 had no known religious affiliation. Of the 240 known to have been Christians, a large share of the 186 Protestants belonged to such relatively liberal or permissive denominations as Quakers (27), Episcopalians (25), Congregationalists (22), Unitarians (16), Universalists (11), and Transcendentalists (3); only 32 were Roman Catholics; and 22 changed their denominational affiliation. The other 65 religiously labeled included 52 "religious," 4 Jews, 3 Theosophists, and 6 Freethinkers.

MARGINALITY AND CREATIVITY

In many ways, nonconformity arises out of marginality, just as creativity arises out of nonconformity. The sociologist Robert E. Park * defines the "marginal man" as a personality type that emerges "at a time and place where, out of the conflict of races and cultures, new societies, new peoples and cultures are coming into existence. The fate which condemns him to live, at the same time, in two worlds is the same which compels him to assume, in relation to the worlds in which he lives, the rôle of a cosmopolitan and a stranger." Park concludes that in consequence the marginal man "inevitably . . . becomes, relatively to his cultural milieu, the individual with the wider horizon, the keener intelligence, the more detached and rational viewpoint." Park has a useful conception here, but it is more serviceable when it is made more relative and seen in its more far-reaching implications. For example, the word "inevitably" indicates an exaggeration. Marginal people also include those who react otherwise than creatively to cross-cultural stimulation. They number some who are more prone to personal disorganization and others who have not internalized the controls of their new culture or subculture intimately and thus may be prone to antisocial behavior. In other words, we have had a great many magnificent intellectual, artistic, political, and business leaders who were immigrants or children of immigrants, and we have also had our immigrant gangsters.

* "Introduction," pp. xiii–xviii, to E. V. Stonequist, *The Marginal Man* (New York: Charles Scribner's Sons, 1937), pp. xvii–xviii quoted.

In the idea of marginality or of the marginal man, Park thus points to the conflict of cultures which takes place "behind the faces" of people who have moved from one culture or major sub-culture to another. Marginality is not enough in itself to explain or predict the kind of personal deviation likely to develop in a given individual or group. The bringing of diverse cultural elements together in individual minds has, as has frequently been shown, a tremendously stimulating effect upon mental processes. It helps to break down traditional barriers to thought and to permit new syntheses, new ways of thinking and doing.

People take on a degree of marginality when they confront a critical situation in which their cultural models fail to meet their needs as they see them. Or this may happen when they see other ways to behave which are apparently superior or more attractive and thus become dissatisfied with their own methods of coping with important personal and social needs. They then come to accept, in whole or in part, the cultural patterns of another group or society. These patterns provide still other orientations (valences) in the complex attitudinal multivalence necessary for personal adjustment to modern society. Taken on later and building less firmly and directly on prototypical group models, such orientations or social personalities are always a little awkward in use.

The kinds of situation in which a culture may dramatically fail or appear to be less adequate or attractive in meeting individual and group life conditions are these eight in particular: (1) *migration* by individuals and relatively small groups, probably the commonest case; (2) *societal change,* in an extreme situation, such as war or a social revolution; (3) *intergroup re-adjustment,* a shift in the power and influence of groups within a society; (4) *personal mobility* within a society; (5) a shocking or traumatic *personal experience;* (6) *conversion* to a different religious or political viewpoint; (7) *psychotherapy,* sometimes a powerful learning or modifying situation; and (8) absorbing and changing *educational experiences* in a more formal school setting.

These pathways to cultural marginality are far from being mutually exclusive. When a person undergoes a shocking experience, one that shakes him deeply, he may decide to emigrate; in addition, he may also undertake membership in a religious cult, become mobile in a society's class groups, seek a psychiatrist's or a group clinician's aid, or enroll for some courses or a whole curriculum in a school of some kind. Learning experiences in our schools sometimes resemble conversion. Skilled teachers, too, have more than a passing grasp of group-clinical techniques. Drastic experiences of this kind may explain why students frequently show more progress at an out-of-town school than they could when continually enmeshed in their earlier environment. Away from home, they may be more stimulated by becoming more marginal, granted that the school has stimulation to offer. The arts, humanities, and physical and biological sciences as well as the social sciences all offer their great and healthily unsettling intellectual and emotional experiences when they are freely and vividly unfolded with the co-operation of a well-motivated student.*

In the United States, the streams of immigrants from many parts of the world through more than three and one-half centuries provided a constant supply of marginal people, people who themselves benefited and often contributed much through the mixing of cultures. To this situation can be attributed much of American nonconformity and creativity. Some of the immigrants and refugees brought well-developed creativity with them. A decline in immigration raised the consequent problem of finding effective substitutes for that source of creativity. A major effort in this direction has been the international exchange of students, teachers, and specialists. The best guarantee of domestic creativity and of international peace would be for Americans to increase such exchanges, during each succeeding generation, with all the other countries of the world.

BRIDGES TO THE COMMUNITY

It is clear that the child has available several types of "bridges" to the larger community outside his family. He has the mental and behavioral equipment assimilated in his prototypical groups with which, granted healthy experiences in them, he can penetrate community groups of similar sorts. The formal and informal groups of school, religious institution, and neighborhood, later of employment, are all bridges which he can tread to a small or large world of experiences throughout the rest of his life.

Adolescents of various social classes seize upon groups which are many times repugnant to adults, and they use them as bridges to the greater autonomy they hope to find in community life. The gang

* Adapted from A. McC. Lee, "Die Weiterentwicklung von Parks Theorie der Grenzsituation," *Kölner Zeitschrift für Soziologie,* VI (1953–54), 234–243.

activities common in urban lower-class neighborhoods frequently have tones of violence, sexual license, and thievery about them. These characteristics are easy to condemn, but they are difficult or impossible for anyone to understand who does not examine the life conditions of such adolescents with care and insight. They are raised in a home atmosphere in which all teachers, policemen, social workers, and ministers are looked upon as surrogates of society, chiefly concerned with manipulating and exploiting them rather than helping them. Hence the mores of such gangs, reflecting those of their families, justify guerrilla warfare with other gangs and with members of other social classes. A great many middle-class professionals and intellectuals fail to understand the nature of the revolt represented typically by middle-class college social fraternities, a revolt against an enveloping and absorbing feminism. Too many of our middle-class leaders assume that social behavior can and should be judged by a single scale of values rather than relatively and multivalently. They do not allow for the many conflicts of social interest and value—the many different subcultures—present in any healthy society and certainly in our own. As A. C. Kinsey and associates conclude in their *Sexual Behavior in the Human Male,** "The existence of the conflict between sexual patterns [of different social levels] is . . . not recognized by the parties immediately concerned, because neither of them understands the diversity of patterns which exist at different social levels. Each thinks that he is in a conflict with a particular individual. He is, however, more often in conflict with a whole culture."

In order to make bridges to the community more surely effective for their child or to help their child select more carefully from among available bridges, parents often consult specialists such as guidance counselors. They hope thus to eliminate some of the inevitable risks from their child's choice of a career. What can the parents "buy" from a guidance counselor? What can he do for their child?

CHILD–GUIDANCE COUNSELORS

There are many types of child-guidance counselor. They have become quite fashionable as technicians who presumably can solve many types of personal and school problems of youth and who can help

---

* Philadelphia: W. B. Saunders Co., 1948, p. 393. Reprinted by permission of the publisher and the Institute for Sex Research, Inc., Indiana University.

give focus to the efforts of pupils. For this reason they are in short supply. There is great pressure to train more and more of them, and many educators who are not well selected or adequately trained are being certified and employed as counselors.

Perhaps we can illustrate this situation by reference to two types of counselor, each of which includes persons who are employed by a school and persons who supply private consultation for a fee. One type might be called a guide to conformity, and the other might be characterized as an aid to self-exploration and self-fulfilment. Neither type actually gives parents the sort of assistance they want, for, most frequently, they want specific answers. The parent asks to be told, as a result of magical tests, the one high road his child can most successfully traverse, but it must be a high road. The guide to conformity generally fails to provide a definite answer, for such a counselor feels insecure about recommending a glamorous career for the child. He knows it is much easier and safer to recommend a conservative and conformist career.

A good counselor can provide or suggest sources for dependable factual information about life-adjustment, careers, and other vital matters, and he can stimulate his client to think things out for himself. He can make available self-probing instruments, such as tests of aptitudes and interests, and he can help interpret to the client the import of the client's responses. In the end, the career possibilities will remain numerous, and the decision will necessarily have to be made by the client himself. There will still remain questions about how the young person will want to live, to work, and to make his contribution to society that no one but he himself can ever answer. A good counselor does not make such decisions for any client. The counselor acts as a friend and an imparter of facts and suggestions; his only magic is that of counseling in a kindly, sympathetic, and permissive manner.

THE CHILD'S STRUGGLE FOR MATURITY

When the child goes from his family home into the community, he can well use the family aid and support given him, but then he must struggle for his own place among men. Maturity, like freedom, love, curiosity, and most other things we cherish, is not so much given to us as won, won in a struggle against our own shortcomings, against the limitations and deprivations of our environment, and with the aid we can gain from other people.

Those who push their child or pupil toward the apparently simple and dependable route of conformity might well ask themselves: Conformity to what? In spite of all the pressures in society to induce people to conform, the definition of societal standards is always vague though dogmatic, and the choice among group standards is never a simple one. As sure as any generalization one can make about society and its groups, too, is the statement that all things human constantly change—even when they appear particularly changeless. The flexible persons can adjust to change, and the flexible persons are always to a degree nonconformist.

When adults are too protective of the child, when schools are too authoritarian or paternalistic, the mentally healthy child may revolt—often quite "unreasonably," as adults may see it—or he may become unhealthily maladjusted. He may fail to mature. What is needed for any child are coaches, not managers. Parents, teachers, and children are ahead, far ahead, in this task when they realize that the struggle is largely the child's. It is his life. After whatever coaching possible has been provided, he must still make decisions and live his own life for better or for worse.

PART THREE

COURTSHIP AND MARRIAGE

Chapter X

LOVE AND IDENTITY

"And then he thought that the countenance of every maiden and every lady he had ever seen was unlovely compared with her countenance." Thus a Welsh bardic tale * written down in the eleventh century tells how Lady Rhiannon appeared at first glance to her future husband, Prince Pwyll of Dyfed. His reaction exemplifies the kind of magic that in many parts of the world gives spice and purpose to life and reproduction. Hosts of young men have had similar feelings toward hosts of young women. Such fervid overevaluations sometimes lead to marriage, but more mundane and durable considerations form the basis of marriage throughout most of the world.

The social anthropologist Ralph Linton † amused himself by noting that the "hero of the modern American movie is always a romantic lover just as the hero of the old Arab epic is always an epileptic." He declared that "the percentage of individuals with a capacity for romantic love of the Hollywood type [is] . . . about as large as that of persons able to throw genuine epileptic fits. However, given a little social encouragement, either one can be adequately imitated without the performer admitting even to himself that the performance is not genuine." In most societies, considerations of a practical sort such as property, expediency, and probable congeniality tend to overshadow romance or love in the initial stages of a marital process. Among many peoples, parents or other go-betweens arrange marriages exclusively in terms of criteria other than the romantic. As Molière puts it in the first act of his play *Sganarelle* (1660), "Love is often a fruit of marriage."

The literature of love is vast and perennially popular. To add another chapter to it seems uncalled for, but we feel it necessary to summarize here certain points that sociologists, cultural anthropologists, and social psychologists make about this essential ingredient in human

---

* *The Mabinogion,* transl. by Gwyn and Thomas Jones (London: J. M. Dent, 1949), pp. 11–12.
† *The Study of Man* (New York: Appleton-Century, 1936), p. 175.

affairs and especially in marriage and the family. We shall be brief and, we trust, as specific as possible.

EFFORTS TO CHARACTERIZE LOVE

Perhaps as good a starting definition of love as any is the one offered by the psychiatrist Rollo May *: "a delight in the presence of the other person and an affirming of his value and development as much as one's own." He thus sees "always two elements to love— that of the worth and good of the other person, and that of one's own joy and happiness in the relation with him."

Love may be a bond between any two human beings. It may be one-sided or mutual. It may be different in character and degree on each side. It is variously motivated, and sexual attraction may or may not enter into it. It is defined in many different ways by the cultures and subcultures of various human societies. Many times it apparently involves a strong element of usage or habituation. It may be many things other than the romantic love of song and story. It is always part of individual and social processes, and thus it changes as individuals and interpersonal relations change. In love the person acquires his strongest awareness of identity with others and, through their reactions, of his own identity. Since they are developed and strengthened early in life, these feelings of identity are bulwarks to the mental security of the person. Individuals for whom such feelings are either weak or negative have little mental security or stability.

The sociologist Joseph K. Folsom † distinguishes four types of feeling which Americans appear to associate with love. He lists them as: (1) erotic feeling, (2) tender affection, (3) rapturous love, and (4) friendly enjoyment. The following brief comments are pertinent:

1. *Erotic feeling* involves sexual pleasure. Whether due wholly to innate biological tendencies or at least partly to cultural determinants, in most societies the expression of erotic feeling by men tends to be more open and aggressive than its expression by women. But the extent of this difference varies with the cultures of diverse societies and the subcultures within any one society.

---

* *Man's Search for Himself* (New York: W. W. Norton & Co., 1953), p. 241. Italics eliminated.

† *The Family and Democratic Society* (New York: John Wiley, 1943), pp. 371–379.

2. *Tender affection* is the sort of feeling a mother has for the child she is nursing. A child's satisfaction in this relationship becomes a powerful basis for such feeling throughout his life. Erotic feeling and tender affection between the sexes were once regarded as somewhat contrary. It was thought that a man could not feel both passion and tenderness for one woman, and a good woman was not supposed to be capable of sexual enjoyment. Today popular belief has it that passion and tender affection are not inconsistent even though each can exist without the other.

3. *Rapturous love* is romantic love "in its moments of full realization and success," as Folsom describes it. "Presumably the feeling is reciprocal. Each lover feels a kind of submissive, reverential attitude toward the other, or perhaps they may say they feel it toward their love as if toward an external reality. They are in love with love as well as with each other." The comments of Linton quoted on page 133 about this type of love are pertinent. The nature of romantic love and its role in American society will be discussed below (see page 139).

4. *Friendly enjoyment* comprises a variety of other emotional experiences associated with love, such as a sense of comradeship, mutual enjoyment of jokes, and fun in play together.

The sociologists Willard Waller and Reuben Hill * make an analysis of the "components of the sentiment of love" that is somewhat different from Folsom's. They see love as involving in varying degrees sexuality and its derivatives, pride, needs for security and respectability, economic considerations, and other miscellaneous factors. Sex, they observe, "may be etherealized so that no carnal element comes to consciousness; it may be completely and frankly of the flesh; an involvement may begin one way and end in another; it may begin with one kind of feeling and end with both or neither." They also mention such individual emotional peculiarities as fetishism, fixations, homosexual tendencies, sadism, and masochism. "Without the sexual element, the process of falling in love could not occur." They distinguish between love and infatuation in terms of social status. "Love is the sentiment which one feels toward a socially acceptable person. Infatuation is a sexual attachment which overrides the bounds of conventionality."

* *The Family* (rev. ed.; New York: Dryden Press, 1951), pp. 110–13. Reprinted by permission of the publisher. Italics eliminated.

LOVE IN PERSONAL DEVELOPMENT

A person's ability to form affectional relationships throughout life is apparently dependent upon his experiences with the mother-child type of love. In discussing the mother-child relationship, the psychologist Harry F. Harlow * summarizes the views of sociologists and psychologists thus: Sex is one of a group of "primary drives." All other "motives" than these primary ones, including love or affection, are "derived or secondary drives." From the time the child is born, the mother "is associated with the reduction of the primary drives—particularly hunger, thirst, and pain—and through learning, affection or love is derived." The child's affection for the mother continues after she "ceases to have intimate association with the drives in question." The feelings developed as "affectional ties to the mother show a lifelong, unrelenting persistence and . . . widely expanding generality." In trying to learn experimentally the basic behavioral determinants of a child's love for his mother, Harlow came to the conclusion that "the primary function of nursing as an affectional variable is that of insuring frequent and intimate contact of the infant with the mother." Children not fondled during their early weeks often become sick and may even die of neglect. Food is not enough.

Many aspects of the psychosomatic relationships between mother and child are still under close study. For example, data suggest the importance of the mother's breast rather than a bottle in helping to implant in the child root feelings of affection and of reciprocity. Other data point to such matters as the utility of the mother's own milk to her child especially during the early weeks of life. Her milk apparently imparts certain valuable antibodies, but it may have other contributions to make of a more emotional sort.

At any rate, at birth a child's sexual equipment and drives related to affection are generalized and have little apparent direction or character. They acquire direction and character under the influence of social interaction. The child's sexual equipment may be masculine, and this will help push him toward functioning socially as a male, but maleness awaits upon a complex of physical-self-personal factors in order to mature. We discussed in Chapter 7 how not only our sexual identity but also our choice of appropriate love objects (maternal, paternal, fraternal, sororal, and other) derive from our early experiences

* "The Nature of Love," *American Psychologist*, XIII (1958), 673–685; pp. 673–674, 677 quoted.

within and near our family circle. We mentioned how our attitudes toward our early love objects are later transferred to other persons. Love for a specific individual may grow out of a great many kinds of association, even out of an exploitative sexual relationship. Sometimes persons have sex relations when they feel contempt and even loathing for one another. In Chapter 7 we also discussed psychosexual maturation in its physical, self, and personal (social) aspects. What we add here is to be considered in relation to that discussion.

Three additional conceptions are useful in considering the relations of love to personal behavior and development. These are: (1) ambivalency, (2) multivalency, and (3) empathy.

1. *Ambivalency* is a term introduced by the Swiss psychiatrist Eugen Bleuler and popularized by Sigmund Freud and other depth psychologists. It refers to the contradictory feelings that one has toward another person and toward himself. It is a recognition of our tendency both to love and to hate the same person and in other ways to combine pleasure and pain, masculinity and femininity, desire for life and for death, and activity and passivity in our thoughts, feelings, and actions. This conception seems to be based too exclusively on biological or instinctual factors and to be a little too easy and simple. To what extent it is an oversimplification of multivalency has not been determined.

2. *Multivalency* is a term introduced by one of the present authors (see Chapter 8) to label the manner in which an individual's thought, affect, and behavior differ from one social situation to another. Even in a group of only two individuals, one may function in relation to the other in terms of a single type of social situation at one time and in terms of another when conditions change. For example, a mother is at one time an intimate, permissive, supportive companion to her child; at another, she is a surrogate of society, an imparter of the controls contained in the taboos traditional in societal culture—in other words, a restrictive character. She changes from one of these two types of relationship with her child to the other, and she is also visible to him performing other roles which imply less identity with him. The two principal types of mother-child relationship Bleuler and others would seek to explain in terms of an instinctual bipolarity even though neither is based exclusively upon biological determinants. When one investigates the matter more carefully, it appears almost always to be more than bipolar, with each valence related to a social context then current or in the individual's life history. Multivalency

helps to explain, upon the basis of physical-self-personal factors, the range of different types of relationship an individual may have with others.

3. *Empathy* is the ability to imagine and to understand the views and feelings of another person and to identify oneself with the other. This ability is a prime ingredient of the tender affection which can bind two or more people together through many years. It is crucial to the formation and maintenance of friendship. To judge from life-history data, it is a capacity which we may possess to some slight degree even in our early years but which we are likely to develop as we grow in maturity.

CULTURAL VARIATIONS OF LOVE

Comparative students of culture give us many fresh insights into love. The romantic type of affection celebrated in Europe and the Americas is a relatively modern idealization. Instead of having a romantic reaction such as that of Pwyll to Rhiannon and letting that lead directly into marriage, primitives usually base their lasting and formal unions upon considerations other than love or even sexual attraction. The consideration may be a property settlement, a choice dictated by some degree of kinship or lack of kinship within limits prescribed by tribal custom, or success in the capture of a wife from another tribe. Later on, after marriage, "spouses may come to cherish considerable mutual affection. . . . Conjugal affection is . . . the result of long use, wont, and dependence upon mutual coöperation, and does not go back to sex-differences so much as to the fact of having lived together." * Only with the decay of traditional paternal authority, "in consequence of the transfer of its various elements to the developing state, with the result that sons and daughters gain increasing independence, does the choice of a wife naturally fall more and more to the son. Then for the first time the motive of expediency, demanded by the organization, is united with the subjective motive in the heart of the suitor." † For that matter, it is probable that personal attraction was in all times and places an individual variant that forced a degree of flexibility in all conventional criteria for mating.

---

* W. G. Sumner and A. G. Keller, *The Science of Society* (New Haven: Yale University Press, 1927), III, 1503.

† Julius Lippert, *The Evolution of Culture,* transl. by G. P. Murdock (New York: Macmillan Co., 1931), p. 318.

Cultural comparisons help to show the extent to which aspects of love may be separated and differentiated. For example, efforts effectively to confine sexual relations and even sexual feeling to persons married to one another are part of relatively recent, Christian, European-American moral mandates. From a survey of kinship institutions among 250 societies, the social anthropologist G. P. Murdock * concludes that "it seems unlikely that a general prohibition of sex relations outside of marriage occurs in as many as five per cent of the peoples of the earth." He calls our own sexual standards in this regard "highly aberrant" in comparison with the rest. On the other hand, he points to only two societies with "a general lack of sex restrictions [sufficient] . . . to justify speaking of them as promiscuous." These two are the Kaingang of Brazil and the Todas of southern India. The Todas are indifferent to adultery, but they observe incest taboos. Murdock believes that "sex regulation hinges only rarely on the fact of sex itself." In 120 of the 148 societies in his sample for which he had adequate data, there were taboos on adultery, but a substantial majority "permit extramarital relations with certain affinal relatives." He also notes that "premarital license prevails in 70 per cent of our cases."

Data such as the foregoing are cited by some who argue that a greater degree of permissiveness should prevail in our own sexual customs and behavior. This conclusion does not necessarily follow. Each society's patterns of morality have deep roots in the society's history and are intertwined with all other cultural patterns of the society and its groups. These patterns are constantly being modified in response to the needs felt for change among substantial numbers of the society, but such needs for change can arise only out of the society's life conditions and continuing social processes.

ROMANTIC LOVE AND ITS PROBLEMS

How did romantic love become "a central prerequisite to marriage in the United States" † today? It has risen to its present status out of a process of basic change in European and American society, but what are the salient aspects of this change? And how can something so idyllic as romantic love be looked upon so generally by social sci-

* *Social Structure* (New York: Macmillan Co., 1949), pp. 264–265.
† F. E. Merrill, *Courtship and Marriage* (rev. ed.; New York: Henry Holt and Co., 1959), p. 33.

entists and marriage counselors as contributory to marital maladjustments?

The beginnings of our tradition of romantic love go back at least to tales told by such professional storytellers as the ancient Greek Homer concerning the Helen-Paris-Menelaus triangle and the second-century Roman Apuleius about Cupid and Psyche. Down through the millennia, the romantic myths of the love exploits of gods, heroes, and royalty were endlessly translated into later idoms, situations, and personality types. These were the Hollywood flights from reality, the television soap operas of their day. Think of the entertainment provided to an English serf by the story of King Uther's magical seduction of Igerna, wife of Gorlois, Duke of Cornwall, with the aid of the famous sorcerer, Merlin. At one point, Uther tells a familiar, "I am consumed of love for Igerno, nor can I have no joy, nor do I look to escape peril of my body save I may have possession of her." * What high and—for the serf—unattainable adventure! From this union, later legitimized, sprang the famous King Arthur of the Round Table. For the latest versions of such romantic affairs, one need only turn to a newspaper yarn about marriage or divorce in "high society" or watch a television serial or play.

Thus the bards, as they endlessly invented and embroidered the characters and exploits of immortals, heroes, and nobles, created an evolving folk theory of romantic love as the privilege of certain superior beings. In its various versions, that theory became identified with the aspirations of the masses. They sought to obtain for themselves this as well as the other prerogatives and advantages of the upper classes—the things of which they had been deprived. With the rise, in recent centuries, of individualism and egalitarianism and the possibility of their achievement through social reform or revolution, the enticing theory of romantic love fell into a cluster with such other powerful and ill-defined myths and theories as progress, democracy, and puritanism. These ideas were associated in varying degrees in the folk beliefs of groups from depressed areas of the British Isles—London slums, the Midlands, Wales, the Scottish lowlands, and the Irish cities and Ulster—who carried their aspirations for religious and politico-economic reform with them when they emigrated to the early communities of the New World. In adopting and

* Geoffrey of Monmouth [1100?–1155], *History of the Kings of Britain,* transl. by S. Evans and rev. by C. W. Dunn (New York: E. P. Dutton & Co., 1958), p. 175.

carrying with them the ideal of romantic love, they heavily edited it. They eliminated such "degenerate" and "aristocratic" practices as seduction and extramarital relations, for romantic love had to go through an anti-aristocratic purification. These puritans (who included not only the Puritans but also members of a great many other sects, notably the Quakers, Presbyterians, Methodists, and, later, some Roman Catholics) in the course of time evolved an ideal, glorified by popular novelists, that had little reference in any overt expression to the erotic. Often the erotic became associated with vile or animal emotion in contrast to romantic notions about chivalry, tenderness, and chaste rapture.

Thus romantic love became part of the birthright of each American adolescent. The idea was so attractive that it helped to extend adolescence, to prolong it even into middle age. The early pagan exultation in the joys and mysteries of sex and reproduction was left far behind in any public sense, albeit not privately. Not until the mid-twentieth century, with Freud and Kinsey as principal midwives, was there any prospect of reviving such exultation and finally overcoming what H. L. Mencken * liked to call "the haunting fear that someone, somewhere, may be happy."

Why do so many social scientists and marriage counselors look upon this idyllic and "purified" folk theory as contributory to marital maladjustment? In general, their objection to romantic attachment as a starting point for a marriage is that romantic love tends to be impressionistic, transient, fragile, unstable. Immature people can have such an attachment, convince each other that they are "madly in love," get married, and then suddenly discover that they scarcely know one another. The comparative strangers may then try to become companions in their intimate enterprise. Whether they do or do not succeed many depend largely upon whether or not they feel it necessary or desirable to try.

Without going into the intricacies here of what is thought to make for success or failure in wedlock, it can be stated categorically that a relationship between a couple who marry and are "successful" in marriage can start with almost any initial event or viewpoint. We are thinking of "success" in a very broad way as "success" by any reasonable set of criteria, and such "success" in marriage is due to the whole interaction experience of the two principals with each other in their

---

* Quoted by R. G. Smith in his *Fugitive Papers* (New York: Columbia University Press, 1930), p. 59.

social environment. As will be explained in the next chapter, dating, courtship, and marriage are parts of a process, an interpersonal adaptive process. The fact that a romantic attachment is an unrealistic sort of thing, necessarily subject to later revision by day-to-day experiences, is no more of a reason for discarding the illusion or delusion of romantic love than are similar considerations reasons for discarding a great many other unrealistic but enchanting and even useful myths with which we embroider the lives we lead. A governmental scandal or even a whole series of such scandals does not disillusion us in our basic attachment to democracy. Romantic love is a part of the folk poetry of our time and society. It may not be very good poetry, but it is our poetry. We accept it and believe in it. The illusion of romantic love, treasured by at least one of the partners to a marriage, may make an otherwise sordid or impossible match an endurable and even a beautiful one.

We have no dependable statistics on how people involve themselves in a relationship which leads to marriage. The testimony of experienced clergymen and family physicians leads candid students to conclude that the whole matter is much too complicated, with too many powerful institutional resistances involved, to be changed dependably in many cases in the near future to knowledgeable, companionable love before marriage. We also do not know that any such development would be intellectually, emotionally, or socially possible at an early enough age level in our society to serve as a useful basis for heterosexual attraction. Moreover, it is doubtful that romantic love could be deflated in our society or that it would serve any useful purpose for it to be replaced suddenly with another love ideal. To overcome many of the problems arising from romantic love, we need chiefly to advocate sound and full sex education, to be given to each boy and girl as early and as rapidly as they can assimilate it. For better or for worse, our love ideals, like all our other ideals, are changing and will continue to change, and we must constantly prepare for this even though the direction is difficult or impossible to predict.

LOVE AND SEX IN MARRIAGE

Culture colors the love relationship. It provides the terms in which love may be expressed. But mature affection in wedlock has much in common in all times, places, and even social classes. It is a sense of interdependence, of having a refuge in one another, and of being able to find identity and worth in one another. Once sex is placed in a friendly perspective between mates, it can become an intimate game played in common and oftentimes serves as a powerful solvent of controversy. Marriages with sexual incompatibility may continue if they are based on personal or social expediency rather than love. This is not to say that there may not be affection between two mates who are both sexually frigid; that can be their basis for compatibility.

Sex is a biological phenomenon, and the various kinds of love are cultural, social, intellectual, emotional, and behavioral products. Sex is so related to the whole human psyche, as the depth psychologists have demonstrated, that it cannot be understood in isolation from the evolving human individual fully considered. Love, regardless of how ethereal it may appear, is so intimately related to all of life that it cannot be considered meaningfully as an abstraction. Thus, while sex and love are not identical, they are forever intertwined and understandable only when so interrelated.

Chapter XI

COURTSHIP AND MATE–SELECTION

Both fiction and popular gossip deal endlessly with rating, dating, courting, and mating. Rating one person or family against another pervades much of the thinking and talking of all human communities, but it comes to an especially sharp focus in courtship and mate-selection. This is the point at which rating may mean the most to an individual's future. How does such a fine girl as Susan come to be spending time with that Frank? Does Bob really know what he is doing in marrying Jane? Aren't Pete and Lynnie an ideal couple?

Our discussion here is an effort to substitute sociological and psychological findings for the folklore criteria used popularly in weighing mate-selection and related problems. For convenience and clarity, we divide this discussion among five chapters: the preceding one on love and identity, the present one on courtship and mate-selection, and the three following. In the next chapter, we consider how an engaged couple may use the engagement period in preparing for the wedding ceremony, the responsibilities and enjoyments of matrimony, and the setting up of the new home. The following chapter takes up premarital counseling and assesses the kinds of studies and clinical findings that may aid those who seek more understanding about marriage or who have special premarital problems. The final chapter of this section provides a brief digest of laws and customs dealing with marriage and the family.

RATING

Rating is the process of social evaluation of individuals by those with whom they come into contact. An individual is rated largely in terms of his social status in various groups and of his uniquely personal qualities.

In all human groups, comparative status is a matter of concern in the ordering of interpersonal relationships. The more fluid the social situation within a group or society, the more likely are its members to stress personal qualities and to redefine or modify traditional conceptions of social status. The more rigid a group or society, the more entrenched it has become, the more likely are its members to rate their fellows in terms of conformity to or deviation from social roles they are expected to play. Social status is a person's recognized position in or relationship to a society or a group. Associated with each status is a social role, or several roles, which are subject to interpretation and adaptation by the person holding the status within socially prescribed limits of deviation.

Rating Disagreements. The social status of an individual is viewed differently by the unmarried who are dating and courting one another and by their concerned relatives. Disagreements regarding evaluation of status are common. In general, social status considerations provide a grid within which rating in more personal terms takes place. The endogamous pressures we discussed in Chapters 3 and 4 are pertinent here. Barriers of social class and of race, national origin, and religion set the limits within which a great many people find themselves obliged to mate. Social-class barriers are apparently somewhat stronger than those defined by ethnoid segments except when the latter are reinforced by color. In the upper social classes in the United States and Europe, the emphasis on class and ethnoid endogamy is very great.

Exogamy. The notion of exogamy is the prescription of marriage outside a certain group. It reflects and may extend the incest taboo. All the states have laws against marriage to a parent, grandparent, sibling, child, grandchild, sibling of either parent, or sibling's child. More than half (29) of the states ban marriages between first cousins. Almost as many (23) forbid the marriage of a stepparent with a stepchild. A half-dozen states even bar marriages between cousins more removed than the first degree. As the sociologist Clifford Kirkpatrick * states: "If incest restrictions between brothers and sisters *were* lacking, there would be certain startling implications for family life." He notes especially that the "nuclear family would become immortal," granted bisexual broods and no desire by offspring to escape.

Popular fiction and parental aspirations often serve to promote another kind of exogamy in the form of interclass marriage, with the mate to be drawn from a higher social class. In our society, such upward mobility is much easier for a woman than for a man.

---

* Clifford Kirkpatrick, *The Family: As Process and Institution,* 2nd ed. (New York: Ronald Press Co., 1963), p. 54.

Labels Rather Than Persons. Such social divisions have many sub-divisions. Much rating, in fact, deals with stereotyped labels and their possible applicability to a given person. For example, in a lower-class environment, membership in a certain gang or a type of vocation or employment may carry a rating of importance. Comparably, a middle-class college group is preoccupied with attendance at a given college or membership in a social fraternity or professional aspiration or achievement. In an established upper-class group, comparable categories would be membership in a prominent family and in exclusive clubs. In gossip, it is frequently more important to say that Susie is dating a policeman, a med student, or a yachtsman than to mention his unique qualities. Just as important may be the categories Badger Gang, Sigma Chi, or Skull and Bones.

Individual claims for prestige or rejection only emerge when they are markedly unusual. The striking presence or absence of physical attractiveness, ability to make and hold friends, conversational talents, personal charm, and many other factors enter into this aspect. Such attributes sometimes combine to shatter social barriers. More often, the revolt of youth against frustrating experiences with family standards and expectations may stimulate in the youngster outgroup interests, dating, and mating.

DATING

Dating is, for most young people, the second important step away from the parental home. (The first step is to join one or more peer groups outside the family circle.) Readiness for dating is stimulated by sexual discussions and even experimentations in early peer groups. At first, dating is, as a rule, clique or peer-group behavior; that is, the peer group of which the adolescent boy or girl is a member starts involving itself as a whole in dating. Dating behavior is a personal and at times an intimate relationship, but the initial making of dates is in many cases a peer-group arrangement.

The series of steps toward independence of the parental home is roughly thus: (1) assimilation in the first of several peer groups of the same sex, (2) membership in a peer group of adolescents, with group dating, (3) individual dating, (4) courting, and (5) marriage.

Some writers on dating in the United States contend that it is an American innovation, something new which was developed early in this century, or perhaps during the period following World War I.

The sociologists E. W. Burgess and Paul Wallin * assert: "Dating is an invention by the mass action of young people in the second decade of the twentieth century. Previously, permanent pairing of couples took place after a few social contacts." They quote a student as defining the practice as "playing the field without going steady with any one person." The rise of this practice of "playing the field" is usually attributed to the easier mobility given by automobiles, a generally high level of prosperity, the prolongation of adolescence through the lengthening of formal schooling, the granting of more and more independence to youngsters, and the growing cult of youth, in which parents wish to participate both directly and vicariously.

Following such American writers, the English anthropologist Geoffrey Gorer † calls dating "the most singular feature of American social life," the activity "which occupies so much of nearly every American's leisure time from before adolescence until betrothal." He claims that dating is "idiosyncratic in many ways, but especially so in that it uses the language and gestures of courtship and love-making, without necessarily implying the reality of either."

This insistence upon the uniqueness and originality of dating in the United States reflects a surprising neglect of the evidence upon the part of such usually perceptive social observers. They forget the old term "dalliance," which perhaps differs from dating chiefly in the greater amount of time devoted to dating. In early New England, "chaperonage seems to have been unknown." Before the Civil War in Virginia, a white young lady "began to have beaux in girlhood and exacted a protracted devotion of her lovers." ‡ Then, as now, some of the young men and women insisted upon and enjoyed "playing the field" for as long a period of time as there seemed to be any point in it.

In a rich country, in a prosperous economic period with a great many adolescents and young adults in school, there is more time for dalliance than there is elsewhere. To *dally* means to play, frolic, and sport with one another. It implies the exchange of kisses and caresses. It is a toying with temptation. With marriage not legally and socially possible until years after the awakening of heterosexual interest, our youth engage in more heterosexual association and talk more about

* *Engagement and Marriage* (Chicago: J. B. Lippincott Co., 1953), p. 64.
† *The American People* (New York: W. W. Norton & Co., 1948), p. 109.
‡ A. W. Calhoun, *A Social History of the American Family* (1917–1919; reprinted, New York: Barnes & Noble, Inc., 1960), I, 51; II, 311.

making a game of it than do young people in most other societies. Of course, most young Americans born and reared in relatively happy families expect sooner or later to make an end of dalliance and get on with courting and marriage.

Our "dating" is at most merely an exaggeration and adaptation of patterns to be found throughout a long period in our society, especially in the more comfortable and secure social groups. Much early hetero-sexual association has long been, in its early stages, a casual and play-ful matter, largely an activity for "bunches" of girls and boys. It has been and is such a thing as a walk to or from school or church to-gether, a "chance" meeting at a store or on the street, and time to-gether at a school event, a movie, or a church picnic or "social." Then and now, as the couples grow older in a rural setting, come hay rides, barn dances, trips to ice cream "parlors" (now drugstores and "coke joints") and young people's meetings at the church, with the trips to and from becoming gradually more a matter of one or two couples than of "bunches." In an urban setting, the equivalents are dances at a settlement house, "Y," church, or commercial hall, trips to soda shops, drugstores, restaurants, and bars, and young people's meetings in a religious center. Now, as earlier—and as at any known time in human history—couples seize opportunities for play, caress-ing, and even love-making as they find them, with or without serious thoughts of marriage.

We in the twentieth century did not invent either dating or petting. A horse could not travel very fast or far, but he required less atten-tion to operate than an automobile. A walk along a country road provided a degree of privacy, and the general absence of chaperonage permitted and encouraged experimentation before pairing. What-ever daters did, and do, they have always been sensitive about the re-lation of their behavior to how they rate. Even in our anonymous urban environment, rating among friends and relatives continues to be important to individuals personally. When they ignore familiar rating standards, they do so in order to revolt against parental controls.

COURTSHIP

Dating and courtship are two stages in the process of maturing, a process of experimentation and education in heterosexual association. In the courting stage, one no longer is dallying, playing the field. One or both of a couple have narrowed the field down to one who is desired, intended, or agreed to be a future marital partner. The sociologist Niles Carpenter * speaks of courtship as having these four functions: (1) "an adjustment to the process of sexual selection": (2) "an apprenticeship in mutual accommodation"; (3) "a stimulus to maturation"; and (4) "an essential link in the chain of allure and pursuit by means of which the prospective mates are ultimately carried on towards biological union." He concludes that the character of courtship is changing in this country chiefly as a result of the modifying status of women through "the relaxation of conventional inhibitions on freedom of action; widened choice of occupation; and coeducational higher education." He notes that "these forms of social change operate to promote both the widening of the range of sexual selection, and apprenticeship in mutual accommodation, through intimacy."

Courtship can be a search for a romantic-love ideal, a calculated effort at social climbing, a "fun and games" exploitation of trusting intimacy, or a mature search for a life partner. "Fun and games" as an approach now has less of the character of a sexual "Russian roulette" than it did before such contraceptive devices as "the pill," but it can open the way to conscious or subconcious entrapment through pregnancy. A little carelessness can cancel the effectiveness of any contraceptive. Educators, counselors, and social scientists are seriously considering just how far and how much premarital intimacy may be desirable in a mature search for a spouse. On some campuses, a few couples have even entered into "super going steady," also called an "unstructured relationship" or just "living together," a step which might or might not lead to marriage. When such relationships do not work out, they often leave deep scars.† In spite of publicity to the contrary, most college and graduate students adhere to more conservative patterns.

Both dating and courtship endlessly adapt to changing social conditions. Let us illustrate this by citing several methods of bringing together the unmarried: (1) bundling, (2) agents and bureaus, (3) advertisements, (4) special dances, and (5) social lectures.

1. *Bundling.* This was a practical courtship arrangement that was

* "Courtship Practices and Contemporary Social Change in America," *The Annals,* CLX (March, 1932), 38–44. Quoted by permission of The American Academy of Political and Social Science.

†" Unstructured Relations," *Newsweek,* July 4, 1966, pp. 78–79.

brought to the American frontier in the northern states by immigrants from Scotland, Ireland, Wales, and probably also Holland
and Germany. Because homes were small and there was a shortage
of fuel, in the wintertime courting couples, after reaching a stage
equivalent to betrothal, spent their "dates" together in bed. They
were fully clothed, and, either through the interposition of a "bundling board" to divide them or through a solemn agreement, limitations were placed on their intimacies. "When, on a sabbath night,
the faithful swain arrived, having, perhaps, walked ten or more weary
miles, to enjoy the company of his favorite lass, in the few brief hours
which would elapse before the morning light, . . . was it not the
dictate of humanity as well as of economy, which prompted the *old
folks* to allow the approved and accepted suitor of their daughter to
pursue his wooing under the downy coverlid of a good feather bed
(oftentimes, too, in the very same room in which they themselves
slept), rather than to have them *sit up* and *burn out uselessly* fire-
wood and candles, to say nothing of the risk of catching their *death
a' cold?*" * This practice flourished especially in the mid-eighteenth
century. "After that it began to be abused and so fell into disrepute." † Bundling still persists in this country, notably among certain Pennsylvania German groups.

2. *Agents and Bureaus.* Intermediaries and marriage brokers to
bring couples together are not new in the United States. Clergymen
often look upon it as one of their duties to introduce likely marriage
partners and to find mates for the lonely. Among the Jews, especially those from Eastern Europe, there is a professional matchmaker
or marriage broker called a *shadchan.* Though stories and novels of
Jewish life often treat the *shadchan* humorously, his profession is considered meritorious and respectable. To judge from current advertisements in Jewish newspapers, "lady marriage brokers" are now at
least as numerous as men.

The largest centers of population, crowded with people unknown
to one another, accumulate many thousands of "lonely hearts" who
cannot resort to a *shadchan.* As a result, numerous agencies have
appeared, which are more or less responsible. They carry such labels
as "friendship service," "social contact bureau," "date bureau," or

* H. R. Stiles, *Bundling: Its Origin, Progress, and Decline* (1871; New York:
Book Collectors Assn., 1928), p. 71.

† J. G. Leyburn, *Frontier Folkways* (New Haven: Yale University Press, 1935),
p. 205.

"matrimonial consultant." Clara Lane, head of the nation-wide Marriage Introduction Service, claimed that in ten years before 1949 she had introduced more than forty thousand people and that eight thousand marriages grew from those meetings. "As I see it," Miss Lane asserted, "I'm simply filling a void created by the fact that America has drifted away from the kind of community life I enjoyed when I was a farm girl living near Davenport [Iowa]. Then, I knew every boy in the county. Today, millions of American girls don't even know the boy next door." She added, "The extroverts can meet. . . . But what about the quiet, reserved ones?" She contended, in agreement with many specialists, that "romantic love has been very badly overrated in America," and she offered in its place four "real, basic pillars required in building a happy marriage." She listed these as need, mutual respect, congenial tastes and ideals, and determination to make the marriage continue. Possibly because they are desperately lonely, Miss Lane's clients may have contracted marriages that endured better than the average; she made such a contention, but she offered no evidence to support it. She has concluded, "People . . . should not have to know loneliness as preparation for marriage, because loneliness is a terrible, corroding, humiliating experience."

Such agents and bureaus maintain a card file for each sex and try to bring together couples likely to be congenial. In order to provide data for such a file, one confidential "personality questionnaire" includes the following:

What movie did you enjoy most in the last year or so? Book? Play? Record? Radio program? . . .
Who is your favorite star of the stage? Screen? Radio? Opera? Sports? Night clubs? . . .
How do you take disappointments, defeats, reversals, adversity?

These and many more questions are on a one-page form.

Unfortunately only a few trained social caseworkers are entering this field of counseling and service. Most of the agencies operate on the basis of hunches and in an atmosphere of intrigue. One "matrimonial consultant" conjures up such an atmosphere in negotiations with parents which begin with this admonition in her advertising circular:

Marriages are not made in Heaven. In fact, sometimes they are the results of the efforts of intelligent and tactful handling by a responsible marriage consultant of long experience.

This "consultant" advises parents how to arrange appointments for a daughter with a young man without embarrassment. Often the daughter is not informed that the bureau made the arrangement.

There is a high degree of specialization among the matchmakers. One bureau in New York City has a clientele exclusively of young professional men who want a wife with sufficient assets to enable them to become established.

Many matchmakers leave their financial arrangements with a client somewhat "open-ended"; they name a small initial fee and make the proviso that total charges will depend upon how easy it is to solve the client's problem. Others use sliding scales and percentage deals which reflect the assets of one or both potential mates. The more ethical agencies charge fixed fees for a given class of clientele and for specified services; these are commonly one-half as much for men as for women because men are expected to pay more of the costs of courtship. The marriage bureau field attracts confidence operators, and from time to time their unscrupulous practices are reported in the newspapers.

In commenting upon commercial "friendship" and marriage agencies, the sociologist Joseph K. Folsom * said that they are in some disrepute because they "advertise and offer to find partners for lonely persons." People do not like the implication that they are unattractive or socially isolated. Many shrink from having their intimate affairs commercialized. Folsom notes the antiquity of matchmaking in many societies and attributes its recent state to its apparent inconsistency with a free choice of partners. He then adds: "Still the idea persists and crops out in newer and more ambitious forms, because the need for some such service is great and is increasingly felt." He contends that "the preservation of the values which romance introduced requires the development of a modern, democratic equivalent for matchmaking."

3. *Advertisements.* One of our female students placed a three-line advertisement in the "Personal" column of a Jewish newspaper. She reported her results as follows:

I was surprised to receive sixteen responses, many of which were from dentists, accountants, and engineers and *none* from "matrimonial consultants.". . . It was a revelation to me to discover that these letters

* "Steps in Love and Courtship," pp. 206–245 in H. Becker and R. Hill, eds., *Family, Marriage and Parenthood* (2nd ed.; Boston: D. C. Heath and Co., 1955), p. 240 quoted.

were very sincere and served a very definite purpose. It is hardly an ideal way to meet people, but it is far cheaper than matrimonial or friendship bureaus. Many of these letters had letterheads or some means of identification, and could be investigated very readily. As a matter of fact, one knows much more than one would when meeting a person at a resort, club, or other meeting place.

Newspapers for many other audiences and some magazines carry more or less veiled advertisements which have as their purpose bringing couples together.

Quite similar to periodical advertising in many ways is the use of correspondence clubs. The chief difference is that the operators of the "club" do a certain amount of screening in terms of the characteristics of the applicant and of those requested in a correspondent. Fictional accounts of racketeering through this medium and of men exploiting one woman after another are common; enough cases also appear in criminal records and newspapers to indicate the hazards of this procedure.

4. *Special Dances.* Many commercial dances have as their purpose easy access to a dancing partner-of-the-moment and the possibility of friendship and even of marriage. The so-called taxi-dance hall provides female dancing partners for all comers, usually at so much for each brief dance with a much higher hourly rate. Their male guests and female employees are mostly from among the economically deprived. Some of the hostesses supplement their earnings with prostitution, but the high turnover in their employment is due chiefly to marriage and to pregnancy within marriage. Catering to a higher class level are agencies offering instruction in ballroom dancing. They are not often thought of as introduction bureaus, but the turnover because of the marriage of their female instructors is substantial.

A recent urban development is the "friendship club." This type of club operates usually on an older age level than the "get-acquainted" dances sponsored by religious organizations, Y's, and lodges. One typical New York City "friendship club" is managed on the assumption that there are more than enough dance halls for socially adjusted men and women and that there is a need to serve the shy, older, socially backward person. This club has the following rules: "No body contacts except during dancing. No smoking. No jitterbugs or 'sharp characters.' No 'glamour girls.' No liquor. Folks over 28 only." Its advertisement adds: "'Welcome Stranger'! Have fun at our 'Small town socials'!" There is television as well as dancing.

A number of male and female staff members take care of introductions and maintain a decorous atmosphere. The head of one such commercial club claims to send about 600 wedding presents a year to clients of his several units who get married to one another.

5. *Social Lectures.* As a get-acquainted arrangement, social lectures are another urban device which has grown in importance in recent years. These use the commercial speech rather than the commercial dance or "rat race" as the basis for bringing couples together. Sometimes the focus of attention is fairly well indicated by such lecture titles as the following: "What Price Chastity?" "How to Tell False from True Love." "What to Look for in Marriage." Interspersed among such titles are a variety of others on psychology, morals, and sometimes political and economic subjects. After the lecture, there is a question-and-answer period to evoke audience participation, and then—the most important part—there are refreshments, usually soft drinks or tea and coffee, as a device for socializing. Interviewers reported:

The women claimed that at social lectures they feel much more secure than they do at a dance because they share a common topic of discussion with the men. They are able to base their opening conversation on the evening's topic. A very large group of women feel that in coming to a social lecture they disguise their real intentions with a veil of intellectual sophistication. . . . Their real aim is to meet a man, and the lecture atmosphere is conducive to their meeting a more intelligent fellow, they say, than they would at a dance.

Our observers at some forty of these lectures reported that the men average about thirty years old and the women about twenty-seven, with considerable range in age from the early twenties on. In the larger cities, effective speakers before such audiences have a fairly steady source of part-time employment.

INCREASED POSSIBILITIES IN MATE-SELECTION

One could not list in brief compass all the old and new ways there are for male to meet female in this country, nor would such an exhaustive list be particularly useful. Any event that brings together unmarried people can serve as a starting point for the processes of rating, dating, and courting. Granted opportunities to meet enough potential wives or husbands, there are very few men or women who cannot find a compatible mate, but many people lack "exposure" to a number of potential mates. Our most effective marriage agencies are the coeducational high schools, colleges, and universities. But a great many young people go through these institutions without finding a mate. Among older groups, the widowed and the divorced, perhaps no longer informed on ways to meet possible mates, are often confused or unduly restricted in their choice.

If our society could rebuild its matchmaking arrangements along democratic lines, as Folsom suggests, we would thereby remedy much loneliness and isolation and also decrease the number of divorces due to inadequate "shopping around." A great many divorces and unhappy marriages arise from the hasty union of incompatible persons.

PREMARITAL INTIMACIES

Ours is one of the few societies in which premarital chastity is expected, especially among women. Even though this situation is changing, it is not clear what pattern will emerge except that it will probably continue to exhibit class differences. Actual behavior has probably never come close to the moral ideal at any time in any society, but the power of social pressures against premarital sex play and coitus cannot be brushed aside. These prohibitions, internalized in individuals as deep-set inhibitions, are related to the whole fabric of marital and other social relations in our society. Although extramarital sexual relations are extensive, the maintence of the social myth of chastity is treasured by many as giving a kind of dignity and sanctity to marriage.

In the Kinsey study of female sexual behavior,* some two-thirds (64 per cent) of the 6,745 married women interviewed had experienced sexual orgasm before marriage. Their experience varied widely and included masturbation, nocturnal dreams, heterosexual petting, heterosexual coitus, and homosexual contacts. One-sixth (17 per cent) of these women had had coitus to the point of orgasm before marriage.

Premarital coitus is more frequent the longer marriage is delayed. The Kinsey group reports it for 3 per cent of the females and 40 per cent of the males under sixteen; 20 and 71 per cent, respectively, for the ages sixteen to twenty; and 35 and 68 per cent for the ages twenty-one to twenty-five. In terms of educational level, there was considerable difference in rates of premarital coitus in the sixteen-to-twenty

---

* A. C. Kinsey and others, *Sexual Behavior in the Human Female* (Philadelphia: W. B. Saunders Co., 1953), pp. 282, 330–332.

age group; 38 per cent of the females and 85 per cent of the males with eight grades or less of schooling had had such experience; among college people, only 17–19 per cent of the females and 42 per cent of the males. Of all females in the sample of nearly eight thousand, one-half had had premarital coitus; four-fifths of these, to the point of orgasm. In addition, there were other types of sexual stimulation which might or might not have led to orgasm. Of the women who had had premarital coitus, 46 per cent experienced it only with their fiancé, 41 per cent with their fiancé and one or more others, and 13 per cent only with others. Coitus with the fiancé frequently took place within a relatively short period (a year or less) before marriage. The degree to which coitus with the fiancé anticipated or precipitated marriage is not clear from the Kinsey studies. Most of these experiences took place in the woman's home. About three-quarters said they did not regret the experience, especially when it was with the fiancé. Of the 2,094 single white women in the study, 18 per cent became pregnant at least once, and 3 per cent more than once. Between 2 and 3 per cent contracted a venereal disease.

Among all men in the Kinsey sample of some twelve thousand, 98 per cent of those with eight grades or less of education had had premarital coitus; 84 per cent of those with 9 to 12 grades; and 67 per cent of those with one or more years of college. Of the total, 92 per cent had had such experience. Kinsey and his associates * generalize about this situation as follows:

There are males, particularly of the upper social level, who may confine their pre-marital intercourse to a single girl, who is often the fiancée. There are males who have some dozens or scores of partners before they marry. In some cases, lower level males may have intercourse with several hundred or even a thousand or more girls in pre-marital relations. There are quite a few individuals, especially of the grade school and high school levels, who find more interest in the pursuit and conquest, and in a variety of partners, than they do in developing long-time relations with a single girl. Some males avoid all repetitions of experience with the same girl. . . . Many a lower level male states quite frankly that he does not like girls [except for intercourse].

In listing considerations restraining them from premarital coitus, the Kinsey group learned that men agreed roughly with women on

* *Sexual Behavior in the Human Male* (Philadelphia: W. B. Saunders Co., 1948), pp. 550, 557. Reprinted by permission of the publishers and the Institute for Sex Research, Inc., Indiana University.

the following ranking of factors: (1) moral objections, (2) lack of desire, (3) fear of pregnancy, (4) fear of discovery and of public opinion, (5) lack of opportunity, and (6) fear of venereal disease. The only differences in the ranking of these factors by the sexes were that men placed lack of opportunity second and fear of venereal disease fourth. On the more positive side, almost one-fourth of the women and about two-fifths of the men said they wanted to marry a virgin.

What do such facts about premarital intimacies mean? We do not wish to give the impression that no other studies of premarital sexual relations have been made or that the Kinsey reports are flawless. But other studies bear out in general the findings of the Kinsey group, and the Kinsey reports are the most extensive and comprehensive efforts of the sort to date. Commenting on these works, the sociologist George Simpson * cautions that "just collating what women [and men] say is their sexual behavior will never give insight into this foundation of human behavior. Yet great good will come from the demonstration of the complete normality of what has heretofore been left to the back stairs and hush-hush talk."

After making an analysis of moral, intellectual, emotional, and social aspects of premarital sexual problems, the social psychologist Lawrence S. Bee † concludes that relatively mature couples should cope with their sexual frustrations by early marriage. He does not advocate prolonged continence; he calls it "possible without damage in the case of only a relatively few couples." He contends that "we must quit kidding ourselves about the ability of young adults to remain virginal very long. Ways must be found to make early marriage possible."

The subject of premarital intimacies between engaged people is discussed further in the next chapter.

WHAT BRINGS MATES TOGETHER?

What are the most significant factors in mate-selection? Available studies reveal that a great many Americans are conformists in this as in numerous other respects. They select mates similar to themselves

* "Nonsense about Women," pp. 59–67 in J. Himelhoch and S. F. Fava, eds., *Sexual Behavior in American Society* (New York: W. W. Norton & Co., 1955), p. 67 quoted.

† *Marriage and Family Relations* (New York: Harper & Bros., 1959), p. 216.

in age, education, race, religion, social-class status, previous marital status, and locality of residence. These similarities reflect our tendencies (1) to conform to the endogamous specifications entrenched in our group subcultures and (2) to find mates in conveniently available groups. But there are those who are not conformists to endogamous standards in mate selection. Like does not necessarily marry like. The marriage of similars is called *homogamy;* that of dissimilars, *heterogamy.* Love is often assumed to be the principal determinant of nonhomogamous selection, but, as we have seen, "love" has many starting points and many meanings.

The sociologist Robert F. Winch * has offered a theory of "complementary needs" to explain individual bases for the choice of a mate. This theory is, briefly, that "where people marry for love, their needs will be complementary." More formally: "In mate-selection each individual seeks within his or her field of eligibles for that person who gives the greatest promise of providing him or her with maximum need gratification."

Winch grants that the ability to select a mate on a basis of complementary needs comes with maturity. The typical adolescent finds his needs to be so vast and pressing "that no mortal love-object could provide gratification for them." He is also "too insecure to allow himself to be known to a love-object." As a result, the adolescent often "accepts the cultural definition of a love-object, a stereotyped and remote object of physical beauty. The fact that the stereotype lacks known personality characteristics allows the individual to project his own ego-ideal onto the love-object with little fear of disillusionment." Personal acquaintanceship may come later, often in marriage.

As Winch analyzed the needs of the typical adult, he formed the opinion that "the reduced demands . . . become more manageable and the person develops a keener sense of the nature of his needs." Such maturity permits one to "abandon the cultural definition of the ideal mate and construct a personal-psychic ideal mate in terms of his idiosyncratic need pattern, a love-object stated in the language of complementary needs."

This theory raises at least as many problems as it tries to solve. Its weaknesses appear in efforts to apply it to specific cases. It fails to

* *The Modern Family,* rev. ed. (New York: Holt, Rinehart and Winston, 1963), chap. 18; *Mate-Selection* (New York: Harper & Bros., 1958), pp. 88–89, 101; *Identification and Its Familial Determinants* (Indianapolis: Bobbs-Merrill, 1962), pp. 15–23.

recognize adequately the adapting, processual character of a couple's interpersonal relations. Winch indicates that there is a certain amount of compromise in selection, but the situation is much more complicated than that. How many members of the other sex can anyone know very well, well enough to make the kind of choice he suggests as an ideal? Such knowledge requires considerable time, a high degree of mutual acceptance and even intimacy, and opportunity to interact with one another in many different situations and in terms of many different problems. The course of a dating-then-courting relationship is usually a zigzag one. Many others than Shakespeare have observed that the "course of true love never did run smooth." Misunderstandings and even quarrels are the "zigs" in the relations between a couple, and more and more intimate and tender makings-up are the "zags"—when there is not a permanent break. Men especially try to use a different set of criteria for selecting a woman who is merely a good "date" and for choosing a woman to court, but in our society this differentiation may break down. Many a man has become deeply enmeshed with a woman who was at first just a possible companion for an evening. Perceptions and misconceptions based upon cultural models and culturally influenced observations operate at all stages of such an interpersonal process. A human being never faces another stripped of cultural equipment; that equipment has too intimately intermingled with and formed the individual's mind and character. A "personal-psychic ideal mate" is thus rarely very far from cultural models, with their oversimplifying mandates. Even when the ideal represents a revolt against group standards, it is influenced by the standards against which it is in revolt.

Our own observations indicate that, granted an accepted basis for the beginning of a relationship and for its continuation, a great many different types of persons can arrive at a sufficiently strong and deep desire or understanding or "love" to wish to marry and to stay married. The couple who first meet are not the couple who get married days, weeks, months, or years later; they change each other. Rarely are matings ideal "fits." Whether or not a marriage lasts and is regarded by its participants as happy or successful depends on the continuing interpersonal processes. It depends thus more upon how they interact with one another, how they influence and can be influenced by one another, than by what they are like at the start of their relationship. A person who delays marriage in his search for an ideal mate may make a poor compromise in the end or, as often happens, remain unmarried. Another person with a more adventurous spirit may marry much younger and then probably find that he and his mate grow into a more and more compatible relationship, a relationship much different from what either might have predicted at the outset.

As we see it, mate-selection inevitably has about it a quality of speculation, of gambling with human potentialities. If a couple are motivated to court one another long enough to "fall into love" and get married, if they are somewhat complementary or at least free of basically antagonistic tendencies, their lives can become intertwined. They can together grow and adapt to one another.

WHAT ABOUT THE NEXT GENERATION?

With the spread of scientific—and pseudoscientific—reports, concern about the consequences to offspring of a given type of mating now tends to go beyond gossip about blood lines. Now one can speak of minute biological determinants; it is estimated that "all of the physical hereditary material which has gone into the formation of the living members of the human race would form a mass of material approximately the size of two and one-half aspirin tablets. This tiny physical bridge carries the total of the hereditary factors from one generation to the next." * What is known about heredity is largely derived, therefore, from the study of successive generations rather than of the minute sperm and egg cells and the genes they contain. Environmental influences are intertwined with hereditary ones, and it is difficult or impossible to separate the operation of such influences.

It is not necessary for the reader to delve into the mechanics of heredity, but he should bear in mind certain basic information pertinent to our discussion of mate-selection. This is summarized by Ray D. Owen † as follows:

Two or more different genes may cause grossly similar defects. An environmental deficiency may copy the effect of a defective gene; a defect so produced will not, of course, be transmitted by inheritance. A

* W. P. Spencer, "Heredity: Facts and Fallacies," Chapter 24 in M. Fishbein and R. J. R. Kennedy, eds., *Modern Marriage and Family Living* (New York: Oxford University Press, 1957), p. 341. Reprinted by permission of the publisher.

† "Heredity and the Family," Chapter 14 in H. Becker and R. Hill, eds., *Family, Marriage and Parenthood* (2nd ed.; Boston: D. C. Heath and Co., 1955), p. 434. Reprinted by permission of the publisher. See also H. G. Hammons, ed., *Heredity Counseling* (New York: Hoeber-Harper, 1959).

gene may be "bad" in one environment, harmless in another. It seems much better, therefore, to urge expert individual consideration of each worrisome case than to provide a table subject to uncritical misuse. "Heredity clinics" located mainly in university centers give qualified guidance to a few people; no doubt such clinics will become more common in the future.

In addition to the possible inheritance of certain types of weakness or abnormality, questions are often raised about the consequences of intermating between different racial types. When one considers that all human beings are already mixed racially, the complexity of such a question is apparent. Specialists generally agree that the problems likely to attend interracial marriage are in their genesis social and not physiological. Our racial strains are so close together that a crossing of them does not even give recognizable hybrid vigor, such as one may obtain in crossing more distantly related animals and plants.

CONCLUSION

Whatever of wisdom and of folly there exists in mate-selection and in courtship in our society rests with individuals and with those who bring pressures to bear upon them. It is part of our democratic way of living together. Some would call it anarchy rather than a system. In our estimation, any improvements should be in the direction of democracy rather than of system. The arrangement could scarcely be improved, for example, through increased dependency upon personal counselors. Professional counselors should be used only for "repair work."

Americans apparently see great merits in their ideals of romantic love, of premarital chastity, and of pair marriage even though many of them fail to model their lives continuously according to these ideals, and divorce persists at a high level. To ease our tensions somewhat, to make for more satisfactory mate-selection, and to diminish the number of premarital pregnancies, abortions, and forced marriages, we could do the following:

1. We could frankly recognize the desirability of much earlier marriages, possibly at the end of high school, as a way of bringing our practices more into line with our moral ideals.

2. We could prepare our sons and daughters for marriage, especially for early marriage. Much of the responsibility for a lack of seriousness about hunting a mate is due to the encouragement of ado-

lescents to regard heterosexual association as a game that should not possibly come to anything very serious for many years. Too often the outcome of the game is decided by a premature pregnancy or by some other precipitating event rather than by mutual choice.

3. We could find ways for adolescents to choose their mates from among larger numbers of their contemporaries.

4. We could then make arrangements to accommodate married couples in college along the lines worked out for married veterans. Then more young men and women who are qualified might continue their higher education after marriage.

Chapter XII

ENGAGEMENT: PLANNING FOR MARRIAGE

Two young people decide to get married. To abide by tradition, to have a period of planning, and also perhaps to learn to know each other better, they become engaged. The groom-to-be in our society usually thinks that he and his bride will have just a simple, little wedding. No "nonsense" of an elaborate and expensive ceremony and reception!

Then the women take over. Planning the wedding often consumes much more time and apparently assumes more importance than planning the home in which the newly wed are to live. It has often been said that a wedding can best be understood as a fulfillment of frustrated ambitions by the mother of the bride. The mother tries to have for her daughter, especially for the first daughter to be married, the kind of an event she would like to have had herself. An elaborate wedding may also be explained as conspicuous extravagance or an effort at display to maintain status.

The bride may resist her approaching glorification, but she can scarcely do so for long or effectively. "Every girl of course wants the nicest wedding she can have. It is something she will always remember. We all want you to have it, dear." The father of the bride stands around confused, overwhelmed, and glowing. He wants his "little girl" to have "everything just right," and he is willing to pay the bills. The groom lives through the sequence of events that he assumes he initiated, but he is typically in a daze. The mother of the groom feels uncomfortably "out of it." It isn't her daughter, and her husband pays little of the wedding expenses in most cases. Granted that his son is well enough employed, the father of the groom is probably the most complacent and relaxed member of the two families.

HOW MANY COUPLES HAVE A FORMAL ENGAGEMENT PERIOD?

How many couples take time to plan for marriage and a home in advance of the ceremony? No statistics are available on these questions. All that we can do here is to summarize what we take to be the enlightened estimates of well-informed social observers. Clergymen and physicians gain the most accurate impressions, and their confidential summaries are especially helpful. Naturally they cannot talk about specific cases.

Engagements, weddings in the presence of a large assortment of relatives and friends, and carefully planned homes have never been the lot of some half or more of the couples who join in matrimony in our society. Mandatory waiting periods, required by church, state, or both, now make more couples take a little time, and sometimes they use it for preparation. Other couples, if they think their marriage is sufficiently urgent, just drive to a "Gretna Green," a town in a state that requires little or no waiting period and no medical examination.

Sometimes a quiet wedding or even an elopement follows an engagement. Older people or people being married a second time often prefer a quiet wedding in the presence of a few friends. Elopements can be carried out to maintain secrecy, just to get married in a hurry, to short-circuit parental opposition or expense, or to cover pregnancy. Secrecy combined with pregnancy may prompt a couple to date their wedding back a few months when they announce it.

Reliable estimates on the proportion of forced marriages resulting from premarital pregnancy or the discovery of extreme intimacy go at least as high as one-half of the marriages contracted. Some clergymen make higher estimates for their particular congregations, but the proportion differs greatly from area to area and from class group to class group. By forced marriage is meant direct and specific pressure for marriage from the woman's family, from the woman herself, occasionally from the man's family, or from the man's recognition of his responsibility. The term *forced* does not necessarily imply a lack of affection or love, and the marriage may be successful. There may or may not be a period of publicly announced engagement and as fancy a wedding as the involved families can afford. Since knowledge of contraceptive devices and methods is widespread and since many girls have premarital sexual relations during a date in their own family home, the "force" may derive entirely from discovery of intimacy by a family member rather than from pregnancy.

In spite of the illegality of abortions for such purposes, through this practice many undesired weddings are forestalled and many desired weddings take place without premature childbirth. Estimates of the number of illegal abortions vary from about 1 in 25 pregnancies to about 1 in 4 and even higher, but there are no trustworthy figures on this matter. It appears that 8 or 9 illegal abortions in 10 are performed for married women between twenty-five and thirty-five years of age, but how many of these situations started as premarital pregnancies is not known. In addition, there are spontaneous and therapeutic abortions. Illegal abortions are sometimes reported in either of these legal categories.

Illegal abortions are performed by physicians, midwives, and the patients themselves. "It is a degrading, soul-searing experience for many women, partly because of the kind of people usually involved in its performance and also because of its clandestine nature. . . . The physical dangers of illegal abortion are death or infection," but often the mental hazards are at least as great. The illegal abortion rate among Jews, Roman Catholics, and Protestants is said to be "approximately equal." Because it requires a specialist to be certain of pregnancy, especially in its early stages, "some women who are not even pregnant die from self-induced abortions." * Such a threat to physical and mental health could be minimized with adequate and early health education. Couples who find themselves forced into marriage often have tremendous unfulfilled needs for affection, and often they do not know exactly what they are doing.

WHAT IS ENGAGEMENT?

The sociologist Francis E. Merrill † has noted that our society regards engagement as "the final triumphant stage in courtship." It climaxes the "years of casual dating, the adolescent social relationships, the period of going steady, the trial-and-error encounters of the college campus, the false starts when each thought he had found the only true love, the initial meeting and increasing involvement with the chosen mate, the doubts and hesitations, the heartaches and palpitations, the loosening of parental ties, and the other accompaniments of the great adventure."

Old World ideas on betrothal, espousal, or engagement were adapted in this country to the social conditions following migration.

---

* A. F. Guttmacher, "Abortions," Chapter 29 in M. Fishbein and R. J. R. Kennedy, eds., *Modern Marriage and Family Living* (New York: Oxford University Press, 1957), pp. 410–412 quoted by permission of the publisher.

† *Courtship and Marriage* (rev. ed.; New York: Henry Holt and Co., 1959), p. 155.

By the eighteenth century, the new towns and the frontier had brought great changes; "marriage and the preliminaries to it were naturally simplified." * A French visitor † at the time reported with regard to the engagement period in the United States as follows:

The time which passes between the proposal and the marriage is given over to mutual observation. The girls insist upon an absolute independence which they devote to testing the character of their future husband. . . . They yield to every fancy . . . and do everything they can to escape the reproach later on of having concealed their imperfections. It is a contest of frankness, inspired by the desire for common happiness.

Something of this tradition has continued and been strengthened. It is a useful one.

Engagement is a period in which a couple have a private and often a public commitment that they plan to wed. The public character of an announced engagement tends to give each person a greater feeling of security in the relationship, a somewhat stable basis for testing out what the other is like. Where association with others of both sexes previously may have been fairly general, after becoming engaged the couple tend to focus their social activities more within their own group of two and with other people in terms of that group.

This definition of engagement is broad, and it is intended to be so. The relationship takes many forms in our society, even in one geographical area, one ethnic group, or among the undergraduates of one high school, college, or university, and it is changing from decade to decade in any group in response to changed life conditions.

Among high school and college students, *four degrees of quasi-engagement and engagement* are often currently found.

1. A couple may be "going together." This involves more than an occasional date. It is dating or courting over a period of time, with sufficient frequency to be noted, but it is not usually an exclusive relationship. The man may ask the woman to wear his school class ring, club pin, or fraternity pin, but they both may still date others. Our informants describe this as "a kind of priority deal" that may be ended without great excitement on either side. It usually implies some degree of intimacy, and either or both of the pair may hope that it will become a firmer commitment. As it is viewed socially, this type of relationship may begin and end informally, or it may lead directly into more formal engagement or into marriage.

* A. W. Calhoun, *A Social History of the American Family* (1917–1919; reprinted, New York: Barnes & Noble, 1960), II, 30.
  † *Ibid.*, p. 31.

2. A couple may be "steadies." They may be going together regularly and exclusively but without having announced themselves to be engaged to be married. Among college students, this relationship may be one of convenience, especially for the man. It gives him a dependable date, without having to spend a lot of time on negotiation, for all important parties and other events. On some campuses, it may also confer a status of greater maturity upon the woman. In this relationship, the man may give the woman some personal item of his own jewelry to wear. How binding and how near a formal engagement this relationship may be depend upon usage and the expectations of associates.

3. A couple may be "formally pinned." This is tantamount to engagement. It may or may not be followed by a "formal engagement" period such as is described below. The formality in the "pinning" is usually provided by the manner in which it is announced. At such a large coeducational city institution as Brooklyn College, women's house-plan clubs and social sororities insert formal announcements of "pinnings" in the campus newspaper. The organization also makes the announcement at a special dinner or dance. This resembles the situation in many large state universities as well as small colleges. "Ivy League" colleges de-emphasize both fraternities and such a derivation from them as "pinning." Formal "pinning" is looked upon as a function of the person's principal peer group at the time as well as of himself. Ordinarily, therefore, parents do not announce a "pinning."

4. A couple may be "formally engaged" in the currently traditional sense. In whatever social class, this is often signalized by a formal announcement party, which may be a tea, cocktail party, "beer blast," dinner, or dance, and by the appearance of an "engagement ring" (often one that is or appears to be a diamond) on the woman's left ring finger. Further public recognition of an engagement may be "showers" for the bride-to-be, parties at which presents other than the "regular" wedding presents are given. These may include a "kitchen shower," a "linen shower," a "gadget shower," a "wedding trip shower." A formal engagement is usually announced by the parents of the bride-to-be if they are available; otherwise by their traditional substitutes or by the couple themselves. Thus engagement, in contrast with "pinning," is a family matter.

Even "going together" somewhat regularly, the first degree mentioned above, once constituted at least informal betrothal, and it is quite binding today in certain parts of Europe and the Americas.

Today in the United States generally it may or may not lead directly to marriage. Today even formal engagements in our society are more easily broken than at previous times. Among one thousand engaged couples, the sociologists E. W. Burgess and Paul Wallin * found that "at least a third of the young men and about half of the young women had one or more broken engagements." The breaks were due to "(1) slight emotional attachment, (2) separation, (3) parental opposition, (4) cultural divergences, and (5) personality problems."

Not only is engagement becoming somewhat more fluid, but both women and men have a great deal more freedom from supervision in dating and courting. Chaperons are now largely a formality at dances and other large social functions and are not often seen elsewhere. Apparently the parents of women now either trust their daughters or assume that several couples going about on dates together are, as it were, self-chaperoning.

HOW LONG DOES AN ENGAGEMENT LAST?

All couples have a period of public or private, formal or informal, understanding that they are going to get married. The period may be relatively short, or it may continue for years. Too little is known about the whole matter, and what we do know deals largely with middle-class behavior.

Studies indicate that of married couples about one-tenth know each other less than six months prior to the ceremony, perhaps five-sixths for a year or more, and two-thirds for two or more years.† But these figures do not refer to engagements, merely to acquaintanceships. A study of the engagement periods of young married college-trained women, their mothers, and their maternal grandmothers reveals that the engagement period has been shortening. "The first-generation women were engaged approximately 11 months, the second generation 8 or 9 months, and the third generation 6 months." During the three generations, the chief concern of couples shifted from planning the details of the home to preoccupation with child-bearing, with whether or not the wife would continue on her job, and with "trou-

---

* *Engagement and Marriage* (Chicago: J. B. Lippincott Co., 1953), p. 273.

† E. W. Burgess and L. S. Cottrell, Jr., *Predicting Success or Failure in Marriage* (New York: Prentice-Hall, 1939), p. 406, and L. M. Terman and others, *Psychological Factors in Marital Happiness* (New York: McGraw-Hill Book Co., 1938), p. 197.

blesome matters which could jeopardize the marriage." Religion and the husband's occupation enjoyed continued interest.* But these findings do not apply to all engagements, even within this limited series of three groups. They refer only to engagements that terminated in marriage, not to those that were broken. They are also necessarily based upon individual memories and interpretations.

Because of differences among class groups and the many other considerations mentioned, we have no way of estimating the average length of engagement. Since an engagement period is part of a long process of interpersonal adjustment, it is also difficult to suggest criteria for judging a suitable duration for an engagement. There is no ideal engagement period that would be best for all couples, in all circumstances.

ENGAGEMENT AS AN ADJUSTIVE AND PLANNING PERIOD

What are the most pressing concerns for a couple during engagement? We shall discuss the following: (1) the new intimacy, (2) physical compatibility, (3) new social roles, (4) interpersonal adaptation, (5) planning the home, (6) planning future community roles, and (7) using educational, planning, and therapeutic aids. For the purposes of this discussion here, it is not possible to be precise about the variety of quasi-engagement and engagement statuses. We shall use the term engagement to cover the relationship of those who expect to marry. It may be an informal or a formal engagement, quasi or full, without outward symbol or signalized by pin or ring.

1. *The New Intimacy.* Greater freedom in talking about personal plans, problems, and anxieties as well as in love-making comes with the agreement to marry. As the previous chapter indicates, roughly half of those engaged have coitus together prior to marriage. If one were to include other types of sexual stimulation to the point of orgasm, the proportion would be somewhat higher. Many times the novelty and excitement of petting and sex play so involve a couple that they find little time for intimate conversation. Such a couple may get really acquainted long after they "fall in love," but the increasing resemblance in our society between engagement and a kind of trial marriage is apparently reducing the time devoted to sexual

* M. R. Koller, "Some Changes in Courtship Behavior in Three Generations of Ohio Women," *American Sociological Review*, XVI (1951), 366–370; p. 369 quoted.

excitement. The young people relieve their sexual tensions and then have more time and inclination to talk intimately and to plan realistically, to work out mutual problems together, as the Ohio study cited above suggests.

Many social scientists and counselors stress the importance of full and free discussions between a couple as a preparation for a stable and satisfying marriage. The sociologists E. W. Burgess, L. S. Cottrell, Jr., and Paul Wallin offer suggestions, in their efforts to assess the success of engagements, which parallel the criteria they use to predict the success of possible marriages. Burgess and Wallin,* building upon the work of Burgess and Cottrell, assume that an engagement ending in marriage is a success. They determine the engagement success of an individual by means of the following considerations:

a) whether the individual has regretted the engagement and contemplated breaking it, and whether it has ever been broken temporarily,

b) the person's extent of satisfaction with the engagement partner,

c) the person's extent of satisfaction with self (included on the assumption that a person who was highly regarded and esteemed by the engagement partner would tend to be less self-critical),

d) the extent to which the couple members confide in one another,

e) the frequency of demonstration of affection and satisfaction or dissatisfaction with it,

f) whether members of the couple engage in leisure-time interests and activities together and their leisure-time preferences,

g) the extent of agreement between the couple in eleven important areas.

The "eleven important areas" are: money matters, recreation, religion, demonstration of affection, friends, table manners, observance of conventions, philosophy of life, ways of dealing with their families, arrangements for marriage, and dates.

Note that all seven points refer to matters that should be the subjects of intimate discussions between the couple. Two weighty ones (*d* and *g*) demand such discussions.

Among one thousand engaged couples, Burgess and Wallin found 123 who broke their engagements and 877 whose engagements were successful in the sense that the couples married. The scores of all these couples on the "engagement-success inventory" did not yield adequate criteria for distinction between couples whose engagements

* *Engagement and Marriage* (Chicago: J. B. Lippincott Co., 1953), pp. 304, 307–308, 314, 317. Reprinted by permission of the publisher.

are likely to be broken and those who will be married. Only at the extremes are there substantial contrasts between the scores for broken and unbroken engagements. The authors admit that for almost three-fifths of the cases the scores "are not a reliable basis for predicting whether an engagement will be broken." Since the scores for both major groups (broken and "successful") span the same range, with substantial numbers of both throughout, it would not be wise to try to use such a test as the basis for guidance to a given couple. The inventory is useful to a couple only as something which they may use as a basis for intimate discussion—for better or for worse.

Such an inventory fails as a test for the following reasons:

a) The data are too incomplete and unreliable. They are based merely upon what the informants were willing to write down on a questionnaire.

b) The questions were apparently selected on the basis of *a priori* considerations, upon the current middle-class view of a "successful" courtship, engagement, and marriage.

c) Only interview and analysis by a well-trained and objective counselor, with adequate time available for his study and with unusually full and candid co-operation from both of the pair, could yield really useful and dependable data.

d) The test fails to reveal and characterize the processes of interpersonal interaction and adjustment. It fails to assess the ways the couple experiment and compromise with one another.

e) The inventory rests upon naïve assumptions regarding "success" and "happiness."

How far should a couple go in intimate discussions? Should each "confess all"? Is that the only "honest" way? There can be no categorical answer to such questions. If one person has something in his past of which he is ashamed, it may have no relevance to the present relationship. If he has a compulsion to confess and the confession might endanger the relationship, it might be well to take it up first with an objective third party, such as a clergyman, physician, or marriage counselor. Many times an urge to confess to a loved one—or to probe for a confession—may cloak other motivations; it would thus be well to try to understand, if possible, what one is doing. The confession might do unnecessary damage. At any rate, it might be better to wait until there is a deep understanding between the two parties. On the other hand, a full and frank statement might achieve a healthful clearing up of doubts and fears on one or both sides. Only an intimate knowledge of a given situation, viewed objectively and helpfully, can lead to an adequate course of action.

Are disagreements in the new intimacy of engagement something to worry about? Once again we must be equivocal, beg for more facts, and counsel an effort to weigh alternatives with wisdom. Often disagreements are needed to stimulate the kind of probing, the kind of breaking down of emotional and intellectual barriers, that leads to a more basic understanding. Disagreements can also lead to a break. There are few engagements that do not involve disagreements, often about sex and sometimes quite serious, but we would question whether an adjustment between a couple can be completely satisfactory without such controversy.

2. *Physical Compatibility.* About five-sixths of the states require some form of blood test and physical examination for males and females prior to marriage, but a more thorough physiological and psychological examination is often valuable. Increasingly, clergymen, educators, and marriage counselors are sending engaged couples to physicians for premarital consultation. Clinics such as those of the Planned Parenthood Federation of America, Inc., are offering this service to groups and to individuals. These clinics are also influencing private practitioners to do more adequate work in this area. Such books as *The Premarital Consultation* by the marriage specialists Abraham Stone and Lena Levine * are providing reliable professional guidance to physicians in this constructive work.

Such examination and consultation can assure a couple that both have adequate knowledge of their own and of each other's sexual anatomy and functions. Sometimes there are physiological or emotional problems that a physician can solve. For example, the hymen may require minor surgery. The vaginal opening may be unusually small and require some stretching. The man may fear that his penis is too small or too large. Where there are physical or psychological obstacles, the first coitus may be painful and disappointing.

The kind of guidance the couple will wish on how to plan their childbearing depends in part upon their religious training and convictions. All of our major religious groups—Jewish, Roman Catholic, Protestant, and other—strongly advise that couples have as many children as they can care for and properly rear. They differ only on the manner in which conception may be limited. (We discuss this matter in some detail in Chapter 15.)

* New York: Grune & Stratton, 1956.

Physicians are learning more about how they may furnish their patients with cautious counsel on the hereditary possibilities of their future offspring. The physicians base their predictions not only on physical examinations and tests but also on available facts about the pair's family backgrounds.

3. *New Social Roles.* In much of early childhood play and later, both girls and boys "try on" future roles as they understand them. They try them on, see how they fit, as it were, before parents, siblings, and other peers. In the new engaged group of two and in the other groups to which the couple belong, the two become accustomed to future identification as the wife of Joe and the husband of Estelle. Since the engaged status is just a preliminary, attention focuses on the future married status. Thought and discussion center about the conditional clauses, "When we are married," "When I am his wife," "When I am her husband," or from parents and friends, "When you are married, . . ."

An engaged couple usually concern themselves with how they will fit into their roles. Doubts may delay and even prevent marriage. Many problems arise before marriage in this regard. Failures to fit or to appear to be able to fit a particular social role may be due to differences in family background or training, or they may be symptomatic—symptomatic of a great many possible covert factors. A woman's ability to cook or to do other domestic work and a man's willingness to "forsake all others" and to become domesticated may be reassuring to the future mate, but failures in these regards may mean many different possible things. For example, a woman's emotional tensions may ruin food in spite of her technical competence as a cook; a man's current problems of emotional adjustment may make him appear to be a "bad provider." Problems of the kind under discussion have their sources in basic aspects of personal and interpersonal adaptation, to be discussed below.

4. *Interpersonal Adaptation.* Many times in our society the relationship between girl and boy in adolescence begins, especially for the boy, in terms of peer-group values. Groups of boys start going with groups of girls, and both groups carry over into the bisexual aggregate at least a part of the peer-group attitudes current in the preadolescent one-sex groups. Even after pair-dating gets well under way, most of the same attitudes continue, but at some point in the processes of dating, the value context usually shifts. The boys and girls become men and women. They start thinking of each other

less as playmates and more seriously as potential mates, especially after pairs start falling in love. Each in terms of his or her own background falls in love with another or at least in love with the idea of falling in love. Then peer-group values give way to those developed in other childhood groups in the characterization of the new and more intimate relationship. The boy may now receive the adoration formerly given to a father, uncle, brother, or popular singer. The girl may succeed, as a love-object, a mother, aunt, sister, family friend, or movie actress.

Thus what starts in peer-group days as a revolt against parental restraints and values, a reaching out for freedom, becomes converted into a relationship based upon emotions originally directed toward a parent, a sibling, or an ideal which met the individual's need for experiences with other human beings. Such a change may create difficult problems of emotional adjustment—temporary or permanent—for the young man or woman. The transference of love from a relative to a sweetheart may stir in a young person deep anxieties based on the incest taboo.

During the years of dating and courting and especially during engagement and the first years of marriage, emotional adolescence normally ends, and emotional maturity is achieved. The young people learn to cope wtih the insecurities and anxieties resulting from the emotional readjustments they must make. Their relationship may not measure up, romantically or passionately, to "soap-opera" standards, but it may meet the realistic needs of the couple and be the sort of thing they can live with rather than merely dream about. They may find in each other something that adequately satisfies their needs and desires.

5. *Planning the Home.* The explosion of our cities has made home-planning complex, precarious, and frustrating. In many areas, urban sprawl and urban anonymity rather than rural neighborliness and difficult access to such conveniences as mass transportation complicate the couple's task of planning their new home. About two-thirds of all Americans live in 168 "standard metropolitan areas" as defined by the Bureau of the Census, and the rest of us are caught up more and more in the urbanization of American life. In 1960, roughly sixty million Americans or one-third of the population lived in suburbia, the wreaths of commuter towns surrounding all our metropolises.

The suburbs and exurbs expand rapidly and planlessly, but the centers of our cities are relatively stable in population. Principally in depressed areas near our downtown business districts exist seventeen million Americans "in dwellings that are beyond rehabilitation—decayed, dirty, rat infested, without decent heat or light or plumbing." This one-tenth of our population includes chiefly Negroes, Puerto Ricans, Mexicans, Chinese, American Indians, and whites from depressed rural areas of Europe and the United States. Migrants, who are now most often underprivileged nonwhites, constantly add themselves to the population of our blighted housing areas, and not a few of them are newly wed when they arrive. Even in cities such as Pittsburgh that are doing spectacular jobs of renovation, "the number of people crowded into slums is growing faster than the population of the city as a whole." * Imagine trying to set up housekeeping in a single room in a walk-up, cold-water slum building with toilet and cooking facilities to be shared with others! More than one-tenth of our fellow Americans have that sort of "home" for which to "plan"!

Large parts of our burgeoning suburbs are called "fresh-air slums." As the journalist William H. Whyte, Jr.,† observes, "Already huge patches of once green countryside have been turned into vast, smog-filled deserts that are neither city, suburb, nor country, and each day—at a rate of some 3,000 acres a day—more countryside is being bull-dozed under." With this expansion has come one transportation crisis after another. Highways become swamped, and bumper-to-bumper driving at peak periods is common. Trains and buses are overcrowded—but allegedly unprofitable. The railroads restrict service and try to eliminate it when they feel they can, but they fight bitterly against proposals for public ownership and control.

In spite of their problems, the suburbs are growing six times as fast as the cities. Millions of new small and medium-sized houses spring up in them each year. It has been estimated that four-fifths of our population growth during the balance of the twentieth century will be in the suburbs. Many families in fast-growing areas are those of the newly wed.

In this whole difficult problem of home-planning, the engaged couple should consider the following in choosing a location for their home:

---

* Daniel Seligman, "The Enduring Slums," Chapter 6 in W. H. Whyte, Jr., and others, *The Exploding Metropolis* (Garden City, N.Y.: Doubleday Anchor Books, 1958), p. 92.

† "Urban Sprawl," Chapter 5 in *ibid.;* p. 115 quoted.

a) Accessibility to the man's (and also frequently to the wife's) place of work has traditionally been a powerful determinant of location, but the automobile and other means of transportation now may broaden the range of areas that are available.

b) Some couples wish to preserve one or both's neighborhood ties with friends, relatives, and institutions. They treasure, or at least do not wish to sever, such identifications, which contribute to a sense of continuity and security.

c) Others wish to assure themselves of the better advantages for continuing study and for access to theaters, museums, and recitals that some neighborhoods offer.

d) An appeal similar to the one described in the second point above (perhaps identical in some cases) is that exerted by certain types of ethnoid neighborhoods. This may apply because the couple are barred from certain neighborhoods. The experience of living in a mixed neighborhood can be very stimulating and valuable.

e) Especially in recent years, with the increasing class stratification of urban areas and suburbs, the status advantages of one or another area or suburb may seem to a couple to be very important. They may wish to sacrifice other things in order to have a "good address." Vance Packard's comments on this factor in *The Status Seekers* * bear thoughtful reading. He notes the "twin trends toward the manipulated one-layer community and toward more straining for a fashionable address" and calls them "a depressing commentary on our success as a civilized people."

So far as the design of an apartment or house is concerned, an engaged couple seldom has much choice. When there is a choice, the couple usually starts with a relatively small apartment or house and then meets increasing needs by moving to a larger living unit. The more funds available to a couple, the greater freedom they may enjoy in planning their home and in carrying out the plans. The fluidity of American life has become such that even home-ownership is not regarded as the rooting influence it once was. Large corporations often encourage their employees to buy homes and then, when it becomes desirable to move the employees to another city, the corporate employer may help to liquidate their investment. The turnover in home-ownership in middle-class suburbs accounts for the droves of realtors they now support.

6. *Planning Future Community Roles.* We have indicated in con-

* New York: David McKay Co., 1959, pp. 91–92.

nection with the selection of a neighborhood that the community roles a couple thinks important do much to influence their choice. In addition to community roles associated with employment, religion, ethnoid segment, education, and recreation, sometimes political affiliations or ambitions figure in the couple's plans for the future. The more satisfying community roles are many times the result of years of association and of gradual rise to a position of leadership. Those who are caught up in the anonymous and rootless tides of modern urban existence have to forego such opportunities on a local basis. Their "neighborhood" or "community" may become chiefly an associational one among members of a trade, profession, church or religious denomination, hobby group, or civic organization rather than one based on local geographical ties.

In planning the kind of employment they wish to have and the sort of lives they hope to lead, a couple's first steps in developing community identities and roles are likely to be significant. Their chief problem is most often one of realizing that they are now entering the main current of life, the "big show," as it were. They may gain by trying to participate in community situations and opportunities, but what they accomplish in this sphere depends upon how they may wish to use their energies and financial resources.

7. *Using Educational, Planning, and Therapeutic Aids.* As has been pointed out, this century has seen a great increase of scientific interest in sex and marriage. Printed materials as well as educators and counselors make scientific findings available in more or less popular form.

Some enthusiasts for premarital and marital counseling assert that that type of service offers the best prospect for solving contemporary problems of sex and marriage. But, in view of the scarcity of well-trained counselors, this enthusiasm cannot be regarded as realistic. There are, of course, experienced professionals who can give useful advice on specific matters: physicians on sexual compatibility and health, bankers on finance, lawyers on legal questions, and others. For special psychological problems, the counsel of a well-trained clinical psychologist or psychiatrist is often a worthwhile investment in mental security and perhaps also in therapy.

Classes, discussion groups, and popular literature of a dependable sort probably offer better guidance to vast numbers of engaged and newly married persons than they could possibly obtain from our limited supply of well-trained premarital counselors. For example, women's magazines are often jokingly called "women's trade journals" because of the extent to which they provide authoritative and useful articles on so many aspects of marriage problems and, more broadly, of heterosexual relations. The nonprofit educational organization, the Public Affairs Committee of New York, constantly keeps revised more than forty pamphlets, all of which deal with aspects of family relations. Another thirty-five of their more than one hundred active pamphlets present carefully checked summaries of scientific findings on specific health problems. These are only a sample of the materials available. A great many religious groups hold special educational classes for youngsters, adolescents, the engaged, and young married people. We have mentioned in the Introduction the extent to which sex education and family-planning classes are now in vogue in schools and other organizations on various levels. This movement is still far short of the need, and many lives are damaged by lack of adequate sex information, but there is constant improvement.

CONCLUSION

For a great many young people, marriage is the climax of a courtship period that may have been all too tense and frightening. For others, engagement is a happy time of preparation for their wedding day, the crowning occasion of their young lives. For too many girls, the long-dreamed-of marriage ceremony seals an unhappy compromise or occurs under the shadow of parental coercion, with discovered intimacy or pregnancy as the precipitating factor. The resulting marriage may or may not be, or become, one satisfying to the couple. The conditions of courtship and engagement being what they are, with the choice of a mate so often based on illusions rather than on the actual characteristics of the individual, it is difficult to predict the probable compatibility of an engaged pair.

The period during which a couple is pledged to marriage is thus of many kinds in the United States. During that short or long time of waiting or during the early months of marriage, the couple needs to adjust to their new terms of intimacy, to experiment with their new social roles, to adapt as well as they can to each other's personality, to plan their home and domestic activities, and to benefit in all this from available printed materials, from classes, and from counsel.

Chapter XIII

WILL THE MARRIAGE WORK OUT?

When a guided missile takes off from Cape Canaveral, Florida, our physical scientists and engineers probably think that they have done the best they can to send it to the target or orbit they have intended. Sometimes they succeed, but they face so many factors, some of which are as yet not very predictable, that they have many failures.

When a couple take off into married life from their wedding, our social scientists are even more in the dark about the probable success or failure of the marital venture. The number of variables is fantastically greater for the couple than it is for any missile, and the influential factors are even more indeterminable than the ones that concern physical scientists and engineers. Among many other things, the "success" of a missile firing is largely recognized and defined. How would one define "success" in marriage?

WHAT IS SUCCESS IN MARRIAGE?

What criteria of success can one use? There are so many conflicting ones. Is it permanence? Is it evidence of the couple's being "well adjusted"? Is it "happiness"? Should it be identified with "satisfaction"? These four criteria have each been used singly in sociological studies as indicative of success in marriage. Although all but permanence are rather vague conceptions, each is really something rather different from the others and from "success." Certainly there are many marriages which continue until one mate dies but in which companionship and happiness are lacking. The other three terms—well adjusted, happiness, and satisfaction—also present difficulties. Chiefly the difficulties are that each society and social class defines them differently.

Rather than rely upon a single criterion, certain sociologists put forward a composite index of marriage adjustment, and still others seek to use multiple criteria, with a resulting "profile" of indexes for each

partner.   To illustrate, E. W. Burgess and L. S. Cottrell, Jr.,* base
their composite index on these five components:

1) Agreements and settlement of disagreements.
2) Common interests and activities.
3) Demonstration of affection and confiding.
4) Satisfaction with marriage.
5) Absence of feelings of unhappiness and loneliness.

They then relate these components to such matters as finance, recreation, religion, friends, in-laws, and thirty-two other items and give a
statistical weighting to each so that in the end there will be a single
figure as the index for each partner.

Since the composite criterion "combines in one index a number of
heterogeneous components," one cannot learn from the total figure
"what aspect of the marriage relation is being measured by the total
score received by husband or wife." E. W. Burgess and Paul
Wallin † turned therefore to the development of multiple criteria.
They came to measure marriage success in terms of the following
eight criteria:

1) Permanence of the union, namely, the absence of separation and
   divorce.
2) Marital happiness of the couple as reported by husband, wife or
   both.
3) Satisfaction of the husband and of the wife with the marriage as
   evidenced by their statements about the marriage and about each
   other.
4) Consensus, as indicated by agreements and absence of disagreements.
5) Love and affection.
6) Sexual satisfaction.
7) Companionship, confiding, and common interests.
8) Compatibility of personality and temperament of husband and
   wife.

These items are each divided into detailed check lists, and the sub-
items are weighted in order to produce eight indexes for each partner.
The first three criteria they regard as dealing with general or over-

---

* *Predicting Success or Failure in Marriage* (New York: Prentice-Hall, 1939),
Chapter 5.
  † *Engagement and Marriage* (Chicago: J. B. Lippincott Co., 1953), pp. 483–484.
Reprinted by permission of the publisher.

all evaluations, and the other five as treating more specific aspects of the husband-wife relationship.

The psychiatrist John Levy and the psychologist Ruth Munroe * place the foregoing notions of success in marriage in a dubious light by making the following point: "Perhaps the quaintest notion man has invented is his belief in his own rationality. We always have a reason for anything we do." They contend that the "first step . . . toward permanent and satisfying marriage is disillusionment, the willingness to accept oneself and one's partner on the level of everyday living, to take the worse along with the better." This and other criticism presents a rather different, a much more earthy, approach to what marital processes may be than the rationalized views of husband, wife, or friends concerning aspects of "success" as listed above. The sociologist Robert F. Winch † has much the same view. Noting that everyone appears to frustrate his or her mate to some degree, he speaks of "the achievement of psychic adjustment in marriage." He apparently regards as basic for a continuing and reasonably satisfying marital relationship "recognizing and accepting that perfect psychic adjustment is illusory." Each must accept and adjust to "the inevitability of imperfection" in the other.

Such considerations and the many kinds of family-drama patterns in terms of which a couple may work out satisfying adjustments to one another demonstrate the futility of either composite or multiple indexes of marital success. We are not convinced of the usefulness of correlations of a complicated statistical nature among highly subjective responses to moralistic questions.

Cultures and group subcultures offer a relatively narrow range of possible relationship patterns for a couple; they influence strongly the persons who try to conform to a society's and group's marriage patterns. Patriarchal, matriarchal, polygamous, monogamous, sexually exclusive, sexually nonexclusive, and variations of these and other forms are patterns that people in various cultures accept and apparently consider good. Within the patterns prescribed for them or permitted to them, a couple work out adjustments to each other as long as they continue to live together.

We do not think any general definition or any set of criteria for success in marriage is tenable outside of a given social-class group in one society. Such general conclusions are chiefly what Burgess, Ter-

---

* *The Happy Family* (New York: Alfred A. Knopf, 1938), pp. 48, 80.

† *The Modern Family*, rev. ed. (New York: Holt, Rinehart and Winston, 1963), pp. 672–673.

man, Cottrell, Wallin, and many others working in this field have produced. This limitation casts doubt on the validity of their work even within the changing culture of one society. A Sicilian immigrant, a Back Bay Brahman, or an American Negro sharecropper would think many of their questions absurd, and for them they would be. The weightings assigned to points are even more absurd in the sense of more precisely specifying one value schema. The psychologist L. M. Terman * himself, one of the pioneers in predictive studies, concludes: "there can be no universally valid test of marital happiness, marital aptitude, or marital compatibility. The things that go to make the 'good' marriage vary from culture to culture . . . or for the peasant and the plutocrat of the same nationality and religion. . . . Regional studies should be made."

There are many conflicting criteria for success even in one couple's marriage, viewed currently or retrospectively. Success in terms of what person or institution? A church may stress the number of pious children raised and the family's tithing and other services to the institution. The state may emphasize the family's loyalty, co-operation in obeying the laws, payment of taxes, ability to be self-supporting and thus not to become a public charge, control of children, and willingness to give sons to the armed forces. A child who has been able to rise in the social scale through educational advantages that his parents won for him may stress their sacrifices for his advancement as evidence of the success of their marriage. A self-centered wife may regard what she has got out of marriage in the way of luxury and ease as evidence of the success of the marriage, and her husband may agree that their marriage has been a success because he has been able to provide such satisfactions for his wife. A self-centered husband may regard as evidence of a satisfactory marriage the ease with which he is able to pursue one sexual adventure after another without his wife's interference or questioning, and his wife may perceive his activities as amusing or admirable or as useful in reducing her husband's sexual demands upon her. What then is success in marriage?

We can most usefully study the processes of adjustment between the members of a married couple and between them and their environment. Such a study requires extensive interviews in depth, as

---

* "Measuring and Predicting Marital Success," Chapter 17 in M. Fishbein and R. J. R. Kennedy, *Modern Marriage and Family Living* (New York: Oxford University Press, 1957), p. 245. Reprinted by permission of the publisher.

well as behavioral data. From our standpoint, the sociologist Constantine Panunzio * defines adjustment quite satisfactorily as the "process by which individuals or groups more or less consciously fit themselves to each other, or fit into, or act in accordance with the prevailing culture. Adjustment may be unilateral in that one person or group compromises, or mutual in that both persons or groups yield to each other." Under the spell of love, even badly disturbed persons may give the impression of having found at last a solution to their personality problems. After marriage, the more neurotic mate is often the one who "calls the tune" in defining the nature of the couple's relationship. The kind of study based on such a viewpoint may not result in statistics, but it can give us detailed and intimate data on living human beings and their interactive processes. It does utilize whatever statistical procedures and resources are appropriate.

WILL A GIVEN MARRIAGE WORK OUT?

Are the couple likely to make a reasonably satisfactory adjustment to and with one another and to their environment? There are a number of ways of trying to answer such questions: (1) soothsaying, (2) popular forecasting, (3) estimating statistical probabilities, (4) diagnosis, (5) personal counseling, (6) group counseling, and (7) education. The first two can be dismissed very quickly, but the other five all serve useful purposes and, as research continues to add to our knowledge, can be increasingly helpful. We shall discuss briefly all seven.

1. *Soothsaying.* This method exploits gullibility, superstition, and coincidence. Readers of tea leaves, phrenologists, palmists, and astrologers may all be considered soothsayers. Unfortunately, people who believe in this sort of thing are not likely to accept our statement that such procedures are delusory and sometimes disastrous, rarely and then only coincidentally useful.

2. *Popular Forecasting.* This procedure is the more or less informed and more or less prejudiced predicting by a parent, other relative, or friend as to whether John or Jane is "getting in too deep with the wrong person" or "has found the right person." This kind of forecasting may be based on such matters as a healthy or unhealthy complexion, physical characteristics, peculiarities in religion, politics,

* *Major Social Institutions* (New York: Macmillan Co., 1939), p. 524.

and economic behavior, and inaccurate assumptions by the forecaster. At its best, popular forecasting is a part of the inculcation of the cultural values of parents and other associates. That it is influential and may be accurate does not establish its predictive dependability. It is most realistically viewed as a part of the social processes of cultural transmission, of personality reproduction.

3. *Estimating Statistical Probabilities.* Studies of engagements, marriages, and divorces have given us some statistical probabilities on conditions related to the durability of an engagement or marriage. The sociologist Clifford Kirkpatrick * evaluates the usefulness of such probability estimates both for self-guidance and as an aid to counseling. He says, "It is not easy to be judicious in regard to the present reality and the future prospect. Couples should not be counseled in terms of present forecasting scores unless they are able to take the evidence with full awareness of the limitations of the scores, especially in the middle of the score range." Here as elsewhere in society, systematic and objective information can make a contribution, even if only to suggest the added effort needed to make a marriage successful. A counselor or educator can thus help individuals to think through the implications for themselves of their probabilities for marital success as a preparation for their marriage. This aid would not rule out a type of mate-selection against which there are highly unfavorable statistical odds, for example, an interracial, interreligious, or interclass marriage or one between a couple of widely different ages, but it might help the couple to a better understanding of their problems.

Kirkpatrick † summarizes a scholarly analysis of "Factors Associated with Marital Adjustment" in two lists of the "factors which, from the evidence, seem proved as most influential." He gives in his first list ten *premarital* factors "roughly in descending order of scientific verification," as follows:

Happiness of parents' marriage
Adequate length of acquaintance, courtship, and engagement
Adequate sex information in childhood
Personal happiness in childhood
Approval of the marriage by parents and others
Engagement adjustment and normal motivation toward marriage
Ethnic and religious similarity

* *The Family as Process and Institution,* 2nd ed. (New York: The Ronald Press Co., 1963), pp. 404–405.

† *Ibid.,* pp. 385–394, 665–672; pp. 389, 393–394 quoted.

Higher social and educational status

Mature and similar chronological age

Harmonious affection with parents during childhood

What Kirkpatrick calls an "impressionistic summary" of *postmarital* factors yields his second list of "general influential factors . . . roughly in order of decreasing substantiation," as follows:

Early and adequate orgasm capacity

Confidence in the marriage affection and satisfaction with affection shown

An equalitarian rather than a patriarchal marital relationship, with special reference to the husband role

Mental and physical health

Harmonious companionship based on common interests and accompanied by a favorable attitude toward the marriage and spouse

Once again, it is well to bear in mind that these considerations and their order of significance reflect the culture and subcultures of the groups upon which such research is overwhelmingly based—American middle-class groups. We must take into consideration, of course, the types of rationality and irrationality common in such groups.

4. *Diagnosis.* The scientific examination and identification of problems that arise between two people can be a simple or an extremely complex and confusing job. It may be simple when the problem is what it seems to be, but it rarely is. The earlier a problem of interpersonal relations is scrutinized fully and objectively by a trained professional counselor, the more likely it is that he will discover within a reasonable time its more significant facets. As time goes on, and a problem between a pair grows more serious, it is increasingly difficult to see clearly what has been happening between them. Remedial procedures become more complicated, and a satisfactory solution becomes more difficult.

The professional counselor on marriage problems carries on with his client couple two basic activities at the same time. On the one hand, he tries to arrive at an adequate diagnosis of the situation. At the same time, he tries to help the client couple to see their relationship and social setting more clearly and, if it seems advisable, to accept other suitable therapy. We have used the expression "client couple" because professional counselors try to work directly with both mates; lacking the co-operation of one, they try to influence the missing one through the single client.

The marriage counselor tries to re-educate his clients, to initiate processes of readaptation to one another and to others who may be involved. Sometimes the most useful contribution a counselor can make is, through informed and wise diagnosis, to refer his clients to another type of practitioner and to help them accept his services. His clients may need the services of a family physician, psychiatrist, group therapist, clergyman, educator, or lawyer.

Fortunately a great many people can get along without the diagnostic aid of a marriage counselor. At any rate, there are far from enough marriage counselors available for couples who have "sick" interpersonal relations. One in every six Americans now living is statistically due for a divorce at some time in his or her life. At least another one in each six is going to consider the idea seriously and perhaps live with a rankling conflict situation that may shorten the lives of the couple and certainly may impair their social contribution.

Both in sociology and in psychology, it is often said that clinical observations provide both our most valuable and our least dependable data. These are observations of client behavior such as are made by a marriage counselor, social caseworker, clergyman, or psychiatrist. The spontaneity of reaction of clients in the clinical situation, their willingness or unwillingness to participate in problem-solving and adaptation, and their presentation of dynamic social and personal problems furnish the most vivid and intimate insights we can get into individual and social behavior. At the same time, clinical students and counselors often become so absorbed in what they are seeing and hearing that their records or memories of observations are impressionistic, vague, and perhaps warped. As the psychologists John Dollard and Neal E. Miller * indicate, "Observations made in the situation of psychotherapy . . . have the advantage of locating significant problems in a realistic setting; by necessity they also have the disadvantage of lacking rigorous control." Such observations are "difficult to condense and transmit to others." They lose precision when reduced to units for statistical purposes. They also "are often not convincing enough to other persons and too convincing to the person who makes them."

University and college departments of sociology and graduate-school programs in marriage problems are leading the way in laying the bases for the emerging profession of marriage counseling. Such graduate programs are greatly aided by schools of social work, depart-

* *Personality and Psychotherapy* (New York: McGraw-Hill Book Co., 1950), p. 6.

ments of psychiatry in medical schools, and graduate training programs in clinical psychology. As marriage counseling evolves professionally, we will have another instrument for dealing with people's marital troubles, and we will also gain significant new data on marital relations from the intimate observations of such specialists.

5. *Personal Counseling.* This type of service shows great promise because of four principal developments:

a) the reorientation through special training of many professional counselors such as clergymen, social workers, attorneys, and educators;

b) the emergence of the profession of marriage counseling, with its own society, the American Association of Marriage Counselors, which is developing standards and accreditation procedures;

c) the substantial growth of popular understanding and acceptance of marriage counseling, even though this development is still far short of what is needed; and

d) the increasing emphasis, stemming from the influence of educators in marriage problems, upon the bringing of couples with maladjustments to counselors before rather than after marriage.

Marriage counseling as a special profession dates from the late 1920's. The training of specialists in this complicated field is designed to help them understand or at least recognize a great many of the problems that may appear in a couple's lives. The sociologist Ruth Shonle Cavan * notes that counselors need to be familiar with marriage laws, the biological aspects of sex, budget-making, psychology, sociology, marriage case material, and many other subjects. Counseling centers may include on their staffs, physicians, lawyers, and psychologists as well as marriage counselors. As Cavan says, "The counselor is able to help a distressed couple partly because he is not personally involved in their problems. The counselor assists the couple in bringing their problems to the surface where they may be examined." To facilitate the process, a counselor usually tries to see each mate separately and then eventually to bring them together with him. A counseling center often turns each mate over to a different staff member, with the two mates and two staff members eventually brought together for discussions. As Cavan contends, "This [latter] method prevents either from feeling that the counselor might 'play favorites' if he sees both husband and wife."

Where can one get adequate premarital or marital counseling?

* *American Marriage* (New York: Thomas Y. Crowell Co., 1959), pp. 361–362.

Certainly one needs to be mindful of the dangers of falling into the hands of quacks, of commercial "psychologists" without adequate training who through incompetence or venality multiply human hardships and anguish with their "expert" snap judgments. The marriage specialist Evelyn M. Duvall and the sociologist Reuben Hill * offer the following criteria by which to assess an acceptable marital counseling service:

1. Doesn't promise quick results or make snap judgments.
2. Doesn't diagnose until after a careful study has been made.
3. Keeps all information confidential.
4. May charge nominal fees which are frankly discussed.
5. May call in other trained specialists to help.
6. Uses only trained professional workers from reputable colleges specializing in such fields as social work, human development, psychiatry, and related areas. (At least a master's degree in the specialized area is the usual professional standard.)
7. Is affiliated with such reliable bodies as local councils of social agencies, and nationally with such professional organizations as the National Conference of Social Work, and the National Council on Family Relations.
8. Does not advertise or try to drum up business, relying instead on slowly building up a clientele of satisfied users through referrals from other agencies and professional persons.
9. May have a membership and a board of directors of reliable citizens who take the responsibility for supporting and interpreting the program to the community.

Instead of using such a list of criteria, useful as it may be, one may be able to locate an acceptable marital counseling service by writing to one of the following national organizations which provide information about agencies and individuals:

American Association of Marriage Counselors, 27 Woodcliff Drive, Madison, N.J.

Family Service Association of America, 44 East 23 Street, New York 16, N.Y.

National Association for Mental Health, 10 Columbus Circle, New York 19, N.Y.

National Council on Family Relations, 1219 University Avenue, S.E., Minneapolis 14, Minn.

---

* Evelyn Duvall and Reuben Hill, *When You Marry,* (rev. ed.; Boston: D. C. Heath and Co., 1953), p. 253. Reprinted by permission of the publisher.

Planned Parenthood Federation of America, 515 Madison Avenue, New York 22, N.Y.

Locally, the council of social agencies or the central office of a religious denomination is probably well informed on commendable agencies and individuals in the marriage counseling field.

Potentially one of the largest groups of marriage counselors are the clergymen of the various denominations. An informed estimate is that only about one-sixth of the ministers in the United States are equipped to do marriage counseling "that can be called competent." Another one-third "are aware that they should do something to help with the changing attitudes, but they prefer not to go out on a limb." For the remaining one-half, "sex is evil. They do not see sex as self-expression, only as self-indulgence. They don't want to teach people how to sin." * Twenty-one Protestant denominations are trying to develop marriage counseling programs of a scientific sort. The United Presbyterians hold seminars for their pastors, and the Methodists offer their clergymen seminars, a correspondence course in counseling, and printed materials. The Episcopalians, Disciples of Christ, United Lutherans, and Unitarians are also notably active. Jewish groups hold special workshops for their rabbis in premarital and marital counseling. Some churches and synagogues have added specially trained staff members for the counseling of people with problems. Many of the so-called "secular" or nondenominational marriage counseling agencies have been developed under the sponsorship or leadership of Jewish and Protestant clergymen and laymen, often with active congregational support.

Roman Catholics are concerned because "today large numbers of Catholics are consulting secular marriage counseling agencies, sometimes with untoward effects upon their Catholic beliefs and practices. A citywide survey indicated that one-third of all the clients of secular agencies are Catholic couples." In consequence, the Catholic University of America has organized a Marriage Counseling Center to train specialists who will work "within the framework of Catholic beliefs and practices." † In addition, a large percentage of the Roman Catholic dioceses have organized "family-life programs," are helping the Pre-Cana and Cana Conference movement (for engaged and

* Gelolo McHugh with J. R. Moskin, "What Ministers Are Learning about Sex," *Look,* XXII, No. 24 (November 25, 1958), 79–80, 83–84, 86: p. 79 quoted.

† Alphonse H. Clemens, *Design for Successful Marriage,* 2nd ed. (Englewood Cliffs, N.J.: Prentice-Hall, 1964), p. 335.

married couples) to develop as effective means of group counseling and study, and are creating special six-week "institutes" on family counseling for priests.

6. *Group Counseling.* This method has its roots in the creative contributions to group psychotherapy of such specialists as J. D. Frank, Helen Hall Jennings, Kurt Lewin, J. L. Moreno, Fritz Redl, and S. R. Slavson. Group counseling takes principally one of these three forms: (*a*) an activity group, (*b*) psychodrama, or (*c*) group discussion.

a) An activity group may be any clublike association of a continuing sort and under intelligent direction from a skilled group-worker or, preferably, a trained group psychotherapist. It provides a medium in which a couple may reorient to each other without approaching their problems in a direct manner. A skilled group-worker and the interaction of other couples can help troubled couples to see each other afresh and to modify their interactive processes toward more constructive patterns. The activity group can devote itself to anything from folk dancing to golf, from dramatics to dining out, from hiking to swimming, or a combination of many activities over a course of time.

b) *Psychodrama* in a "spontaneity theater" is the invention of J. L. Moreno. It involves the acting out of an unrehearsed drama in which the therapist uses as the actors one or more clients plus necessary extras. The drama theme is chosen with the patient's problems in mind. The patient is asked to re-enact incidents in his life on a stage and before an audience. In doing so, as Moreno * comments, the client "finds himself, as if trapped, in a near-real world." In this near reality, the patient or patients spontaneously reveal much about themselves both to the psychotherapist and to themselves. The reactions of the psychodrama's audience add to the therapeutic value of the experience. "As the strangers from the group [the audience] begin to rise and relate their feelings as to what they have learned from the production, [the patient] . . . gains a new sense of catharsis, a group catharsis." The psychodrama thus becomes a very vivid sharing of behavioral and emotional experiences in which many may participate. Attendance at a series of such sessions, sometimes as performer and sometimes as spectator, can help to draw two mates away from their obsession with their own problems and can encourage

* *Who Shall Survive?* (Beacon, N.Y.; Beacon House, 1953), pp. 86–87.

them to see themselves anew, to make their processes of interaction more constructive and satisfying. The social psychologist Hubert Bonner * concludes that "people can be induced through participation to express freely their private and concealed emotional and ideational trends . . . [and] that in a psychodramatic relationship highly constricted and inhibited persons experience a liberation of feelings and develop a health-inducing spontaneity."

c) *Group discussion* of marriage problems and of such related concerns as child-rearing can be useful as a form of marriage therapy. These might be called "third-person experience meetings" or even "third-person group confessionals." The "third-person" refers to the characteristic form in which a person introduces his problems into the discussion of such groups; personal problems are presented as case histories that allegedly deal with a person or persons not in the group. Group discussions under somewhat professional leadership are popular in many urban and suburban districts. The professional leader usually starts a session with brief remarks and then throws the discussion open to those present. The meetings are typically held in private homes and are concluded with refreshments. Some groups are independent; others are sponsored by a religious body. If the group adheres closely to a program of marriage and family problems, it usually has a gradual turnover of member couples. As couples find themselves benefited by the discussion experience, they drift away from it, either because they no longer need it or because they decide to try something else with or without their mate.

7. *Education.* People can also participate in education in marriage and the family as a form of personal and group therapy. Education depends for its effectiveness as therapy upon a great many things but notably upon the interest and co-operation of the couple, the skill of the teacher, the soundness and relevance of the printed materials, films, and other materials used, and the dynamics of the class situation as it is more or less controlled and manipulated by the teacher or class leader. Because classes are ostensibly for the purpose of informing people intellectually rather than of providing psychotherapy, as the term is popularly understood, the classes should be conducted by well-motivated and well-trained high school and college instructors who understand their therapeutic role. In our estimation, no one

* Hubert Bonner, *Group Dynamics: Principles and Applications.* Copyright, 1959, The Ronald Press Company. (P. 474.)

should be assigned to teach subjects in this area who does not appreciate the need for maintaining a highly responsible professional attitude toward his students.

CONCLUSION

As applied to marriage, "success" is such a vague term that it has little or no scientific value. It is more fruitful to look upon premarital and marital relationships as processes of adjustment rather than in terms of their possible "success" or "failure." From such studies as those discussed in this chapter, we now have much useful information concerning the statistical probabilities for different types of marriage to work themselves out in reasonably satisfying ways. Our growing body of case materials, now being enlarged by the expanding marriage-counseling profession, applies psychological and sociological knowledge relevant to the diagnosing, personal counseling, group counseling, and educating of couples with marital problems.

Here is another and perplexing side of the counseling picture: There is nothing like the diagnosing of other people's problems to harden one's own prejudices and to inflate one's sense of power and control. In order to avoid this possibility and to increase their effectiveness, marriage counselors try to make their counseling nondirective. It would be unfortunate if they were to presume to give specific instructions rather than to serve (as they do) as aids to self-help.

Counselors of all sorts must constantly struggle to maintain their intellectual and emotional modesty, their curiosity, and their flexibility. Human problems are so harrowing and human ignorance so disastrous that it takes no little fortitude to remind oneself, so confronted, that there is often little one can do directly for a couple. One can provide information, can help diagnose, can indicate therapeutic facilities which are available, and thus can help a couple to clarify for themselves alternatives between which they can choose.

In the best professional sense, a counselor of individuals or groups on emotional and behavioral matters is a friendly guide. He is a somewhat objective participant who disguises his role as much as he can. By maintaining a spirit of open-mindedness, knowledge, and helpfulness, the marriage counselor helps couples with problems to work out ways to modify *their own* living processes.

Chapter XIV

MARRIAGE CUSTOMS AND LAWS

A great many of our customs and laws concern the family, its ceremonials, its organization, and the rights and duties of its members. Our history books are full of wars, diplomatic deals, and personal incidents in the lives of the powerful; but the history of the customs and laws relating to marriage and the family would be far more meaningful as a basis for understanding our past and its bearing upon our present and future. For example, for all that we read concerning government and industry in the Soviet Union and Red China, a constantly recurring question is: How do the people actually live? In other words, what customs and laws influence their day-to-day family life?

Social history can enter into this chapter only to the extent of suggesting a little of the background of current practices, but the chapters in Part One of this book help to piece out such information further.

WEDDING CUSTOMS

An experienced Protestant clergyman * tells how he has "sometimes felt that as officiating clergyman I was accomplice in—or, at least, accessory to—two of the country's leading rackets: weddings and funerals." He is speaking of the "big wedding" with its expensive setting in a large, elaborately decorated church, followed by an even more expensive reception in a hotel or club. We now even have the "wedding director" who does for that ceremony what the "funeral director" has done more and more exploitatively down through the years for the family afflicted with death. Both events are heavily charged with emotion and irrationality. The family members responsible have anxieties about doing "the right thing" on such a crucial occasion, and the director finds her suggestions readily ac-

---

* F. H. Ferris, "Of Weddings," *Harper's Magazine,* CXCI (1945), 496–499; p. 496 quoted. See "The Bride Business," *Newsweek,* May 2, 1966, p. 100.

cepted. The clergyman mentioned tells of what it is like "to be visited by a mother and daughter who contemplate a wedding which will rate notice in the society columns and are trying to find an appropriate site. He [the clergyman] stands by while they discuss the pros and cons of what is to him a holy place . . . as a theater for staging a show. It seems to him a desecration."

Regardless of how fancy or how simple it is, a couple's marriage ceremony can be a most memorable occasion for them and for their relatives and friends. It is difficult to decide which of a variety of ceremonies might be thought most appropriate. A wedding's character comes from the significance the couple and their families and friends feel it to have. The pretentiousness of a wedding has nothing to do with the permanence of a marriage or the satisfactions of the couple in their new relationship. It correlates principally with the wealth, social ambitions, and extravagance of the bride's parents. Other than such considerations, the part of marriage custom that deals with

> "Something old, something new,
> "Something borrowed, something blue,"

and with Mendelssohn's ubiquitous "Wedding March" does not concern us here.

Our purpose is to sketch salient aspects of the body of custom and law which defines the nature of the marriage contract, the rights, privileges, and obligations of family members, and other related matters as found in the United States. *Custom* in this sense is common law or unwritten tradition that has the force of law. We do not discuss here legal matters taken up in other chapters except to relate them to the general legal situation.

TYPES OF MARRIAGE LAW

As Justice Oliver Wendell Holmes, Jr.,* observes, "The distinctions of the law are founded on experience, not on logic." Our marriage and family laws have a complex social history running back through the common law, statutes, and judicial decisions of the federal and colonial periods to English common law and Celtic and Germanic tribal customs, to civil law derived from the French and Spanish civil codes and ancient Roman, Greek, Hebrew, and even earlier

---

* *The Common Law* (Boston: Little, Brown and Co., 1881), p. 312.

customs and laws, and to American social experience. Our laws take the form of constitutional provisions, statutes, and judicial interpretations (so-called judge-made law). Unwritten law, called "common law," consists of traditions and customs as interpreted by judges. It thus often enters into "judge-made law." It continues in force until it is replaced or modified by a constitutional provision or a statute that may or may not contain a similar principle.

Much of American marriage and family law is within the jurisdiction of the states, and there is thus considerable variation in it. On the other hand, the similarity of the heritage of our states has tended to limit this diversity. Popular pressures for the standardization of domestic legislation and the increasing mobility of our population are very slowly eroding state differences. We need to remember that differences in such laws among states have fortunate as well as unfortunate aspects. Such differences help to provide flexibility and to introduce the opportunity for observing the consequences of a variety of legal experiments.

Interstate co-operation in the enforcement of marriage laws runs into some problems. These have to do chiefly with efforts to avoid the jurisdiction of a state and with differences in public policy among the states. The validity of a common-law marriage depends upon the laws of the jurisdiction in which the couple took up notorious cohabitation. An exception to this rule would be some matter of a state's public policy having to do with marriage, such as a ban on the marriage of the mentally incompetent. As our mobility has grown, interstate co-operation in enforcement becomes increasingly complex. An old legal maxim has it that the "presumption is always in favor of the validity of a marriage," and about one-half of the states accept a marriage as valid if it is valid in the state in which it was performed. On the other hand, one-third of the states declare a marriage invalid if it violates a statute of the state or is contrary to the state's public policy. One-fourth do not recognize marriages performed outside their jurisdiction for the purpose of evading their laws. One-tenth of the states deny the validity of marriages within their own limits when such marriages are for the purpose of circumventing a law in the couple's own state of residence. A growing number of states now refuse to accept divorces or annulments obtained by their residents elsewhere. A Uniform Reciprocal Enforcement of Support Act is now in effect throughout all United States jurisdictions. Under this statute, a person liable for the support of a mate or child may be made to furnish such support wherever he may be.

In discussing here selected details of marriage and family law, we do not presume to do more than to outline certain principles and problems. Those who have legal problems are advised to seek the counsel of a lawyer. We recommend one with a reputation as a "family lawyer" rather than as a "divorce lawyer." The fees charged by an ethical practitioner of the law are usually a modest enough investment in personal peace of mind and security.

The five groups of laws to be discussed in this chapter are those having to do with: (1) the marriage relationship, (2) the termination of marriage, (3) parents and children, (4) political rights of women, and (5) other civil rights of women. These matters are closely related to the subjects of other chapters, and we do not try to bring together here all aspects of marriage and family law. We wish rather to give some general information on various legal matters related to our subject.

1. *The Marriage Relationship.* The table of state marriage laws on pages 198–199 sums up many basic aspects of statutes and common-law provisions related to getting married. Quite briefly we wish to note points regarding: (*a*) prenuptial promises, (*b*) the age of consent, (*c*) prohibited marriages, (*d*) physical examinations, (*e*) waiting periods, (*f*) common-law marriages, (*g*) marriage ceremonies, and (*h*) marital obligations.

a) *Prenuptial promises* include agreements to marry and to carry out a mutually acceptable program concerning ways of life, the religious education of children, and property arrangements. Suits for breach of promise to marry may seem reasonable enough when one thinks of an occasional bride left waiting at the church, but considerable controversy exists as to the wisdom of permitting such actions. The practice can become, and often has become, a racket. Many states now bar such actions. The legal specialist John S. Bradway [*] comments, "When such a suit is begun, or even threatened, the reputation of the male defendant suffers even though he may never have made a promise. An experienced and attractive woman plaintiff has opportunities to impress the jury, which may never be available to her more timid and retiring sister who might be more definitely vic-

---

[*] "What Family Members Should Know about Law," Chapter 19 in H. Becker and R. Hill, eds., *Family, Marriage and Parenthood* (2nd ed.; Boston: D. C. Heath and Co., 1955), p. 562. Reprinted by permission of the publisher.

timized." As to breaches of other types of prenuptial promise, the courts often hold that the formal marriage vows and their implications in law take precedence over any previous agreement. Bradway * illustrates this point thus: "At common law, the father and not the mother could decide how the child should be educated. The statutes in this country usually give the parents equal powers in this respect. With few exceptions, courts have generally refused to enforce antenuptial contracts regarding religious education of the children." Such matters are so difficultly technical and complicated by so many exceptions that we can only introduce them here in our limited space.

b) *The age of consent* in common law was 14 years for a male and 12 for a female. As the table on pages 198–199 indicates, all of the states have now set by statute higher ages for consent to marry. Without parental consent, more than one-fourth of the states place the age of 21 years for both sexes; more than one-half set 21 years for the man and 18 for the woman. All of the states permit lower ages with parental agreement; the most common age with parental consent is 18 for males and 16 for females. Courts usually can waive age requirements for pregnancy or other weighty reasons.

c) *Prohibited marriages* in common law are those between persons of different race or color and of a person with mother, father, brother, or sister. If contracted, they are void. Statutes replacing common law continue the ban on interracial marriages in 21 states, but the 1948 state supreme court decision invalidating the California interracial marriage law and other judicial decisions concerning race cast doubt on all such racist legislation as being contrary to the guarantees in the federal Constitution of equal rights to all citizens. The definition of a person's racial background is impossible in a scientific sense and depends in practice upon social labeling. We are all of mixed racial background in varying and indeterminate proportions. Thus in many states little or no effort is made to enforce such interracial laws. There are a range of other prohibited marriages in addition to those involving close kin and race. For example, 24 states will void a marriage in which one of the parties was of unsound mind at the time of the marriage. Epilepsy provides such a basis in 14 states; communicable venereal diseases in 9 states; bigamy in 19 states; and there are a variety of other bases, such as alcoholism and tuberculosis.

d) *Physical examinations* are now required by all but five states

* *Ibid.*, p. 563.

MARRIAGE LAWS – As of July 1, 1966

State or other jurisdiction	Age at which marriage can be contracted with parental consent — Male	Female	Age below which parental consent is required — Male	Female	Common-law marriage recognized	Physical examination and blood test for male and female — Maximum period between examination and issuance of marriage license	Scope of medical examination	Waiting period — Before issuance of license	After issuance of license
Alabama	17(a)	14(a)	21	18	*	30 da.	(b)		
Alaska	18(c)	16(c)	21	18		30 da.	(b)	3 da.	
Arizona	18(c)	16(c)	21	18		30 da.	(b)		
Arkansas	18(c)	16(c)	21	18		30 da.	(b)	3 da.	
California	18(a,d)	16(a,d)	21	18		30 da.	(b)		
Colorado	16(d)	16(d)	21	18	*	30 da.	(b)	3 da.	
Connecticut	16(d)	16(d)	21	21		40 da.	(b)	4 da.	
Delaware	18(c)	16(a,c)	21	18		30 da.	(b)		(e)
Florida	18(a,c)	16(a,c)	21	21	*	30 da.	(b)	3 da.	
Georgia	18(c,f)	16(c,f)	19(f)	19(f)	*	30 da.	(b)	3 da.(g)	
Hawaii	18	16(d)	20	20		30 da.	(b)	3 da.	
Idaho	15	16	18	18	*	30 da.	(b)		
Illinois	18	16	21	18		15 da.	(b)		
Indiana	18(c)	16(c)	21	18		30 da.	(b)	3 da.	
Iowa	18(c)	16(c)	21	18	*	20 da.	(b)	3 da.	
Kansas	18(d)	16(d)	21	18	*	30 da.	(b,h)	3 da.	
Kentucky	18(a,c)	16(a,c)	21	21		15 da.	(b)	3 da.	
Louisiana	18(d)	16(d)	21	21		10 da.	(b)		72 hrs.
Maine	16(d)	16(d)	21	18		30 da.	(b)	5 da.	
Maryland	18(c)	16(c)	21	18				48 hrs.	
Massachusetts	18(d)	16(d)	21	18		30 da.	(b)	3 da.	
Michigan	(i)	16(j)	18	18		30 da.	(b)	3 da.	
Minnesota	18(a)	16(i)	21	18				5 da.	
Mississippi	17(d)	15(d)	21	21		30 da.	(b)	3 da.	
Missouri	15(d)	15(d)	21	18		15 da.	(b)	3 da.	
Montana	18(d)	16(d)	21	18	*	20 da.	(b)	5 da.	
Nebraska	18(c)	16(c)	21	21		30 da.	(b)		
Nevada	18(a,d)	16(a,d)	21	18					
New Hampshire	(k)	(k)	20	18		30 da.	(b)	5 da.	
New Jersey	18(d)	16(d)	21	18		30 da.	(b)	72 hrs.	

State								
New Mexico....	18(c)	21	16(c)	18	......	30 da.	(b)	......
New York	16	21	16(d)	18	......	30 da.	(m)	24 hrs.(1)
North Carolina..	16	18	16(c)	18	......	30 da.	(o)	......
North Dakota ..	18	21	15	18	......	30 da.	(b)	......
Ohio..........	18(c)	21	16(c)	21	...*	30 da.	(b)	5 da.
Oklahoma......	18(j)	21	15(j)	18	*	30 da.(q)	(b)	72 hrs.(p)
Oregon........	18(j)	21	15(j)	18	*	30 da.	(r)	7 da.
Pennsylvania ..	18(d)	21	16(d)	21	***	30 da.	(b)	3 da.
Rhode Island..	18(d)	21	16(d)	21	*	40 da.	(s)	(t)
South Carolina	16(c)	18	14(c)	18	*	......	...	......
South Dakota..	18(c)	21	16(c)	18	......	20 da.	(b)	......
Tennessee	16(d)	21	16(d)	21	......	30 da.	(b)	3 da.(u)
Texas.........	16	21	14	18	...*	15 da.	(b)	3 da.(p)
Utah..........	16(a)	21	14(a)	18	*	30 da.	(b)	......
Vermont.......	18(d)	21	16(d)	18	......	30 da.	(b)	5 da.
Virginia......	18(a,c)	21	16(a,c)	21	......	30 da.	(b)	......
Washington....	17(d)	21	17(d)	18	......	......	(o)	......
West Virginia ..	18(a)	21	16(a)	21	......	30 da.	(b)	3 da.
Wisconsin	18	21	16	18	......	20 da.	(b)	3 da.
Wyoming.......	18	21	16	21	......	30 da.	(b)	5 da.
District of Columbia.....	18(a)	21	16(a)	18	*	......	...	3 da.

(*) Indicates common-law marriage recognized.

(a) Parental consent not required if minor was previously married.

(b) Venereal diseases.

(c) Statute establishes procedure whereby younger parties may obtain license in case of pregnancy or birth of a child.

(d) Statute establishes procedure whereby younger parties may obtain license in special circumstances.

(e) Residents, 24 hours; nonresidents, 96 hours.

(f) If parties are under 19 years of age, proof of age and the consent of parents in person required. If a parent is ill, an affidavit by the incapacitated parent and a physician's affidavit to that effect required.

(g) Unless parties are 21 years of age or more, or female is pregnant, or applicants are the parents of a living child born out of wedlock.

(h) Feeblemindedness.

(i) No provision in law for parental consent for males.

(j) Parental consent and permission of judge required. In Oregon, permission of judge required for male under 19 years of age or female under 17.

(k) Below age of consent parties need parental consent and permission of judge.

(l) Marriage may not be solemnized within 3 days from date on which specimen for serological test was taken.

(m) Uncontrolled epileptic attacks, idiocy, imbecility, mental defectiveness, unsound mind, infectious tuberculosis, and venereal diseases.

(n) Forty-eight hours if both are nonresidents of the State.

(o) Feeblemindedness, imbecility, insanity, chronic alcoholism, and venereal diseases. In Washington, also advanced tuberculosis and, if male, contagious venereal diseases.

(p) If one or both parties are below the age for marriage without parental consent.

(q) Time limit between date of examination and expiration of marriage license.

(r) Venereal diseases, feeblemindedness, mental illness, drug addiction, and chronic alcoholism.

(s) Infectious tuberculosis and venereal diseases.

(t) If female is nonresident, must complete and sign license 5 days prior to marriage.

(u) Unless parties are over 21 years of age.

Prepared by the Women's Bureau, United States Department of Labor. Reprinted by permission.

before a couple may obtain a license to marry. The table on pages 198–199 gives in detail the principal state requirements on physical examinations and also on the time period within which such examinations must be made prior to marriage. Note that pregnancy is made a reason for exception to marriage prohibition, but the infected party must undergo prescribed treatment.

e) *Waiting periods* are now thought to be a way of cooling impetuosity and making for more stable unions. The table on pages 198–199 lists state requirements of this sort. When good cause is shown, the waiting period can be shortened or waived.

f) *Common-law marriages* were recognized in colonial common law but not in that of England. In England the temporal courts upheld the requirement of Anglican Church canon law that a marriage should be properly solemnized. With the shortage of clergymen in the colonies and the widespread and bitter resentment of English efforts to enforce the Church of England's established status, a more practical view of common-law marriages emerged, and they were recognized as valid in a great many jurisdictions. A common-law marriage is one without formal license or ceremony but accepted and enforced by the community as binding, a *de facto* marriage. The criteria of validity for a common-law marriage differ from state to state. They emphasize chiefly evidence of mutual agreement that the pair take each other as husband and wife, of known cohabitation as man and wife, and of community recognition of the marriage as such. Once a common-law marriage is held valid in one state, it has general validity in all states. In all but fifteen of the states (and the number is decreasing) statutes or judicial decisions now deny the legal basis for establishing new common-law marriages.

g) *Marriage ceremonies* with witnesses, a marriage certificate later recorded, a formal place for the ceremony, and performance of the rites by, or under the supervision of, an authorized person are required to make a marriage valid in states where common-law unions are not permitted. Except for Maryland, where a religious ceremony must be held, either a civil or a religious ceremony satisfies legal requirements.

h) *Marital obligations* reflect the general recognition that marriage is more than a legal contract between two people. The agreement also involves as its principals the state and, when accepted by the couple, a religious institution. Unlike other contracts, marriage cannot be ended legally merely by mutual consent. Both under common law and under existing statutes, the husband and father is required to assume the duty of supporting and maintaining his wife and family. In only one-fourth of the states is the wife obliged to support her husband out of her own resources when he cannot support himself. Three-fourths of the states make nonsupport by a husband a criminal offense, but none has such a liability laid upon a wife. In general, marital obligations in our society carry the indelible stamp of the middle-class mores of our legislators and judges—those we principally trust with the making and interpreting of law. The laws give the husband the right to select, within reason, the place where the couple is to live and the right to enjoy his wife's conjugal fellowship, co-operation, and services; they entitle the wife to the support and conjugal companionship of her husband and permit her to serve as his agent for certain types of purchases and activities.

2. *The Termination of Marriage.* Marriages end in: (*a*) annulment, (*b*) divorce, (*c*) desertion, or (*d*) death. Chapter 21 deals with the social and personal aspects of those events, but here we wish to bring together briefly their legal aspects.

a) *Annulment.* When a judge issues an annulment decree, his purpose is to return the couple to their previous status with their pre-existing rights re-established as if the marriage had not taken place. Almost all states specify one or more grounds for annulment. Most of them indicate that children of an annulled marriage, void though it be, may be legitimized. A compilation by the Women's Bureau of the United States Department of Labor * lists the following principal grounds for marriage annulment (the numbers refer to the jurisdictions included): nonage (32); mental incapacity (30); fraud (23); prohibited degrees of kinship (22); duress or force (21); physical incapacity (19); former undivorced spouse still living (19); and interracial (7). Note that three times as many states prohibit interracial marriages as specify race difference as a basis for annulment; in the other states, the discovery of race difference may be accepted as the basis for an action alleging fraud. At least 14 states take the position that cohabitation makes a marriage valid in spite of nonage, fraud, duress, or force.

b) *Divorce.* Prior to the American Revolution, English common law recognized two types of divorce, both of ancient lineage. One was *legal separation* (from bed and board) without the right of mar-

* *The Legal Status of Women* (Women's Bureau Bulletin No. 157, rev.; Washington, D.C.: Govt. Printing Office, 1956), pp. 69–72.

DIVORCE LAWS AS OF JULY 1, 1966

State or other jurisdiction	Residence required before filing suit for divorce	Grounds for absolute divorce								
		Adultery	Mental and/or physical cruelty	Desertion	Alcoholism	Impotency	Non-support	Insanity	Pregnancy at marriage	Bigamy
Alabama	(a)	*	*	1 yr.	*	*	*(b)	5 yrs.	*	..
Alaska	1 yr.	*	*	1 yr.	*	*	*	18 mos.	..	..
Arizona	1 yr.	*	*	1 yr.	*	*	*	.....	*	..
Arkansas	2 mos.	*	*	1 yr.	*	*	*(h)	3 yrs.	..	*
California	1 yr.	*	*	1 yr.	*	..	*	3 yrs.	..	..
Colorado	1 yr. (j)	*	*	1 yr.	*	..	*	3 yrs.	..	..
Connecticut	3 yrs. (j)	*	*	3 yrs.	*	..	..	5 yrs.	..	..
Delaware	2 yrs. (j)	*	*	2 yrs.	*	..	*	5 yrs.	..	*
Florida	6 mos.	*	*	1 yr.	*	*	..	.....	..	*
Georgia	6 mos.	*	*	1 yr.	*	..	..	2 yrs.	*	..
Hawaii	2 yrs.	*	*	6 mos.	*	..	*	3 yrs.	..	..
Idaho	6 wks.	*	*	1 yr.	*	..	*	6 yrs.	..	..
Illinois	1 yr.(j)	*	*	1 yr.	*	*	..	.....	..	*
Indiana	1 yr.(t)	*	*	2 yrs.	*	*	*	5 yrs.	..	..
Iowa	1 yr.	*	*	2 yrs.	*	..	..	.....	*(av)	..
Kansas	1 yr.(w)	*	*	1 yr.	*	..	*	5 yrs.	..	..
Kentucky	1 yr.	*	*	1 yr.	*(x)	*	..	5 yrs.	*	..
Louisiana	(aa)	*	..	....	..	..	..	.....	..	..
Maine	6 mos.(j)	*	*	3 yrs.	*	*	*	.....	..	..
Maryland	1 yr. (ad)	*	..	18 mos.	..	*	..	3 yrs.	..	..

State										
Massachusetts	*	5 yrs.(j)	*		*	*		*		
Michigan	*	1 yr.(j)	*	*	*	*		*		
Minnesota	*	1 yr.(j)	*	*	*		5 yrs.			
Mississippi	*	1 yr.	*	*	*		3 yrs.	*	*	*
Missouri	*	1 yr.(j)	*	*	*			*	*	*
Montana	*	1 yr.	*		*	*	5 yrs.	*	*	
Nebraska	*	2 yrs.(j)	*	*	*	*	5 yrs.	*		
Nevada	*	6 wks.(j)	*	*	*	*	2 yrs.		*	
New Hampshire	*	1 yr.(j)	*		*					
New Jersey	*	2 yrs.(j)	*	*	*	*				
New Mexico	*	1 yr.	*	*		*	5 yrs.	*	*	
New York	*	1 yr.	*						*	
North Carolina	*	6 mos.	*	*	*		5 yrs.	*	*	
North Dakota		1 yr. (t)	*	*	*	*(h)	5 yrs.		*	*
Ohio	*	1 yr.	*	*	*	*				
Oklahoma	*	6 mos.(w)	*	*	*	*	5 yrs.	*	*	
Oregon	*	1 yr.	*	*	*		2 yrs.			
Pennsylvania	*	1 yr.	*					*	*	
Rhode Island	*	2 yrs.(al)	*		*	*				
South Carolina	*	1 yr.	*	*	*			*		
South Dakota	*	1 yr. (j)	*				5 yrs.			
Tennessee	*	1 yr.	*	*	*	*		*	*	*
Texas	*	12 mos.	*		*		5 yrs.			
Utah	*	3 mos.	*		*	*	*	*		
Vermont		6 mos. (ar)				*	5 yrs.	*		
Virginia	*	1 yr.	*		*				*	
Washington		1 yr.	*	*	*	*	2 yrs.	*		
West Virginia	*	2 yrs.(j)	*	*		*		*	*	
Wisconsin	*	2 yrs.	*			*				
Wyoming	*	60 days(j)	*	*		*	2 yrs.	*	*	
District of Columbia	*	1 yr.								

DIVORCE LAWS AS OF JULY 1, 1966

State or other jurisdiction	Grounds for absolute divorce						Period before parties may remarry after final decree		
	Separation or absence	Felony conviction or imprisonment	Drug addiction	Fraud, force or duress	Infamous crime	Prior decree of limited divorce	Other	Plaintiff	Defendant
Alabama	....	*	*			(c)	(d)	60 days (e)	60 days(e)
Alaska	....	*	*				(f)		
Arizona	5 yrs.	*			*		(g)	1 yr.	1 yr.
Arkansas	3 yrs.	*			*				
California	....	*	*					(i)	(i)
Colorado	3 yrs.	*	*			(c)			
Connecticut	7 yrs.	*		*	*	(c)			
Delaware	3 yrs.		*				(k)	3 mos.(l)	3 mos.(l)
Florida	....	*					(m,n,o)	(l)	(l)
Georgia	....	*					(o,p)	(l)	(l)
Hawaii	2 yrs.(q)	*	*			(c)		(i)	(i)
Idaho	5 yrs.	*					(r,s)		
Illinois	....	*			*			(u)	
Indiana	....	*			*				
Iowa	....	*						1 yr.(o,l)	1 yr.(o,l)
Kansas	....	*		*			(r,y,z)	60 days	60 days
Kentucky	5 yrs.	*		*		(ab)			
Louisiana	2 yrs.	*						wife,10 mos.	wife,10 mos.,10 mos. (ac)
Maine	....		*						
Maryland	18 mos.	*					(ae)		

State							
Massachusetts						*	
Michigan	(af)	(n)	(c)			*	
Minnesota	6 mos.	6 mos.				*	
Mississippi	(ag)	(o,p)		*		*	2 yrs.(q)
Missouri		(g,ah)				*	
Montana	6 mos.					*	
Nebraska	6 mos.					*	
Nevada		(y,ai)		*		*	3 yrs.
New Hampshire							2 yrs.
New Jersey	3 mos.(l)	3 mos.(l)					
New Mexico		(f)				*	
New York		(d)				*	2 yrs.(q)
North Carolina						*	1 yr.
North Dakota	(l)	(l)	(c)			*	
Ohio		(aj)			*	*	1 yr.
Oklahoma	6 mcs.	(f,n)			*	*	
Oregon	6 mos.	6 mos.				*	
Pennsylvania	(ac)	(o,ak)				*	
Rhode Island	6 mos.						
South Carolina		(am,an) 6 mos.					
South Dakota	(ao)					*	2 yrs.(ap)
Tennessee	(ac)	(s,ak)		*		*	7 yrs.
Texas	(aq)	(aq)				*	3 yrs. (q)
Utah	3 mos.(1)	3 mos.(1)				*	3 yrs.
Vermont	2 yrs.(l)	6 mos.(l)				*	2 yrs.
Virginia	(av)	(d,au)	(at)			*	2 yrs.
Washington	6 mos.	(aw)			*	*	
West Virginia	60 days(ax)	6 mos.	(ay)	*		*	5 yrs.
Wisconsin	1 yr.	60 days				*	2 yrs.
Wyoming		(g,ah)				*	1 yr.
District of Columbia	6 mos.	6 mos.	(az)			*	

Notes to Preceding Table, pages 202-205

(*) Indicates ground for absolute divorce.

(a) No specific period, except 1 year when ground is desertion or defendant is nonresident or 2 years if wife sues husband for nonsupport.

(b) To wife, living separate and apart from husband, as resident of the State for 2 years before suit and without support from him during such time.

(c) May be enlarged into an absolute divorce after expiration of 4 years; in Connecticut, any time after decree of separation; Hawaii, 2 years after decree for separate maintenance or from bed and board; Michigan, 5 years after decree of limited divorce.

(d) Crime against nature.

(e) Except to each other.

(f) Incompatibility.

(g) Crime before marriage.

(h) Also to husband in certain circumstances.

(i) Final decree is not entered until 1 year after interlocutory decree.

(j) Under certain circumstances a lesser period of time may be required.

(k) Female under 16, male under 18, if complaining party under age of consent at time of marriage has not confirmed the marriage after reaching such age.

(l) In the discretion of the court.

(m) Habitual violent and ungovernable temper.

(n) Defendant obtained divorce from plaintiff in another State.

(o) Relationship within prohibited degrees.

(p) Mental incapacity.

(q) Under decree of separate maintenance.

(r) Loathsome disease.

(s) Attempt on the life of the spouse by poison or other means showing malice.

(t) Five years if on ground of insanity.

(u) Two years where service on defendant is only by publication.

(v) Unless at time of marriage husband had an illegitimate child living, which fact was not known to wife.

(w) Five years if on ground of insanity and insane spouse is in out-of-State institution.

(x) If on part of the husband, accompanied by wasting of husband's estate to the detriment of the wife and children.

(y) Joining religious sect disbelieving in marriage.

(z) Unchaste behavior on part of wife after marriage.

(aa) No statutory requirement for adultery or felony conviction; 2 years when ground is separation.

(ab) Limited divorce may be enlarged into absolute divorce after 6 months for the party who obtained the limited divorce and after nine months for the other spouse.

(ac) When divorce is granted on ground of adultery, guilty party cannot marry the accomplice in adultery during lifetime of former spouse.

(ad) No specific period required, except 1 year if cause occurred out of State and 2 years if on ground of insanity.

(ae) Any cause which renders marriage null and void from the beginning.

(af) Not more than 2 years in court's discretion.

(ag) When divorce is granted on ground of adultery, court may prohibit remarriage. After 1 year, court may remove disability upon satisfactory evidence of reformation.

(ah) Husband a vagrant.

(ai) Wife's absence out of State for 10 years without husband's consent.

(aj) When husband is entitled to a divorce and alimony or child support from husband is granted, the decree may be delayed until security is entered for payment.

(ak) Incapable of procreation.

(al) Or a lesser time in court's discretion.

(am) Void or voidable marriage.

(an) Gross misbehavior or wickedness; loss of citizenship rights of one party due to crime; presumption of death.

(ao) When divorce is for adultery, guilty party cannot remarry except to the innocent person, until the death of the other.

(ap) To husband for wife's refusal to move with him to this State without reasonable cause, and willfully absenting herself from him for 2 years.

(aq) When divorce is granted on ground of cruelty, neither party may remarry for 12 months except to each other.

(ar) One year before final hearing, and 2 years if on ground of insanity.

(as) Intolerable severity.

(at) A limited divorce granted on the ground of cruelty or desertion may be merged with an absolute divorce after 1 year.

(au) Wife a prostitute prior to marriage.

(av) When divorce is granted on ground of adultery, court may decree the guilty party cannot remarry. After 6 months the court may remove the disability for good cause. Remarriage of either party forbidden pending appeal.

(aw) Want of legal age or sufficient understanding.

(ax) In court's discretion, guilty party may be prohibited from remarrying for a period not to exceed 1 year.

(ay) Living entirely apart for 5 years pursuant to a judgment of legal separation.

(az) Limited divorce may be enlarged into absolute divorce after 1 year. Also, absolute divorce may be granted for any cause arising after a divorce from bed and board, sufficient to entitle complaining party to an absolute divorce.

This table was prepared by the Women's Bureau, United States Department of Labor. Reprinted by permission.

riage to another. This was controlled by the ecclesiastical courts. The other type, *absolute divorce,* a termination of the marriage bonds, could be obtained only in special cases and then by an act of Parliament. Since the United States authorized no ecclesiastical courts, early divorces were at first obtained through a special act of a legislature and then, in more and more states, under statute through a court.

All states now provide some form of divorce. One-half prescribe bases for both absolute and limited divorces. *Limited divorces* may be a type of legal separation without the right of marriage to another person or a decree *"nisi"* ("except") that delays for a period permission to marry again. The decision as to which type of divorce is to be granted depends not so much on the grounds as on the judgment of the court. The other half of the states permit action only for absolute divorce.

The table of state divorce-law provisions on pages 202–206 highlights the current situation in our states and other jurisdictions. The only grounds for absolute divorce to be found in all states is adultery; but even where adultery is alleged as grounds for action, it is often not the cause of a divorce. In 1966 New York State finally abandoned adultery as the only basis for divorce and added cruel and inhuman treatment, abandonment (two years), imprisonment (three years), and living apart (two years) after legal separation. Adultery was redefined to include homosexuality and sodomy.

The most common basis specified for divorce action in the Northern states is "cruelty (often "mental cruelty") and in the Southern states "desertion." In commenting on such generalizations, the sociologists Mabel A. Elliott and Francis E. Merrill* note the need to probe the "real" reasons for divorce. They note "that most people do not 'air their dirty linen in public' and the spouses tend to get a divorce for the least embarrassing reasons unless they are incensed." Thus the pleas of the litigants may have little relation to the marital problems involved. Collusion and frame-ups are common in states with limited grounds for divorce.

Divorce is an interpersonal problem that should be viewed by a representative of the state with as much social and psychological wisdom as possible; but it frequently must go through a court of law in a spirit of prosecution, of trying to prove guilt. By traditional consent, the wife most frequently brings the action, and the husband obligingly co-operates in providing enough evidence so that he will

* *Social Disorganization* (4th ed.; New York: Harper & Bros., 1961), p. 421.

be the "guilty" party. Actually guilt is often felt deeply on both sides. Both have usually contributed to the situation which brings about the divorce. Sometimes a divorce does not solve the problem and leaves both persons more miserable than before. Sometimes efforts to remedy or relieve the interpersonal situation in ways other than divorce are more successful.

All states show their concern with the custody, education, and maintenance of the children of a divorced couple. Legally, neither parent is given a superior claim on the children; but where possible, courts usually favor the mother for custody and care even though the father must continue to contribute to their support. The father is also usually given an opportunity to visit with his children. When children are sufficiently competent, their preferences as to custody may have weight with the court. When the husband obtains a divorce on the grounds of his wife's adulterous behavior, the courts sometimes are given the right to decide the legitimacy of children born after the act of which the husband complains.

The legal complications of divorce are endless, but we wish to mention further only certain aspects of alimony. Only the wife may obtain alimony in 30 states; either spouse in 15; and no provision exists in 4. Three states limit alimony to one-third of the husband's income, and one to one-half. Elsewhere the size of the alimony payments is up to the court.

Is alimony justifiable? The issue is controversial. Alimony grew out of the principle that a husband should support his legally separated wife, and then it was continued and made part of the doctrine of absolute divorce in many jurisdictions as it entered its more recent phases. Out-of-court financial settlements are common. Some women decide they want to have nothing whatsoever to do with their former husband, financially or otherwise. Few ex-wives apply for alimony. Even though alimony has placed permanent and at times unwarranted burdens on some husbands and may encourage sharp legal practices, most specialists agree that it would be wise to continue alimony statutes in a form protective both of the ex-wife unable to fend for herself and of the husband from exploitative grants. Alimony may be necessary so that a mother may give adequate attention to the couple's children. It may also be a deterrent or punishment which a judge may think it wise to use.

c) Desertion might be defined as a separation arrived at unilaterally without benefit of a court. It has been called a "poor man's divorce." As we mention above, three-quarters of the states establish by statute the criminal liability of the deserting husband. The chief legal concern here is usually one of finding the missing supporter of a family and forcing him to contribute. Rarely does the wife want him back when he does not wish to come. As we have noted (page 195), the Uniform Reciprocal Enforcement of Support Act now enacted in all United States jurisdictions facilitates this process.

d) *Death* raises legal problems chiefly related to inheritance and to guardianship for minor children. In inheritance, the "homestead" or place of residence of a couple is often given to the survivor with a special status, exempt from seizure for debt, but the value of such exemption is usually limited to $5,000 or less. A wife has certain "dower" rights in her husband's estate. In common law, this is a widow's lifetime right to use one-third of her husband's lands; her claim takes precedence over any liens or mortgages she did not join in sanctioning. "Curtesy" is a similar common-law right that the widower possesses during his lifetime. His right is contingent on the birth to the union of a legitimate heir. He has a prior claim on the use of all lands owned by his wife during their marriage to the extent that he has not given up that right. As applied to personal property, a widow with children is entitled to one-third of her husband's assets of that sort after his debts are paid. Without children, she gets one-half. A widower can have whatever personal property his wife leaves after her debts are paid.

State statutes show the influence of the common-law provisions, but they modify such provisions in many ways. For example, about one-half of the states do not distinguish between real and personal property. Where there are no children or other heirs, all states now give the surviving spouse all real and personal property after obligations have been met. The variations in proportions and conditions of dower and curtesy in various states is too complicated for discussion here. There are also variations in such matters as the degree to which each spouse may will property to others.

More and more people, even those of modest means, are recognizing the wisdom of reviewing their estate plans with a family attorney. This may or may not mean having a will written, signed, attested, and properly filed. Where a state permits man and wife to own such property as their home, common stocks, or bonds as "tenants in common," each has an undivided interest in the property. Each is sole owner after the death of the other. During life, either can dispose of such property without the consent of the other. So far as the inheritance—or rather, assumption—of such property is concerned, items so owned would not need to be covered by a will, but further inheritance possibilities of all property holdings prompt a review from time to time in order to be assured of sound estate-planning. For this, the services of an attorney are urged. In some circumstances, the lawyer may recommend no will for a given person on the grounds of one not being necessary or of intestate status upon death being preferable. A will is usually advantageous and prevents possible misunderstanding among heirs.

3. *Parents and Children.* Other than the family matters mentioned above, legal problems relating to the relationships of parents and children arise chiefly out of considerations of: (*a*) custody, (*b*) guardianship, (*c*) adoption, (*d*) inheritance, (*e*) lack of wedlock, and (*f*) services and earnings.

a) *Custody* is a term to be considered in connection with guardianship and adoption. One or both natural parents usually have custody of their own minor child, and they are also his guardians. When a court or other authority finds it necessary to interfere with parental custody, such care and control may be turned over to some other person, couple, or agency as parent-substitutes. In a change of custody, responsibility for the raising and training of the child is shifted, but the child retains his original family name and family identity.

b) *Guardianship* somewhat overlaps the conception of custody, but it may not involve custody. For example, the court usually makes the minor children of a divorced or annulled marriage its wards and then grants their custody to mother, father, or other person as it deems wise. In common law, the father was regarded as a minor child's natural guardian, but he did not have the right to control the child's property. If the child died, the father was likely to be made guardian of the child's estate. In the father's absence, the mother usually assumed such rights. Under our more democratic statutes and judicial interpretations today, all but a few states make the parents when living together the joint guardians of their minor children. When a choice must be made between parents for this purpose, the father usually has preference. Upon the death of one parent, the other usually becomes sole guardian. As regards the guardianship of a minor's estate, there remains in effect in all states the common-law principle that a qualified person must be chosen by the court and must function under court supervision. If there are no special problems, the parents (or surviving parent) are the ones usually selected.

c) *Adoption* makes a child legally a member of a family, with foster parents of whom he is not a natural offspring. The adoptive parents become the guardians of the child's person and also have the child's custody. The child takes the family name of his foster parents and in every way becomes legally their child.

d) *Inheritance* is usually from parent to child, but it may also be in the opposite direction. If a parent dies without a will, the children usually receive equal shares of whatever part of the estate does not go to the other parent by dower or curtesy right. If a child dies without a will and without spouse or offspring, the parents usually share equally in the child's estate. If one parent is dead, the surviving parent usually inherits the whole. About one-fifth of the states also give brothers and sisters inheritance rights. If there is a spouse but no children of the deceased child, one-half of the states give the parents a share in the estate. These and a great many other complexities, plus the needs of an individual family situation, point again to the wisdom of careful estate-planning, modified from time to time to meet changed family conditions.

e) *Lack of wedlock* of a child's parents involves legal problems of his support, of the ways in which he may be legitimized, and of his inheritance. The mother has to support her illegitimate child or to place this responsibility upon the father through proving paternity. In general, the marriage to each other of a child's acknowledged parents legitimizes the child. In one-half of the states, the marriage alone is enough; in one-fourth, some form of acknowledgment alone is adequate. If an illegitimate child dies without a will, the mother may inherit all or part of his estate. In some one-fourth of the states, the legally acknowledged father may also inherit. So far as inheritance by a child born out of wedlock is concerned, the various jurisdictions are apparently moving in the direction of giving the child as many of the rights of a legitimate child as possible. After all, the fault is not the child's.

f) *Services and earnings* of a minor child were, under common law, the due of the father, and the mother inherited this right. In about one-half of the states, the parents share a claim on the services and earnings of their minor children. In about one-third, the common-law rule continues.

4. *Political Rights of Women.* In summarizing our gains in po-

litical rights for women, writers for the United States Women's Bureau * note, "In 1848, when a few women met at Seneca Falls, N.Y., to draw up their complaint of women's treatment under the law, women could not vote, they had no share in lawmaking, jury duty was barred to them, as was the holding of public office." They then contrast with that situation the one a century later. Now women have achieved legally what amounts to a political status substantially equal to that of men. As they conclude,

In all States, women are eligible for election to public office on the same terms and conditions as men. Generally, women are eligible for all types of State appointive office. There are some types of offices in which State law may require the appointee to be of a designated sex. Examples of such offices are those in State penal or corrective institutions in which the sexes are segregated.

A remaining political impediment is the fact that in a very few states women are not eligible for federal or state jury duty, but this situation is rapidly being changed. As a practical matter, the domicile of a married woman and of her minor children is specified as being that of her husband, but for such specific purposes as voting many states permit separate domiciles. A woman no longer loses her citizenship (unless she so choses) upon marrying an alien. Since 1952, too, all discrimination on the basis of sex is eliminated from the immigration laws.

5. *Other Civil Rights of Women.* A century ago, the following statement in the famous *Commentaries* (1765–69) of the English jurist, William Blackstone, still applied to the legal status of married women:

By marriage, the husband and wife are one person in law: that is, the very being or legal existence of the woman is suspended during marriage, or at least incorporated and consolidated into that of her husband.

An unmarried woman then had considerable civil autonomy even if her political rights were limited, but the married woman had very little. As Mrs. Alice K. Leopold,† head of the United States Women's Bureau, concludes, "Today a married woman's power to make a contract, run a business, convey a lot, or sue a defendant is only slightly

* *The Legal Status of Women* (Women's Bureau Bulletin No. 157, rev.; Washington, D.C.: Govt. Printing Office, 1956), pp. 1, 98.

† "The Legal Status of Women," in *The Book of the States* (1958–59 ed.; Chicago: Council of State Governments, 1958).

different from that of her husband." The legal gains of women have been tremendous, but some restrictions and inequalities still remain, many of which are attributed fairly or unfairly to sex differences. The sociologist Ray E. Baber * estimates that about one thousand laws in the United States still "discriminate against women, whether for men's advantage or women's protection, blocking the road to the 'equality' which some want and some do not." Most of these laws restrict women in employment, rather than in the inheritance, management, and disposition of property. In most states women are limited in the number of hours and time of day when they may work. They often must have better conditions of sanitation and relief than men. They are barred in more than one-half of the jurisdictions from certain types of employment for reasons of danger or health.

The fight over the proposed "equal rights" Amendment to the federal Constitution illuminates the issues over which there is controversy in this area. The National Woman's Party put forward in 1923 this proposed Amendment: "Men and women shall have equal rights throughout the United States and every place subject to its jurisdiction." The powerful League of Women Voters, supported by many other women's societies, secures the defeat of this Amendment each time it is introduced into Congress. Their objections to the proposal are that it would wipe out all legislation protective of women. The advocates of the Amendment think it would do such desirable things as lay the basis for equal pay for equal services by men and women. Labor-union pressures (chiefly masculine) have helped get equal-pay legislation in about one-fourth of the states; such legislation has not increased the employment of women. Opponents of the Amendment proposal raise such questions as: Where the age for marriage is lower for women than for men, as it is so often, which age would prevail and how would that decision be made? The League of Women Voters and other opponents of the proposed Amendment offer as a constructive alternative a joint Congressional resolution that would specify "no discrimination based on sex except those differences in physical structure, biological and social function and similar reasonable justifications in fact." The proposed Amendment would not take into consideration such "reasonable" differences.

* *Marriage and the Family* (2nd ed.; New York: McGraw-Hill Book Co., 1953), p. 340.

CONCLUSION

In spite of the democratic principles for which the American Revolution was fought, conservatively trained American lawyers preserved for a time the property, family, and sex conceptions of the aristocratically oriented English common law. Gradually the more egalitarian aspirations and conditions of the new country forced revisions of marriage and family law by statute and by judicial decision. Many students of marriage law are concerned with the wide variations in regulations that now exist among our states and other jurisdictions. However, if one is not too impatient with the processual character of legal as well as of other human affairs, the virtues of our range of legal experimentation become apparent. We are developing a wealth of experiences which more homogeneous and monolithic countries could never accumulate.

Like physicians, clergymen, and other professional men in the community, lawyers can be helpful in resolving some of the increasingly overwhelming complexities of life. In the family field, they are beginning to establish quite constructive relationships with sociological and psychological specialists in marriage counseling. Nevertheless, in confronting the mysteries of the law, many people worry about placing themselves in the hands of an attorney. To meet this uncertainty, responsible community leaders such as social workers, clergymen, bankers, union officials, and others can furnish the names of attorneys who are known as "family lawyers" rather than "divorce lawyers." The legal profession itself tries to police its ranks and eliminate from practice those who exploit clients in times of anxiety. Most cities have legal aid societies which serve those who cannot afford to hire an attorney.

PART FOUR

PARENTHOOD

Chapter XV

CHILDREN IN PROSPECT

In the language of the Hebrew Bible's King James version,* "Therefore shall a man leave his father and his mother, and shall cleave unto his wife: and they shall be one flesh." Eve was told that "in sorrow thou shalt bring forth children." Both she and Adam were instructed, "Be fruitful, and multiply, and replenish the earth, and subdue it." To which John † adds: "A woman when she is in travail hath sorrow, because her hour is come: but as soon as she is delivered of the child, she remembereth no more the anguish, for joy that a man is born into the world." In so few words were the ancients able to describe the fundamentals of human reproduction.

In most times and places during the history of the world until modern medicine began to lower the death rate, the survival of family and tribe meant the maintenance of as high a birth rate as possible to combat the frightful ravages of death. In most societies and on all social levels the stress upon family ties further reinforces the preoccupation of mankind with fertility and reproduction.

Concern with the mysterious gift of fertility rarely equals that with death, but it is a deep-set social preoccupation. Fertility rites among the Celts of Ireland in ancient times were typical of similar practices in many other regions. The Celts focused their rites on Imbolc, the feast of Brigit, held early in February. Brigit was the goddess of fertility, learning, and healing, her qualities reminiscent of the great Mediterranean fertility goddesses. ‡ Appropriately enough, Brigit was the daughter of the good, all-competent god, Dagda, and of the queen of the demons, Morrígan. The observance of Brigit's rites marked the beginning of the lambing season and thus tied in symbolically with all fertility. It apparently had a profound hold on the Irish people; it was only slowly displaced by the Christian festival of St. Brigit. §

* Genesis 2:24, 3:16, 1:28.
† 16:21.
‡ E. O. James, *The Cult of the Mother-Goddess* (New York: Frederick A. Praeger, 1959), esp. Chapters 2, 5, 6, and 7.
§ T. G. E. Powell, *The Celts* (New York: Frederick A. Praeger, 1958), pp. 117–119.

PARENTHOOD IN PROSPECT

When talking about possible future offspring, young couples generally assume that they are fertile. Under the current industrial, urban, and scientific conditions, their concern is likely to be with the control of fertility. The question of whether or not to have children—and when—is related to the factors in the "man/land ratio" discussed in Chapter 6.

As has been explained, in a general societal perspective, the man/ land or population ratio involves four principal factors. Stated in relationship to one another, these are: (1) *the numbers of people,* who tend to press against (2) *the supporting power of their environment* on (3) *their current level of technical competence* in industry, distribution, service, and control and in terms of (4) *their average mode of living.* From the point of view of one family, these societal factors might be interpreted as follows: A couple may believe that (1) *the number of children* they should have ought to depend upon (2) *the possibilities of their environment* as they are able to exploit it through (3) *their grasp of techniques* available to them and in terms of (4) *the mode of living* they feel they want to maintain. These factors confront all couples everywhere, but tradition rather than rational analyses most commonly dictates what a couple will do. As noted in Chapter 6, certain major religious and political organizations are strongly opposed to such considerations as reasons for limiting reproduction. Many couples so thoroughly assimiliate the views of these organizations that they are unaware that they could apply birth-control measures to avoid the damaging physiological and social consequences of unplanned reproduction.

The following questions may clarify the relationships of the above-mentioned factors: If the first child is delayed, is it not possible that the couple will be enabled to give their children a better start in life? What will one, two, or more offspring do to a family's mode of living, to its probable future, to the advancement of the parents and the education of the children? For how long and to what extent will motherhood withdraw an employed wife from income-producing employment? What price in personal welfare will the other members of the family have to pay for each additional child? Would a change in environment make possible better earnings and thus more children? How might such a change be planned?

Less directly related to the man/land ratio are these other kinds of questions: What is likely to happen to a wife's health if her children are not spaced out enough to permit adequate recovery after each birth? What are the social, intellectual, and emotional consequences of a child's membership in a large or a small family?

Social pressures may serve to raise or lower the desirability of having a large family, quite apart from the parents' personal wishes or financial considerations. For example, during the 1920's young college graduates came to regard more than one or two children as unfashionable, careless, or ostentatious. By the 1950's, young college graduates looked forward to three-child families.

Here is an account of the reactions of a middle-class American, a salaried professional man, to such social pressures: "We get so tired of telling people that we *wanted* our four children! When we are out in public with them, we are stared at curiously and asked in amazement, 'Are all those yours?' When we had the first one and then the second, our friends and relatives congratulated us and were delighted along with us. When we had the third, enthusiasm waned and we heard veiled hints about our carrying a good thing too far. When, according to our wishes, we had a fourth child, our intimates frankly said, 'This is surely all, isn't it? You couldn't have meant to have *four* children. People nowadays just don't have that many on purpose. If you did, as you say, well, all right then, but it is pretty hard to believe.' The inference is clear; we are rationalizing. The one thing that seems to make our protests credible is that our son is our second child. If we had had three girls and then a boy, nobody would ever have believed that we deliberately set out to have four children." Such pressures differ from one class group to another and from period to period.

With parenthood an approaching possibility, how can one best prepare for that status? What is meant by "planned parenthood"? What different approaches are there to such planning? How can conception be avoided, prevented, or controlled? If a wife does not become pregnant, what can be done about it? These questions introduce such topics as fertility clinics and artificial insemination; artificial ovulation may be a future possibility. What social issues and personal problems are to be considered in the sterilization of those who should not have children, do not wish to have children, or think they have had enough children? What about involuntary sterilization? Should anyone be denied by governmental authority the privilege of becoming a parent? What needs to be said about sexual relations as an intimate social activity? These are topics with which we deal briefly in the present chapter.

PREPARATION FOR PARENTHOOD

In spite of our appalling traffic-accident statistics, we do a much better job of preparing our children to drive automobiles than we do of preparing them for the vastly more important opportunities and duties connected with sexual relationships. Think of the slaughter we would have in our streets and on our highways if people could get a motor vehicle operator's license with as few prerequisites as those for a marriage license! Young men enter marriage who associate sex chiefly with filthy jokes and illicit practices. Young women still enter wedlock who do not know why they menstruate or how one becomes pregnant. With sexual preparation so often lacking, what can one expect concerning intellectual and emotional preparation for other interpersonal aspects of marriage?

As our society has become less rural, sex education is imparted less by the practical example of barnyard animals and more by the private conversations of children or by the instruction of parents, schoolteachers, physicians, and clergymen. To insist, as some groups do, that sex instruction is properly to be given only by parents or the clergy is evasive. Too often the adults fail in this responsibility either entirely or attempt to do too little instructing too late. Even now, after all the discussions in recent years about the need for such instruction, children still usually get their first information about sex either by experimentation or by gossip. The resulting misinformation and unhealthy emotional conditioning are to be expected.

Fortunately, the fight for more realistic and helpful sex instruction in the public schools is slowly gaining ground through the efforts of dedicated teachers and informed parents. The public schools are the only medium whereby those who most lack such instruction are likely to get it. In connection with the trial of a Van Nuys, California, high school instructor for having "gone too far" in sex instruction, the Los Angeles *Mirror-News* * asserted editorially: "The outraged indignation of a few parents whose 18-year-olds were apprised of some of the not unusual aspects of sex . . . seems a little far-fetched and silly. . . . We've come too far along the path of common sense to revert to a birdsies-and-beesies approach to sex education."

The emotional and intellectual preparation of people for parenthood best begins in infancy and continues steadily until and after

* Quoted in the *New York Times,* August 9, 1959.

they become parents. If they are fortunate, their parents and the parents of their friends furnish them with models of desirable family life, and their parents answer all their questions as they go along. Neither child nor parent should have to face an embarrassing discussion in which sex is finally "unmasked." Neither should be able to remember when the child first started to learn, little by little, as rapidly as he could understand, the nature of reproductive processes. In the absence of such ideal circumstances, the school or the church, or both, should provide sex information in an atmosphere of friendliness, naturalness, and dignity. One can be moral without having one's sex life fraught with feelings of anxiety and guilt.

There is, of course, a great deal more than sex information to preparation for parenthood. Other types of preparation are discussed elsewhere in this book.

PLANNED PARENTHOOD

Anything having to do with the control of human conception is controversial. That is one reason the old term and notion of "birth control" is now often replaced by the more comprehensive "planned parenthood." *Planned parenthood* has been defined as "the utilization of medical knowledge for the procreation of the number of children any given couple want to have, born when the family is ready for them. For some couples this means the correction of infertility. For others it means severe limitation of offspring. For still others it means spacing pregnancies in terms of the mother's health and strength, the father's education or career, housing facilities, economic security, and all the other factors that intelligent parents regard as important for their children's well-being. For a few couples, planned parenthood may mean simply allowing nature to take her course." *

Those concerned with planned parenthood now concentrate principally upon (1) conception control, (2) treatment for infertility, (3) education for marriage and parenthood, and (4) research in human reproduction. We discuss (1) and (2) below and (3) elsewhere. Research in human reproduction (4) involves technicalities not relevant to this book, but the results of such investigation are mentioned in appropriate connections. Even though the funds

* David Loth, "Planned Parenthood," *The Annals*, CCLXXII (November, 1950), 95–101; p. 95 quoted by permission of The American Academy of Political and Social Science.

available to subsidize research in human reproduction are far from adequate, minute in contrast with those expended for research in animal breeding, the Planned Parenthood Federation of America and co-operating organizations base their work on such research; they are especially effective through bringing research findings to the attention of physicians. Oddly enough, relatively few physicians were informed on techniques for conception control until recently.

Conception control is of many kinds. It is achieved by sexual abstinence, by interrupting coitus before the male ejaculates, by limiting intercourse to the part of the woman's monthly cycle when she presumably cannot conceive (the "safe period"), by the use of mechanical barriers, such as condoms and pessaries, by the employment of intrauterine chemical preparations or mechanical devices, by medicines taken by mouth, and by combinations of these.* Oral contraception, commonly called "the pill," is said by many to be ideal because it is effective and can be taken in a manner independent of the sex act. The pill was introduced in the United States in 1960, and it was estimated that six million American women, almost one-fifth of those of child-bearing age, were using it in 1966. The pill is supposed to be available only upon prescription, and physicians try to check their patients twice a year for side-effects. It is still on trial. Less costly but not so effective is the intrauterine device (I.U.D.), which consists of a small piece of plastic, nylon, or metal shaped as a loop, coil, ring, or bow inserted in the uterus by a physician. The device may remain there and be effective indefinitely, but it may be expelled from the uterus without the woman's being being aware of it.

Still in the experimental stage are once-monthly pills (rather than those taken twenty days a month or daily as now), retroactive pills that would counteract unwanted pregnancies after coitus or up to a week later, and even a possible pill that would make a woman sterile until she took a second fertility-restoring pill weeks or years later.

Comments on "the pill" contrast sharply. One mother typified the views of many when she asserted: "We have three children, and we can't afford any more. I have a job now to help put the children through college, and another pregnancy would ruin our plans. A diaphragm didn't work for us, as the birth of our third child showed. After that, I felt we had to limit sexual relations to times of the month when I'm almost certain I won't get pregnant. That's not too often, you know. But now with the pills, we don't have to worry any more.

* Population Council, *Family Planning and Population Programs—A Review of World Developments* (Chicago: University of Chicago Press, 1966).

It's just great—like a second honeymoon."* Others charge that the use of the pill makes for promiscuity. Lewis Frank,† executive director of the Information Center on Population Problems, replies: "A lot of nonsense.... Many youngsters ... are practicing contraception on the level of the ancients. We get the results of that in foundling homes and shotgun marriages."

In a survey published in 1966 of the use of pills in the United States, Charles F. Westoff and Norman B. Ryder‡ estimated "no less than 21 per cent of Catholic wives under 45 have used oral contraceptives, compared with 29 per cent of non-Catholic women.... One important difference between Catholics and non-Catholics, according to Westoff and Ryder, was the way in which they used the pill. Non-Catholics apparently used birth control to space their children, while Catholics seemed to take the pill, after having some children, to keep their families from growing larger."

The following is part of a statement prepared by scientific specialists associated with the Planned Parenthood Federation as advice on the choice of a birth-control method:

Selection of the method which is best suited to the needs of your family should be done with the assistance of a qualified physician. When properly prescribed and used, these methods can never cause harm or illness. Nor are they uncomfortable. By removing fear of unwanted pregnancies they should make married life happier.

These methods will not prevent you from having a child when you are ready. When you want to have a child, you simply stop using the method.

Contraception should not be confused with abortion. An abortion destroys life after it has been started. Birth control merely postpones the beginning of life.

In commenting upon the two nonmedical methods usually mentioned—abstinence and the "safe period" or "rhythm method"—the Planned Parenthood specialists raise significant doubts. Abstinence is regarded as "neither feasible nor desirable. It is usually considered physiologically and psychologically unsound." For the "rhythm method" to be "at all reliable, . . . the so-called 'safe period' must be carefully calculated under the guidance of a trained physician. Even then, anxiety, a cold, a journey or other simple cause may throw the calculation into error."

The Legal Status of Contraception. Both federal and state statutes which restrict the manufacture and distribution of contraceptive de-

* Quoted by Jane E. Brody in *The New York Times,* May 31, 1966.
† *Ibid.*
‡ *Newsweek,* May 16, 1966, p. 94.

vices and the imparting of contraceptive information appear to be more stringent than recent applications have proven them to be. Federal laws specify that the importation of contraceptive articles and literature and their distribution through the mails may be only for scientific and medical purposes. Aware of the widespread support of birth-control measures, federal judges have brought considerable wisdom to the interpretation of such laws. Their decisions tend to focus upon the issue of obscenity rather than of contraception as such. For example, a federal judge held in 1931 that Marie C. Stopes's book, *Contraception,* was not obscene, "for the reading of it would not stir the sex impulses of any person with a normal mind"; he therefore permitted its delivery through the mails.*

After a half-century of struggle against restrictive legislation, the proponents of birth-control and planned-parenthood programs now find more and more positive programs being worked out by the states and local units of government as well as by agencies of the Federal government. The Planned Parenthood Federation of America's legal specialists* make these summary comments concerning the general status of birth-control legislation:

It is important . . . to bear in mind that the laws on the books mean what the courts say they mean. Thus, while the federal and a few of the state statutes read as if they were absolute prohibitions, the courts have generally interpreted such statutes to permit considerable freedom with respect to the distribution of contraceptives and contraception information.

Where there have been no court interpretations of a statute on the books, guidance as to its actual impact can be gleaned from the attitude of enforcement agencies. Thus, although in some states the statute reads as an outright prohibition without any exception, the fact that it is not so construed is apparent from the inclusion of contraceptive services as part of the public health program of the state.

With this background, we present the table, "Legal Status of Birth Control in the United States," set forth on pages 226–227. Also relevant as background for this table is the general Federal legal and policy stance toward planned parenthood, and this, too, is briefly summarized by the Planned Parenthood specialists as follows:

The Federal law governs the importation, mailing and interstate transportation of contraceptives and contraceptive literature. Under the relevant court decisions, it is now well-established that these federal laws do not interfere with distribution of materials and information in the interests of

---

* "Survey of Laws Relating to Planned Parenthood in the United States as of January 1965," mimeo., pp. 1–3 quoted.

life and health. As the courts have ruled, these laws were not intended: ". . . to prevent the importation, sale, or carriage by mail of things which might intelligently be employed by conscientious and competent physicians for the purpose of saving life or promoting the well being of their patients." . . .

In addition, administrative agencies of the Federal government and of some state and local governments have recently issued liberal directives and rulings in connection with the applicable laws in particular jurisdictions.

As the table indicates, twenty-one states now operate family planning programs, and twenty others permit or encourage programs through local governments and other agencies. Only ten have no program or are merely in a planning stage. Seventeen states have no restrictive laws concerning contraceptives, and these include eight of the twenty-one states now sponsoring family planning programs.

The changed spirit that is entering into our legislative assemblies when dealing with planned parenthood is well suggested by statements from the July 3, 1965 issue of *The Pilot,* organ of the Boston Roman Catholic Archdiocese: "We can be confident that the General Court [the Massachusetts legislature] will bring to this matter a willingness to adjust the law to wide community needs and while remaining faithful to their personal moral commitments in whatever tradition they may be, seek also to satisfy the proper demands of others insofar as this is possible. Catholic legislators certainly have no obligation to oppose a change in the law and should work for a law that protects freedom of conscience for all the people."

How Religious Leaders Judge Birth-Control Methods. All religious bodies sanction the limitation of family size through one or more procedures, but they disagree sharply on which procedures are moral and useful. Here are some representative positions taken by organizations and their leaders:

Central Conference of American Rabbis: "We urge recognition of the importance of the control of parenthood as one of the methods of coping with social problems."

Pope Pius XII, in speaking of the "rhythm method" of birth control: "[The] Church knows how to consider with sympathy and understanding the real difficulties of the married state in our day. Therefore . . . we affirmed the legitimacy of a regulation of offspring, which, unlike so-called 'birth control,' is compatible with the law of God." To this, the head * of the Marriage Counseling Center

---

* Alphonse H. Clemens, *Marriage and the Family: An Integrated Approach for Catholics.* (C) 1957. Prentice-Hall, Inc., U.S.A. (P. 230.)

LEGAL STATUS OF BIRTH CONTROL IN THE UNITED STATES†

States	No Laws	Advertisement Prohibited	General Sale Prohibited	Allowed Through Physicians	Allowed Through Pharmacists	Special Licenses for Distribution	Family Planning Programs
Alabama	*						S
Alaska	*						P
Arizona		*					LG,P
Arkansas		*	*	*		*	S
California		*	*	*		*	S
Colorado		*	*	*	*	*	S
Connecticut		*	*	*	*		O
Delaware		*	*	*	*		S
District of Columbia		*	*	*	*		F
Florida	*						S
Georgia	*						S
Hawaii		B	V				P
Idaho		*	*	*	*	*	LG
Illinois	*						S
Indiana	*						O*
Iowa		*	*	*	*		S
Kansas	*						S
Kentucky		*	*	*	*	*	S
Louisiana		*	*				O
Maine		*	*				P*
Maryland			V				S
Massachusetts		*	*	*	*		O
Michigan		*	*	*	*	*	S
Minnesota		*	*	*	*		LG
Mississippi		*	*				S
Missouri		*	*	*			LG
Montana		*	*	*	*		LG
Nebraska		*	*	*			LG
Nevada		*		*			S
New Hampshire	*						O
New Jersey		*	*	*	*		O*
New Mexico	*						R
New York		*	*	*	*		R*
North Carolina	*						S
North Dakota			V				LG
Ohio	*						O
Oklahoma	*						O
Oregon		*	*	*	*	*	S
Pennsylvania		*					P*

LEGAL STATUS OF BIRTH CONTROL IN THE UNITED STATES†
(continued)

States	No Laws	Advertisement Prohibited	General Sale Prohibited	Allowed Through Physicians	Allowed Through Pharmacists	Special Licenses for Distribution	Family Planning Programs
Rhode Island	*						O
South Carolina	*						S
South Dakota		*					O
Tennessee	*						S
Texas				*	*	*	P*
Utah		*		*		*	LG
Vermont	*						R
Virginia			*		*	*	S
Washington		*	*	*		*	S
West Virginia	*						LG,P
Wisconsin		*	*	*	*	*	R*
Wyoming		*	*	*	*		LG

*This symbol alone means that that is the approximate position of the State. The asterisk beside a letter in the last column means that the Planned Parenthood Federation of America reported (January 1965) these States to be making planned parenthood services available through public health and/or welfare agencies, either on a State, county, or local basis. The letters in that column summarize the U.S. Senate publication, *Population Crisis*, cited below.

†Compiled by the authors from Planned Parenthood Federation of America, "Survey of Laws Relating to Planned Parenthood in the United States as of January 1965," and supplements dated June and July, 1965; U.S. Senate Committee on Government Operations, Subcommittee on Foreign Aid Expenditures, *Hearings . . . on S. 1676*, Appendix, Part 4, *Population Crisis* (Washington: Government Printing Office, 1966); and Norman St. John-Stevas, *Birth Control and Public Policy* (Santa Barbara, California: Center for the Study of Democratic Institutions, 1960).

B — Outdoor advertising prohibited.

F — The District of Columbia, Puerto Rico, American Samoa, and the Virgin Islands have centralized programs under governmental auspices.

LG—Local government programs.

O — No State or local government program; no State study under way.

P — State program in development.

R — State refers patients to private physicians.

S — State-operated program.

V — Sales from vending machines prohibited.

NOTE: Private agencies, such as the Planned Parenthood Federation of America and its affiliates, also operate in all States and especially in those marked O and P.

of the Catholic University of America adds: "However, it is often forgotten that even in the presence of compelling reasons rhythm cannot usually be employed. . . . Every couple contemplating its use should consult their confessor or a priest to determine whether their alleged reason is a justifiable one and whether all the conditions which free it from guilt are present."

John Cogley, Editor, *The Commonweal,* in a statement approved by the Roman Catholic Archdiocese of New York: "Strictly speaking, it is artificial birth prevention (by means of contraceptive devices, chemicals, etc.) which the Church condemns as intrinsically evil. 'Natural' birth control—the so-called rhythm theory—is permitted (as the Pope stated) in cases where undue medical or economic hardship makes family limitation imperative."

Dr. Norman Vincent Peale, Methodist minister, well-known author, and radio speaker: "It is no more wrong to control scientifically this natural force [human reproduction] than it is to harness and direct any of God's forces in this universe."

General Conference, Methodist Church: "Planned parenthood, practiced in Christian conscience, may fulfill rather than violate the will of God."

William B. Lipphard, Editor, *Baptist Missions:* "No parish Baptist church and no ecclesiastical convention of Baptists has ever by resolution expressed approval or disapproval of birth control or planned parenthood. Most Baptists would resent and repudiate any such resolution as an unwarranted intrusion into the private life of husband and wife."

General Convention, Protestant Episcopal Church: "We endorse the efforts being made to secure for licensed physicians, hospitals and medical clinics, freedom to convey such information as is in accord with the highest principles of eugenics and a more wholesome family life, wherein parenthood may be undertaken with due respect for the health of mothers and the welfare of their children." To this, the National Council of the same church added: "Some form of family planning, particularly in those areas of rapidly growing population, is an urgent necessity."

Philadelphia Yearly Meeting of Friends (Quakers): "Married couples vitally need the varied benefits of a rich and harmonious sex experience. The full expression of the sex relation requires a large measure of freedom and spontaneity. It is clear that the fear of pregnancy creates an atmosphere in which such freedom and spontaneity are impossible. Birth control does not necessarily mean family limitation alone but planning for and spacing children as the whole welfare of the family may indicate. The proper use of approved contraceptives may contribute to the social and economic welfare of the home, and to the physical and mental health of parents and children."

The National Council of the Churches of Christ in the U.S.A. (Protestant) adopted a general statement on birth control (February 23, 1961) which contains these key paragraphs:

Within the purposes of marriage ordained by God, there are a number of considerations concerning parenthood which need to be taken into account in trying to determine the number and frequency of pregnancies. These include:
1. The right of the child to be wanted, loved, cared for, educated, and trained in the 'discipline and instruction of the Lord.' . . . The rights of existing children to parental care have a proper claim.
2. The prospect for health of a future child, if medical and eugenic evidence seem negatively conclusive.
3. The health and welfare of the mother-wife, and the need for the spacing of children to safeguard it.
4. The social situation, when rapid population growth places dangerous pressures on the means of livelihood and endangers the social order. . . .
Most of the Protestant churches hold contraception and periodic continence to be morally right when the motives are right. They believe that couples are free to use the gifts of science for conscientious family limitation, provided the means are mutually acceptable, non-injurious to health, and appropriate to the degree of effectiveness required in the specific situation.

A very influential and conclusive statement on birth control is that of a study group of the World Council of Churches, the 1959 publication of which had the authorization of the Council's secretariat. This council represents 171 Protestant, Anglican, and Orthodox denominations. Here are excerpts from the study group statement:

Limiting or spacing of children is a morally valid thesis. . . . There appears to be no moral distinction between the means now known and practiced—whether by the use of estimated periods of fertility [*i.e.,* rhythm method], or of artificial barriers to the meeting of sperm and ovum [*i.e.,* contraceptives], or indeed of drugs which would, if made effective and safe, inhibit or control ovulation in a calculable way.

The group stresses the "extremely high rates of abortion in many regions, Eastern and Western, with their toll of human suffering and violation of personality" and other aspects of the "population explosion." The group contends that true marriage and parenthood are areas in which the Christian is given two sorts of freedom. "This means freedom from sensuality and selfishness which enslave. It also means considerable latitude of choice, when the motives are right, in regard to mutually acceptable and noninjurious means to avert or defer conception. . . . Sexual intercourse within marriage has in itself a goodness given by God, even when there is neither the possibility nor the immediate intention to beget children."

The Planned Parenthood Federation sums up its position on the moral issues involved in medically recommended methods of birth control in these terms: "Objections have been raised that birth control is against the law of nature. This is no more true than that anesthesia, immunization against disease, control of infection or any other great advance in medical science is against the law of nature. The latest and best scientific information should be available for dealing with problems of maternal health and parenthood, in the same way that scientific knowledge is applied in other areas of life."

Do Members Follow Church Teachings on Contraception? Studies of the degree of adherence by members to the official mandates of their denomination, when the denomination has any, apparently reveal that social-class status outweighs religious sanctions in the determination of the birth-control methods to be used. This is an area in which it is difficult to obtain data convincing to partisans. Msgr. Irving A. De Blanc, director of the National Catholic Family Life Bureau, told his organization's 1960 convention that there is some evidence American Roman Catholics are using contraceptives as much as their non-Catholic neighbors. The sociologist Pascal K. Whelpton,* reporting on interviews with a cross section of American white wives aged 18 to 39, furnishes some of the evidence behind De Blanc's concern. He and his associates found that "only about 6 per cent [of the wives] . . . conceived easily and did not expect to use some method of birth control to space children or limit their number." Whelpton adds: "If we consider only the fecund couples—those that

* "A Generation of Demographic Change," Chapter 7 in J. E. Nordskog, ed., *Social Change* (New York: McGraw-Hill Book Co., 1960), p. 67; he is summarizing Ronald Freedman, Whelpton, and A. A. Campbell, *Family Planning, Sterility, and Population Growth* (New York: McGraw-Hill Book Co., 1959).

conceived easily—we find that about 83 per cent had already used contraception, another 7 per cent expected to do so, and only about 10 per cent said they would not try any type of family planning. The latter group contains a substantial number of younger couples who have not been married long, some of whom are likely to change their minds after they have three, four, or five children. The experience of the older couples shows numerous additions to the ranks of family planners after the birth of an additional baby. In fact, having an additional child seems to be a strong incentive to the practice of contraception." More than twenty per cent, rather than only six per cent, of the married women in the population are Roman Catholics.

Is Contraception Harmful? In the speech mentioned, De Blanc asserted that contraception is harmful morally and also "psychologically, socially and emotionally." He added that there are even some "weak indications that birth control affects the body physiologically."

In response to De Blanc's statements, William H. Genné, the Congregationalist clergyman who has a comparable position to De Blanc as director of the Department of Family Life for the National Council of Churches (Protestant), asserted: "Contraception can bring beneficial emotional and spiritual effects when morally used. Protestant clergymen at home and abroad have seen not only the debilitating physical and socio-economic effects of haphazard child-bearing, but have also been deeply concerned with the spiritual devastation wrought by fear of bearing children unable to be provided for." Dr. Alan Guttmacher, director of obstetrics and gynecology at Manhattan's Mount Sinai Hospital, noted: "Contraception promotes health rather than illness. A good contraceptive device—the right one found for a particular patient—causes the complete blooming of the emotions during sexual intercourse because of the sense of freedom." The psychoanalyst Lawrence S. Kubie asserted: "There isn't one shred of evidence that birth control is physically or physiologically harmful. If someone is made to feel guilty, on this or any other subject, the internal conflict can of course be disturbing; but that's all." *

COPING WITH INFERTILITY

If a wife does not become pregnant and a child is desired, what can be done about it? About fifteen per cent of American marriages

* "Contraception & Catholics," *Time*, July 4, 1960, p. 38.

are childless. Two-thirds of these couples are estimated to want children. Medical specialists believe they can help one-fifth to one-third of such couples to have at least one child, but specialists who know how to deal with infertility are not easy to locate. The Planned Parenthood Federation has done much to help develop and publicize this specialty, and there is also an active American Society for the Study of Sterility.

Birth control is physiologically a relatively simple problem in contrast with infertility and its treatment. The infertility of husband or wife or both may be due to one or more of hundreds of conditions. If it is due to a relatively simple obstruction in the male or female, the problem may be quickly and easily solved; if it is more complicated, an extensive course of treatments may be required. Both psychotherapy and medical or surgical aid may be needed. Such a recourse as artificial insemination may be advised in a small proportion of the cases. If the source of the semen is to be a man other than the husband, this would be an expedient which both husband and wife would have to understand, consider carefully, and accept or reject in all its psychological, moral, and legal implications. There has been considerable experimentation with artificial ovulation in animals, and this too may become a human possibility. In this arrangement, a woman would carry a donated egg fertilized by either her husband's or a donor's semen. In due course, she would give birth thus to another woman's child. Here again, both husband and wife would have serious psychological, moral, and legal problems with which they would have to cope.

Families which have had children after a fight against infertility are often more closely bound together as a result of their struggle than are more fertile families.

VOLUNTARY AND INVOLUNTARY STERILIZATION

Tubectomy is the term given to the principal modern operation for the sterilization of both men and women. In such an operation, the surgeon removes nothing from the body. He blocks the small tubes that lead from the glands producing male or female cells, the sperm or the ova. The body then absorbs such minute cells, and the sterilized person undergoes no change in appearance and has much the same feelings and desires except that he or she can no longer reproduce. The removal of the fear of pregnancy may make sexual intercourse more enjoyable and may greatly improve the relationship between a husband and wife.

A male tubectomy is called a *vasectomy*. It is done quickly with a local anesthetic. The female tubectomy, called a *salpingectomy*, is compared by surgeons to the simple removal of a quiescent appendix and involves a relatively slight risk. A tubectomy is something quite different from castration. A sterilized man will not develop a soprano voice; a sterilized woman is not fated to grow a beard. Both retain the heterosexual attractions they had.

What conditions make sterilization advisable? Except in rare cases, a tubectomy is an irreversible act, and a physician therefore advises it only as a means of assuring a permanent obstacle to reproduction. For a temporary problem, he would recommend another kind of conception control. Four principal types of condition may point to voluntary sterilization. These are:

1. When a future pregnancy would be hazardous to the mother.
2. When well-defined inheritable defects exist in either husband or wife. These include certain blood conditions, types of blindness, and other abnormalities.
3. When one or both parents are feeble-minded. Even though feeble-mindedness may not be inheritable, a mentally deficient parent cannot recover from his or her affliction and may contribute to making the home a damaging one for the child.
4. When one or both parents are chronically ill. Physical or mental illness may create a condition not necessarily related to physical inheritance in which further childbearing or even any childbearing would be unwise or tragic.

As long as sterilization is voluntary and for relatively pressing medical reasons, it involves little social controversy. Beginning with an Indiana law in 1907, more than half of the states have enacted laws to provide for the performance of sterilization operations at state expense. When such laws specify a procedure for involuntary sterilization, they usually call for a careful review of each case by a state board of medical and other specialists. Appeal to the courts from the decision of such a board is made available. Once both patient and family fully understand the nature of the operation, legal action seldom results. On the contrary, the operation is usually welcomed.

The genocidal sterilization of Jews in Nazi Germany haunts discussions of involuntary sterilization, but involuntary sterilization is not in itself necessarily an instrument of terror and extermination. The opposition of certain religious bodies also beclouds the development of sound policies and procedures for protecting the clearly unfit from parenthood and society from the burden of their offspring. As the burden of the unfit continues to grow, sterilization becomes a more and more indicated type of social prophylaxis. Our laws are far from adequate in this area, and American officials in applying them have demonstrated their avoidance of extremes.

The sterilization operation is now generally regarded not as a sacrifice by the patient but as a protection for the patient and his family and for society. Sterilization operations are ordinarily performed with the consent of either the patient or the patient's family. When the Virginia law was tested before the United States Supreme Court, Justice Oliver Wendell Holmes, in his majority decision, uttered the often-quoted words: "It is better for all the world, if, instead of waiting to execute degenerate offspring for crime or to let them starve for their imbecility, society can prevent those who are manifestly unfit from continuing their kind. The principle that sustains compulsory vaccination is broad enough to cover cutting the Fallopian tubes. . . . Three generations of imbeciles are enough." One need not enter into the problem of the relative influences of heredity and environment in order to recognize and accept the wisdom of the Justice's words.

COITUS AS A SOCIAL ACTIVITY

Sexual relations between husband and wife color all aspects of their lives together. The easing or eliminating of misunderstandings, tensions, repressions, and resistances in their sexual activities may do much to bring a husband and wife closer together and to make other kinds of friction less irritating.

In addition to initiating pregnancy, sexual relations can also bring immediate physical pleasure, a profound sense of closeness and identification, and deep emotional satisfaction. But too often sex relations do not bring these benefits because of anxieties about pregnancy, scruples or inhibitions regarding marital sex play, or the man's impatience to complete the sexual act. Such frustrating attitudes are products of a sex code which is fortunately changing but which still exists and has powerful support. In writing about that code in the 1920's, the sociologist Russell Gordon Smith * told his students:

It renders impossible intelligent sex education, and the ultimate consequences are sexual perversion, insanity, suicide, and marital tragedy. It opposes venereal prophylaxis, and the ravages of syphilis and paresis continue almost unabated. It hinders eugenics and sterilization, and the epileptics and the feeble-minded produce their kind without restraint. It permits barbarous divorce laws, based upon an outworn religious imperative, and the sequel is degraded homes and the geometric increase of human misery. It prohibits birth control, and thereby sentences thousands of women to death or to chronic invalidism, to say nothing of the vast increase in population which makes for lowered standards of living and ultimate disaster. . . .

The current moral code in America, especially as it relates to sex, is a survival of primitive supernaturalism and apostolic bigotry. It is perpetuated by the stupidity of parents, and rigidly maintained by Puritan neurotics . . . It was conceived in the hatred of the Elders for that youthful charm and beauty which they had irrevocably lost, and dedicated to the proposition that the sexual impulse is not only sinful but that, officially, it does not exist at all. . . . [The] moral code in America seeks to thwart and to destroy the strongest human impulse, to degrade below the level of swine the love-life of man. With this code youth can have no compromise. Not until this code is eliminated from human living can we hope for the renaissance of the blessed Hellenic trinity —beauty, laughter, and love.

In the three decades since Smith thus lectured to his Columbia College undergraduates, perceptible changes have taken place in the sex code of the United States. These are chiefly modifications in the code to fit more accurately what had already become common patterns of behavior. As Alfred C. Kinsey and his associates † conclude: "coitus, both before and after marriage, is had primarily because it may satisfy a physiologic need and may serve as a source of pleasure for one or both of the individuals who are involved. No appreciable part of the coitus, either in or out of marriage, is consciously undertaken as a means of effecting reproduction." More

* *Fugitive Papers* (New York: Columbia University Press, 1930), pp. 58–59. Reprinted by permission of the publisher.

† *Sexual Behavior in the Human Female* (Philadelphia: W. B. Saunders Co., 1953), p. 313. Reprinted by permission of the publisher and the Institute for Sex Research, Inc., Indiana University.

and more couples are apparently learning to face this opportunity for intimacy frankly and willingly. They are now able to separate considerations of sexual pleasure from those of reproduction and in doing so to face both more healthily.

In a thoughtful paper on "Sex as Play," the sociologist Nelson N. Foote * offers these insights into marital intimacies:

Even within happy marriage, variations in sexual response are indicative of fluctuations in the level of trust attained between partners. Thus intimacy is not an inheritance but a social-psychological achievement; it is the acme of communication and exposure of self. Every act of human coitus has something of the quality of a drama; it commences with some form of pursuit and may be climaxed by total intimacy, but often is not. By itself, sex cannot substitute for intimacy; at best it then becomes mutual masturbation, a counterfeit currency of interpersonal relations. . . . Though their bearing is still only dimly understood, it is the improvement of specific social conditions to which we must look for explanation of trends in sexual functioning, in the life of the individual and in society at large.

What does coitus mean then as a satisfying social activity in marriage? It means at the outset of such relations a willingness to explore and to yield to exploration, to find artistic and exhilarating techniques of sexual expression, and to make them reciprocal. Ideas of smut and shame are to be left behind. Sex play in marriage should require no explanations and no embarrassments. As such requirements disappear in the growing intimacy of a happy marriage, the couple grows closer and closer together.

CONCLUSION

Now that the death rate has been lowered, the birth rate has become the pressing business of individual families, of nations, and of human society at large. With modern contraceptive procedures providing a basis for the separation of the enjoyment of sex play from the production of offspring, sexual relations can be more relaxed, and society can benefit from the many advantages of voluntary parenthood.

Education for parenthood is becoming more common. Parents

* Chapter 21 in J. Himelhoch and S. F. Fava, eds., *Sexual Behavior in American Society* (New York: W. W. Norton & Co., 1955), p. 242. Reprinted from *Social Problems,* I (April, 1954). Reprinted by permission of the publisher.

of teen-agers and many clergymen and educators now more frequently insist upon adequate sex education and try to help provide it. The evils of sex ignorance become clearer as social scientists and psychiatrists give us more precise and dependable knowledge about our sexual behavior. Actually, sex education is just a start toward education for parenthood. We need quite comprehensive parenthood education for as large a segment of our teen-agers as possible—better still, for all our unmarried.

This chapter has described various birth-control measures. Physicians now learn in most medical colleges that a rubber diaphragm used with a vaginal jelly or cream is the most dependable conception-control method. A physician should fit the diaphragm and specify the appropriate accompanying preparation. Such specialists look upon the so-called "rhythm method" of conception control as undependable, at best a gamble.

The program of the Planned Parenthood Federation of America has included attention to the stimulation of fertility as well as to conception control. It also helps develop research projects, brings research findings to the attention of specialists, and educates sex educators, the unmarried, and married couples.

With relatively simple sterilization procedures available that do not make a person less masculine or feminine in appearance or behavior, those to whom parenthood is hazardous or who are clearly unfit for it now accept the operation more readily. Pressure groups still make it difficult or impossible to sterilize a great many who are far from being marginal cases.

In raising so many significant issues in connection with anticipated parenthood, we need also to remind ourselves that sexual relations are a basic activity throughout married life. A couple owes it to each other as well as to themselves to devote enough time and thought to those relations so that they will be as satisfying as possible down through the years. As the sociologist Nelson N. Foote * notes, "The drama of human development does not end with adolescence; that is only the first act, with a second and third to follow." Those acts include far more than coitus, but coitus when viewed without anxiety and shame can make the drama more intimate and exciting.

* "Family Living as Play," *Marriage and Family Living*, XVII (1955): 296–301; p. 298 quoted.

Chapter XVI

CHILDBIRTH AND CARE
OF THE NEWBORN

Within a few decades, we have markedly reduced the anxiety and the hush-hush so long associated with pregnancy and childbirth. In about forty years (1915–57), maternal deaths connected with pregnancy dropped from 1 in 165 births to 1 in 2,300 births. During this period, the number of live-born babies who failed to survive the first year of life dropped from 1 in 10 to 1 in 40. In the same years, gravid women also ceased to be ashamed to appear in public. Now there are attractive maternity frocks, and their wearers go wherever they wish without embarrassment. The pregnant woman's bulging figure has become a badge of honor. The pregnancies of film stars, of the Queen of England, and of other popular figures may be announced shortly after their onset.

Advances in medical and psychological knowledge have combined with a "new ingredient" in maternity care to make these dramatic and useful changes possible. In describing this new ingredient, Hazel Corbin,* director of the Maternity Center Association notes: "Fathers and mothers learn together what to expect from the first moment of pregnancy until they meet their baby face to face. With this knowledge, there is less anxiety, less discomfort and more—much more—satisfaction. The parents are happier and better able to cooperate with each other and with the doctor and nurse because they understand why. The baby is more contented because he is being cared for by parents who are not tense and unfamiliar with their tasks. The doctor and nurse are more satisfied with their parts in the drama of new life because they work with informed, cooperative people who, with their guidance and help, take a truly active part." The new ingredient described by Miss Corbin should not be overlooked in our admiration for specifically medical contributions. The pioneering activities of the Maternity Center Association under her direction have contributed to this development.

* In her foreword to Ruth Carson's "Having a Baby," *Public Affairs Pamphlet* No. 178 (New York, 1952).

The ramifications of this shift in life conditions and attitudes are tremendous but unclear. Adequate data on this subject are lacking. At this point we shall merely sketch some of the over-all implications of the trend and review briefly the most important of the practices related to childbirth and to the care of the newborn. The topics to be discussed in this chapter will include: (1) the value of medical care, (2) the value of special instruction, (3) stages of pregnancy, (4) "natural" childbirth, (5) parental participation in birth and in neonatal life, (6) multiple births, (7) malformations, (8) infant care and feeding, (9) the financing of childbirth, and (10) the next time.

THE VALUE OF MEDICAL CARE

A missed menstrual period may or may not mean pregnancy, but it is indication enough to warrant a visit to the family physician. Consultation with a specialist in obstetrics offers many advantages because of his experience with both the psychological and the physical aspects of pregnancy and also because of his possible hospital connections. It is wise to use a hospital approved by the American College of Surgeons and the American Medical Association.

In addition to determining whether or not a woman is pregnant, a physician can from the outset perform many other services for an expectant mother. By means of a thorough physical examination of the woman early in her pregnancy (including consideration of her complete health history and the results of blood and urine tests), he can ascertain the stage of gestation and start to study her adjustment to pregnancy before any great changes have taken place. With such information, he can better advise her on diet, physical activities, and any corrective measures needed, and he can also better judge the significance of subsequent developments.

Data for New York City during the year 1955 disclosed that nearly one-half of the women who later gave birth to live children began to receive their physician's prenatal care during the first three months of pregnancy; only one in six either began to receive such care in the last three months or received none at all. During the period 1935 to 1963 for the United States as a whole, the proportions of births attended by physicians changed very little (the proportion was about 7 in 8 births in 1935, and 99 in 100 births in 1963). During the same period, the proportion of births in hospitals rose from a little more than 1 in 3 to 99 in 100. Data obtained by the Health Information

Foundation of the University of Chicago in 1963 disclosed that women in the United States had 10.5 out-of-hospital visits with their physicians (for prenatal care) before each live birth. The Foundation reported (November, 1958): "Recent maternal mortality committee studies indicate that 50 to 90 per cent of the maternal deaths that now occur are associated with 'preventable' factors. As we overcome these factors and reject more forcefully than at present the philosophy of 'irreducible minimums,' risk may be virtually eliminated from childbearing. The lowest maternal mortality rates achieved anywhere today may come to seem ridiculously high, as those of former years seem now." Further gains in medical knowledge and particularly in the application of such knowledge will be required in order to achieve this anticipated reduction in maternal deaths.

What should a woman take up with her physician during pregnancy? In her excellent pamphlet, "Having a Baby," * Ruth Carson advises: "Nothing is too silly or simple to discuss with your doctor. He is busy, but he realizes that your peace of mind is important. Certainly any pain or any change that you do not understand should be reported to him. Pregnancy isn't meant to be painful. Headaches, dizziness, chills—they may just mean you are tired or have a cold coming on. Tell the doctor anyway." Bleeding and a sudden rush of water from the vagina are examples of danger signals indicating that medical attention is immediately needed.

Other than matters of health, perhaps the commonest questions raised by a couple have to do with the probable date of confinement, the sex of the child, and the possibility of a multiple birth. A physician can be fairly precise about the date, granted adequate opportunities to examine the patient from an early stage, but at this time he cannot predict the baby's sex. Folklore is full of sex-indicators, and according to chance about one-half of the time any predictive method may appear to be verified. A scientific indicator would have to do better than fifty-fifty. With the aid of X rays, the physician can find out the number of babies to expect and, what is often more useful, their position, but physicians have become more cautious in their use of X rays because of possible genetic consequences.

If the date of conception is known, one may add 266 days to it and arrive at the approximate date for the confinement. Another procedure is to add seven days to the date on which the last menstrual period started and then subtract three months. Thus, if the

* *Public Affairs Pamphlet* No. 178 (New York, 1952), p. 15.

first procedure is used and conception assumed to have taken place on June 1, delivery about February 22 will be anticipated; if the second procedure is used and the last menstrual period began on May 18, then February 25 would be the predicted date of birth. In the case of a first baby, the child's first felt movement may precede confinement by 22 weeks; for subsequent babies, 24 weeks may elapse between the first feeling of movement and the probable birth date. Note, however, that for a variety of reasons such datings are not very dependable. It is not known precisely how long sperm may remain alive and still be able to join with an ovum. A fetal movement is sometimes easily confused with a sudden internal gas pressure. A physician's calculations should be sought, for they are likely to be much more accurate than the formulas described above.

THE VALUE OF SPECIAL INSTRUCTION

Articles in the better magazines, pamphlets, and books and special classes for expectant mothers and fathers are now widely available and more and more commonly used. Important among publications are the booklets, such as *Prenatal Care,* of the United States Children's Bureau, Washington, D.C.; the pamphlets on many aspects of the subject published by the Public Affairs Committee, 22 East 38 Street, New York 16, N.Y.; and many of the standard high school and college textbooks on marriage and the family.

The Maternity Center Association's program has done much to stimulate the interest and participation of nurses, physicians, educators, and expectant parents in instruction in prenatal care, childbirth, and postnatal care. The Association's pioneering exhibit at the New York World's Fair of 1939–40 of life-sized sculptures that portrayed a baby's development from conception to birth became a popular attraction, even though it evoked as much criticism as had been predicted. During the following decades, the Association's educational program in this field, as in related ones, helped to bring about more realistic attitudes toward reproduction.

STAGES OF PREGNANCY

At the moment when a sperm cell finds and combines with an ovum, the characteristics of the new individual's physical heredity are determined. As these characteristics develop, they are modified by the individual's environment before birth and throughout life. Environment stimulates, impedes, and changes the individual's processes of physical development. During the period of gestation, the fetus undergoes an evolution and growth which are fantastically complicated and rapid, but it is difficult for the mother to realize what is going on until the abdomen is noticeably enlarged and the baby starts to move. Even then it is a long and tiresome wait until the little creature actually appears.

During the waiting period, the following questions often arise.

Should sexual intercourse be continued during pregnancy? Ordinarily no objection is raised to sexual relations during the early months of pregnancy, though gentleness and care are advised. During the last two months of pregnancy, physicians often advise against sexual intercourse. They point out that it may introduce harmful bacteria into the vagina and that it may also precipitate premature birth.

How much does a mother ordinarily gain in weight during pregnancy? Will she lose it again? As a rule, women gain about fifteen pounds as a direct result of pregnancy. About one-half of this is the weight of the fully developed infant, and the rest is due to the bag of water, the placenta, and the enlargement of the uterus. Other weight that women gain during pregnancy may be controlled in part or lost afterward under the guidance of their physician. Self-doctoring and the use of patent medicines for weight control are both hazardous during such a critical period. Each woman differs, and no physician can guarantee to his female patient that she will regain her premarital figure. Some women just have to accept having more substantial proportions, and this may not be nearly so disturbing to their husbands as they might anticipate.

Do the mental and emotional states and experiences of expectant mothers result in birthmarks or other changes, physical or mental, bad or good, in the infant? Normally mother and child have separate blood streams. The nervous systems of mother and child are also separate. Although relationships between mother and fetus are far from being fully understood, there is no scientific basis for the popular belief that birthmarks result from the mother's thoughts, emotions, or experiences. The mother is not likely to be predestining a child for a literary life by reading or for a musical career by listening to symphonies during pregnancy. Her general mental and physical condition may, however, make the infant's earliest environment more or less beneficial. The mother's physical health and nutrition are especially important. If she should have a serious disease, the fetus may suffer drastic ill effects. Severe and lasting glandular disturbances also affect the growing unborn child.

Should the expectant mother radically change her mode of living? Other than taking the prescribed medical precautions and preparing as best she can for motherhood, a gradual transition rather than a drastic change is indicated. For a great many women, the pregnancy period is a time of excellent health. Pregnancy is the greatest adventure of all. In her pamphlet cited above, Ruth Carson * says, "The theme song of all good advice about having a baby is to enjoy yourself. . . . If you can relax and appreciate each phase of it, you will get real pleasure from having a baby." As she admits, this is easier advice to take for the second than for the first child. If girls were given the opportunity to observe the birth of animals and also of human beings, they would feel much less anxious about childbirth—and boys also should have this opportunity. As an excellent substitute for such firsthand observation, motion pictures of childbirth are now available and should be shown for the benefit of young people.

Fortunately the woman who is awaiting her first child is busy preparing the infant's layette—diapers, clothing, and other equipment. (A current fashion note regarding an expected baby's wardrobe is worth mentioning. At one time, the expectant mother felt obliged to be prepared with pink trimmings for a girl and blue for a boy. Now yellow trimmings are being accepted as a bisexual alternative.) Toward the end of pregnancy, the woman also has to have her suitcase ready for the trip to the hospital.

Possibly the greatest anxiety that faces a young father is what in the world he would do if he should be the only person present when the baby suddenly demanded to be delivered. This and other anxieties of the expectant father should be alleviated by information, preferably by the actual observation of persons performing such acts.

"NATURAL" CHILDBIRTH

This expression seems at first glance to be a redundancy. Is not childbirth usually as natural as it can be? The expression is based on the assumption that in a more "natural" or primitive state of human affairs, childbirth was not nearly so painful as it sometimes now is. The obstetrician Grantly Dick Read, in his book *Childbirth*

* *Ibid.*, p. 2.

*without Fear,** advocates utilizing as fully as possible the normal processes of labor with little or no employment of medical relaxants and pain-killers. His application of his techniques to his own patients resulted in the management of an average of almost three in five normal births in relative comfort without drugs for relaxing or pain-relieving.

This method of Read and others might better be called "childbirth with understanding." It consists of providing useful information to physicians and to expectant mothers, of developing techniques for the emotional and muscular conditioning of expectant mothers, and of evolving new delivery-room techniques.

The assumption about the primitive painlessness of childbirth is an oversimplification, but the roles of tension and anxiety in producing severe pains in childbirth are now coming to be recognized and dealt with. As a result of experimentation and advocacy in this field, a great many women now face childbirth with more knowledge and confidence than did their mothers and grandmothers. Of great emotional significance is the fact that they participate consciously in the delivery.

PARENTAL PARTICIPATION IN BIRTH AND IN NEONATAL LIFE

The standardization of birth procedures in our hospitals had gone far and without adequate attention to the psychological needs of mother, father, and child when the naturalism trend got under way just before World War II. The baby was separated from his mother at birth; they got together only at precisely timed feeding hours. Many hospitals discouraged breast-feeding and encouraged bottle-feeding as a more efficient way of dealing with mother and child. The father was kept at as great a distance from mother and child as possible. These evidences of tidy systematization still prevail in most hospitals.

The findings of practicing psychiatrists, especially of the psychoanalytically trained, are just beginning to make themselves felt in maternity ward organization. They emphasize the great gains to be obtained from the participation of both parents in the act of birth and in the early life of the newborn in the hospital as well as later at home. Now some hospitals are seeing the wisdom of permitting

* 2nd ed., rev.; New York: Harper & Bros., 1959.

the father to be present in the delivery room in order to caress and give assurance and security to his wife. This practice also creates another close bond among mother, father, and offspring. A few hospitals permit the infant to be continuously near his mother, to be fondled and fed as needed. The psychiatrist Margaret A. Ribble * claims that breast-feeding "brings 'immunization' against anxiety, and this is even more important than the chemical protection which it is supposed to give the child." Such offsetting of anxiety, it needs to be added, depends not merely upon the act of breast-feeding as such but also upon the rest of the physical and social environment that the mother provides for her infant. Conversely, a mother's anxieties in our anxiety-laden society can be communicated in a great many ways to her newly arrived offspring.

Granted that there are no complications indicating another course of action, the father may now be encouraged to visit his wife and baby often in the hospital and to have opportunities to hold and fondle the infant. His sense of participation and his wife's sense of his participating are thought significant by the specialists responsible for such modifications in current practice.

MULTIPLE BIRTHS

In a little more than one per cent of the deliveries in the United States, the mother gives birth to more than one child. On the average, one human being in 43 or 44 is a twin, but twinning and other multiple births do not occur with similar frequency among all peoples. For example, one in 47 or 48 Americans is a twin; one in 95 confinements resulting in one or more live infants yields a set of twins. American Negroes have five pairs of twins for each four pairs born to a similar group of their white fellow citizens; they are said to have the highest twin birth rate of any civilized group in the world. The Japanese record the lowest rate, about one-sixth lower than that of Americans. In general, the very hot countries have a low twin rate, and the colder lands, such as those populated by Eskimos and Lapps, have a high one.

The commonest type of twinning is fraternal. This type derives from two separate ova which are fertilized at roughly the same time and develop side by side in the mother's elastic womb. Such twins may or may not have the same birthday; a Bengali woman in India

* *The Rights of Infants* (New York: Columbia University Press, 1943), p. 106.

had fraternal twins born 45 days apart. A difference of one or two days in the birth date is not unusual. Fraternal twins may, and frequently do, differ in sex. In some cases, the twins may even have different fathers. The tendency toward fraternal twinning is thought to be inherited solely through the female line. A female fraternal twin has a high chance of producing fraternal twins. Some women have two or more sets of fraternal twins. Three sets are not uncommon. A Sicilian woman earned a place for herself in the annals of obstetrics by giving birth to eleven pairs of fraternal twins in eleven successive years.

About one in four pairs of twins is not fraternal but identical. Such a set derives from one ovum which is fertilized and then is separated into two different but identical eggs. Identical twins are practically duplicates of one another and are always of the same sex. The degree of similarity they exhibit in development is almost uncanny. Occasionally, but quite rarely, the separation is not complete. About once in some ten million births, the two babies are joined together as Siamese twins. They may, in such a case, take the form of a trunk with two heads or possibly with four arms and legs. Such malformed infants ordinarily die before birth or within a few days thereafter.

Other than a female fraternal twin, who are the women most likely to give birth to twins? In confinements of teen-age mothers in the United States, there is about 1 chance in 167 of twins; in confinements of women in their late 30's, about 1 in 59. A married woman between 35 and 39 with a family of eight children is the most likely person to give birth to twins at her next parturition. In declining order, the women next most likely to have twins are those of 35 to 39 with seven, six, five, and fewer children, and then those of 30 to 35 with eight, seven, six, and fewer children. Women outside of the 30–39 age range and those with more than eight children have much less chance of giving birth to twins.

What about triplets, quadruplets, and even larger multiple deliveries? All such births combined are not numerous in the United States—less than one in 10,000 or about 400 sets a year, to judge from recent figures of the United States Public Health Service. Of these, all but a very few are triplets. From none to eight sets of quadruplets with at least one live member are reported as having appeared in each year in recent decades. Larger multiple deliveries are even rarer, no more than one in an occasional year.

MALFORMATIONS

In spite of the extreme complexity of the human reproductive processes, there are relatively few malformed infants. Nevertheless, pregnant women and prospective fathers are often anxious, many times due to sexual guilt feelings, about the possibility of their having an abnormal child. In discussing malformations, the obstetrician Alan F. Guttmacher * points out, "Minor abnormalities of the infant occur approximately once in every sixty births, and abnormalities sufficiently severe to cause the fetus to be stillborn or die shortly after birth occur about once in two hundred and twenty-five deliveries. In this enlightened era, few obstetricians are cruel enough to fan the spark of life in a hapless monster unless sincere religious conviction dictates such a conservative policy." No one can say whether the low rate of malformation can be maintained. For example, it is not clear to what extent the by-products of nuclear fission, by contaminating milk, water, air, and other parts of our environment, may increase malformations and produce other genetic damage. Such matters are currently being investigated; they will require much greater attention than heretofore.

INFANT CARE AND FEEDING

Now, increasingly, families place their newborn baby under the care of a pediatrician shortly after birth. This procedure assures special supervision of care and feeding as well as needed medical attention. Those who cannot pay for a private practitioner can often find similar aid in a pediatric clinic.

For information about details of child care—that is, of clothing, cleanliness, and feeding—the reader is referred to the useful guidebooks already mentioned (see list of titles in the Bibliography for this chapter at the end of the book). What must be noted here is the fact that the infant's early experiences responsible for his growth and development take place within his family circle. He forms therein his prototypical impressions of his mother and father which provide starting points for his views of himself, of other people, and even of human society. Siblings, other peers, and strangers later fill in details and even modify this prototypical world, but the parents or their substitutes provide the first vague yet substantial and

* *Having a Baby* (rev. ed.; New York: New American Library, 1950), p. 55.

significant outlines. (See the more extensive discussion of this topic in Chapters 7 and 8.)

How does one try to make the early learning processes of an infant—his early conditioning with regard to hunger, evacuation, fatigue, and sex—as helpful as they might be? The psychologist Robert R. Sears * concludes: "There is abundant psychiatric evidence to show that improper training, involving serious frustration or the arousal of anxieties or inconsistent over-permissiveness, can create motivational distortions that will prevent a normal and healthy personality development in later childhood and adult years. The consequences of such distortion not infrequently manifest themselves most seriously in the breakdown of interpersonal relations depending on love and the adoption of mature and responsible emotional roles in marriage. On the other hand, effective training leads to secure personalities whose capacities for adjustment to the needs of others is sufficient to ensure wholesome and mutually satisfying relationships throughout life."

Since, as Sears notes, the child "must learn to satisfy his needs in a culturally conforming manner," the best general guidance in parent-child relationships is apparently a compound of these elements: Parents need to know and understand the culture and subcultures in which they live and into relationship with which they have brought their child. Those patterns provide the norms with which their child will probably have to deal and which he will have to assimilate in a more or less discriminating manner. Tolerance, a sense of humor and proportion, and an ability to avoid taking exaggerated intellectual and emotional stances are commended. The world outside the home is tense and full of very real problems. A child who finds reinforcement and security within his home is better equipped to see, understand, and try to cope with the problems outside of it.

THE FINANCING OF CHILDBIRTH

As more and more women have preferred to give birth in a hospital instead of at home, childbirth has become safer, and new ways of financing its costs have been devised. In its surveys of the extent of maternity care in the United States in 1953, 1958, and 1963, the

* "Personality Development in the Family," pp. 215–239 in R. F. Winch and Robert McGinnis, eds., *Marriage and the Family* (New York: Henry Holt and Co., 1953), p. 219 quoted by permission of the author.

Health Information Foundation of the University of Chicago found steady improvement in the use of protective services. In the decade, births occurring in hospitals with a physician in attendance increased from 90 to 99 per cent of the total. The average stay of obstetric patients had declined from a traditional twelve days to 4.7 in 1953, 4.4 in 1958, and 3.7 in 1963. Even though maternity patients account for about one-fifth of hospital admissions, they use only one-seventh to one-eighth of the beds.

Because of the decline in days hospitalized, the costs of childbirth have not increased as much as increasing technology and price levels would suggest. Expenditures for the medical aspects of live births represented a mean gross of $193 in 1953, $272 in 1958, and $316 in 1963. Counting only hospitalized births, the increase in 1953-63 has been from $213 to $316. Of the families involved, 45 per cent in 1953, 55 per cent in 1958, and 58 per cent in 1963 received maternity insurance benefits. For the three years, these benefits amounted respectively to $129, $187, and $236 (53, 58 and 63 per cent of the totals). Considered a little differently, voluntary health insurance benefits amounted to 30 per cent of all payments for live births in 1953, 38 per cent in 1958, and 43 per cent in 1963.

The various forms of health insurance, especially of hospital insurance, are now usually paid for by payroll deductions. This has made the costs of deliveries as well as of other major types of medical care more of a continuing payroll tax than a special expenditure to meet a crisis. Now about three-fifths of all obstetrical patients, as the Health Information Foundation has discovered, are covered by some type of insurance that pays all or part of the various costs. With about three-fourths of Americans—principally employed persons and their families—enrolled in hospitalization plans in the United States, a very large part of the hospital costs for obstetrical care is paid through insurance programs of the Blue Cross and its affiliated agencies. Unfortunately, the underprivileged financially and educationally do not have such insurance so extensively available to them, and they fail to benefit from such services as prenatal examinations and instruction. Future improvements should be focused especially upon these families in this as in so many other aspects of life.

THE NEXT TIME

The great majority of primitive peoples required mothers to regard the period following parturition as a period of uncleanliness, one during which they were taboo and thus were not permitted to engage in sexual relations. Leviticus 12:2–5 states that a woman shall be unclean for forty days after bearing a son and for eighty days after the birth of a daughter. The period ends with a sacrificial atonement ceremony. The situation in modern times is more often considered medically rather than religiously. If all goes well for the mother, physicians will examine her and frequently permit a resumption of coitus as early as six weeks following delivery. This period is thus roughly the same length as the shorter of the two periods mentioned in Leviticus.

When a couple discusses the resumption of sexual relations, they frequently turn again to such questions as the number of children desired and what spacing there should be among them. For women in their twenties, granted good health and the ability of the family to provide for the next child as they would like, physicians often advise an interval of at least two years and of no more than four years. For healthy women in their thirties, the interval between the end of one conception and the beginning of the next one may be shortened to six months, but medical advice regarding the time element should be sought.

CONCLUSION

The nature, availability, and use of medical care in maternity cases have all improved spectacularly during the decades following World War I. The perinatal deaths of infants (those before, during, and just after birth) and deaths of women due to childbirth have both declined to a point where investigators no longer are sure what the "irreducible minimums" in such deaths may eventually turn out to be. Carefully planned programs for the early and continuing care of the mother during pregnancy, at parturition, and after parturition by a trained obstetrician and of the child by a trained pediatrician are being widely recommended and implemented. To supplement available professional services, expectant parents may obtain useful information and guidance from books and pamphlets on childbirth and infancy.

The trend toward "naturalism" in the management of childbirth and in the early care and feeding of children is not so much a reversion to primitive procedures as it is an application of scientific findings. Scientists have pointed out that the bureaucratization of hospital procedures has placed major emphasis on efficiency in the handling of routine matters, rather than upon the whole interrelated physiological, psychic, and social development of the newborn. The phrase "childbirth with understanding" reflects the new attitude which emphasizes the attempt to eliminate both physical pain and unnecessary mental and emotional stress and to help adjust the mother, father, and infant more fully and directly to the processes of parturition. Thus, mothers are encouraged to make use of breast-feeding, and fathers and siblings are given information and advice about their roles in dealing with mother and infant. While enthusiasts have possibly claimed too much for this trend toward naturalism, it is influencing medical practice and hospital organization in useful ways.

Psychologists and sociologists are especially concerned with the neonatal period as one most significant in the reproduction of a family, of social groups, and of mankind.

Chapter XVII

ADOPTION

Many couples seeking to adopt a child encounter in placement agencies and in the courts attitudes which are most difficult for them to accept.

Let us assume that a couple has decided to provide a good home for an unfortunate child. They have come to their decision slowly and painfully. They may have finally realized that they cannot have a child of their own. Perhaps they believe that a child would give their marriage a firmer foundation. Possibly they want a second child so that their first one will not grow up as an only child.

The couple are then shocked to discover during their first contact with a child-placing agency that their offer is not received with overwhelming gratitude. A great many such offers are made, and for a great many reasons. Estimates place the number of couples wishing to adopt children at a figure some ten or twelve times the 127,000 children, more or less, who are legally adopted in this country each year. One in seven American couples is childless. Agencies, in all fairness to the child and to the community, have to concern themselves with finding the pair of adoptive parents most likely to match the child intellectually, emotionally, and socially.

A couple wishing to adopt has usually gone through an emotional struggle of an excruciating sort as they made up their minds to adopt a child rather than to wait longer for pregnancy. They then find that they have a new type of waiting period before them, the period of investigation, both of themselves and of possible adoptive children. They also face heavy odds of not being given a child at all. They may not match an available child. For that matter, they may not be so desirable as adoptive parents as other couples whom the agency already has listed. As a result, they sometimes turn bitterly to "black-market" channels which are often productive of unanticipated difficulties, expenses, and even dangers.

The principal problems connected with adoption are discussed in this chapter under the following headings: What is adoption? What children are available for adoption? What kinds of adoptive parents are sought? How are children placed for adoption? What about nonagency adoptions? What are the advantages of using child-placing agencies? How should an adopted child be treated?

WHAT IS ADOPTION?

Adoption is the process that makes a child legally a member of a family into which he has not been born. It gives him a new set of parents. The child takes the name of his adoptive parents, and in many states he is given a new birth certificate on which the names of his adoptive parents appear.

Until a child is legally adopted, his foster parents cannot perform many legal acts in relation to him which become possible for adoptive parents. For example, they are unable to grant parental permission for such acts of a minor as getting married or joining the armed forces, to the extent that such consent is necessary. They also are ineligible to receive governmental benefits which might arise out of military services of a nonadopted foster child.

WHAT CHILDREN ARE AVAILABLE FOR ADOPTION?

As one would anticipate, many facts regarding adopted children are hidden from inspection and even falsified. We lack the kinds of inspection that would furnish us with comprehensive data on the number and characteristics of children available for adoption, of children actually adopted, of couples seeking to adopt, and of adoptive parents. In the interests of maintaining the citizen's right to privacy, it is just as well that we do not have the kind of inspection necessary for such fact-gathering. For our purposes here, it will suffice to make use of approximations, the best available estimates in the field.

The following descriptive terms have frequently been used in referring to the types of children most frequently available for adoption: (1) the physically defective, (2) the mentally defective, (3) the disturbed, (4) the delinquent, (5) the neglected, (6) the dependent, (7) the ethnically and the racially different, (8) the related, (9) the legitimate, and (10) the illegitimate. These are certainly not labels for exclusive categories; they overlap. One child may represent several such types, and that is why we call them *types*.

1. *The Physically Defective.* The sociologist Francis R. Duffy *
notes, "In theory any child is adoptable if there are adoptive parents
available, willing and able to meet that child's needs in a way that
will compensate him for his handicaps. In practice, however, except
in rare cases, the defective child is unadoptable for lack of enlightened, informed and sympathetic demand." Such children thus generally spend their lives in institutions. Recently, however, there has
been some change in attitude toward them, and, in fact, wise social
workers now take the position that many defectives are not unadoptable. Some couples may regard the adoption of a defective
child as an opportunity for service and for self-fulfillment. They
may, perhaps, have a defective child of their own for whom they
wish a foster sibling with a similar problem. Thus, some physically
defective children are now finding adoptive parents, but usually
such couples must specifically request and insist upon such a child.
In this, as in other cases discussed below, the child bound by ties of
kinship may be adopted, despite his handicap, as a familial and possibly also a religious obligation.

2. *The Mentally Defective.* It is clear that some children are
mentally defective, and hopelessly so, but it is more than probable
that some so-called mental defectives are marginal types. In commenting upon this problem, the social work specialist Leontine
Young † contends that an intelligence test to determine adoptability
may be "valuable as a guide, . . . a menace as a god. . . . Only a
happy and secure baby can give anything like an accurate picture of
his potential development. At best the results can serve only as general indications; yet too often they are used as determinants of
whether or not a child shall have an opportunity for a home and
family of his own." To a degree, getting a child by adoption is, like
getting one by birth, a lottery. In the case of adoption, one can
improve the odds somewhat, but in human affairs there is no such
thing as a sure bet.

3. *The Disturbed.* This term applies chiefly to children old
enough to exhibit symptoms of mental and/or emotional disturbance. Most children who have been abandoned or neglected are
more or less disturbed. Whether or not they are likely to react fa-

* "Adoption—A Social Problem Unsolved," *Marriage and Family Living,* XV
(1953), 292–296.

† *Out of Wedlock* (New York: McGraw-Hill Book Co., 1954), pp. 164–165. Reprinted by permission of the publisher.

vorably to treatment and to loving foster-home care is a decision that requires skilled, intelligent, and objective investigation by well-trained social workers and psychiatrists—investigation of both the child and the prospective parents. This is asking much more than is usually available. Unfortunately, few couples, seeing the child's current symptoms of disturbance, can visualize the desirable, better-adjusted child they might help to develop. The exceptions are usually couples bound to the child by ties of kinship. On the other hand, some disturbances are so deep-set that the child's personality may be twisted hopelessly for many years or for life, even in the most favorable home. Our curative techniques and facilities are far from adequate, and few adoptive parents are competent to co-operate fully in them. Thus, in actual practice, few disturbed children are adopted by couples who are not their kin.

4. *The Delinquent.* Some disturbed children are delinquent. Some delinquents are merely misguided or unguided children with drive and imagination who rebel against intolerable conditions. Some are in search of an identity and autonomy they cannot find through socially acceptable channels. Those who are arrested, brought into juvenile or other courts, and labeled delinquents are usually of deprived background. The more privileged children who do similar things in about the same proportion contribute very few cases to delinquency statistics.* Whether or not carefully selected foster parents could help them, delinquent children are not commonly selected for adoption, but more and more often in recent years they have been placed in foster homes rather than in detention institutions. Too many, however, are still given opportunities to socialize, under restraint, with other delinquents in so-called reformatories which are all too often preparatory schools for future criminal behavior.

5. *The Neglected.* Duffy † describes the neglected child as "one who is suffering privation or positive abuse at the hands of those whose duty it is to see that no undue privation or positive abuse comes his way." Such a child "is usually found under-protected or over-disciplined" and often lacking adequate food, shelter, clothing, and affection. As Duffy continues, "The normal legal procedure is to reprimand or punish the parents and to remove the child from the

---

* A. McC. Lee, "Crime and Conformity," *Fellowship,* XXVI, No. 13 (July 1, 1960), 26–27.

† *Op. cit.*

home. If any hope is given that the parents will correct their behavior and establish a normal home, the child may be returned there under supervision." In such cases, the law does not permit the placing of a child for adoption over the protest of a parent. One or both parents often protest.

6. *The Dependent.* These are the orphaned, the partly orphaned whose remaining parent cannot or will not provide a home, the abandoned, the illegitimate given for adoption or found to be in a hostile environment, the offspring of insane parents, and the child of a broken, unstable, or poverty-stricken family. In other words, "dependent" children are those without the physical and human resources needed for reasonably wholesome development. Most adoptive children are of this type. As we see in "How Are Children Placed for Adoption?" below, the determination of whether or not a child really is legally abandoned may present a difficult legal problem. Public policy, too, usually provides that every effort possible be made to keep family groups together, and public funds are made available for this purpose. As a result, a mother with six or eight children by unspecified fathers sometimes figures in sensational newspaper stories because she is given family-assistance funds in proportion to her fecundity. How social agencies can protect the integrity of family groups worth maintaining and at the same time not subsidize irresponsible breeding is only one of the complicated problems in this area.

7. *The Ethnically and the Racially Different.* The courts and child-placing agencies try to match the ethnic and religious backgrounds and apparent racial characteristics of the child with those of the adoptive parents. A couple with a mixed or unclear religious identity may have difficulty in being accepted as adoptive parents. They may find it necessary to work with an agency under specific religious auspices and to make commitments to meet that agency's requirements. Even though many couples in American society are not affiliated with churches, the courts and agencies almost always assume that a child should have Jewish, Roman Catholic, or Protestant adoptive parents; the choice depends upon available evidence (or often on mere assumptions) concerning his real parents' religious affiliations. Conversely, the ethnic, religious, and racial groups most heavily represented among the underprivileged which furnish the largest numbers of adoptable children provide disproportionately few adoptive parents. Child-placing agencies have even advertised

for foster homes and adoptive parents for Negro and Puerto Rican children. At the same time, there have been long lists of couples awaiting children of other origins. When adoptive parents insist, it is possible to break the ethnic and racial barriers, but the religious ties are jealously guarded by representatives of religious institutions.

8. *The Related.* Approximately two in five petitions for adoption in the United States are filed by stepparents or other relatives. An indeterminate number of other children are placed, through family channels, with friends and acquaintances. These related children may be of almost any type here listed. They are subject to controversy chiefly when religious lines are crossed. A great many petitions by stepparents and others merely seek to legalize a relationship which has already developed between foster parents and a child.

9. *The Legitimate.* Very frequently a child conceived outside of wedlock has been legitimized by the way in which the family physician filled out the birth certificate. By such an act, for example, many a teen-age girl's child has become identified as a belated brother or sister. Of the children legally adopted in the United States, about one-half are believed to have been born of married parents. How many of these are adopted by relatives and how many through other adoptive channels, it is not possible to report. But certainly not all children placed for adoption through agencies are illegitimate.

10. *The Illegitimate.* As Federal Judge L. R. Yankwich asserted in a 1928 California case (*Zipkin* v. *Mozon*), "There are no illegitimate children—only illegitimate parents." Among such cases, as Leontine Young * notes, babies resulting from an incestuous relationship are "not as rare as is popularly presumed." The mother of such an infant is frequently a teen-age girl; her emotional problems are in many ways the most tragic of all and the least accessible to treatment. Often she will talk with no one.

In discussing adoption for children born out of wedlock, Young concludes that it "is in and of itself no magic key. It is an opportunity, the best life chance for both mother and child in the great majority of cases. For the child it is as good and as bad as the kind of adoptive parents selected." She is of the opinion that the three major problems connected with such adoptions "are the timing of surrenders, the validity and meaning of surrenders, and the stand-

* *Op. cit.,* pp. 109, 160–161.

ards of adoptability of the child." Both for adoptive parents and for many unmarried mothers, it is best for the infant to be surrendered as early as possible. If the mother succeeds in meeting and building some rapport with her child, the wrench of separation may become more and more intolerable, in spite of all the difficulties of maintaining a relationship with him. Those in search of a baby to adopt would do well not to forget, however, that there is a shortage of small babies and that many more older children of a desirable sort are available for adoption.

WHAT KINDS OF ADOPTIVE PARENTS ARE SOUGHT?

Adoptive parents are sought who are well-motivated, of a suitable age and emotional stability, of the same sort of religious and racial background as the child, and with adequate and fairly dependable financial resources. Other natural or adopted children in a family may be an advantage; it depends upon their mental and emotional health. Generally speaking, younger parents are sought for the younger children; older parents may adopt the older ones and find the arrangement a happy one. As we note above, some exceptions to this formula take place; the claims of kinship ties are sometimes involved in such exceptions. Especially when an agency finally informs a couple that it has no baby for them, the red tape of formal adoptive procedures through agency channels may seem endless and pointless, perhaps obstructive. When one understands the reasons for carefully establishing the legality of adoptive proceedings and also for finding for each child the best available parents, an unfavorable decision may still hurt just as badly, but it will seem better than facing the hazards that lurk in black-market or gray-market channels (described below).

HOW ARE CHILDREN PLACED FOR ADOPTION?

The United States Children's Bureau once estimated that child-placing agencies are responsible for about one-fourth of the introductions of children to adoptive parents. Another one-fourth the Bureau attributed to arrangements made by parents, friends, relatives, physicians, lawyers, and others. All but another one-tenth of the children, in other words about two-fifths of the total, are adopted by relatives, as we note above. The other one-tenth are placed through friends and relatives with whom the child has lived. Who, then, are the gray-market operators? They are the physicians, lawyers, friends, and relatives who succeed in placing children without reference to agencies and without any thought of personal financial gain. As they view it, they are merely trying to be helpful to all concerned. Who are the black-market operators? They are chiefly lawyers and physicians of a highly unethical sort who traffic in human infants for profit. They operate locally, nationally, and even internationally.

In each state, some appropriate court has jurisdiction over the granting or withholding of a final adoption order. The judge or judges are supposed to be convinced that the interests of the child, of its natural parent or parents if living, and of society are all adequately considered and satisfied. Because court dockets are crowded and many judges lack specialized knowledge, more and more states have set up juvenile and family courts to exercise jurisdiction in such cases. The judges in these courts are expected to be specialists (as some of them are) in the social as well as the legal aspects of adoption.

When an adoption takes place through a professional child-placement agency, its specialists try to minimize the possibilities of legal hitches in the adoptive processes. More than that, they try to maximize the possibilities that the nonlegal aspects of the adoption will also work out as well as can reasonably be expected. Nevertheless, every act of adoption, even after the usual trial period of six months to a year or more, is always and necessarily a gamble.

WHAT ABOUT NONAGENCY ADOPTIONS?

The weaknesses of a gray-market adoption are those inherent in a well-meaning, sentimental act. If everyone involved in the transaction is lucky (or amazingly well-informed), it may work out all right. It can also have some of the disastrous consequences possible in a black-market adoption. A gray-market adoption, without adequate psychiatric, medical, and legal counsel, may be legal, sanctioned by a court, but it can be very unwise.

The evils of a black-market adoption are those which issue from dealing with corrupt members of professions enjoying a high ethical reputation. The so-called "baby brokers" exploit the desperation of unmarried mothers and the longing of would-be adoptive parents. They cash in for whatever the traffic will bear. Prices up to $10,000 for a baby are reliably reported. Often these brokers work as physician-lawyer teams, sometimes aided by nurses and ex-social-workers. The physicians and nurses are likely to work in private hospitals. Some attempt to justify their activities by railing against the rigid procedures of child-placement agencies. News stories of local, national, and even international baby rings, usually centering in New York City and Chicago, appear year after year. Recently, for example, the journalist Homer Bigart reported (in the *New York Times*) testimony before a joint legislative hearing on the bringing of black-market babies to New York City from Chicago, Miami, and Greece. He found that "tentative arrangements for adoption could be made by telephone, without a personal interview." A Greek baby brought $2,800, of which the ring took $1,600 in profits.

WHAT ARE THE ADVANTAGES OF USING CHILD–PLACING AGENCIES?

Some of the advantages have already been mentioned above. The main advantage is that the agencies make their placements for the sake of the best interests of the adoptive child and of society rather than of the natural or the adoptive parents. The agencies seek for the child the kind of family which will apparently best meet his intellectual and emotional needs and fulfill his potentialities. They are interested in making certain that the natural parent or parents have legally relinquished their child and that, after the usual trial period, the adoptive parents will legally adopt that child. These matters involve many subtleties and technicalities, and they are likely to be handled most effectively by the skilled professional staffs of the agencies. The child is thus provided with the best possible opportunity to find a family of his own and to develop into a useful citizen.

There are many reasons a couple might have for wishing to adopt a child that would not be acceptable to an agency entrusted with the child's future. Agencies do not permit a child to be used to satisfy the emotional cravings of a psychoneurotic woman or man, or to patch together a badly damaged marriage. A single man or woman is almost always rejected; the agencies know that the child should have the experience of living with both a father and a mother and that plenty of couples are available.

A large proportion of the adoptive babies were born out of wedlock. What is done to assist their mothers? One defense of the black-market operators for their high fees is that they pay the expenses of the mother and perhaps also give her a "present." The Jewish, Roman Catholic, Protestant, and secular homes for pregnant unmarried women usually adjust their charges—if any—to the financial situation of the woman, and then they do what they can to help her fit herself again into the community.

HOW SHOULD AN ADOPTED CHILD BE TREATED?

Adopted children should be accorded, so far as possible, the same advantages and relationships as the parents' own child. But there are three important questions: (1) What should one tell the adopted child? (2) If he was born out of wedlock, are sexual problems likely to plague him? (3) What should be done if he tries to locate his natural mother or parents? The following answers to these questions have been found helpful and dependable.

What should one tell the adopted child? The consensus is that the parents should tell the child the truth; they should let the fact of adoption be apparent to the child from as early an age as possible and not wait until he starts asking questions. Fascinating accounts of adoption are available for reading to the child (for example, Valentine Wasson's *The Chosen Baby,* published by Lippincott, 1951). The Bibliography for this chapter lists some of the best books for parents on this subject. The *Public Affairs Pamphlet* "You and Your Adopted Child" (No. 274), by Eda J. LeShan, is especially helpful.

Are sexual problems likely to plague the child born out of wedlock? Whether or not a child, as he grows up, learns how to live wisely with the problems of sex depends chiefly upon how his adoptive parents regard sex and educate him concerning sex. There is no more reason for an adopted child to get into sexual scrapes than for a natural-born child—possibly less, because his adopted parents are likely to be all the more conscious of the need for intelligent sex education from early childhood.

What if the adopted child expresses a desire to meet his natural mother or parents? Usually the question ceases to agitate a child when he is assured that his mother or parents gave him up only after convincing themselves that it would be best for him and that they also helped to create a barrier to investigation which is either exceedingly difficult or impossible to pass. When a child persists after such an explanation, it is probably because of problems of adjustment of which his adopted parents and the child himself are not aware. Such persistence is best handled with the aid of a professional counselor in problems of personality adjustment—a psychiatric social worker or a psychiatrist.

CONCLUSION

Those who wish to adopt a child and are able to see the adoptive situation broadly and with tolerant understanding can find emotional fulfillment in the experience. The child they adopt may or may not be a baby. He may turn out to be of the same or of a different ethnic or racial stock from that of the adopting couple. He may be an orphan, the victim of war or revolution, and from a distant land. Couples who fail to be given an adoptive child through regular child-placement-agency channels may find opportunities to adopt if they express a willingness to accept a child from among the less easily placed types mentioned in this chapter. In any event, they should not run the risk of being exploited (and then, probably, disillusioned) through resorting to the gray or black markets. In fact, the so-called scarcity of children for adoption is due mainly to the fact that seven in ten couples seeking to adopt a child are looking for infants who are girls. What about the unadopted children who are neither girls nor infants? Adoptions of older girls and of boys have been among the most striking success stories in adoption records.

Chapter XVIII

THE SINGLE PARENT

To what extent is a single parent likely to be handicapped in trying to serve as both mother and father to a child? Should a single
mother or father remarry primarily in order to create a two-parent
home for the children? How can a parent induce a son or daughter
to accept a new mother or father?

These questions often worry a parent faced with the prospect, or
actuality, of the death of a mate, separation, desertion, or divorce.
Similar questions concern unmarried prospective parents. Both the
unmarried mother and the unmarried father may find themselves
tormented by conflicting desires and by social pressures converging
on their problem of whether or not to marry in order to create a
home for the anticipated offspring.

Single parents are so diverse that it is difficult to generalize about
them. The most special cases are perhaps those of the unmarried
mother and the unmarried father, and we shall consider them first.
We shall then discuss the problems of the broken family—of the lone
mother as a family head, of father-substitutes, of the lone father as a
family head, of mother-substitutes, and of remarriage. We shall give
special attention to the problem of explaining the temporary or permanent absence of the other parent and to the difficulties which may
arise out of a child's visits with his nonresident parent.

THE UNMARRIED MOTHER

Official estimates (1963) numbered total births out of wedlock in
the United States at 259,400, some 6.3 per cent of all births, but such
estimates are considered by well-informed students to be too low.
The actual number is probably at least double the official figure. Of
the some four million live births each year in the United States, possibly one birth in ten may be illegitimate, whether so recorded or not.
Unmarried women who are pregnant include a great many more
than those who become the mothers of the 60,000 or more children

born each year out of wedlock who are legally adopted. Some of these women solve their pregnancy problem by (1) abortion, (2) marriage, or (3) acceptance of the child by a married woman as her own. Public concern focuses chiefly on the women known to be unmarried mothers.

Who are the unmarried mothers? What are they like? In 1963, four in ten of them were under twenty years of age, and seven in ten were under twenty-five. Generally, they were neither the sophisticated nor the delinquent; such girls usually know how to avoid pregnancy, and they do not hesitate to use their knowledge. A great many unmarried girls who became pregnant knew about birth-control methods but for reasons of religious scruples, emotional confusion, or subconscious need did not use their knowledge. In contrast with general opinion, the social-work specialist Leontine Young * concludes from her extensive study of unmarried mothers that they "are by and large representative in their social, economic, and educational backgrounds of the population as a whole." Young contends that such a "girl's wish to have a baby without a husband is neither an adult nor a normal desire. . . . The baby is not desired for himself but as a symbol, as a means to an end. . . . In mistaking an unmarried mother's tremendous drive for a baby for love, we have overlooked the fact that the one invariable trade-mark of all real love is concern for the loved person. An unmarried mother who is bound hand and foot by the iron bonds of her own neurotic needs has little freedom for concern for the needs of the infant she has to bear." In response to the question of why a girl feels impelled to bear a child at such a personal cost, Young replies, "The answer can only be sought in her past life, her home and her childhood."

How can preventive work be done in this field? Two other specialists † advise: "Young people must build up their own controls, but adults have to find ways of making young people think. What do they want out of life? What dilemmas do they face in regard to dating, sex relationships? These are real problems, and young people have to think them through. To do this, they need trust, appropriate guidance and protection—and a minimum of clichés and moralizing." Too many young people feel that they are withheld too

* *Out of Wedlock* (New York: McGraw-Hill Book Co., 1954), pp. 18, 36, 38, 39. Reprinted by permission of the publisher.

† Ruth L. Butcher and M. O. Robinson, "The Unmarried Mother," *Public Affairs Pamphlet* No. 282 (New York, 1959), p. 28.

long from participating in adult activities. Barriers to communication and association between youth and adults grow much higher and more impenetrable in our society than many parents suspect. Such barriers help to promote in the young a feeling of being shut-in and isolated, even unwanted. In their desire to break down this feeling, girls may be driven to sex relationships in order to try to find a sense—however brief—of being needed and wanted, of being close to another person. The possibility that pregnancy may result is a chance to be taken, little considered at the time. Young contends that such girls have a subconscious drive toward pregnancy. Other specialists stress, instead, the girls' ignorance of reproductive processes, coupled with loneliness and desire for acceptance by the other sex; they believe that these are the factors responsible for the initiation of sex relationships, with possible pregnancy given little or no consideration.

What facilities are available for unmarried pregnant women? For reasons of secrecy, as well as to find well-equipped maternity hospitals which will admit unmarried females, such women usually prefer to go to the large cities, often to places remote from their home communities. Each year, about 20,000 of them apply for admission to some 150 maternity centers located in all parts of the United States. The Florence Crittenton Homes Association is a federation of 46 such centers and of two other service agencies. The Salvation Army operates 35 centers. The standards of service developed by these two groups have beneficially influenced such agencies generally in this country. Recently, the Sheltering Arms Service of Philadelphia and Inwood House of New York City have resorted to placing pregnant girls in foster homes or in family boarding homes. When necessary, the agency pays the girl's expenses in whole or in part. Even when the agency pays all the costs, the arrangement is not only less expensive but frequently more constructive mentally and emotionally for the unmarried mother than an institutional maternity home. Voluntary and tax-supported hospitals in one way or another can usually provide free care and aid before and after the delivery period. Community Chests, United Funds, and tax moneys are used for this purpose. According to a 1959 report of the United States Department of Health, Education, and Welfare, children born out of wedlock cost American taxpayers about $210,000,000 a year on the federal, state, and local levels combined. This figure does not include charitable, family, and personal expenditures.

To avoid being exploited and to receive as good care as possible, the unmarried pregnant woman should seek the counsel of a social worker connected with the local council of social agencies or the central family service agency.

Should the girl keep her baby? She should discuss this question from every point of view with professional advisers when she seeks aid through recognized social-work channels. The advisers will usually encourage her to make up her own mind after carefully considering her own future situation and that of her child. Often, the more mature decide that their child would be better off in an established family with two parents and a sense of stability and security from the outset. Those who have the most pressing personal need for a child try to hold on to the baby; these are usually the ones less likely to succeed in the very difficult task of being both mother and father. Now it is common practice for the girl to see and nurse her infant but to give him up as soon as possible. She gains emotional reassurance from seeing and realizing briefly the miracle of motherhood. Commenting upon the decision to give up the child, the two specialists quoted above * assert: "There seems no question but that, with many girls, the making of this decision is a maturing process in itself. A girl who may have considered herself bad—even doomed—can experience elation and tremendously increased self-esteem to know she could decide something so difficult." Thus, the unmarried mother gains a vivid realization of what she has accomplished and of what she is giving to her child. She is given confidence to go on and to make a new, more satisfying adjustment to life.

THE UNMARRIED FATHER

The traditional "solution" for pregnancy out of wedlock in our society is marriage, either voluntary or forced. As we have mentioned in Chapter 12, a great many more marriages are to some degree forced than is popularly admitted. Under these circumstances, even though nontherapeutic abortion is illicit, immoral, and often physically dangerous, it is sometimes used to eliminate the social embarrassment of premature pregnancy for the newly married. Far fewer illegal abortions are performed on the unmarried, perhaps less than one-fifth of such abortions, than one might anticipate.

Unmarried fathers who do not yield to personal or social pressures

* *Ibid.*, p. 22.

or to a sense of personal involvement and obligation are often young and retarded socially and emotionally. To illustrate, in a 1959 study of a boys' gang in a deprived area of Brooklyn, made under the supervision of one of the authors of this book, one young man of nineteen was found to be enjoying high prestige among his fellows because they believed four neighborhood girls currently to be pregnant by him. For religious reasons, all four girls planned to permit their pregnancies to run the full course. Granted that the young man actually was the father in all four cases, no responsible professional person informed about the situation in detail contended that he should marry any of the four girls, a judgment apparently shared by the girls as well. The case is an extreme one, but the male exploitation of sexual notoriety to achieve higher status among male associates is common on a great many social levels. Such behavior is to be found among members of college social fraternities and residents of Ivy League college quadrangles as well as among street gangs and factory workers. Whether or not pregnancy is a suitable reason or excuse for marriage depends upon the individual case. Marriage offers great benefits, but it is scarcely a panacea.

THE SINGLE PARENT: A STATISTICAL SUMMARY

Data of the National Office of Vital Statistics indicate that the lengthening of the American life span is gradually bringing with it larger percentages of unremarried widowed and divorced men and women. As a result, more and more families are coming to be headed by a single parent.

Information for the year 1965 disclosed that because of the longer life span of women there were roughly four widowed women for every widowed man who had not remarried. Women whose current marital status was "divorced" outnumbered men about four to three. Among some 65 million men over 13 years of age in 1965, 3.3 per cent were widowed, 2.2 per cent divorced, 1.6 per cent separated, and 1.2 per cent with wife absent for some other reason. Among more than 71 million women over 13 years of age, 12.5 were widowed, 2.9 per cent divorced, 2.3 per cent separated, 0.3 per cent with husband absent in military service, and 1.4 per cent with husband otherwise absent. Thus, 8.4 per cent of the men and 19.1 per cent of the women were no longer living with their mates and were not remarried. Of the widowed, 96.1 per cent of the men and 94.8 per cent of the women were over 44 years old; this means that there were a little more than four times as many widowed women as men in that older segment of the population. After age 74, 57.1 per cent of the 2.7 million men remaining alive were still married, but only 1 in 5 of the 3.9 million comparable women were so classified; 1 in 3 of the men and 7 in 10 of the women were widowed.

As the foregoing data would lead us to expect, the reports of the National Office of Vital Statistics reveal a gradually rising proportion of female family heads in the age groups beyond 34 years. Of the family heads 30 to 34, females headed in 1965 one-tenth of the families. In the 45–54 age level, they headed one-sixth; in the 65–74 level, one third; and at 75 and more, one-half. Women headed 11.2 million families in 1965, about one-fifth of the 57.3 million total.

A variety of factors complicate the affairs of younger married people, particularly the young wives. For example, data for the year 1965 showed that, whereas only 0.3 per cent of all husbands were absent in military service, the percentage absent for this reason was much higher among husbands of wives in certain age groups: 1.1 per cent of husbands with wives 20–24 years old, 0.6 per cent of those with wives 18 and 19 years old, and 0.5 per cent of the group with wives 25–29 years old. The percentages for other groups were even lower.

EXPLANATIONS OF A PARENT'S ABSENCE

No matter what type of broken home is involved, it is difficult for a parent to explain the situation to himself and even more difficult to explain it to a child. In the case of bereavement, many who are not personally familiar with such situations would think that for an adult, if not for a child, death in itself is all-sufficient as an explanation of absence. Such a notion misses the haunting questions asked by so many generations of men in so many times and places, "Why? Why did my husband [wife] have to die?" It also misses the deeply anxious sense of guilt implied in the further question, "What did I do or leave undone that might have helped?" This question leads often to the lament, "Oh, if only I had tried a little harder to make our life together more pleasant!" The promises of religion are sometimes accepted, but the fact of death is a hard and shocking one. It sometimes makes the surviving spouse question, at least for a time, the wisdom of divine guidance. When a child is told that "God has taken your mother [father] to a better world," his realistic reaction may be quite different from what one might expect. The abduction of a beloved parent by a relatively unknown deity may turn the child for a time bitterly against religion and even undermine his confidence in the surviving parent's judgment. A death within the family has been compared to an amputation. Time is needed to heal the wound and to permit the adaptation of patterns of living to the new situation.

Explanations for the absence of a deserting, separating, or divorcing spouse are often even more difficult. Such explanations may drag the child directly into the conflict between his parents and, if anything, do even more damage to his orientation to them and through them to other human beings. When possible, the child should be spared involvement in the controversy. Extended visits with grandparents or with the family of an aunt or uncle are advisable at such a time, especially for the young child. In the case of an older child, one might as well assume that he knows a great deal more about a souring parental relationship than he has been told directly. Probably the best net impression he can get out of the disruption is that both his parents are fundamentally decent and that they just could not continue to get along together.

THE BROKEN FAMILY

An estimate (1958) based on reports of the National Office of Vital Statistics indicated that six million children, or almost one in ten, live in one-parent homes. In such homes, the children are often confronted not only with the absence of one parent but also many times with the necessity of sharing the other with a job and with social activities outside the home.

For any of numerous reasons, a man or woman may prefer making a home alone for the child rather than seeking another mate. For example, a divorced person's religious convictions may rule out remarriage. If widowed, a parent may not wish to make the additional break with the past that remarriage and the reorganization of the home would represent. Because of her unhappy experiences in her first marriage, a woman may not care to face another possible marital failure; she may not wish to perform the supportive role in relation to a man so often expected in our society. For similar reasons, a man may prefer to hire a housekeeper or send his children to a boarding home or boarding school rather than try again to cope with a woman in a position of wifely power. Such personal reasons for remaining unmarried may prevail among the widowed as well as among the divorced.

The lone mother tends to create a home environment which a son or a daughter may find to be oppressively feminine. The son's succession to some of the responsibilities and even prestige of the "man of the house" can scarcely offset his sense of feminine domination and his lack of an understanding masculine model, competitor, and friend. The daughter may have a brother, but he usually cannot be accepted as more than a sibling competitor; she, too, lacks and needs in her intimate environment paternal affection and a model of adult masculine companionship. If a male relative of the mother—her father, brother, or uncle—is available, he may be able to fill such a void in the child's life. He might be even more helpful to the boy as a guide toward maturity than would a natural father, but the model of parental interaction would still be lacking within the home. A father-substitute other than a relative might be found. He might be a neighbor, teacher, part-time employer, professional man who serves the family, or close personal friend of the mother. With the help of such a person, a lone mother can provide the child with masculine companionship. If the child is a boy, such companionship will steer him away from being a "mama's boy"; if the child is a girl, it can exemplify masculine roles in family life.

The lone father can usually find a maternal substitute more easily, but the results may be much more difficult to foresee than he anticipates. Whether or not he really has found a solution to the problem, he may never know, at least not until too late to repair whatever damage may have been done to his children. Common procedures are to enlist the aid of a mother, aunt, or sister, to employ a motherly housekeeper, or to bundle the offspring off to a boarding school for much of the year. The ties of a mother-substitute may become so close that both she and the child find the relationship deeply satisfactory. In such a situation, the father may become emotionally involved with the mother-substitute and may—if she is single and unrelated to him—marry her. On the other hand, the stories of substitute mothers and stepmothers who resent and persecute their charges represent a real possibility. The resentment and persecution may take very subtle forms which are not recognized by the fathers as such.

THE CHILD'S VISITS WITH THE OTHER PARENT

In discussing the problems of children in broken homes, the sociologist Willard Waller * observes: "Only one type of situation seems to be peculiar to divorce, the situation in which the custody of the child is divided. In many of the cases of divided custody, the parents compete for the love of the child; sometimes they continue the bitter contest of the divorce process into later life and continue to degrade one another in the eyes of the child." Because of the conflict situation out of which divorce ordinarily arises, the child's visits with the other parent have a strained character. They continually remind everyone involved of old mistakes, recriminations, and sufferings. If both parents are married again happily, the potential damage to the child as a result of such visits is reduced to a minimum through demonstrating that a reasonably happy family life is possible for his parents and thus, by example, for him. The sociologist Kingsley Davis † points out, however, that the "child may thus have to divide his life between two radically different milieus, with a resulting confusion in his personality development."

REMARRIAGE

This solution is more likely among the divorced than among the widowed. Analyses of data (1965) about American widows and divorcées showed that there were about five times as many widows as divorcées. Studies indicate that divorcées have about two and one-half times the widows' chances of remarrying. The corresponding data for widowers and divorced men were much the same. This situation is due at least in part to the relative ages of the widowed and the divorced. In 1955, the median age for remarriage by widowed women was 47.5 years, but for the divorced, it was only 31.4. For widowed men, remarriage came at 56.8 years, and for the divorced at 35.7. In 1962, women were 20.2 years old at first marriage and 35.8 at remarriage; men were 23.0 at first marriage and 40.2 at remarriage.

* *The Family* (New York: Dryden Press, 1938), p. 569. Reprinted by permission of the publisher. See also ed. rev. by Reuben Hill (1951), p. 543.

† "Children of Divorce," *Law and Contemporary Problems*, X (1944), 700–710; p. 709 quoted.

The sociologist Jessie Bernard * classifies divorced men and women into four types: (1) the "hard core" of the nonremarrying, consisting of the one-seventh of those divorced who do not remarry within 14 years, "the rejected, the physically or mentally ill, and the suicide-prone"; (2) the "divorce-prone," the one-fifth who will probably be in and out of marriage again; (3) those "lacking in marital aptitude," constituting roughly another one-seventh who will remarry but "whose success in remarriage, for reasons not determined, is below average"; and (4) "those capable of average marital success," a little over one-half of the total divorced.

Thus while a spinster 30 years old has about a 50–50 chance of still getting married, a divorcée at the same age has 94 chances in 100, and a widow has 60 chances in 100. Two-thirds of the men unmarried at 30 years of age will marry, but 96 in 100 of the divorced and 92 in 100 of the widowed men at this age level will remarry. The lower remarriage rate for the widowed woman is usually attributed to her having children; this may make her less interested in remarrying and may make her less attractive as a potential mate. At the age of 45 years, however, the divorcée is still given a 50–50 chance of remarriage to 9 in 100 chances for the single woman and 18 in 100 for the widow. (These odds were worked out some years ago by the Metropolitan Life Insurance Company.)

Popular lore has it that children tend to discourage divorce. The social statistician P. H. Jasobson † notes that the "relative frequency of divorce is greater for families without children than for families with children," but he goes on to say that "the presence of children is not necessarily a deterrent to divorce. It is likely that in most cases both divorce and childlessness result from more fundamental factors in the marital relationship. Moreover, while children may hold some marriages together, in others pregnancy itself and the additional strains involved may disintegrate rather than cement the marriage. It is also probable that some unsuccessful marriages are not legally dissolved until the children have grown up. However, their number is undoubtedly less than is popularly believed in view of the small difference in the divorce rate between the two groups at the later years of marriage." The relative frequency of divorce in 1960 for couples with children under 18 years of age was 56.7 per cent, the

---

* *Remarriage* (New York: Dryden Press, 1956), p. 107.

† In collaboration with Pauline F. Jacobson, *American Marriage and Divorce* (New York: Rinehart & Co., 1959), p. 135.

result of a steady rise from 36.0 per cent in 1940. In terms of the number of children under 18 years of age in a family, the divorce rate drops regularly as the number rises from none to one, two, three, and then four or more.

If a satisfactory remarriage can be arranged, that is the most direct way to assure growing children of intimate association with parents of both sexes. The adjustment between child and new parent is not easy, and it may turn out to be far short of something ideal, but it is well to remember that even natural parents are not always as adequate in their parental roles as they might be. Provided that the lone mother or father does not search out and marry another person with some of the same faults as the first mate or overcompensate by going to the opposite extreme in mate-selection, remarriage can offer a child a great deal more than a home torn by tension or one broken by separation, desertion, divorce, or death.

CONCLUSION

Single parents are a varied lot. On any age level, however, they appear to include more people with emotional and physical problems than are found in that age level as a whole. The widowed are usually older than the divorced and apparently either less able or less willing to start over again with a new partner.

Unmarried parenthood and divorce occur chiefly among people whose parental families did not give them an adequate sense of the affectional values of family life. A great deal more wisdom and considerably enlarged social resources are needed to deal with the problems of broken homes in order that the children of the unmarried and the divorced will not pass on their unhappy heritage. Such a heritage can be changed and is being changed—but not in enough cases.

Chapter XIX

THE POST–CHILD FAMILY

Our lives grow longer. Our health and vigor are improving. Consequently, an individual is more likely than ever before to be a member of a family circle in which there are four, five, or even six generations alive at the same time. This experience develops in him a keen sense of human continuity.

Grandmothers were once pictured as sitting beshawled in quiet decadence by the fire with their trembling fingers busily knitting. Their fussiness and meddling in the affairs of children and grandchildren were proverbial. Grandfathers were depicted as gossipy oldsters who did odd jobs around the house and retold accounts of events long past; they needed much more attention and loving care than they were likely to get. Now such stereotypes scarcely apply to surviving *great*-grandparents.

As a result of the increase in life span and improved health, more and more people tend to think less bitterly about old age and death and to consider more the opportunities of later years of life.

On the subject of old age, the lament of the ancient Roman writer Horace in his *Epistles* expressed a viewpoint which has been widely accepted in many societies, ancient and modern alike: "Waning years steal from us our pleasures one by one; they have already snatched away my jokes, my loves, my revellings, and my play." Today, at least in Western society, old people are convinced that they can replace the vanished pleasures of youth with new jokes, loves, revellings, play, work, and special interests. Death is known to be an inevitable eventuality and its approach, along with possible suffering, is still feared; but many opportunities for concern with life and the living can keep people involved in meaningful events and contributing to the welfare of others and of themselves to the end.

In the home, the birth of the first child and the departure of the last child in order to make his own way in the world usually mark the greatest changes in the domestic life patterns of both wife and husband. From the time of their own birth until their first child is born, they often gradually achieve the series of goals which their society and class group prescribe for them. The newborn then may change their objectives drastically. Even marriage and the organization of their separate home scarcely exerted modifying experiences as sweeping as those associated with a family's first tiny human addition. Until that event, many couples act merely as though they were dating regularly or playing at housekeeping. Then, after fifteen to thirty or more years of centering their family life about the task of physical and social reproduction, they suddenly realize that their "nest" is empty. Women find themselves entering a "third life." Husband and wife may discover that they can return to the former intimate pair relationship—or that they do not care to return to it. They may—and should—start planning realistically for retirement and for activities with which to occupy themselves in retirement.

The end of the daily mothering and fathering of children brings a new freedom from responsibility, but for a great many couples it initiates a critical period. The husband, the wife, or both of them may welcome their new lack of parental responsibility as an opportunity to end the pretense of marital bliss or the continuance of an armed truce. Unless the wife has independent means or job possibilities, she may find it more difficult to break with her husband than it would be for him to leave her. To complicate the wife's situation, she may be tormented by the physiological or emotional effects of the menopause. Both she and her husband may anxiously try to escape the implications or reminders of aging. Each may try to avoid contemplating the diminishing powers and aging appearance of the other. Accustomed to the glorification of youth in our culture, some elderly people brush aside the contention that each period of life can bring with it its own beauty and enjoyments. On the other hand, many couples welcome their freedom from daily parental duties and embark with a sense of release upon plans for personal development and enjoyment deferred during their child-rearing stage.

THE MOTHER'S "THIRD LIFE"

In 1920, less than 17 per cent of all women 45–64 years of age had employment outside their homes, but by 1964, almost 46 per cent had such jobs. This trend created new problems of training, education, and refresher instruction, as well as of domestic reorganization. As the sociologist Daniel Bell * concludes: "[The] return of the older woman to work denotes a new conception of her role. As her life expectancy rises, a woman faces the problem of fruitfully occupying the twenty years or so of life after her children are completely grown. Significantly, perhaps, for the light it casts on the American character, most working women would rather have a job than full leisure." In a study of a representative national sample by the Survey Research Center of the University of Michigan, almost three-fourths of all the working women told interviewers that they wanted to continue to work outside the home even if they should become financially independent. Most of them also stated that they would prefer to continue in the same sort of job. As Bell comments, "Work fills a deep social need for these individuals."

Even though large family conections may no longer make demands upon a woman after her children establish their own homes, she can still do the kinds of work she would traditionally have done for her relatives. She may perform these services for nonrelatives as a nurse, nurse's aid, settlement worker, family-assistance worker, or the like— as an employee or as a volunteer. Commenting on the work of volunteers from the standpoint of his own experience in organizing them, Melvin A. Glasser † says, "Many women whose children are grown find volunteer work an antidote to feelings of emptiness and loneliness." As to the value of the services of volunteers, Glasser states: "Volunteers are particularly essential in our private health and welfare agencies. Without them there would be no organization. There would be no funds. Few services would be performed. Research and experimental projects would be at a standstill. . . . Through a wise use of trained volunteers, the agency can spread its services over wide areas and reach great numbers of people." The Gray Ladies of the American Red Cross perform one of many such valuable volunteer services.

More and more young women are beginning to plan so that they will be prepared to continue or renew their activities outside the home during the post-child period of their lives.

* "The Great Back-to-Work Movement," *Fortune,* July 1956, pp. 90–93, 168, 170, 172; p. 172 quoted.
  † "What Makes a Volunteer?" *Public Affairs Pamphlet* No. 224 (New York, 1955), pp. 5, 8.

WHAT ABOUT THE MENOPAUSE?

In spite of worrisome folk tales to the contrary, menopause is (like menstruation and childbearing) "a natural process in the life history of a healthy woman." The following advice reflects the attitude of modern specialists * regarding the health problems of women: "The majority of women today go through the menopause with little or no distress. . . . When you can accept the need for change as one of the inevitable facts of life, then the menopause will take its rightful place. As a natural event that terminates one productive activity of your life, it sets you free to use your skills, old and new. This, in turn, should strengthen you, your family, and the larger community."

The menopause is the period of final cessation of menstruation, but it does not mark the end of female sexual responsiveness. In their study of 930 cases, the Kinsey investigators † discovered that for almost one-fifth of the women the menopause had begun by age 46; for a little more than one-half, by age 50; for seven-eighths, by age 54; and for all but one in thirty, by age 56. Inquiring about the effect of the menopause on sexual response in 127 cases, these researchers learned that two-fifths of the women discerned no effect on their response and no change in their sexual activity, but about one-half reported decreases in both respects. Some of the cases of decrease are attributed to the women's never having been much interested in sexual relations.

Suggestions as to how a given woman can best adjust to her menopause are obtainable from publications such as the *Public Affairs Pamphlet* quoted above, but the most specific and practical advice can be obtained only from a medical specialist in this field or from another physician. In most cases a quite satisfactory adjustment can be made. With a "third phase of life" to give the woman new interests and involvements, the menopause becomes far less of a physical and mental hurdle than it has traditionally been regarded. Occurring as it usually does at about the same time as the last child leaves home, in most cases it need not interfere with the development of the third-phase interests and activities of the mother. On the contrary, such

* Stella B. Applebaum and Nadina R. Kavinoky, "Understanding Your Menopause," *Public Affairs Pamphlet* No. 243 (New York, 1956), pp. 1, 27.

† A. C. Kinsey and others, *Sexual Behavior in the Human Female* (Philadelphia: W. B. Saunders Co., 1953), pp. 719, 736.

interests and activities help to overcome the possible mental and emotional implications of the menopause.

Surgical sterilization of the female creates a situation similar to that of the menopause. This operation takes many different forms, but its effects "on the sexual behavior of a fully mature female have generally been reported to be minor, or none at all." * If she has had as many children as she and her husband wish, the chief difference between menopause and sterilization is that the latter usually takes place ten to fifteen years earlier.

THE FATHER'S CRITICAL LIFE CHANGES

The departure of the last child from the home frequently alters the father's ways of life as much as the mother's or more. He may find himself much more often the recipient of his wife's concern and attention than he has been for many years, and he may also discover— if he is perceptive enough—that she wants and needs a great deal more attention from him than he has been accustomed to give her. The routines of many years will be broken or greatly modified.

The father's critical life changes are thus (1) domestic and (2) sexual as well as (3) occupational, (4) financial, and (5) intellectual and emotional (affecting his self-confidence as he becomes part of an aging generation). His wife's menopause requires him to show sympathetic understanding and to co-operate in helping her to build a new orientation to their children and to society. His wife needs to realize that, while her own level of sexual responsiveness is likely to remain relatively high after the menopause, that of her husband will continue to decline as it has been declining since his early twenties. The investigations of the Kinsey group † into the differences between the male and female life-curves of sexual responsiveness in terms of its early development in the male and later development in the female indicate "the location of the period of maximum responsiveness for the male in the late teens and early twenties and for the female in the late twenties, the subsequent decline of the male's sexual capacities from that peak into old age, and the maintenance of female responsiveness on something of a level throughout most of her life." Why do men experience this steady decline for such a long period? Kin-

* *Ibid.*, p. 734. Reprinted by permission of the publisher and the Institute for Sex Research, Inc., Indiana University.
† *Ibid.*, p. 759.

sey and his associates * conclude that it is "partly, and perhaps primarily, the result of a general decline in physical and physiologic capacity. It is undoubtedly affected also by psychologic fatigue, a loss of interest in repetition of the same sort of experience, an exhaustion of the possibilities for exploring new techniques, new types of contacts, new situations. . . . Under new situations, their rates materially rise, to drop again, however, within a few months, or in a year or two, to the old level." Women may be impatient with or shocked by the insistent interest of their husband of many years in sexual experimentation beyond practices they regard as proper. Older men are sometimes tempted to find sexual partners other than their habit-bound wife because of the stimulation novel experiences can give them. On the other hand, the continued sexual needs of women in later life when their husbands' attentions diminish bring to many women frustration and neurotic symptoms which are incorrectly attributed to the menopause. Many of them have heightened sexual desires and freer responses once the menopause or surgical sterilization has removed the fear of pregnancy. Both husband and wife need to understand the sexual needs and problems of their mate and to do the best they can to meet them tolerantly and helpfully.

Men ordinarily center more of their time and energy outside the home in gainful occupation than do their wives. Hence retirement from accustomed work among old associates can be a very serious blow to a man's sense of having a hold on life. It is much like the departure of her last child from home for a woman. The presence of so many elderly men in the modern community serves to remind younger men of their future problems, and the younger men are giving more thought to planning not only for their financial future but also for activities that will keep them interested in living and will give them a sense of being self-reliant—activities, moreover, into which they can enter prior to retirement.

INTERESTS OF ELDERLY PEOPLE

The "third lives" of both men and women thus have much in common as well as much that can be complementary. An article in *Time*

---

* *Sexual Behavior in the Human Male* (Philadelphia: W. B. Saunders Co., 1948), pp. 227, 229. Reprinted by permission of the publisher and the Institute for Sex Research, Inc., Indiana University.

magazine (October 20, 1958) * stresses the importance of serious interests during this period: "The one common denominator that sociologists, psychiatrists, gerontologists and geriatricians see in all the actively productive oldsters of this or any other time in history is a keen continuing interest in some activity, which carries with it a revitalizing sense of participation in life. This may be . . . a continuation of earlier activity, but with a switch from administration to policy, or a new career in public service. It may be a former avocation can be turned into a vocation. But 'make-work' hobbies will not do. The oldster, like the human being of any age, must feel that what he is doing is useful, needed and appreciated."

ON BEING AN IN–LAW

Proverbs about in-laws are universal, such as, for example, the old Scottish one, "Happy is she who marries the son of a dead mother," and the Jewish proverb, "A mother-in-law and a daughter-in-law in one house are like two cats in a bag." Too often parents cannot resist the temptation to interfere in the lives of their married children. It is especially difficult for a mother to remember that her child has become an adult.

Parents who have had the wisdom gradually to relinquish controls, to permit and encourage their sons and daughters to learn self-direction and independent judgment, will usually understand the necessity of avoiding involvement in the affairs of their married children. Even under the most wisely planned conditions, the struggle of young couples to work out their own problems freely and to achieve autonomy is difficult. Interference by in-laws usually leaves emotional bruises which require time and maturity to heal. Problems often arise not from what a mother-in-law or father-in-law says or does but from what she or he stands for symbolically in the thoughts and emotions of the son- or daughter-in-law.

The total isolation of parents from their child's family is not suggested. They can be friendly and helpful; they can visit and be visited. When requested, they can do odd jobs of sewing, cooking, baby-sitting, nursing, carpentry, painting, or gardening; but they need to see and understand that their child is a member of a new family unit, with all that that implies. If one or both parents should have to live with a child's family, a policy of noninvolvement in the affairs of the younger family does a great deal to ensure tolerance on

* Courtesy *Time;* copyright Time Inc., 1958.

both sides and the possibility of continuing such a relationship under the same roof in reasonable harmony. A private workroom for the single parent and at least a small private sitting room for a parental couple are conducive to such disengagement.

On their part, adult sons and daughters can help create a good relationship between themselves and their parents and parents-in-law by trying to keep them informed, by contributing and accepting services of a modest sort, and by understanding as fully as possible the gradual modification taking place in the reciprocal roles of parent and child. Aging parents may react to their changed situation more and more like dependent children and require attention from their children or child-substitutes much like that which they once gave to their children.

Both parents and children would do well to avoid what is commonly, and often whiningly, called "self-sacrifice." The self they sacrifice is usually not their own.

ON BEING A GRANDPARENT

Grandparenthood is a status, not a career. When a grandparent—usually a grandmother—tries to turn that status into a career, periodic tensions and crises are likely to follow. Those grandparents who live their own full and interesting lives generally become pleasant companions for their children and grandchildren. They can be valuable friends who are quite different from any others. If they have the wisdom not to try to relive their lives through their grandchildren, they can lend stimulating variety to the family circle. They can listen sympathetically and speak words of reassurance to one and all in times of trouble—but only when such services are needed and requested. They must avoid intrafamilial controversy or intrigue as they would a plague.

Grandparents can give their grandchildren a sense of the continuity of generations which can help them in many ways. They can help grandchildren realize that their parents were once immature and that the path to maturity is not impassable even though it may appear to take a very long time and an awesome amount of effort to traverse.

PROBLEMS OF THE AGED

Among the most critical problems of the aged are those of money and housing. The lack of financial resources handicaps the mental and physical health of elderly people, intensifies their loss of interest in and zest for life (discussed above), and casts a shadow of insecurity over their last years.

The federal social security program has provided modest assistance through its old age and survivors' insurance benefits, supplementing other pension and insurance schemes (see Chapter 5), but the economic condition of the aged remains generally dismal. Most of these people have retired from the labor market and whatever income they might obtain from pensions or investments is usually of the fixed type which shrinks in buying power with the short-term and long-term inflationary trends of the economy. In an attempt to meet this situation, federal social security benefits have been increased slightly—exhibiting more flexibility than most types of insurance. In general, however, the inadequate assets of the aged cannot keep pace with the inflating cost of living.

As one might expect, there is a greater proportion of homeowners among families the head of whose household is sixty-five years old or older than there is in the total population. Statistics (as of 1950) showed that about two-thirds of the families with elderly heads lived in their own homes, often mortgage-free; the other one-third lived in rented quarters. A little more than one-half of all families were homeowners.

In most cases the elderly homeowners possess homes purchased in their youth and therefore designed to accommodate their growing families. Now they must cope with the problems of unused space, maintenance, repair, obsolescence, and diminished market value. Nevertheless, although old people might like to trade a burdensome (and perhaps hazardous) house for a nearby dwelling on one floor with all modern conveniences, the tug of safe, familiar surroundings impels them to remain where they are. For the sake of this feeling of security, this may be a wise decision for those who can maintain their home reasonably well and keep themselves occupied with everyday tasks, hobbies, and absorbing interests. Many a widow or widower has found it possible to retain a treasured home by renting rooms; besides avoiding the need for reorientation in living, this has the additional advantage of providing opportunities to develop contacts with new personalities.

CONCLUSION

More and more people pass through the middle years and, either alone or with their spouse, live to enjoy old age—the period of their "third life." For a woman, this period ordinarily begins with the departure of her youngest child from the home, the onset at about the same time of her menopause, and a feeling of loneliness impelling her to occupy her newly found leisure time with interests outside the home. For a man, the comparable period begins at about the same time; he first notices and reacts to his wife's experiences and shortly thereafter to his own retirement from steady gainful employment. For both husband and wife, problems of sexual adjustment may arise. Surgical sterilization or the menopause apparently has little influence on the sexual responsiveness of women, which generally declines slightly yet remains at a relatively high level throughout life. In contrast, the sexual responsiveness of men tends to decline rather steadily from the early twenties onward, even though it often continues as long as health is good.

Parents who can grow in maturity and who can permit and encourage the growing autonomy of their children usually become good parents-in-law and grandparents. Such parents recognize their children's own family as a separate unit to be treated with respect and friendship.

PART FIVE

FAMILY CRISES

Chapter XX

ILLNESS, DISABILITY, UNEMPLOYMENT, WAR SERVICE

For many individuals and their families, the great changes in human society are largely "off stage." People may learn something from the mass-communication media about what is going on in one country or many, but they often get at best a vague and colored impression which does not touch them personally. Many changes are so vast and complex that at the time of occurrence no one fully understands their nature. Thus the innumerable factors responsible for the spread of a disease or for the cure of a disease, for the ups and downs of the national and the world economy, and for the conflicts and accommodations in international affairs largely transcend individual comprehension.

The ordinary person can grasp vividly only those specific experiences that happen to himself, to a close relation, or to a friend. For this reason, the mass media typically report national and world events in terms of individual experiences—the activities of "big names" and exceptional happenings to ordinary people. People rejoice with those who benefit from social change, but they are not at all clear about how the benefit occurred; they see the individual without reference to his setting. They sympathize with persons who encounter misfortune or injustice, but they rarely relate such ills adequately to great social events or changes. Yet many problems of individuals and of families (illness, disability, unemployment, and war) stem directly from large-scale trends in society.

Commenting on war as one type of social change which profoundly affects every individual, the sociologist Willard Waller * concludes: "The madness of our world usually escapes observation because it is on such a fantastically large scale. Each one of us plays reasonably his part in the great human drama. We are all sane, more or less, but the play which we enact is utterly mad." In discussing more spe-

* "Editor's Introduction," pp. vii–xi in *War in the Twentieth Century* (New York: Dryden Press, 1940); p. vii quoted.

cifically the "senseless butchery" of World War I, Waller illustrates our confused reactions to societal changes by reminding us that "while it was going on we somehow deluded ourselves with the notion that a better world would come of it. How many times we uttered, with the orotund voice considered appropriate for such speeches, the words 'not in vain!'"

TYPES OF PROBLEMS

Certain types of family crisis may arise out of the inability of one or more members of the family (especially the parents) to fulfill their customary roles. This difficulty may appear as a consequence of the following emergency situations: (1) serious physical illness, (2) physical handicap, (3) mental illness or defect, (4) addiction, (5) unemployment, (6) mobility in employment and housing, (7) disaster, (8) war service, and (9) imprisonment. In these emergencies, the afflicted or absent person is usually still considered to be a family member, and even when broken or in process of change the family is, nevertheless, regarded as continuing. When the problem is that of absence from home (the reason may be war, imprisonment, hospitalization, or search for employment), the family looks upon it as temporary even though it may actually turn out to be permanent. Family crises in which the family circle is permanently broken by some form of separation or by death will be discussed in Chapter 21. Note that the preceding list makes a distinction between physical and mental problems, but only for convenience in discussion. The physical and mental factors are of course intertwined in human behavior.

GROUP DIFFERENCES

Before discussing the major types of crises listed above, we should consider the factor of group differences. Sex, occupational, ethnic, and geographical groups experience these crises in varying degrees. For example, women are ill more often than men. Sedentary employees differ from workers performing physical labor in regard to their patterns of illness and accidents, frequency and extent of unemployment, and permanence of residence. Negroes and other underprivileged minorities face too often the injustice of being "last hired, first fired." Law violations among the more deprived and less educated groups more often result in imprisonment than do the more subtle and better-disguised depredations of middle-class and upper-class individuals.

As explained in our discussion of the welfare roles of families (Chapter 5), there are striking group differences in reactions to family crises. With the close interfamilial ties and sense of neighborly responsibility common in rural areas and small towns, a crisis in one family tends to bring other families closer. For example, the person who goes to prison or is known to have a venereal disease is sharply rejected in most cases, but personal aid and sympathy are often given to his family. In the more anonymous life of larger urban centers, ethnic and religious associations sometimes succeed in maintaining neighborly relations resembling those in a small community, but ordinarily it is left for the professional workers in governmental and voluntary agencies to show social concern for the unfortunate. This urban approach has the advantage of applying greater technical competence to a problem but at the cost of personal warmth and of a sense of community identification. In both the urban and rural areas, the lack of medical and hospital facilities for colored and other underprivileged groups is a matter of concern to leaders in social reform.

SERIOUS PHYSICAL ILLNESS

We have learned how to cope more and more effectively with the so-called mass diseases, the bacterial, viral, and nutritional diseases which are common in societies of scarcity. In our society of abundance, although epidemics of influenza and poliomyelitis have struck, medical researchers and practitioners have learned to cope with these diseases, and tuberculosis has declined sharply. If we could locate all the cases, syphilis would be eliminated. Major health problems in this country now consist of the degenerative diseases of old age (as a result of the constantly greater longevity of the population) and of the diseases arising from stress, strain, and anxiety. These two types of diseases are characteristic of a "fat" industrialized society of abundance.

On the average throughout the year, about one-seventh of the population is classifiable as incapacitated to some degree by illness. The estimated proportion is indefinite because the conceptions of what constitute illness and incapacitation are necessarily fuzzy. Significantly enough, the infectious and nutritional diseases for which preventive and remedial measures are available afflict our underprivileged people much more heavily than the upper strata, whereas the incidence of degenerative illnesses varies to a much less extent with social-class differences.

Two thirds of Americans of all ages in 1963 were found by the Health Information Foundation of the University of Chicago to visit a physician at least once a year, but the figure varies with age, sex, and social-class group. It was highest for those under six years of age and lowest for those six to seventeen. The mean number of visits to physicians per person a year was four for males and five for females.

Women have more disabling illnesses at all ages beyond ten years than do men. In 1964, the following figures for illness were compiled by the National Center for Health Statistics: restricted-activity days per person, male 14.5, female, 17.8; bed-disability days, male 5.3, female 6.8; work-loss days, male 5.6, female 5.3; school-loss days, 4.9 male, 5.1 female. Women apparently take better care of themselves; in other words, they are less likely to "go out anyway" when ill. Men are subject to illnesses and injuries which are more likely to be fatal. Thus, according to the report, a larger proportion of men than women died as a result of accidents, heart disease, pneumonia, cancer, and vascular lesions affecting the central nervous system.

Some evidence exists that women are biologically the more durable sex, but this difference is probably due in part to environmental factors and mode of living. The Health Information Foundation has stated (December, 1957): "[The] higher mortality differentials by sex in the larger cities and in the upper occupational groups suggest that certain modes of living may place an unequal stress on males. Perhaps men more than women are subject to internal stress, with a consequent higher incidence of coronary artery disease and ulcers. Exercise or lack of it, smoking, changing dietary habits, the propensity of women to take greater advantage of medical facilities—all these have been suggested as possibly related factors. But whatever the reasons, it would be well to concentrate medical research upon this problem before American males—especially those at age 45 and beyond—become in effect an underprivileged segment of the population."

As the public has sought to benefit from recent advances in medical knowledge and facilities, the percentage of family income expended on medical care has increased markedly. In 1929, the cost of medical care in the United States amounted to 3.7 cents in each dollar of national expenditures on consumer goods. In 1960-61 the total, as reported by the U. S. Department of Labor, had amounted to 6.7 cents for whites and 4.8 cents for Negroes. The Health Information Foundation learned that family expenditures for health came to 4.6 per cent of average family income in 1953, 5.6 per cent in 1958, and 5.5 per cent in 1963.

Medical advances and increased expenditures on remedial measures have shown how we can deal with the so-called "social diseases," which have created special problems in human relations through recorded history. Venereal disease is usually thought of as including syphilis and gonorrhea, though there are at least three other venereal diseases of some significance. All varieties of venereal disease: (1) are due to microorganisms introduced into the body; (2) are transmitted in most cases through sexual intercourse and practically never without direct contact with an infected person; and (3) are found, so far as is known, only in human beings.

Recent methods of treatment, control, and education have reduced the incidence of venereal disease in the United States to a new low; but the struggle against syphilis and gonorrhea is not over, despite the fact that from 1938 to 1964 the venereal disease death rate declined from about 16 to 1.4 per 100,000 of the population (whites 1.1, nonwhites 3.2; males 1.9, females 0.8). The Health Information Foundation issued a warning (November 1959) : "The very successes recently achieved threaten to lull the public into a false sense of security about the future course of these diseases. Today, even though successful treatment is available, it is generally agreed that control measures, designed to bring in all cases for treatment, are far from adequate. Case reservoirs of unknown size still exist in this country, and reported incidences of the two [principal] diseases are no longer declining." Special problem groups are migratory agricultural workers (interstate and international), military personnel, American Indians on reservations, and homosexuals. Specialists in social investigation are co-operating with public health experts in the development of more effective ways to discover cases for treatment and to encourage people to seek examination and care.

PHYSICAL HANDICAP

The average number of Americans incapacitated for all reasons totals about 8 million individuals. This is a very broad and varied group. Of the total, about 5 million or 1 in each 36 of the population have disabilities lasting six or more months. The whole group includes the crippled, blind, deaf, palsied, and other unfortunates who require a very large share of the medical, nursing, and social-work attention of the country. Two million of those with disabilities lasting six months or more are 65 years and over; these comprise about one-sixth of the total population in the "old-age" category. Surveys report some 2 million of the physically handicapped to be gainfully employed; about 275 to 300 thousand of the disabled are initiated into such employment each year, and it is estimated that another 2 million physically handicapped persons await such rehabilitation. Out of more than 5 million with continuing handicaps, more than one-fifth are being treated in hospitals or other institutions.

Whether or not more of the handicapped will be rehabilitated depends in large part upon the speed with which our welfare agencies learn to utilize more effectively and more extensively the aid of related and adoptive families and to convince employers that handicapped employees can do tasks for which they are fitted as well and as dependably as the unhandicapped.

Two types of program for meeting the social problems of the disabled are followed by agencies in this field. One is segregative, and the other, assimilative. The former program calls for special schools or special classes, for working arrangements whereby people with similar defects are brought together, and for attempts to encourage men and women similarly afflicted to socialize and even, in some cases, to marry each other. The assimilative approach recognizes the problems arising out of the tendency of similarly handicapped people to create for themselves a tight little social world separated from the rest of society. Agencies using this approach try to bring about as frequent and as normal relations as possible of the handicapped with the nonhandicapped. Perhaps the best approach is somewhat of a compromise between these two extremes, adapted with wisdom to the needs of the individual case.

MENTAL ILLNESS OR DEFECT

A total of 9 million Americans, or about 1 in 20, suffer from emotional or other personality disturbances or defects. Of these, about 1.5 million are classified as mentally ill, and an equal number as mentally deficient. At any one time, about 1.2 in 200 Americans or some 1.1 millions are undergoing long-term hospital care for treatment of their mental problems.

Mental illness is a vague label for all those who exhibit symptoms which bring them for aid to psychiatric specialists or which take such forms as detected criminal behavior, alcoholism, and narcotic addiction.

The magnitude of the problem of emotional disorder and mental defect and deficiency is further indicated by the statistics for rejections and separations of men examined for military service in World War II. Of 18 million men examined, 970 thousand, or more than 1 in 20, were rejected for "emotional disorder," and another 716 thousand, or 1 in 25, for "mental or educational deficiency." Of 2.5 million army male personnel separated from the service in 1942–45 for reasons other than demobilization, about 1 in 8 were certified as psychiatric cases, but other categories, such as "inaptitude," may have included many with emotional problems.

Responsible estimates indicate that, while a great deal more research in this area is urgently needed, we are now probably applying not more than a small fraction of current psychiatric knowledge to the mentally ill in hospitals, and those outside the hospitals probably benefit even less from such knowledge. More psychiatrists and more counselors and workers of other types with psychiatric training, such as psychiatric social workers and nurses and psychiatrically informed clergymen, are needed to narrow the gap between what is known and what is applied. Chemotherapy is opening up new and promising possibilities for more effective and less costly treatment, especially with certain of the new tranquilizers, but it is not yet emptying the hospitals. On the contrary, a growing understanding and acceptance of psychiatry constantly brings forward more people who need psychiatric attention, and the complexities of our society and the disturbing by-products of modern living are making ever greater numbers become aware of their personal inadequacies.

Wisely or unwisely as the case may be, many a family feels itself compelled to orient much of its household activity around the mental or emotional problems of one or more of its members. A group of psychiatrists * contend that in their professional experience they have found it wise "to treat the patient and the family as a totalized unit."

* P. Lefebvre, J. Atkins, J. Duckman, and A. Gralnick, "The Role of the Relative in a Psychotherapeutic Program," *Canadian Psychiatric Association Journal*, III (1958), 110–118; p. 110 quoted.

They advocate, therefore, "a therapeutic approach which seeks the family's useful participation and collaboration." Whenever such a co-operative approach is possible without distorting further the lives of growing children or helping to create additional mental and emotional problems, it can be useful. On the other hand, sometimes a great deal can be gained by breaking the situational pattern to which a patient and his family have habituated themselves and thereby helping them to gain a fresh perspective upon themselves and their problems. The merits of leaving or not leaving a disturbed person in a given family situation or of transferring him elsewhere require careful study, analysis, and counsel by a professionally competent person.

ADDICTION

Some 68 million Americans—40 million men and 28 million women—drink some form of alcoholic beverage with a degree of regularity. More than four million are said to have one or more of the disorders called "alcoholism" to such an extent that they are disabled physically, socially, or economically. Among alcoholics, there are reported to be one woman to five or six men. About one-fourth of all alcoholics are ones "with complications," in other words, "those who exhibit a diagnosable physical or psychological change due to prolonged excessive drinking." * Another sixty thousand or more are addicted to narcotics. Thus at least four million Americans cast heavy shadows of addiction to alcohol or narcotics across their families and their own lives. Fortunately, fewer people now try to handle relatives and friends addicted to alcohol or narcotics by means of biting personal recriminations. Constantly more people are coming to realize that such deep-set psychosomatic problems can be approached only by more objective and constructive methods.

The relations between an alcoholic and his family are complicated and reciprocal. In terms reminiscent of the co-operative approach to other mental and emotional problems, the sociologist Joan K. Jackson † concludes: "It is now believed that the most successful treatment of alcoholism involves helping both the alcoholic and those members of his family who are directly involved in his drinking be-

---

* Mark Keller, "Alcoholism," *The Annals,* CCCXV (January, 1958), pp. 1–11; p. 5 quoted by permission of The American Academy of Political and Social Science.

† "Alcoholism and the Family," *ibid.,* pp. 90–98; pp. 91, 98 quoted by permission of The American Academy of Political and Social Science.

havior." She continues: "Most families have little awareness of what treatment involves and are forced to rely on the alcoholic patient for their information. The patient frequently passes on a distorted picture in order to manipulate the family situation for his own ends. What information is given is perceived by the family against a background of their attitudes towards the alcoholic at that point in time. The actions they take are also influenced by their estimate of the probability that treatment will be successful. The result is often a family which works at cross purposes with therapy." Under the leadership of the organization Alcoholics Anonymous (described below) and of certain clinics, the combined treatment of alcoholics and their families is growing and revealing useful possibilities.

A highly significant program to cope with alcoholism has been carried on by the voluntary organization called Alcoholics Anonymous (A.A.). Formed in 1934–35, this movement has grown to more than 7,000 groups with some 200,000 members. The guiding principles of A.A. are: to admit being addicted to alcohol and powerless to cope alone with the problem; to have belief in "a Power greater than ourselves" which can "restore us to sanity"; to use prayer and self-help; to confide freely with other alcoholics; to abstain totally from alcohol; and to help others who have an alcohol problem. These principles are spelled out in A.A.'s famous "twelve steps." No one knows how many people of all sorts A.A. has helped, but observers agree that it is a substantial and constructive supplement to the more formal psychiatric efforts dealing with alcoholism. A.A. includes many influential and articulate people whose pressure has helped to expand and improve psychiatric care and research.

One of the principal differences between alcoholism and addiction to narcotics is that the selling of narcotics is illegal, largely in the hands of racketeers who exploit the addicts they supply. Eventually the community may adopt the sensible way to cope with this problem, that of placing the distribution of narcotic drugs in the hands of trained personnel who would assure all certified addicts of a cheap and dependable supply. This procedure would help to reduce narcotic addiction in several ways. It would undercut the commercial recruitment of addicts by unprincipled dope-runners and peddlers. Moreover, it would give addicts a feeling of being helped, rather than only threatened with persecution and punishment, by government agents. This would make it easier to obtain the co-operation of addicts in coping with their problem. Like the varied types of alcoholism, the numerous kinds of narcotic addiction are afflictions which an addict can learn to combat, but he can scarcely anticipate a cure. He can learn how to live with his problem and how to minimize it. Narcotics Anonymous, organized in 1950 and patterned after Alcoholics Anonymous, is proving helpful in this direction.

UNEMPLOYMENT

Unemployment comes about in many ways in our society and varies widely in amount and duration from year to year, region to region, and type to type of employment. Strikes, technological changes, business failures, marketing problems, and business ups and downs of a seasonal and so-called cyclical nature all can throw employees out of work locally or in larger areas. The welfare legislation which grew out of the depression of the 1930's divides the burden of unemployment between the unemployed and governmental agencies, but a great many families still face crises or chronic poverty through drastic changes in the employment situation.

The rapid development of machines for all sorts of manufacturing, agricultural, distributive, financial, communicational, and even educational purposes suggests that in the future the automation of American life may far outrun anything we have yet seen. What this will do to the redistribution of employment and earnings cannot be foreseen. One's analysis of the problem may depend to a large extent upon the values and units of our society to which one gives most attention. For example, social economists * often contend that mechanization and increasing productivity need not "cause increasing unemployment in the working force as a whole. For a worker is never displaced by a machine; he is displaced by other workers who build, maintain, and operate a machine. If production costs are reduced— and this is generally the motivation for the innovation—prices to consumers may be reduced and profits increased, thus tending to increase demand for other consumer and investment goods throughout the economy."

The point that such optimistic generalizations gloss over is that male and female workers and their families are not constituents in some automatically adjusting fluid. They are specific people. They have habitual skills and attitudes toward work and life. Their small

* A. J. Jaffe and C. D. Stewart, *Manpower Resources and Utilization* (New York: John Wiley & Sons, 1951), p. 267.

assets are tied up in homes which can be worth little or nothing after their factory or market is automated out of usefulness or even existence. They have little sense of security, and they often have no one to whom to turn for aid and guidance in their possible readaptation to changed conditions. Statistics may reveal over-all gains in employment, but for individuals technological change may mean permanent unemployment.

When trade unions fight to maintain "feather-bedding" or make-work jobs, they are attempting to diminish the cost to workers of technological change. Both employers and union leaders too often struggle for static conceptions of gain or protection rather than for means to help their constituencies adapt to continuing processes of social change in ways involving less chance of personal disaster.

MOBILITY IN EMPLOYMENT AND HOUSING

Many have speculated about how far the "trailerization" of our society is likely to proceed and about the nature of its consequences. (How many Americans actually *inhabit* trailers for part or all of the year, we do not know, but reliable estimates place them at three and one-half millions.) The increasing use of trailers resulted from the housing shortage during World War II. A trailer is often less expensive than a house, and it has the advantage of keeping the shelter part of a family's assets mobile if not liquid. The trailer camps on the edge of many communities pose problems of sanitation, health, education, and policing—for the costs of which the owners of trailers or their employers do not provide sufficient municipal taxes. Trailer-dwellers seldom have local ties or community responsibilities. When they are confronted with some local irritation, they always have the open road before them to follow to another trailer camp and job.

According to the United States Bureau of the Census, about one in five families change each year from one dwelling unit to another. The average worker lives in about eight different dwelling units during his working career. Moving to a new location may result from considerations such as itchy feet, an opportunity for self-improvement, or compliance with an employer's request.

The mobility of the numerous technologists and managers in the employ of large corporations appears to be increasing with the continuing expansion of these vast enterprises. These people are frequently assured by the corporation of a market for their home in the event that they have to move at the request of the organization. Such mobility destroys the sense of belonging to a geographical community which an employee, his wife, and his children might otherwise possess, and apparently replaces it with a sense of belonging to a corporation community or to a scattered social-class community of mechanical engineers, advertising copywriters, salesmen, medical specialists, lawyers, factory managers, or some other vocational group.

DISASTER

Floods and tidal waves, fires, explosions, earthquakes, hurricanes, epidemics, riots, and a great many other types of disaster disrupt families suddenly and often violently. Lives may be lost, and homes and other assets be destroyed. The Red Cross and other voluntary and governmental agencies help, but the main burden is always upon the families most directly involved.

Families living in river valleys or in hurricane or tornado country, families with members employed as coal miners or in connection with dangerous manufacturing processes, and families with memories of relatives or close friends struck down by disaster try to prepare themselves as best they can for "whatever may come." Recent efforts to fan concern about possible atomic bomb attacks are met in part with complacency or a sense of futility. Today we expect to receive disaster warnings from agencies operating an extensive system of fact-gathering and scientific analysis, but disasters usually strike not only suddenly and unexpectedly but also with novel variations and problems.

The disasters commonly referred to as "accidents" take the lives of almost a hundred thousand Americans each year. All types of accidental injuries together number, according to the National Safety Council, almost ten million a year. The greatest problem areas for accidents are street traffic and the home. More than four in ten accidental deaths involve motor vehicles, and about three in ten are in the home. Even though the number of accidents per unit of miles driven has been declining for three decades, the total number of traffic accidents tends to increase because of the rising number of miles being driven. A bright spot in the accident situation is the fact that on-the-job or "work" accidents have declined in recent years. More and more business organizations are learning that they can introduce a greater degree of safety into their operations. The workmen's compensation laws, the educational work of the insurance companies, the development of safety engineering, and the campaigns of agencies such as the National Safety Council have all contributed to this improvement.

Not so bright is the accident situation within the home. As indicated above, the rate of incidence within the home remains at a very high level. Moreover, serious defects in home background are reflected in the fact that more than one in four drivers in fatal traffic accidents are between eighteen and twenty-four years of age, and almost one in four fatal accidents involve a driver or a pedestrian under the influence of alcohol.

WAR SERVICE

The main consequences of war are destructive for the individual, for the family, for the nation, and for the world community. Millions of families are broken or gravely handicapped by wartime and postwar disruption of lives, economic affairs, and moral values. On the other hand, millions of people seize upon participation in war as a socially sanctioned way to solve temporarily or permanently some personal problem. Wars offer a temporary divorce, a temporary flight from vocational boredom or failure, a temporary vacation from responsibilities of all kinds, or simply a cloak for suicide.

The 165 "lost" divisions of the United States in World War II who were separated from the services for medical or psychological reasons focus attention once again on the age-long contrast between constructive and destructive social policies. Why did so many Americans presumably "fail?" Was it failure of American families and homes? The authors * of a comprehensive study of the 2.5 million men in the "lost" divisions conclude: "There is no way of calculating how many soldiers, resenting the fact that the Army was unable to be equitable simply refused, consciously or unconsciously, to continue in a combat assignment. A man's willingness to sacrifice depends on his faith in the integrity of the organization to which he belongs." Many men "who had been brought up in a strict religious community and who, until their induction, had lived according to their beliefs . . .

---

* Eli Ginzberg and others, *The Ineffective Soldier*, 3 vols. (New York: Columbia University Press, 1959). Vol. I, *The Lost Divisions*, p. 200; Vol. II, *Breakdown and Recovery*, pp. 112–113, 275; Vol. III, *Patterns of Performance*, p. 5. Reprinted by permission of the publisher.

experienced emotional conflicts in the Army which finally prevented them from performing effectively." To this the investigators add: "Even a brave and patriotic man can be broken by the agonies of combat. . . . Even if he breaks down, he is likely to recover if he is aided by a loving family, a sympathetic government, and there is a place for him in an expanding economy." As much has often been said of juvenile delinquents and criminals. They, too, can often function well in a sane society.

The authors of this study note that certain clergymen "found a direct connection between the decline in religious training of youth and the unwillingness of many soldiers to endure hardships when their country was in danger." This point of view is not uncommon; yet it seems strange to blame lack of religious training for reluctance to kill one's enemies. One may well ask, what clergymen accept this point of view and to what kind of "religious" training is reference made? Other leaders, the authors contend, "pointed to the hidden toll resulting from the inroads of pacifism which had swept the country after World War I—if the waging of war is pronounced by many leaders to be totally unjustified, young people will not rush to the colors when their country is attacked." In the military frame of reference, the teachings of such pacifists as Jesus are a perennial problem. Mothers and fathers, preoccupied with raising sons and daughters who will be useful citizens in a peaceful society, rarely wish to prepare their children as well for an aggressive role in battle.*

IMPRISONMENT

When a man or woman is imprisoned, the imprisonment is symptomatic—like so many problems we have been discussing—of a deep-set family problem or pattern of problems. It is symptomatic, among other things, of a family situation in which obeying the law is not regarded as a practicable virtue. Furthermore, compared with typical families of the general population, the families of delinquents and criminals are more likely to be broken families, to include other members apprehended for law-breaking, and to exhibit low education, poor economic status, and high mobility.

A little more than one American in each thousand is in prison, federal or state, at any one time. A program of social therapy for

* A. McC. Lee, "They Failed as Killers," *Fellowship*, XXV, No. 17 (September 1, 1959), 12–13.

the families of prisoners, backed with adequate personnel and other resources, might help to assure the community that such families will not continue to produce as many candidates for imprisonment. Such social therapy can be of many different sorts and should be prescribed only after social workers have made an adequate study of the family and community situation. The obstacles in the way of such an effort are suggested by the criminologists E. H. Sutherland and D. R. Cressey * thus: "During a period when rather strict discipline is the fad in child rearing, homes without such discipline are likely to be designated as delinquency-producing; but when permissiveness is the fad in child rearing, then the homes using strict discipline are likely to be so designated." Efforts to deal with criminals and their families are handicapped by the fact that criminological generalizations tend to be based upon the small percentage of delinquents and criminals who are actually convicted.

CONCLUSION

Such family crises as illness, disablement, unemployment, and war service are rightly considered, for the purposes of diagnosis, both as symptomatic of vast social changes and in their more particular interpersonal contexts. Many of these crises would be far less burdensome to the groups they especially afflict were it not that social-class groups in our society experience many such problems with unequal frequency. The more powerful policy-making groups have had greater attention given to their pressing problems both by voluntary and governmental agencies. Actually we all pay for such problems, among whomever they exist, even though we cannot always understand the ways in which payments are exacted of us. We lose especially through the impairment of millions of families as reproductive units through physical or mental illness or defect, addiction to alcohol or narcotics, unemployment, disaster, war service, and imprisonment. We may never be able to eliminate such problems, but we can learn through research and experimentation to understand them and to understand how to minimize a great deal more than we have both their incidence and their costs.

* *Principles of Criminology* (7th ed., Philadelphia: J. B. Lippincott Co., 1966), p. 174.

Chapter XXI

SEPARATION, ANNULMENT, DESERTION, DIVORCE, BEREAVEMENT

For a member of a family circle, it is difficult to realize that that circle will one day be broken or even that, once broken, it is in fact changed or destroyed. We learn that "all men are mortal," but we cushion ourselves against the forthcoming deaths of our loved ones and ourselves by assuming that the events are still distant from us in time.

The family circle is a social entity which has great persistence as a social phenomenon and even greater persistence in the minds of its surviving members as an influential image. Even though a family be broken by divorce or death, once we have been assimilated into it we can never again completely separate ourselves from its influence. Some marriages terminated by divorce owe their end to the fact that one or both of the couple were so habituated to their parental family that they never could enter fully into the new social unit. Another possibility, among many, is that one or both mates may have been so habituated to family unhappiness as to be incapable of participating in relatively happy family processes.

In the present chapter, we deal with the permanent breaking up of a marriage or a family circle as a major personal and family crisis. We are not concerned here with the factors making for the disruption of marriages, with customs and laws concerning marriage termination, or with ways in which an ex-mate adjusts to his new status, but rather with the shock of disruption and with ways in which the members of families try to deal with the break.

KINDS OF SEPARATION

At least temporarily, separation may be of an undefined, *de facto* sort. It may be a matter of mutual agreement between a couple or of judicial decree. When it is a desertion, it is illegal. A formal legal separation, sanctioned or ordered by a court of law, can take one of four forms: (1) separation pending agreement or judicial decree, (2) annulment, (3) divorce without the right of remarriage, and (4) divorce with the right of remarriage. As stated in Chapter 14, the third form is the permanent separation of a couple's "bed and board." It is what is most often meant by "separation" or "legally separated." It is the modern American equivalent of the sort of limited divorce once available through the Church of England's ecclesiastical courts. Most common in the United States is the fourth form, divorce which is either absolute when granted or limited only in the sense of there being a delay in the right to remarry.

Statistics for annulments, limited divorces, and absolute divorces are usually lumped together in this country and are not available for all the states. Together they produce a rate of incidence which steadily increased to an all-time high in 1946 and then began to decline. The divorce rate per 1,000 married females 15 years of age and older moved from 4.0 in 1900 to 4.7 in 1910, to 8.0 in 1920, to 7.5 in 1930, to a low of 6.1 in 1932 and 1933, then to a peak of 17.8 in 1946, back down to about 10.0 in 1951–53, and then below 10.0 in 1954–57 and approaching 9.2 in the 1960's. The marriage rate per 1,000 unmarried females 15 years and older moved from 68 in 1900 to 77 in 1910, to 92 in 1920, to 67 and down to 56 in 1930–32, to a wartime peak of 94 in 1942, to postwar high of 121 and 107 in 1946–47, and then to a level of about 77 in the 1950's and about 72 in the 1960's.

On the average, about one divorce or annulment is obtained for each four marriages performed. Only slightly more than two in each hundred legal separations of an absolute sort are annulments. These proportions, based on the situation prevailing during the 1950's, vary somewhat from place to place and from time to time. Even though the combined divorce and annulment rate has tended to rise for many years, so also has the percentage of Americans living in a married state. These trends are related.

Census reports contain the grab-bag categories, "wife absent" and "husband absent," for separated people who are presumably still married. These groups are then further subdivided into "separated," "other," and, in the case of married women, "husband in Armed Forces." Those "separated" are defined as "those with legal separations, those living apart with intentions of obtaining a divorce, and other persons permanently or temporarily estranged from their spouse because of marital discord." In the "other" group are "married persons employed and living for several months at a considerable distance from their homes, . . . in-migrants whose spouse remained in other areas, husbands or wives of inmates of institutions, and all other married persons (except those reported as separated) whose place of residence was not the same as that of their spouse." In 1964, the ratio of men to women who said their spouses were separated from them was about 1 to 10 (82 to 791 thousand). The ratio of men to women who reported themselves to be married but their spouse absent was about 1 to 8. These figures resemble those for persons married; more than one million more women than men claim to be married.

The large differences between men and women in the "absent" and the "separated" figures are due in part to the larger proportion of men held in institutions as prisoners or mental patients, and men absent in military service. Another reason for these differences is that both men and women make inaccurate statements about their marital status. Moreover, the terms "absent" and "separated" are often used to disguise multiple female mates or the fact that one or more existing children were born out of wedlock.

EROSION AND THEN SHOCK

Stories are told of apparently happy marriages that suddenly fall apart through the intrusion or discovery of the "other woman" or "other man." This is exciting melodrama, but the suddenness of the break is almost always more apparent than actual. Just as a marital relationship is a process of living and adapting to one another, so some form of permanent alienation and separation comes as a climax in a disintegrative process, or it may serve as a certification of the results of such a process. One or both mates may be shocked to have to realize that such a disintegrative process has been going on, but this does not alter the fact that the process has indeed been going on. In this "process of alienation," the sociologist Willard Waller * perceives an interdependence of the mates even in the destruction of their union. In this process, "each one needs for his role the continued support of the other. . . . The person who plays the active role must take upon himself the full responsibility for breaking the relationship, and this is a real burden, but he is helped in his struggle by

* *The Family* (rev. by Reuben Hill; New York: Dryden Press, 1951), pp. 520–521. Reprinted by permission of the publisher.

the continued opposition of the other." As Waller * puts it in another study, "He is quarreling with his wife, and he is falling in love; neither is an easily arrested process, and here they set up in such a way as to reinforce each other. The more he falls in love with the other woman, the more he quarrels with his wife; the more he hates his wife, the more he turns to her rival."

Our custom of treating a divorce proceeding as a legal struggle between two contenders rather than as a problem in disturbed interpersonal relations aggravates the disagreeableness and deepens the psychological wounds. As Waller † notes, "If a couple have escaped bitterness before, they are likely to fall into it when the time comes to go to court. And when the judge says the time has come, they talk of many things. Now it comes out, all the essential nastiness of tearing the blanket in two; each person blames the other."

At best, separation is a traumatic experience. It wounds both parties deeply regardless of the pose each may be able to assume and maintain. To meet the shock of realization that finally the struggle is over, that finally the excitements of the process of alienation can no longer absorb the attention of the participants, and that finally the marriage has ended in desertion, annulment, or divorce, often the most comforting procedure is to fall back on available routines, to lose oneself in tested and satisfying rituals.

The routines or rituals cannot be those of the broken marriage unless the couple, in exhaustion and in fear of the hazards of another relationship with an unknown, decide they might as well marry each other again. More often, the routines are those of the parental family, or other old rituals are applied to a new heterosexual relationship. Often enthusiastic involvement in a job can help in a short-term sense to tide a person over the first period of adjustment. The familiar satisfactions of the parental family and the preoccupations of a job do not in most cases provide a sufficient basis for a permanent reorientation of the individual to his basic new problems of socialization. A new and more stable heterosexual relationship is the most satisfactory and permanent solution to the problem. On the other hand, the current sex ratio, with men dying so much earlier than women, deprives a great many divorced women and even more widows of the opportunity to obtain another husband.

* *The Old Love and the New* (New York: Liveright Publishing Corp., 1930), p. 126.
† *Ibid.*, p. 133.

The shock of separation comes, on the average, at an earlier age than that of the death of a spouse. It also is more often followed by remarriage, and the new marriage of persons whose unions have ended in divorce or annulment is apparently often taken by the new mates to be successful.

ETHNOID PATTERNING OF SEPARATION

Among Roman Catholics, the ban on absolute divorce makes annulment the favored method of dissolving a marriage. In civil annulment, a judge declares that no valid marriage has existed between the parties, that it was null from its inception. Among Roman Catholic bases for annulment, church authorities sanction others than those recognized in American civil courts; their church legislation permits them to dissolve "the marriage bond in the following four instances: (1) unconsummated marriage, (2) the privilege of the faith, (3) unconsummated marriage in which one of the parties afterwards takes solemn vows in a religious order, and (4) the Pauline privilege." In commenting on these ways to dissolve a marriage so far as the Roman Catholic church is concerned, the sociologist John L. Thomas * "emphasized that, although these cases involved valid marriages, the marriage was either unconsummated (type one and three), or nonsacramental (type two and four, since they were contracted between baptized and unbaptized or between two unbaptized partners). A valid marriage contracted by baptized partners and consummated can be dissolved by no human power and by no cause other than death." Cases under the "privilege of the faith," type (2), "arise when there has been a valid marriage in which one of the spouses was unbaptized and a subsequent breakup of the marriage followed. . . . This privilege is granted only by the Pope. . . . The Pauline privilege cases [type (4)] occur when there has been a valid marriage between two unbaptized persons, the subsequent conversion to the Catholic faith of one of the spouses, and the refusal of the nonconvert to live in harmony with the converted spouse. . . . This is called the Pauline privilege since it dates back to St. Paul in his dealings with the converts at Corinth." When a couple of one of these types gains a divorce in the civil courts, the Roman Catholic member may also be granted annulment through

---

* *The American Catholic Family* (Englewood Cliffs, N.J.: Prentice-Hall, 1956), pp. 84–85. Reprinted by permission of the publisher.

ecclesiastical channels. In addition, the Roman Catholic judicial authorities can find and declare that a valid marriage has not existed or can sanction a temporary or permanent separation from "bed and board," a legal cessation of cohabitation.

Certain of the more orthodox or puritanical Protestant and Jewish denominations also sanction few bases for divorce.

In the United States, religious and civil obstacles to divorce are circumvented in several ways. We have the phenomena of "migratory divorce" (divorce through the establishment of residence and the initiating of proceedings in a jurisdiction with "easy" divorce laws) and of annulment. Migration for divorce removes the case not only from religious controls expressed in the laws of a state but also from the community expressions of those religious controls. Mexico, the Virgin Islands, and Nevada are meccas of easy divorce with relatively short required periods of residence. The restrictive divorce laws of New York state gave its residents the highest rate of annulment in the United States (3 annulments to 10 divorces) until they were broadened in 1966 to include bases other than adultery.

In Roman Catholic countries such as Italy, Spain, and the Latin-American states, marriages are rarely dissolved formally. In a great many activities, social life is so arranged that married men need not include their wives. Men who can afford to do so often keep a mistress, usually a woman from a lower social class. Such practices are more expensive and legally more difficult or hazardous in the United States. Here alcohol and work substitute, in part, for such extramarital activity.

CLASS PATTERNING OF SEPARATION

Desertion is most common among the poor and shiftless, those who cannot afford divorce and find it practical and easier to disappear. Divorce becomes more common among social-class groups with some financial security. Migratory divorce and freer sexual experimentation of an extramarital sort are most common among the *nouveaux riches,* especially those in the business and entertainment worlds. Marriages in middle-class professional and bureaucratic groups and in established, old-family, upper-class groups are notably stable. In general, groups with less education and lower social status have higher divorce rates as well as the bulk of desertions.

As for deserters, it is estimated that each year at least 100,000 fathers abandon their families and that from 5 to 8 in 10 are repeaters. About four times as many Negro as white fathers desert their families. The median age of deserting husbands is 33 years. Only 3 in 5 deserters are apprehended. The greater ease with which men find an excuse to leave home in order to look for work makes them the deserters more frequently than their wives, especially in families with children. Social workers sometimes succeed in getting male deserters to return and settle down in jobs found for them. The laws against desertion are helpful in exerting pressure upon the deserters.

Individuals who have some financial security and mobility are more apt to solve their marital problems, when they have them, by extramarital experimentation or by divorce. As might be expected, periods of financial prosperity are accompanied, as noted above, by increases in the rates both of marriage and of divorce.

MEETING THE SHOCK OF DEATH

The death of a near one means so many things to survivors that it is difficult to characterize its impact. In it, one finds more than a little of what cross-cultural students * imply when they say that "there has existed a consistent and sharp antagonism of interest between the dead and the living." In tribal life, grief is a constant feature of death and funerals, but, as the anthropologist William Howells † points out, "so is a tendency ritually to separate the dead from the living." The living take the occasion to terminate their involvement with the dead. This may come to require the destruction or abandonment of a house and other property. Howells states that "the living cannot go on and on sorrowing . . . or the society would become morbid." They also cannot pay too great a price for quieting the spirit of the departed, for assuring themselves that he will not return, and they therefore invent symbolic substitutes for more expensive procedures.

In one of his thoughtful essays on bereavement, the sociologist Thomas Dawes Eliot ‡ comments: "Fore-warnings and 'rehearsals'

---

* W. G. Sumner and A. G. Keller, *The Science of Society* (New Haven: Yale University Press, 1927), II, 929.

† *The Heathens* (Garden City, N.Y.: Doubleday & Co., 1948), pp. 163–164.

‡ "War Bereavements and Their Recovery," *Marriage and Family Living*, VIII (1946), 1–6.

and the experience or observation of other sorrows may lessen the shock of bereavement. I believe that if one knows in advance some of the reactions to expect in grief, and recognizes them when bereavement comes, it may help a person not to be sunk by his own unexpected reactions. . . . There remains the basic adjustment to the actual presence of absence, the finality, the absoluteness, the irrevocability and inexorability of death itself. . . . The real show is very different from even a dress rehearsal, but it is also very different from what it would have been if it hadn't been rehearsed."

Organized religions devote considerable attention to preparation for death and for the impact of a loved one's death. Eliot * puts it, "As sex dominates the first half of life so death dominates the latter half. As sex was dodged in vain, so death is dodged in vain. . . . We are 'acquainted with grief,' but while some of us have won out, it has been 'by grace of God and force of habit,' not by knowing 'the truth which makes us free.' . . . It remains to apply modern techniques of case histories, group studies, and documentary analysis to the attitudes and actual behavior of people toward death. Only upon such a basis, slowly to be accumulated, compared and worked over, can a social psychology of death be built up which can be of social value." He contends that the "art of death should be part of the art of life, even as the art of love, but all three are as yet in their infancy, and uncoordinated."

Reactions of Families to Bereavement. Eliot † sums up some of their reactions as follows:

1. The role of a family member exists in relation to the configuration and functioning of the family as a unit. A death tends to disturb this unity. The shifting of the roles of the various members under bereavement represents a reshaping of the configuration.

2. The consensus of the family in respect to these roles, i.e., in respect to its own pattern, may result; or, family conflict may develop as a sequence to incompatible conceptions of the role of certain members under the new conditions.

3. Such conflicts or jealousies, or the lack of a common personal or domestic object or symbol of affectional attachment (conditioning stimuli) may result in decreased family solidarity.

* "A Step Toward the Social Psychology of Bereavement," *Journal of Abnormal and Social Psychology*, XXVII (1932–33), 380–390; pp. 380–381 quoted by permission.

† "The Bereaved Family," *The Annals*, CLX (March, 1932), 184–194; p. 188 quoted by permission of The American Academy of Political and Social Science.

4. Acceptance of new interpersonal responsibilities may increase family solidarity.

5. Removal of authority, of habit-stimuli, of home, or of support may lead to revision of family folkways.

6. Maturity of children who lose their parents may lead to individualism or turning to their own families.

7. The will, or personality, of the deceased, acting psychologically as a dynamic complex in each member's memory, and reenforced by consensus, may activate the behavior of the entire family.

Possible Secondary Reactions to Bereavement. Eliot * has offered another list of reactions—possible secondary reactions—to bereavement, as follows:

1. Escape, or attempted escape, from conflict. E.g., disbelief, use of drugs, moving of residence, suicide, social distractions, or illusions.

2. Defense and repression. E.g., removing all reminders, deliberate forgetting, postural self-control, or certain 'mental diseases.'

3. Compensation (in the narrower sense). E.g., rationalizations, beliefs and cults, rituals of guilt or contrition, perpetuation of memory of deceased, or of wish or supposed will of deceased, revenge, penance, or 'overdetermined' grief.

4. Masochism and exhibition. E.g., voluptuaries of grief, recluses, ascetics, and the like.

5. Identification (introjection). E.g., stepping into the role of the deceased, or 'carrying out the spirit' of the deceased.

6. Transference and substitution (involving projection). E.g., reattachment of affections to new mother, child, or spouse; espousal of charities or causes.

The works of many poets, novelists, and playwrights have elaborated upon the themes in Eliot's two lists of reactions. For example, identification, or stepping into the role of the deceased, is a part of the theme of *The Late George Apley,* a popular novel by J. P. Marquand. Similarly, the reactions of relatives of the six dead soldiers who refused to be buried, portrayed by Irwin Shaw in his play *Bury the Dead* highlight some of the ways in which individuals and families try to cope with the death of a near one.

"Purpose" in Death. In the preceding chapter, we discussed the familial setting of physical and mental illnesses. To a degree, death, too, is psychosomatic and situational, a product of processes and conditions in the individual's family circle. In referring to such factors, *purpose* is perhaps not the correct term to use. Although

---

* *Ibid.,* p. 186.

the behavior of people often portrays tendencies toward both self-preservation and self-destruction, the extreme desire or drive to "end it all" is generally a subconscious one. Subconscious motives of self-destruction may impel some individuals and families to indulge in excesses—eating too much, competing too tensely, sleeping too little, and neglecting health and safety. Suicides and murders of spouses do not cause the loss of as many years of human life as the quasi-suicides and quasi-murders listed as "natural" deaths. Psychiatrists know that guilt feelings associated with the death of a close family member may arise from a subconscious sense of having contributed to the event—and, for that matter, may reflect a subconscious antagonism shared by other members of the family circle.

In societies imbued with a sense of the presence of the spirits of the dead and of magical manipulations, all deaths are thought to be caused by a human or superhuman agent. Even though we may not accept such a notion of agency, the family setting of life, of illness, and of death, the intimate interrelationships of all persons in the family circle—all emphasize the influence of little-known interpersonal factors in major life events.

The Funeral. In the United States during the present century, the advent of the automobile and the fast pace of urbanization have transformed the character of funerals. The plumed horses and black carriages are gone. Few widows wear what were once called "widows' weeds." Few men wear black sleevebands. The hair of the dead is no longer enshrined in the parlor under a glass bell jar. Since the dead person now rarely lies in state in his home, the drawing of shades, the door wreath, the mirrors turned to the wall, and the men "sitting up with the body" are now largely things of the past.

Just as babies now often emerge from behind the aseptic façade of a hospital, so a great many Americans go through the final portal behind the same façade. Death is thus most often off stage, in an atmosphere of depersonalized efficiency. In what are taken to be the dependable hands of the hospital's personnel, we are given assurance that "everything possible was done."

From the impersonal efficiency of hospital functionaries, the body passes to the "funeral director" in his "funeral home" or "funeral parlor." The sociologist LeRoy Bowman * has provided the most

---

* *The American Funeral: A Study in Guilt, Extravagance, and Sublimity* (Washington, D.C.: Public Affairs Press, 1959).

competent survey and analysis of the operations and facilities of this specialist. In attempting to meet emotional and traditional needs in an increasingly depersonalized setting, distraught widows, widowers, and other relatives are often exploited by the funeral specialist. Frequently lacking in experience and in precedents, they agree to everything indicated by the specialist as being proper. They feel it indecent to bargain or economize in the face of their awesome loss. The funeral director, with his carefully polished manner and his daily experience in similar situations, often reaps outrageous profits.

Class differences in funerals continue. Proportionate to their income, lower-class families often spend the most money on undertakers, automobiles, and burial facilities. Among the better educated, cremation is gradually replacing burial. Memorial services after burial or cremation are gaining over large funeral ceremonies, with cremation or entombment a more private family matter. Many such families now urge friends to contribute an equivalent amount to a charity rather than to spend it on flowers. Monumental cemeteries and mausoleums still expand, but burial parks, with unobtrusive brass or bronze memorial markers, are becoming more common; they are a park for the living as well as a depository for the remains of the dead.

Life Minus One. As with permanent separation, so with the death of a loved one, life for others must go on and can enter new and rewarding avenues. Even though today fewer prospective husbands for widows may be available than in the past, the lone woman has increasing opportunities for self-support. Insurance and social security benefits make the lot of widows with small children and of the dependent widowed much more tolerable. As we emphasized in our discussion of the post-child family, the newly divorced and the widowed, as well as the aging, need to find absorbing and useful interests and activities, to continue to be active, to seek to help others and to look outward rather than to withdraw mentally and emotionally into themselves.

Social scientists have in general neglected the more intimate aspects of death. Perhaps the cultural anthropologists, in describing the ways in which a great many societies deal with the possibility and actuality of death, have given us the most useful bases for sociological and psychological guidance. Now social scientists and social practitioners may begin to help us face death and bereavement with more wisdom.

Death occurs quickly, but a person's brooding about it, fear of it, and preparation for it may absorb a large segment of his life, especially in the later years. To prepare to cope with the death of a loved one or of oneself is thought by some to help bring on the event. Once one gets beyond this superstitious belief, much can be done by science and religion to place death in such a perspective that life can be lived more fully prior to its inevitable termination.

PART SIX

CONCLUSION

Chapter XXII

SCIENTIFIC RESEARCH

Together with society as a whole, our families and we ourselves are constantly changing. In the future, we are likely to have to change more rapidly than ever before in response to the new environment being created by the labors of physicists, chemists, and engineers. Fortunately, to meet the challenges of such change as wisely as possible, particularly in solving problems of family life, we shall have recourse to the substantial aid made available through the scientific research of psychologists, sociologists, and cultural anthropologists.

BACKGROUNDS OF RESEARCH

Research in marriage and the family began as an effort to meet human needs, to cope with drastic social changes, and to apply scientific methods to urgent problems of human relations. Its history is intertwined with that of moral philosophy, sociology, anthropology, and social psychology. It has gained much from psychiatry, criminology, public health, social work, and education. Since the family has been a factor in world history from the earliest times, research in this field draws heavily upon the work of historians. Finally, the contributions of moral philosophers, including utopians, theologians, and scholars in the philosophy of law must be acknowledged, for they were the predecessors of modern social scientists concerned with the study of family life.

As modern social science developed during the eighteenth and nineteenth centuries and divided into its present specialties, the study of marriage and the family did not become a separate discipline built solely around familial activities, interests, and problems. It did not follow the example set in the study of economic or political activities; its data did not form the core of a special social science, similar to economics or political science. However, as sociology, social or cultural anthropology, and social psychology grew into closely related general or integrative social sciences, they recognized the basic function of the family in individual maturation and socialization and in the maintenance and persistence of social groups. Special research in marriage and the family is thus largely carried on by scientists trained in those subjects, aided substantially by the findings of counselors who have clinical experience in mental health, social work, law, and education.

STIMULI TO SOCIAL–SCIENTIFIC RESEARCH

The impact of events in world history upon the development of family life has emphasized with ever greater urgency the need and the value of social-scientific studies of marriage and the family. In preceding chapters, references have been made to the trends of social change during the Renaissance and the Industrial Revolution, as well as the consequences of subsequent migration, industrialization, and urbanization. Early scientific approaches to the study of the family emphasized biological aspects. Charles Darwin (1809–1882) and other biologists considered man in his animal context, and their conceptions of evolution, challenging traditional absolutes about the individual and the family, inspired studies of society and of such institutions as the family from their point of view. A contrary approach came from the politico-economic attacks of Karl Marx (1818–1883) and his followers upon the family institution, which stressed social-scientific research as the most trustworthy way to benefit from social experience.

The influx of millions of Europeans into the United States dramatically focused attention upon the social problems arising out of attempts by immigrant families to adapt to new conditions. Further impetus to the social-scientific approach was provided by the investigations of sexual factors in family life. Even though the English physician and man of letters Havelock Ellis (1859–1939) overemphasized biological factors, his forthright *Studies in the Psychology of Sex* (7 vols., 1897–1928) turned increased concern toward the persistence of inaccurate beliefs and unwise practices. As Ellis observes in the "General Preface" to the *Studies,* "Sex lies at the root of life, and we can never learn to reverence life until we know how to understand sex." An extremely influential conception of this subject was developed by the great Austrian neurologist and psychoanalyst Sigmund Freud (1856–1939); he altered the entire trend of thinking and research concerning the nature of the parental family as the principal social matrix of the child and of society.

Events during the past half-century have profoundly affected family relationships. The dislocations of World War I featured especially (1) the beginning of great internal migrations of Negroes to the Northern states and (2) the achievement of national suffrage by women with the ratification in 1920 of the Nineteenth Amendment to the U. S. Constitution. During the 1920's, the growth of cities and the spread of urbanization resulted in the overthrow of small-town domination of national moral standards, a change signalized in 1933 by the repeal of Prohibition. The depression of the 1930's turned renewed attention to the families of the unemployed. World War II then brought with it private crises occasioned by the removal of father, mother, or both from the home for war-related duties. The personal uncertainties of both depression and war, with the divorce rate mounting, intensified the search for methods of increasing stability in family life and stimulated interest in the possibility of predicting accurately whether or not two persons should marry. In the 1950's, the challenges have been the depersonalization of family life through its invasion by television; the moral unsettlement due to East-West tensions; and the devastating potentialities of atomic bombardment and biological warfare. The publication * of interviews by Dr. Kinsey on the sexual behavior of large numbers of Americans came as an invigorating assault from the physical science realm on lack of realism in popular thinking and on lack of enterprise among social scientists. In 1966, a gynecologist and a psychologist † published a book which carried such observation through and beyond interviewing. They observed individuals masturbating and couples engaging in coitus under controlled laboratory conditions replete with sound recorder, color cinema camera, electroencephalograph, and electrocardiograph.

EMERGENCE OF FAMILY RESEARCH

Most of the early examples of social-scientific research in the family field were not specialized but rather were aspects of more general studies. An illustration of such research was *Le réforme sociale en France* (1864) by Frédéric Le Play (1806–1882), which reported

* A. C. Kinsey, W. B. Pomeroy, and C. E. Martin, *Sexual Behavior in the Human Male* (Philadelphia: W. B. Saunders Co., 1948); Kinsey, Pomeroy, Martin, and P. H. Gebhard, *Sexual Behavior in the Human Female* (Philadelphia: W. B. Saunders Co., 1953).

† William Masters and Virginia Johnson, *Human Sexual Response* (Boston: Little, Brown & Co., 1966).

observations on religion, property, association, private enterprise, and government, as well as family life. Another work by Le Play, his *L'organisation de la famille* (1871) was exceptional in that it dealt more specifically with a survey of family behavior.

Stimulated by Darwin's theory of evolution, such early social anthropologists as Herbert Spencer (1820–1903), Edward B. Tylor (1832–1917), and Lewis Henry Morgan (1818–1881) laid the bases for comparative studies of cultures and institutions and contributed substantially to the development of a theory of the relativity of moral values to cultural heritage and to life conditions. Spencer also brought that comparative viewpoint into sociology with the appearance in 1873 of his *The Study of Sociology* and in 1876 of the first volume of his three-volume *Principles of Sociology*. This approach was given its most powerful and original exemplification in social science in 1906 with the publication of the famous *Folkways* by William Graham Sumner (1840–1910), a former Episcopalian clergyman who had become an esteemed Yale professor of social science. These works led to long series of valuable social-historical and comparative studies of marriage and family patterns as well as of other aspects of society.*

---

* Notable among social-historical studies of the family have been E. A. Westermarck's *The History of Human Marriage* (London and New York: Allerton, 1891; rev. and enlarged, Macmillan Co., 1921, 3 vols.), George E. Howard's monumental *History of Matrimonial Institutions* (University of Chicago Press, 1904, 3 vols.), Willystine Goodsell's *A History of the Family as a Social and Educational Institution* (New York: Macmillan Co., 1915; rev. as *A History of Marriage and the Family*, 1934), W. G. Sumner and A. G. Keller's "Self-Perpetuation" in their *The Science of Society* (New Haven: Yale University Press, 1927, Part 5, Vol. III), Robert Briffault's *The Mothers* (New York: Macmillan Co., 1927, 3 vols.), and Carle C. Zimmerman's *Family and Civilization* (New York: Harper & Bros., 1947).

Friedrich Engels gave an authoritative Marxian theory of family social history in his *The Origin of the Family* (in German, 1884; in English, transl. by E. Untermann, Chicago: Kerr, 1902).

A useful account of the American family's history is A. W. Calhoun's exhaustive *Social History of the American Family* (1917–1919; reprinted, New York: Barnes & Noble, 1960, 3 vols.).

The comparative study of nonliterate peoples' family patterns has been continued in such works as Ernest Crawley's *The Mystic Rose* (1902; rev. ed. by T. Bestermann, New York: Boni and Liveright, 1927, 2 vols.), A. J. Todd's *The Primitive Family as an Educational Agency* (New York: G. P. Putnam's Sons, 1913), Nathan Miller's *The Child in Primitive Society* (New York: Brentano, 1928), Leo Simmons's *The Role of the Aged in Primitive Society* (New Haven: Yale University Press, 1945), G. P. Murdock's *Social Structure* (New York: Macmillan Co., 1949), a treatise on "family and kinship organization and their relation to the regulation of sex and marriage," and C. S. Ford's and F. A. Beach's *Patterns of Sexual Behavior* (New York: Harper & Bros., 1951).

The fields of sociology and psychology developed with sufficient rapidity in the United States and elsewhere from the 1890's to meet some of the challenges outlined above beginning in the World War I period. It was in 1907 that the influential sociologist William I. Thomas (1863–1947) published his unconventional *Sex and Society* through the University of Chicago Press. Among other points, Thomas sharply criticized the subordination of women. He wrote, with Florian Znaniecki (1882–1958), the famous study of individuals and families in migration and adjustment, *The Polish Peasant in Europe and America* (1918–1920; 2 vols. New York: Alfred A. Knopf, 1927). The authors demonstrated in that work the utility in sociological research of personal documents such as letters and autobiographies. We also wish to mention the important work of Charles Horton Cooley (1864–1929), another noted sociologist, especially his *Human Nature and the Social Order* and *Social Organization* (1902, 1922, 1909; Glencoe: Free Press, 1956), with which he contributed weightily to the study of the socialization of the individual in the family matrix.*

QUESTIONNAIRE AND INTERVIEW SURVEYS

These studies of marriage and the family by sociologists and social psychologists have centered chiefly on efforts to isolate and to determine the relative influence of factors making for success and failure in marriage. Such studies help to clarify what is happening to marital patterns. They fill in factual details with which to interpret gross census trends. They also aid in the development of procedures and in the provision of data with which to predict the probable suc-

---

There are also a great many studies of the marriage and family practices in one or a small group of tribes. These include Bronislaw Malinowski's *The Sexual Life of Savages in Northwestern Melanesia* (New York: Liveright Publishing Co., 1929, 2 vols.), Margaret Mead's *Sex and Temperament in Three Primitive Societies* (New York: William Morrow and Co., 1935), W. Lloyd Warner's *A Black Civilization: A Social Study of an Australian Tribe* (New York: Harper & Bros., 1937), E. E. Evans-Pritchard's *The Nuer* (Oxford: Clarendon Press, 1940), and A. R. Radcliffe-Brown's and D. Forde's *African Systems of Kinship and Marriage* (New York: Oxford University Press, 1950).

* More recent studies of families which, like those studied by Thomas and Znaniecki, are largely in one general ethnic tradition, are represented by Conrad M. Arensberg and S. T. Kimball's *Family and Community in Ireland* (Cambridge: Harvard University Press, 1940), John and Mavis Biesanz's *Costa Rican Life* (New York: Columbia University Press, 1944), and Olga Lang's *Chinese Family and Society* (New Haven: Yale University Press, 1946).

cess or failure of a given type of proposed marriage. Katherine B. Davis, a social economist and penologist, is said to have initiated this type of inquiry in this country in 1923, while she was serving as director of the Bureau of Social Hygiene in New York City. She contributed an outstanding work in her *Factors in the Sex Life of Twenty-Two Hundred Women* (New York: Harper & Bros., 1929). Because of the challenges to traditional family values during the prosperous 1920's as well as the depressed 1930's, many other social scientists participated in such research.*

More recent survey reports have continued to reflect improvements in the quality of research, particularly in the application of more basic sociological and social psychological findings to the study of family problems.

THE PREDICTION OF SUCCESS OR FAILURE

The study by Ernest W. Burgess and Leonard S. Cottrell, Jr., which was published in 1939 under the title, *Predicting Success or Failure in Marriage,* was begun in 1931. At that time they set up a program of research to test the predictability of marital success or failure. They sought to adapt to the study of marriage partners and of marriages the procedures and theories which Burgess and others had used with some promise to predict the probable success or failure of prisoners released on parole.† Research studies of this kind make use of background questions dealing with the subject's state of health, years of schooling completed, current occupation, amount

* G. V. Hamilton's *A Research in Marriage* (New York: Medical Research Press, 1929) and Robert L. Dickinson's and Lura Beam's *A Thousand Marriages* (Baltimore: Williams & Wilkins, 1931) are examples of the monographs which began to appear.

Out of the depressed 1930's came such research reports on family success and failure, strength and weakness, as Robert Cooley Angell's *The Family Encounters the Depression* (New York: Charles Scribner's Sons, 1936), Ruth S. Cavan's and Katherine H. Ranck's *The Family and the Depression* (University of Chicago Press, 1938), and Mirra Komarovsky's *The Unemployed Man and His Family* (New York: Dryden Press, 1940).

There also appeared these important monographs dealing with the success and failure of individuals as marriage partners: Lewis M. Terman's *Psychological Factors in Marital Happiness* (New York: McGraw-Hill Book Co., 1938) and Ernest W. Burgess' and Leonard S. Cottrell, Jr.'s *Predicting Success or Failure in Marriage* (New York: Prentice-Hall, 1939).

† See A. A. Bruce, A. J. Harno, E. W. Burgess, and John Landesco, *The Workings of the Indeterminate-Sentence Law and the Parole System in Illinois* (Springfield, Ill.: Division of Pardons and Parole, 1928), esp. pp. 205–249.

of savings, and church membership and activity; characteristics of his parents; his attitudes toward parents and others; his knowledge of sex; and pertinent aspects of his environment. The question-naire employed by Burgess and Paul Wallin in their *Engagement and Marriage* (Chicago: J. B. Lippincott Co., 1953) also includes queries about the subject's personality, his engagement history and attitudes, and the contingencies which he expects in marriage. In processing replies to these questions, a variety of positive and nega-tive weights are assigned to the items in order to apply past experi-ence to the computation of the most useful predictive index for each subject.

Burgess and others have apparently assumed that subjects can and will reveal, before or during marriage, information upon back-ground, environment, and personality traits from which one may predict the outcome of their prospective or existing marriage. Un-fortunately the validity or utility of this assumption lacks support. A basic research problem to be tackled is to what extent subjects can and will reveal such information in response to a questionnaire or in an interview. Are extensive interviews in depth necessary to achieve dependable data? How and by whom are such data best assessed and interpreted?

Burgess and other scientific investigators are cautious about the application of their research findings to counseling. For example, the sociologist Clifford Kirkpatrick, a careful analyst of prediction studies, insists that couples counseled in terms of present prediction scores should be given detailed information about the limitations of such scores, especially in cases where the score is not at either ex-treme but in middle range. In his book on *The Family,** Kirk-patrick comments: "If marriage is recognized as still a gamble, it is proper to peek at the cards dimly lighted by present scientific knowledge."

Such are some of the difficulties confronting those who would at-tempt predictions of marriage success. In addition, critics of these research procedures have brought up the following questions:

1. What is happiness in marriage? How is it related to success in marriage? Is persistence of a marriage the most significant criterion of marital happiness? Of marital success? Is it not the situation that happiness and success are very complex conceptions which are variously defined? And is it not the case that each individual's

* 2nd ed. (New York: Ronald Press Co., 1963), p. 405.

definitions depend upon his cultural and subcultural backgrounds, as well as life history and current personal experiences?

2. How important are the nonpredictable events that follow a marriage in determining the outcome of that marriage? A war, a depression, a boom, an accident, or an illness may drastically change conditions for a newly married couple. Any such development may strengthen or destroy a marriage.

3. Do contemporary research studies aimed at prediction of marriage success or failure reflect too superficial or too outmoded a view of personal characteristics and of interpersonal behavior? This question is frequently asked by psychoanalysts because of their interest in studies in depth.

STUDIES IN DEPTH

These studies of marital relations have been inspired especially by the work of Freud and by the writings of Havelock Ellis, Charles Horton Cooley, and Alfred C. Kinsey. In the main, such studies report and interpret the clinical experience of psychoanalysts and other counselors.*

In reviewing much of the research on marriage and the family that was completed during the first decade after World War II, the sociologist Robert F. Winch remarked on the extent to which studies in that period tended to be either anti-Kinsey or anti-Waller. The noted sociologist Willard Waller (1899–1945) achieved this controversial status through his books and shorter publications in

* An influential early work of this sort is J. C. Flügel's *The Psychoanalytical Study of the Family* (1921; London: Hogarth, 1948), but in this connection mention should also be made of the many stimulating insights in the more general psychoanalytical literature of Alfred Adler, Sandor Ferenczi, William Healy and Augusta Bronner, Carl G. Jung, Otto Rank, Harry Stack Sullivan, and William Alanson White, as well as a great many others, and the works of Sigmund Freud himself.

John Dollard, with his *Criteria for the Life History* (1935; reprinted, New York: Peter Smith, 1949) and other works, has led in the adaptation and assimilation of psychoanalytical findings into sociology and social psychology. John Levy's and Ruth Munroe's popular interpretation, *The Happy Family* (New York: Alfred A. Knopf, 1938), has gone through a great many printings and continues to make an important contribution to marital adjustment.

Attention may well be drawn here to another important book, *Childhood and Society,* 2nd ed. (New York: W. W. Norton & Co., 1963), by Erik H. Erikson, who approached the problems of personal maturation and of the family matrix from a psychoanalytic starting point, prepared by considerable anthropological field work and historical study.

which he built especially upon the work of Cooley and Freud and contributed his own incisive observations.* The "covert psychological processes" to which Waller often refers lead many, according to Winch, to question his findings. It apparently worries such critics to have suspicions raised as to the relative superficiality of their own observations and to the inconclusiveness and even instability of their trusted moral guides. Winch admits a "suspicion that in these [anti-Waller] studies there has been some tapping of the official ideology . . . rather than of the level which concerned Waller. It may be that Waller, whose formulations and literary style were highly refreshing, was largely wrong, but before this conclusion becomes importunate, we shall need to design studies more indisputably relevant."

SPECIALIZED STUDIES

In addition to the aforementioned broad types of research on marriage and the family, there has been a great increase in the number of specialized investigations. Inquiries into the customs and problems of youth and marriage have dealt with rating, dating, courtship, and social adjustment; sex knowledge; the nature and role of "love"; and mating. Significant, but with a biological emphasis, have been the continuing studies of the nature of sex and of the problems of fertility and differential fertility. The roles of parents have not been neglected; social scientists have been investigating mother-infant and other parent-child relations and more generally the processes of socialization. They have also been analyzing juvenile delinquency. Studies have been made of the advice which counselors give to children, teen-agers, the young married, and parents. Some of the social scientists have studied the changing problems of our growing population of elderly parents. Others have specialized in problems of divorce or of deviant individuals such as homosexuals and the mentally ill. Still others have investigated the family as it is found in one or another group or type of group, whether areal (for example urban, rural, regional), ethnic, or occupational.

* See Winch's "Marriage and the Family," Chapter 11 in J. B. Gittler's *Review of Sociology* (New York: John Wiley & Sons, 1957), esp. p. 373. See also Waller's *The Old Love and the New* (New York: Liveright Publishing Corp., 1930), *The Family: A Dynamic Interpretation* (1938; rev. ed. by Reuben Hill, New York: Dryden Press, 1951), and *War and the Family* (New York: Dryden Press, 1940).

NEEDED DIRECTIONS IN SCIENTIFIC RESEARCH

Many unsolved problems of Western civilization have been mentioned in this chapter. These problems prod us ever more urgently to re-examine and to try to strengthen our most intimate interpersonal relationships. Certainly global tensions do not diminish. Industrialization, urbanization, and bureaucratization proceed apace toward eventualities which are difficult to predict and which are likely to create a strange world resembling some of today's "science fiction" fantasies.

Modern conditions of living have given us greater mobility and more time for leisure, together with more freedom and with a tendency toward greater equality between the sexes. Married couples are free to plan the size of their family, and their decisions join with those of others to aggravate further or to help solve the problem of overpopulation. A great many earthlings look romantically to the possibilities of settlements on other planets, but they had better ponder the fact that in any event the human race will still have to live on on this globe and deal here with the frightening problem of overpopulation.

Fortunately Americans have a growing conviction that we all can benefit from scientific contributions to our understanding of ourselves and others and of our society, and to the development of techniques to promote mental hygiene. As a part of this, our attitudes toward the mentally strange or ill are becoming more tolerant and wise, even though this process of cultural modification still has a long way to go to absorb fully the findings of our social scientists and psychotherapists.

These considerations highlight needs for scientific research on marriage and the family, particularly for investigations of the most fundamental and pressing problems in this field. Too much effort has been expended upon the relative superficialities which are easily and precisely studied. Research specialists are needed who will investigate the most controversial problems and will use methods so novel and imaginative that they are likely to be called "unscientific." We are not advocating irresponsible prying. A respect for the rights of personal privacy as well as objectivity and other standards of responsible social-scientific research must be observed, but we must encourage bold exploration in new directions in order to achieve substantial gains in theory and in therapeutic procedures.

Those who are interested in pursuing this field of research as a career might consider types of questions in need of immediate investigation, such as the following: What is a "successful" family? To what extent are the divorce laws in any given state well-devised and beneficial? What can social scientists do to improve the techniques of family case workers? What are the best methods of dealing with the problems of the many varieties of "sick families"? What are the conditions of family living conducive to alcoholism, delinquency, divorce, vocational success and failure, intelligence, intellectual dullness, sexual health, sexual deviation? These are but a few of the problems which are available to challenge the prospective research scientist.

CONCLUSION

Family life did not become the subject of a special academic discipline as did business and government, but it became recognized as basic in the subject matter of sociology, social anthropology, and social psychology. The scientific investigation of marriage and the family gained stimulus during the past century from the rapid changes that swept society, threatened the stability of our institutions, and prompted a re-examination of treasured values and behavior patterns. Notable scientific innovators influential in this field have been Havelock Ellis, William Graham Sumner, Sigmund Freud, Charles Horton Cooley, William I. Thomas, Alfred C. Kinsey, Ernest W. Burgess, and Willard Waller.

A great deal of research energy has gone into efforts to develop questionnaire methods for the prediction of success and failure in marriage. These efforts have come to little because of their dependence upon relatively superficial and uncertain data. Beginnings of importance have been made in the examination of the more covert aspects of family processes. Research along such lines looks promising, even though it is difficult and controversial. In this field, investigators are urgently needed who will be concerned with the possibility of making constructive scientific contributions rather than with gaining the quick plaudits of colleagues or of the functionaries of social institutions.

Chapter XXIII

THE HAPPY FAMILY

Some families are called "happy." A great many others are judged to be "unhappy." The verdict on this at any given time by the family members or by the community will depend upon factors which are constantly subject to change.

In societies less preoccupied than ours with happiness, people do not understand what the terms "happy" and "unhappy" mean when they are used to characterize family life. For them, a family may be simply the principal group within which one lives, works, plays, contends, and has deep ties—a group which one at times avoids, yet accepts as a natural ingredient of each member's destiny. In such societies, family members do not ask themselves whether they are happy or unhappy; their culture does not permit them to raise such an issue.

DISTINCTIONS BETWEEN HAPPY AND UNHAPPY FAMILIES

The first sentences of Tolstoi's highly perceptive *Anna Karenina* * contain two poetic truths: "Happy families are all alike; every unhappy family is unhappy in its own way." The first clause in this comment parallels the conclusion of John Levy and Ruth Munroe † that a "successful and enduring" marriage "has one requirement . . . two people shall be ready to sink themselves in the creation of a new unit bigger than either of them." Levy and Munroe comment further thus: "Acceptance of the relationships is the big thing—not careful adjustment of money and interests and in-laws. A man and woman who are sure of their marriage, of each other, can fight openly about the other problems and work through to some sort of solution. The experimental approach is fine in the laboratory. In marriage it has a signpost: 'To Reno.'"

* Transl. by C. Garnett (New York: Modern Library, 1950), p. 3.
† *The Happy Family* (New York: Alfred A. Knopf, 1938), pp. 45–46.

From all we can learn, there appear to be a great many more unhappy than happy families in our society. Be this as it may, the second clause in Tolstoi's comment, his reference to the uniqueness of family unhappiness, points to a basic characteristic of the unhappy family: each society and its chief groups provide accepted models for the happy family, and the unhappy family is thought to deviate more or less from them. Even in widespread adversity, dissatisfaction with one's own family is regarded as resulting from acts or misfortunes which have made the family deviate somehow from accepted standards. The contention is that if the family had been more "moral," it would not have been torn by dissension, would not have produced delinquents or alcoholics, or would not have terminated in divorce. Depending upon the community's information and values, a member of such a family or the whole family may be either pitied or condemned.

If we are to use the term as we usually do in our society, a "happy family" is one favored by fortune. It is one that is prosperous or productive or content. A happy family is one in which its members are pleased with their lot, with what they do together, or with what the family group does or means to each member.

THE BASIS OF A HAPPY FAMILY

The patterns and processes of behavior in any family, whether happy or unhappy, depend in large part upon the customs prevailing in its society, community, social-class group, and ethnic tradition. These customs permit and encourage human biological potentialities to unfold and to be shaped, and they provide models for human association and interaction. In every community, the customary social processes reflect the influences of physical facilities, neighborhood, ethnic and ethnoid background, and class group as well as societal culture. The individual participates and is himself molded by this matrix of customs. Consequently, the family owes much to the personal and family ideals, experiences, and group memberships which have been most influential in the life of each mate before marriage and which continue to shape the shared life of the married couple.

The association in marriage of two people with necessarily somewhat different backgrounds may in any given case prove to be wise or fortunate, foolish or unfortunate. Rarely can the result be foretold with a high degree of certainty. The predictions—that is, the judgments, more or less informed but more or less prejudiced—of marriage counselors about the probable success or failure of a marriage are chiefly useful in stimulating thoughtful consideration of pertinent factors by a couple before marriage and careful planning afterward. Helpful marriage counselors devote themselves to stimulating such a process of thoughtful discussion between an engaged or married couple.

How does a happy family get started? According to Levy and Munroe,* people "marry because they lived in a family as children and still cannot get over the feeling that being in a family is the only proper, indeed the only possible, way to live." There is no wholly adequate substitute for the profound desire to live in a family similar to an intimately experienced and successful model and to make it the medium for a good life. But even if one or both partners in a marriage have not developed this intensely felt interest in family living, the situation may not be entirely hopeless. A sound basis for happiness in marriage can still be found by such a person or couple by observing the behavior of happy families and making up their minds to shape their own family life similarly. Sometimes the determination of a couple to avoid making the same mistakes as their parents helps to assure them of a happy and durable marital relationship—especially when the couple understand fully the positive goals they are trying to achieve.

CRITERIA FOR IDENTIFYING A HAPPY FAMILY

How do family members and others know that a given family is "happy"? The four major types of answer to this question reflect four major sets of criteria which are common in our society. These four major sets of criteria may be classified as follows: (1) traditional, (2) functional, (3) popular, and (4) processual. Let us briefly examine these diverse ways of looking at happiness in a family.

1. *Traditional Definitions.* Each moral tradition offers an ideal model for *the* happy family. It appears precise and rigid and, in terms of the tradition's criteria, rewarding. In our society, the major Jewish, Roman Catholic, Protestant, and other (chiefly humanist) religious groups agree on a number of points in their mod-

* *Ibid.,* p. 3.

els and disagree on others. They all tend to place a high value on religious conformity as evidenced by adherence to and support of the religious institution, on marriage within the religious tradition, on marital fidelity, on the bearing of children, and on hard work, generosity, and responsibility. They all condemn divorce, even though all make allowance for ways to terminate intolerable marriages. They have ideological differences about birth control, the justifiable reasons for divorce, whether or not remarriage may follow divorce, the extent to which the family should be separated from or assimilated into the larger society, the control of education, and the source of moral authority (in the institutional structure, in direct personal communication with God, or in an "inner light" of inspiration or reason). Such differences are often more official and formal than behavioral. Differences in behavior do not reflect religious teachings as often as they do the mores of social-class and ethnic groups which cut across religious traditions. An instructive illustration of this is to contrast behavior typical of Roman Catholics recently derived from Ireland with that of those recently from Italy. It is just as instructive to contrast the behavior of Jews or Baptists drawn from various social-class or ethnic groups.

2. *Functional Definitions.* Traditional moralistic definitions fail to supply a family model as acceptable under urban and industrialized conditions as under those of the rural Old World and of the rural America of an earlier generation. Wars and threats of wars and of nuclear fission bombardments, not to mention dreadful rumors of possible biological warfare, stimulate reassessments of all our values. To a degree, they unsettle all authority and faith in authority. Thus boys and girls now meet, rate one another, date, and even mate under conditions less controlled by parents than tradition would require or even wholly without parental knowledge. Problems of middle-class competition for jobs and status and of the expansion of the middle class to vast new proportions, with the accompanying prolongation of adolescence and of education, were delaying the age of marriage until the prosperity of the 1940's and 1950's lowered it again. The old models are requiring a lot of patchwork and of rationalizing to remain influential in the face of such new situations and needs.

In consequence of these pressures against traditional definitions, leaders of the more adaptive religious denominations are now assimilating many ideas which are called social scientific. Rather than "scientific," these ideas are often mores of middle-class intellectual groups translated into the modish guise of social-scientific patter. Nevertheless, the wide acceptance of these ideas makes it necessary for moral standards to be reinterpreted in ways said to be more "functional"—in ways asserted to be more adapted to today's social conditions and aspirations. Family ideals thus tend to shift toward meeting the new conditions of social competition and toward the rearing of children who can better exemplify contemporary class standards and competitive demands.

To find a source of authority with which to justify the new interpretations of moral principles, many intellectuals turn to a physiological or a societal determinism. In some respects, their conceptions of authority thus are not unlike the mystical ones of traditional religions. Some of these intellectuals refer to the "innate wisdom" of the human organism. They see in the characteristics of the human organism a mandate for transforming all society into a middle class whose families will somehow idealize and practice individual freedom, democracy, and humanitarianism while at the same time they prepare children to compete sharply in the interpersonal scramble for status and influence. Others see in the superorganic forces of society the ever changing conditions of life which require the modification of traditions. They contend that there is a kind of social Darwinism in which families devoted to intellectual pursuits are not always but, for the survival of our way of life, should be given the greatest survival value. In attempting such revisions of traditional moral standards, the functional determinists try to preserve a sense of continuity in the midst of change by claiming to be merely "clarifying" or "revitalizing" interpretations of traditional symbols and forms. It is indeed true that traditional patterns constantly require rethinking but in much broader terms than such determinisms can provide.

Upper-class and lower-class people have generally treated moral prescriptions for the life of a happy family and a happy individual as being distorted by the special pleadings of such middle-class specialists in morality as clergymen, teachers, judges, and writers. As a rule, entrenched upper-class groups try to present to the public an image of their family life which resembles the traditional moral pattern. This is a part of their customary *noblesse oblige,* now more commonly and accurately called "public relations." However, other upper- and lower-class people find justification in their group mores for abridging or circumventing societal morality. For example, being contemptuous of the anxious desire of middle-class persons to be accepted as "respectable" members of the community, they prefer to exploit heterosexual opportunities as they present themselves. This contempt takes the form, among others, of jokes aimed at alleged sexual impotence of middle-class men.

The societal determinists, seeking a more functional basis for ideal family living, try to find an authority for their ideas in "the social system" or in characteristics of social interaction which they take to be inescapable and universal. The fact that any social "system" is a shifting approximation, a social fiction, is an unsettling thought they do not wish to face. Also, the fact that the world's cultural traditions provide many strikingly different patterns for interaction is also difficult to comprehend unless one has somehow gotten outside one's own society and inside another one. The societal determinists neglect physiological (and neurological) as well as cultural and processual factors.

The societal determinists who advocate a less traditional and more "functional" definition of the happy family say that a family is more likely to be happy if it is not handicapped by "cultural lag," by the persistence of outworn imperatives. This statement is too dogmatic. Chronological age may or may not be a basis for criticism of a cultural pattern. The culture of any time and place is a patchwork of symbols, forms, and conceptions drawn from many other times and places. Many symbols and forms have very ancient roots. The fact that Halloween is in derivation an ancient Druidic festival does not keep it from being an entertaining annual event to the observation of which there would be no point in attaching the label, "cultural lag."

The physiological determinists, seeking a more functional basis for ideal family living, like to speak of "self-actualizing" or of "self-realizing" persons and families. These are persons or families who do not permit traditional culture to prevent them from realizing fully their organic potentialities. These determinists appear to believe that physiological capacities can somehow be separated from environmental influences. They fail to see that cultural patterns not only impede and limit intellectual and emotional development but that they are also intellectual and emotional tools which are used in successful family living. They insist that, for the sake of ideal family life, society should be remolded so that every person will enjoy the fullest and freest possible growth and expression. This is an oversimplification which attempts to reduce social phenomena to mere derivatives of physiological characteristics—derivatives which are more or less distorted or perverted by tradition and environment and thus require modification. They subordinate social phenomena to physical, and mainly to organic, influences.

These deterministic advocates of more "functional" definitions of family happiness have failed to take into account the facts of social history, particularly the significance of cross-cultural differences, and the nature of personal and social processes. They need to search more deeply into the relationships between culture, group interaction, and personality, and to understand the variability of culture and related processes. In this way, instead of overemphasizing physiological factors or societal controls, they would develop a much broader and more substantial basis for evaluating happiness in the modern family.

New conceptions of the happy family now taking shape must yield to demands for greater flexibility and for an expedient recognition of the conflicts between sexual maturity, sexual fulfillment, and vocational preparation. Because preachers, teachers, advertising copywriters, and politicians have great power in redefining public standards and are mostly esteemed members of middle-class groups, they will somehow need to take a view broader than that provided by their class mores and interests if they are to help provide the needed reformulations.

3. *Popular Definitions.* In recent years, popular notions of family happiness have included not only the judging of unusual individual cases of happiness or unhappiness as neighbors see them but also the reports of formal social surveys.

The individual happy family may become the popular yardstick in the community or among relatives. Whether or not it is actually happy may be beyond the point. Popular judgments depend heavily upon appearances and upon the ability of family members to cope with rumor.

Sample surveys of sexual behavior and opinion on sexual practice such as those made by the Kinsey group are popularly cited to justify the breaking of traditional models of the ideally happy family and of the moral person. "Everybody is doing it. Why not us?" Some people thus take such surveys as warranting the acceptance of prevalence as an adequate reason for breaking traditional sexual taboos. Such did not appear to have been the intention of Kinsey and others in making their cross-sectional surveys. They apparently were concerned primarily with learning as accurately as they could the nature of contemporary American sexual behavior and opinion. Those who try to make such findings the grounds for a "new ethic" are, in most cases, merely seizing an easy and satisfying excuse for doing what they would have done in any event but with less comfort. The reports of survey studies of this sort help to eliminate some of our pretense and hypocrisy and some of our emotional and factual blocks against more accurate analysis. They encourage but do not provide more realistic and constructive rethinkings of our problems.

Our discussion elsewhere of differences among the mores of various groups in our society and of the multivalent ways in which individuals adapt themselves to such differences suggests that nation-wide or even community conformity in sexual attitudes and behavior is neither likely nor desirable. Let us mention a few considerations bearing on this: As is often noted, sexual repression is a deep-set aspect of culture-and-personality among many of our middle-class groups. Before advocating ways to lessen or eliminate that repression, we need to study most carefully what such a change would do to the straining of middle-class men and women for higher social status, income, and recognition. Many lower-class groups do not accept such repressive ideas, emotions, and behavior patterns as part of their typical mores. To what extent are their more permissive sexual mores related to their relative lack of concern with upward mobility through study and hard work? Sex cannot be considered apart from the whole social situation of an individual, family, or class group, and sexual patterns are a crucial aspect of family ideals and organization. A society requires many different sorts of individuals and groups in order to carry on its wide range of activities, and diverse patterns of sexual expression help to make them different.

4. *Processual Definitions.* In the present book, we have analyzed American marriage and the family in a way that recognizes the family's processes as basic to an understanding of it. Forms may change or they may have an illusory appearance of changelessness, but family processes are constantly at work. These social processes are the continuing actions, the dynamic continuities in social interrelations within families as they take form out of others, carry on

their activities, and eventually disappear or merge into other families.

Family processes are more like a continuing novel than like a mathematical problem. In the latter, regardless of its complications, the participant goes from the description of the problem to its solution by the shortest possible route. In family living, the common threads of the narrative are the daily, weekly, monthly, annual, and lifetime cyclical patterns. All that we do in a family is a web of tangled elaborations of those time cycles which may or may not possess a certain rationality currently or later. What rationality family activities may appear to possess is usually visible only in retrospect and then only because of the selectivity and even flexibility of our memories.

When we try to study these tangled processes, as so many other subjects of social-scientific investigation, we tend to stress static methods and principles rather than the constantly shifting social reality. Somehow we need to learn how to study social processes without the use of distorting short cuts; such short cuts are those mentioned in connection with the discussion of functional definitions. We need to see and interpret the rich multivalence of personality and culture, not an artificial monovalence or an oversimplified determinism. "[Every] human being, by virtue of his humanity, has mingled with generous, altruistic feelings, self-seeking aims, petty vanities and ambitions, hostilities, resentments, and competitive attitudes even toward those he loves best, as well as a variety of erotic impulses." * We need to see as fully as we can, and with courageous objectivity, the constantly modifying character of social phenomena, even of those which look most sure and stable, even of those on which we place our greatest dependence.

In a happy family, as seen processually, much of the interaction among its members is pervaded with a spirit of playfulness. People do many things in their families which are related to organic and other basic needs, but, as the sociologist Nelson N. Foote † points out, much of family living has a playful character, "quite different from operating a family business, raising a family, or visiting relatives." Play is not always fun. It may involve hard—even grim—competition, possibly a bitter emotional struggle, but the privacy and the repetitiousness of family living give it among us a

---

* John Levy and Ruth Munroe, *The Happy Family* (New York: Alfred A. Knopf, 1938), p. 187.

† "Family Living as Play," *Marriage and the Family,* XVII (1955), 296–301.

gamelike quality. In the processes of family interaction and cultural transmission, play joins with ritualizing as major aspects of family life. In a secure and content family, young and old can play again and again with one another in terms of understood and evolving rituals. They experiment with varying the social roles they perform within and without the family. They exercise their fantasies. They make a game of such homely events as face-washing and table-setting. Examples of this are found in jokes and slang commonly developed or selected and treasured within a family circle and in their playful punning with names and nicknames. As the family specialists James H. S. Bossard and Eleanor S. Boll * conclude, "A ritual, appealing in content and manipulated wisely, becomes a powerful and constructive weapon in the integration of a family; and an ill-adapted ritual or a good ritual misused may become an agent in its disintegration."

What are the processual criteria for a happy family? We really do not know them at all well, but we have some helpful glimmerings. Only from the work of such incisive and courageous investigators as William James, Sigmund Freud, W. G. Sumner, C. H. Cooley, and other more recent social scientists can we gain such knowledge. These social scientists have not been afraid to deal with moral problems of great human concern in ways that are direct and fresh. As the sociologist George Simpson † wisely and hopefully observes, "Sociologists are more than technicians; they are the keepers of the conscience of the social sciences, and the critics of the very social process which tries to make them merely technicians." And he comments in another study,‡ "We have come to realize that achievement of mental, social, and cultural rationality involves basic understanding of the pervasive infiltration of irrationality into all facets of human behavior." Such students of social dynamics are greeted by the many academic keepers of the *status quo ante* with anguished cries of pain and with such name-calling terms as "moralist," "amoralist," and "speculative philosopher," but the work of those so criticized points to important bodies of knowledge. They have immeasurably enriched our understanding in this field of human relations.

---

* *Ritual in Family Living* (Philadelphia: University of Pennsylvania Press, 1950), p. 202.

† *Science as Morality* (Yellow Springs, Ohio: Humanist Press, 1953), pp. 43–44.

‡ George Simpson, *Man in Society* (Garden City, N.Y.: Doubleday & Co., 1954), p. 44.

From what we know of family processes today, our families have not only changed but are likely to continue to change for many years to come. In what directions are those changes likely to be? Let us consider a few of the contemporary trends.

More and more Americans now must make the best of urban and suburban living. They are therefore beginning to devise social inventions with which to compensate for or offset the tendencies in modern life making for isolation and anonymity. Among these inventions are voluntary baby-sitting and child-chauffeuring clubs, self-help discussion groups to deal with problems of child-rearing and family solidarity, toy "libraries," and systems for sharing or passing along other equipment and clothes.

In social welfare work, family agencies are becoming more selective and are working in a more concentrated manner with the relatively few families that require the greatest amount of free social service. Such agencies are also constantly trying to raise their standards and performance levels of professional competence.

In counseling, the shortage of adequate professional personnel is likely to continue, but do-it-yourself and voluntary-group procedures are becoming more common and more helpful. As we discover and learn to interpret more tenable goals for happiness in family processes, such do-it-yourself and group efforts will gain in effectiveness. Much can be learned through reading a good book—and more through group discussion of it. The growth of the mental-hygiene movement and the dissemination of information about mate-selection are both making would-be mates more cautious and also more confident in their marital decisions.

When a marital problem reaches the stage of a legal action for annulment, separation, or divorce, we are still confronted with the insistence of many courts upon treating the problem like the general run of controversies between interested parties rather than in a diagnostic and therapeutic fashion. Many legal specialists, however, have gone far beyond this practice, and efforts are being made to create an atmosphere in which the damage arising out of such court struggles may be minimized and in which the chances of new and more durable marriages are increased.

In spite of the criticisms of contemporary family patterns and the many substitutes offered, there are many reasons for thinking that our patterns and processes of family living are at least as firmly treasured as they have ever been.

SELECTED READINGS

SELECTED READINGS

Textbooks and volumes of readings on marriage and the family appear in the Tabulated Bibliography of Standard Textbooks and the Quick Reference Table to Standard Textbooks on pages xiv–xxvi and the Tabulated Bibliography of Readings Books on page 355.

Introduction: The Study of Marriage and the Family

Hess, Robert D., and Gerald Handel. *Family Worlds: A Psychosocial Approach to Family Life.* Chicago: University of Chicago Press, 1959. Five case studies that answer such questions as: How does a family function? What is a "normal" family?

Marriage and Family Living. Published quarterly by the National Council on Family Relations, Minneapolis, Minnesota. Articles by specialists on many aspects of the study of marriage and the family.

Nye, F. Ivan, and Felix M. Berardo, eds. *Emerging Conceptual Frameworks in Family Analysis.* New York: Macmillan Co., 1966. Essays outlining eleven approaches to family study.

Part One: The Changing Family

I: *Varieties of Family Life*

Blitsten, Dorothy R. *The World of the Family:* New York: Random House, 1963. Comparative study of families throughout the world.

Farber, Bernard, ed. *Kinship and Family Organization.* New York: Wiley & Sons, 1966. A study of a wide range of family types.

Mead, Margaret. *Male and Female.* New York: William Morrow and Co., 1949. A cultural anthropologist looks at the significance of sex differences.

Nimkoff, M. F., ed. *Comparative Family Systems.* Boston: Houghton Mifflin Co., 1965. Major variations in family organizations.

Queen, Stuart A.; Habenstein, Robert W.; and Adams, John B. *The Family in Various Cultures.* Rev. ed. Chicago: J. B. Lippincott Co., 1961. Descriptions of family life among ancient, primitive, and modern peoples.

Stephens, William N. *The Family in Cross-Cultural Perspective.* New York: Holt, Rinehart & Winston, 1963. Anthropological discussion of plural marriage, kinship groups, courtship and mating rules, roles of husband and wife, and related topics.

II: *America's Family Heritage*

Calhoun, Arthur W. *A Social History of the American Family.* 3 volumes. New York: Barnes & Noble, 1960. Standard historical work divided into volumes on the colonial period, the period from Independence through the Civil War, and the period from 1865 to 1919.

Goodsell, Willystine. *A History of Marriage and the Family.* Rev. ed. New York: Macmillan Co., 1934. A broad social historical treatment with special attention to the American colonies and the United States.

Stein, Herman D., and Richard A. Cloward, eds. *Social Perspectives on Behavior: A Reader in Social Science for Social Work and Related Professions.* Glencoe, Ill.: Free Press, 1958. Pp. 53–170. Authoritative discussions of American ethnic family patterns: Negro, eastern European Jewish, Italian, Puerto Rican, and Mexican.

III: *Is an American Pattern Emerging?*

Black, Algernon D., "If I Marry Outside My Religion?" *Public Affairs Pamphlet* No. 204. New York, 1959. Should young people of different religions marry? What difficulties are they likely to face?

Bossard, James H. S., and Eleanor S. Boll. *One Marriage: Two Faiths.* New York: Ronald Press Co., 1957. A sociological study of inter-religious marriage.

Glick, Paul Charles. *American Families.* New York: John Wiley & Sons, 1957. A digest and analysis of data from the United States Bureau of the Census.

Ogburn, William Fielding, and Meyer F. Nimkoff. *Technology and the Changing Family.* Boston: Houghton Mifflin Co., 1955. Mechanical invention and scientific discovery are related to social change and especially to the modification of family processes.

Whyte, William H., Jr. *The Organization Man.* New York: Simon and Schuster, 1956. Chapters 19–29. A perceptive journalist reports on family and community life in the "new suburbia" among "corporation families."

IV: *Socioeconomic Aspects of the Family*

Bigelow, Howard F. *Family Finance.* 2nd ed. Philadelphia: J. B. Lippincott Co., 1953. A text on family financial problems and planning.

Farber, Seymour M., and Wilson, Roger H. L., eds. *The Potential of Woman.* New York: McGraw-Hill Book Co., 1963. Symposium on experimental studies, feminine roles, consequences of equality, and male revolt.

Kyrk, Hazel. *The Family in the American Economy.* Chicago: University of Chicago Press, 1953. A study of incomes, prices, and standards of living of American families and of their economic role as a part of the institutional framework.

Nickell, Paulena, and Jean Muir Dorsey. *Management in Family Living*. 3rd ed. New York: John Wiley & Sons, 1959. Methods of homemaking, simplification of procedures, handling of financial problems, housing, and meeting changing responsibilities.

Nye, F. Ivan, and Hoffman, Lois W. *The Employed Mother in America*. Chicago: Rand McNally & Co., 1963. Why women work outside the home; consequences for their children; how their husbands react; how working mothers adjust to outside work.

Packard, Vance. *The Status Seekers*. New York: David McKay Co., 1959. Subtitled: "An Exploration of Class Behavior in America and the Hidden Barriers That Affect You, Your Community, Your Future." Oversimplified but stimulating.

V: *Welfare Roles of the Family*

Foote, Nelson N., and Leonard S. Cottrell, Jr. *Identity and Interpersonal Competence: A New Direction in Family Research*. Chicago: University of Chicago Press, 1955. Special attention by two sociologists to the roles of family-serving agencies.

Gordon, Henrietta L. *Casework Services for Children: Practices and Principles*. Boston: Houghton Mifflin Co., 1956. Systematic treatment of boarding-home care, institutional care, adoption, day care, supervised homemaker service, protective service, and service to children in their own homes.

Margolius, Sidney, "Medicare—Benefits and Gaps: Social Security—Your Rights." *Public Affairs Pamphlet* No. 289. New York, 1966. A summary of this important legislation.

Porterfield, Austin L. *Marriage and Family Living as Self-Other Fulfillment*. Philadelphia: F. A. Davis Co., 1962. Text which stresses psychological, value, and counseling considerations.

Thorman, George, "Family Therapy." *Public Affairs Pamphlet* No. 356. New York, 1964. Services performed by family welfare specialists.

Zietz, Dorothy. *Child Welfare: Principles and Methods*. New York: John Wiley & Sons, 1959. Historical and contemporary treatment of child welfare in its social, economic, educational, psychological, and governmental aspects. An interprofessional approach.

VI: *Population Characteristics and Problems*

Bogue, Donald J. *The Population of the United States*. Glencoe, Ill.: Free Press, 1959. Detailed reference work, with charts and discussions for nontechnical readers.

Freedman, R. *Population: The Vital Revolution*. Chicago: Aldine Publishers, 1965. A detailed study.

Thompson, Warren S., and David T. Lewis. *Population Explosion*, 5th ed. New York: McGraw-Hill Book Co., 1965. A standard reference work.

Tomlinson, Ralph. *Population Dynamics: Causes and Consequences of World Demographic Change*. New York: Random House, 1965. A basic analysis of processes at work.

Part Two: Childhood and Adolescence

VII: *The Child in the Family*

Archer, Jules, and Dixie Leppert Yahraes, "What Should Parents Expect From Children?" *Public Affairs Pamphlet* No. 357. New York, 1964. Careful discussion of attitudes and methods.

Brim, Orville G. *Education for Child Rearing*. New York: Free Press, 1965. A discussion of efforts to increase the competence of parents in raising their children.

Hart, Evelyn, "How Retarded Children Can Be Helped." *Public Affairs Pamphlet* No. 288. New York, 1959. A far greater proportion of the retarded can be trained and educated.

Hymes, James L., Jr., "Enjoy Your Child—Ages 1, 2 and 3." *Public Affairs Pamphlet* No. 141. New York, 1958. Advice to parents and child-study workers on what to expect from children.

Hymes, James L., Jr., "Tell Your Child About Sex." *Public Affairs Pamphlet* No. 149. New York, 1959. A specialist in nursery education tells what children will ask and do about sex.

Lee, Alfred McClung, *Readings in Sociology*. Rev. New York: Barnes & Noble, 1960. Section II, "Socialization of the Individual." Ten articles on various aspects of the subject.

Lee, Alfred McClung, "Socialization of the Individual." Lee, ed. *Principles of Sociology*, 2nd ed., rev. New York: Barnes & Noble, 1960. Part VI. An outline of the literature on aspects of life-history and of family living.

LeShan, Eda J., "The Only Child." *Public Affairs Pamphlet* No. 293. New York, 1960. How parents can bring sensitivity, understanding, and imagination to the circumstance of being an only child.

Ross, Helen, "The Shy Child." *Public Affairs Pamphlet* No. 239. New York, 1958. Written by a leading consultant on child care and addressed both to parents and to teachers.

Sears, Robert R., Eleanor E. Maccoby, and Harry Levin. *Patterns of*

Child Rearing. Evanston, Ill.: Row, Peterson and Co., 1957. An outstanding text.

United States Children's Bureau. *Your Child from One to Six.* Rev. Washington, D. C.: Government Printing Office, 1956. Widely distributed guide on child care.

Wolf, Anna W. M., "Your Child's Emotional Health." *Public Affairs Pamphlet* No. 264. New York, 1958. What about rivalries between brother and sister? What are the new baby's needs? Suggestions concerning the over-aggressive child, the under-aggressive child, hidden fears and anxieties, and family crises.

Wylie, Philip. *Generation of Vipers.* New annotated ed. New York: Rinehart and Co., 1955. A sensational attack on "momism" and problems Wylie thinks are related to it.

VIII: *The Child in Group Processes*

Erikson, Erik H. *Childhood and Society,* 2nd ed. New York: W. W. Norton & Co., 1963. An outstanding and readable book which brings together psychoanalytical, anthropological, sociological, and historical findings.

Hymes, James L., Jr., "Three to Six: Your Child Starts to School." *Public Affairs Pamphlet* No. 163. New York, 1959. How to help children during this restless age to bridge the gap from home to school.

Kluckhohn, Clyde, Henry A. Murray, and David M. Schneider, eds. *Personality in Nature, Society, and Culture.* 2nd ed. New York: Alfred A. Knopf, 1953. Part II, Sections 3–7. An important collection of articles on social roles, group memberships, and situational determinants.

Lee, Alfred McClung. *Multivalent Man.* New York: George Braziller, 1966. Esp. Part Two. A discussion of the prototypical roles and groups and their successors through which the individual learns socialization.

Lambert, Clara, "Understanding Your Child—From 6 to 12." *Public Affairs Pamphlet* No. 144. New York, 1958. Suggestions on child-rearing during the latency period.

Lee, Elizabeth Briant, and Alfred McClung Lee, eds. *Social Problems in America: A Sourcebook.* Rev. ed. New York: Henry Holt and Co., 1955. Part III, "Problem Periods in Family Life." Selected readings on problems of socialization.

IX: *The Child in the Community*

Aries, Philippe. *Centuries of Childhood: A Social History of Family Life.*

New York: Alfred A. Knopf, 1962. A perspective on childhood in Western cultures with special reference to education.

Carson, Ruth, "Your Child May Be a Gifted Child." *Public Affairs Pamphlet* No. 291. New York, 1959. How parents can work with the school to provide greater opportunities for development. How significant are mental tests?

Haimowitz, Morris L., and Natalie Reader Haimowitz, eds. *Human Development: Selected Readings*. New York: Thomas Y. Crowell Co., 1960. Parts III–V. An extensive collection of notable papers on the child's views of his world, distortions of those views, and educational and other institutional controls.

Henry, Nelson B., ed. *Citizen Co-operation for Better Public Schools*. 53rd Yearbook of the National Society for the Study of Education, Part I. Chicago: University of Chicago Press, 1954. The needs for and the possibilities of citizen co-operation. Addressed both to parents and to teachers.

Lee, Alfred McClung. *Fraternities Without Brotherhood*. Boston: Beacon Press, 1955. A report on racial and religious prejudice in our high schools and colleges.

Neisser, Edith G., "Your Child's Sense of Responsibility." *Public Affairs Pamphlet* No. 254. New York, 1957. How to help children become trustworthy, reliable, and responsible.

Part Three: Courtship and Marriage

X: *Love and Identity*

Foote, Nelson N., and Leonard S. Cottrell, Jr. *Identity and Interpersonal Competence: A New Direction in Family Research*. Chicago: University of Chicago Press, 1955. An original discussion of the family in terms of the ends that it can serve in modern society.

Fromme, Allan. *Sex and Marriage*. New York: Barnes & Noble, 1955. Chapters 1–3, 6. A popular and informed discussion by a psychologist of the intimate everyday problems of married life.

Landis, Paul H., "Coming of Age: Problems of Teen-Agers." *Public Affairs Pamphlet* No. 234. New York, 1958. A sociologist offers insights into the kinds of problems that face adolescents.

Rainwater, Lee. *Family Design: Marital Sexuality, Family Size, and Contraception*. Chicago: Aldine Publishing Co., 1965. A comprehensive survey of factors determining family size.

XI: *Courtship and Mate-Selection*

Barron, Milton L. *People Who Intermarry*. Syracuse, New York: Syracuse University Press, 1946. A sociological study of interethnic and especially interreligious marriages.

Bernard, Jessie, Helen E. Buchanan, and William M. Smith, Jr. *Dating, Mating & Marriage: A Documentary-Case Approach.* Cleveland: Howard Allen, 1958. A collection of intimate personal documents illustrative especially of dating and mating problems.

Kirkendall, Lester A., "Too Young to Marry?" *Public Affairs Pamphlet* No. 236. New York, 1958. Pros and cons of early marriage.

Kirkendall, Lester A., with Elizabeth Ogg, "Sex and Our Society." *Public Affairs Pamphlet* No. 366. New York, 1964. How sex problems are discussed in our society and how they might better be discussed.

Turner, Ernest Sackville. *A History of Courting.* New York: E. P. Dutton & Co., 1955. A popular and informed history of dating and courting.

Winch, Robert F. *Mate-Selection: A Study of Complementary Needs.* New York: Harper & Bros., 1958. This is an elaboration of the author's sociological theory of mate-selection, with case illustrations.

Woods, Ralph Louis, ed. *The Catholic Concept of Love and Marriage.* Philadelphia: J. B. Lippincott Co., 1958. An anthology of views by earlier and contemporary Roman Catholic writers.

XII: *Engagement: Planning for Marriage*

Burgess, Ernest W., and Leonard S. Cottrell, Jr. *Predicting Success or Failure in Marriage.* Englewood Cliffs, N. J.: Prentice-Hall, 1939. A pioneer work which emphasizes the study of personal qualities operative before marriage, especially during engagement.

Kinsey, Alfred C., and others. *Sexual Behavior in the Human Female.* Philadelphia: W. B. Saunders Co., 1953. Especially chapters 6–8 deal with premarital behavior; a study of sexual data concerning almost 8,000 females, with some comparable male data.

Terman, Lewis M., and others. *Psychological Factors in Marital Happiness.* New York: McGraw-Hill Book Co., 1938. Chapter 12 contains an extensive treatment of engagement.

XIII: *Will the Marriage Work Out?*

Note: The titles for the preceding chapter also apply here.

Cuber, John F. *Marriage Counseling Practice.* New York: Appleton-Century-Crofts, 1948. An influential discussion of marriage counseling written by a sociologist.

Duvall, Evelyn M., "Building Your Marriage." *Public Affairs Pamphlet* No. 113. New York, 1959. Advice on money problems, in-laws, arguments, and other topics.

Eisenstein, Victor William, ed. *Neurotic Interaction in Marriage*. New York: Basic Books, 1956. Useful collection of papers on irrational factors in family life.

Locke, Harvey James. *Predicting Adjustment in Marriage*. New York: Henry Holt and Co., 1951. A comparison of divorced with happily married persons to find factors making for success or failure in marriage.

Mace, David, "What Is Marriage Counseling?" *Public Affairs Pamphlet* No. 250. New York, 1957. When and where to seek marriage counseling. How to use it. The costs and possible gains.

Mace, David, "What Makes a Marriage Happy?" *Public Affairs Pamphlet* No. 290. New York, 1959. A summary of major studies on how to help and guide men and women in their quest for marital happiness.

Mudd, Emily H. *The Practice of Marriage Counseling*. New York: Association Press, 1951. A leader in marriage counseling outlines the history, character, techniques, and theory of the emerging profession.

Mudd, Emily H., and others, eds. *Marriage Counseling: A Casebook*. New York: Association Press, 1958. A symposium of case histories edited for the American Association of Marriage Counselors.

Skidmore, Rex A., Hulda Van Streeter Garrett, and C. Jay Skidmore. *Marriage Consulting: An Introduction to Marriage Counseling*. New York: Harper & Bros., 1956. A survey of the background, functions, training, and roles of marriage counselors.

Vincent, Clark E. *Readings in Marriage Counseling*. New York: Thomas Y. Crowell Co., 1957. An anthology of text materials.

XIV: *Marriage Customs and Laws*

Pilpel, Harriet F., and Theodora Zavin. *Your Marriage and the Law*. New York: Rinehart & Co., 1952. A summary in lay language of laws and legal precedents dealing with engagement, marriage, and the family.

Vernier, Chester G. *American Family Laws*. 5 volumes and Supplement. Stanford, Calif.: Stanford University Press, 1931–1938. A comprehensive compendium.

Part Four: Parenthood

XV: *Children in Prospect*

Carson, Ruth, "Nine Months to Get Ready." *Public Affairs Pamphlet* No. 376. New York, 1965. This can be used with a film (color, 25 mins.) of the same name, issued by the Public Affairs Committee, 381

Park Ave. So., New York, N. Y. 10016.

Freedman, Ronald, Pascal K. Whelpton, and Arthur A. Campbell. *Family Planning, Sterility, and Population Growth.* New York: McGraw-Hill Book Co., 1959. A study of a national sample of white wives aged 18 to 39 (in 1955) to determine the relation of planning to family size.

Fromme, Allan. *Sex and Marriage.* New York: Barnes & Noble, 1955. Chapters 4–6 furnish a basic and simple psychological discussion of sex and reproduction.

Gebhard, P. H., W. B. Pomeroy, C. E. Martin, and C. V. Christenson. *Pregnancy, Birth and Abortion.* New York: Hoeber-Harper, 1958. Based upon detailed interviews.

Guttmacher, Alan Frank. *Having a Baby: A Guide for Expectant Parents.* Rev. ed. New York: New American Library, 1950. A compact and authoritative work by a physician, written in clear .language.

Prenatal Care. Children's Bureau Publication No. 4. Washington, D. C.: Government Printing Office. Detailed description of each stage of pregnancy.

So You Are Expecting a Baby. Children's Bureau Publication. Washington, D. C.: Government Printing Office. Questions and answers for pregnant women, with pictures.

Sulloway, Alvah Woodbury. *Birth Control and Catholic Doctrine.* Boston: Beacon Press, 1959. An analytical study.

Thomas, John Lawrence. *Marriage and Rhythm.* Westminster, Maryland: Newman Press, 1957. An official Roman Catholic treatise on the use of the "rhythm method" of birth control.

Wiedenbach, Ernestine. *Family Centered Maternity Nursing.* New York: G. P. Putnam's Sons, 1958. A practical reference book for young couples.

XVI: *Childbirth and Care of the Newborn*

Carson, Ruth, "Your New Baby." *Public Affairs Pamphlet* No. 353. New York, 1963. A practical summary.

Gell, Barbara. *ABC of Natural Childbirth.* New York: W. W. Norton & Co., 1954. A simplified guide.

Gilbreth, Frank B., Jr. *How to Be a Father.* New York: Thomas Y. Crowell Co., 1958. An amusing and instructive volume.

Goodrich, Frederick W., Jr. *Natural Childbirth.* New York: Prentice-Hall, 1950.

Gould, Joan, "Will My Baby Be Born Normal?" *Public Affairs Pamphlet* No. 272. New York, 1958. Things that happen from inception to birth that make for defects in babies born in this country.

Rainwater, Lee, and Karol Kane Weinstein. *And the Poor Get Children*. Chicago: Quadrangle Books, 1960. The results of depth interviews with working-class people in the United States.

Read, Grantly Dick. *Childbirth Without Fear: The Principle and Practice of Natural Childbirth*. 2nd rev. ed. New York: Harper & Bros., 1959. The work of a famous medical specialist and advocate of "natural" childbirth.

Riker, Audrey Palm, "Breastfeeding." *Public Affairs Pamphlet* No. 353S. New York, 1964. A discussion of advantages, problems, and methods.

Spock, Benjamin. *Baby and Child Care*. Rev. ed. New York: Pocket Books, 1957. A sound and popular work. Handy for reference.

XVII: *Adoption*

Cady, Ernest and Frances. *How to Adopt a Child*. New York: William Morrow and Co., 1956. A helpful discussion of each step.

LeShan, Eda J., "You and Your Adopted Child." *Public Affairs Pamphlet* No. 274. New York, 1959. A guide to relations between parents and adopted children.

Lockridge, Frances. *Adopting a Child*. New York: Greenberg, 1947. The coauthor of the Mr. and Mrs. North mystery stories discusses the problems and opportunities in adoption.

Smith, I. Evelyn, ed. *Readings in Adoption*. New York: Philosophical Library, 1963.

XVIII: *The Single Parent*

Brown, Helen Gurley. *Sex and the Single Girl*. New York: Random House, 1962. A frank treatment.

Butcher, Ruth L., and Marion O. Robinson, "The Unmarried Mother." *Public Affairs Pamphlet* No. 282. New York, 1959. Unwed pregnancy as a personal, family, and social problem.

Despert, J. Louis. *Children of Divorce*. Garden City, N. Y.: Doubleday & Co., 1953. A specialist in child psychiatry tells how children react to divorce. Simply written with specific examples.

Thorman, George, "Broken Homes." *Public Affairs Pamphlet* No. 135. New York, 1958. A discussion of consequences and of what can be done to ameliorate them.

Vincent, Clark E. *Unmarried Mothers*. New York: Free Press, 1962. A careful survey and analysis.

Wolf, Anna W. M., and Lucille Stein, "The One-Parent Family." *Public Affairs Pamphlet* No. 287. New York, 1959. Should a lone parent try to be both mother and father to children? How does one explain separation or divorce? Is a boarding school the answer?

XIX: *The Post-Child Family*

Applebaum, Stella, and Nadina Kavinoky, "Understanding Your Menopause." *Public Affairs Pamphlet* No. 243. New York, 1959. A practical effort to distinguish facts from folklore and fancies.

Barron, Milton L. *The Aging American: An Introduction to Social Gerontology and Geriatrics.* New York: Thomas Y. Crowell Co., 1961. A comprehensive and readable text on problems of aging, retirement, and the post-child family.

Greeley, Ogden, "Private Nursing Homes: Their Role in the Care of the Aged." *Public Affairs Pamphlet* No. 298. New York, 1960. Such homes often furnish services that cannot be done so well in the home of a son or daughter.

McKinney, John C., and Frank T. de Vyver, eds. *Aging and Social Policy.* New York: Appleton-Century-Crofts, 1966. Twelve contributors summarize recent research findings.

Neisser, Edith G., "How to Be a Good Mother-in-Law and Grandmother." *Public Affairs Pamphlet* No. 174. New York, 1959. How to cope with such problems as "emotional unemployment." How grandmothers can and cannot help.

Ogg, Elizabeth, "When Parents Grow Old." *Public Affairs Pamphlet* No. 208. New York, 1958. How to help older people to live happily. How to avoid conflict or resentment on the part of either parents or children.

Stern, Edith M., "A Full Life After 65." *Public Affairs Pamphlet* No. 347. New York, 1963. A careful and popular summary.

Part Five: Family Crises

XX: *Illness, Disability, Unemployment, War Service*

Angell, Robert C. *The Family Encounters the Depression.* New York: Charles Scribner's Sons, 1936. A noted study of the family during a grave crisis.

Applebaum, Stella B., "Your Family's Health." *Public Affairs Pamphlet* No. 261. New York, 1958. Suggestions for a family health program of medical care, dental care, immunization, nutrition, and home safety.

Block, Irvin, "How to Get Good Medical Care." *Public Affairs Pamphlet* No. 368. New York, 1965. Discussion of problems with practical suggestions.

Doyle, Kathleen Cassidy, "When Mental Illness Strikes." *Public Affairs Pamphlet* No. 172. New York, 1959. Concise digest of what families need to know about emotional breakdowns.

Hart, Evelyn, "Homemaker Services for Families and Individuals." *Public Affairs Pamphlet* No. 371. New York, 1965. How to meet a short or continuing emergency.

Hill, Reuben. *Families Under Stress: Adjustment to the Crises of War Separation and Reunion.* New York: Harper & Bros., 1949. A study of a group of Iowa families of which the husband served in the armed forces during World War II.

Johnson, Harry J., "Your Health Is Your Business." *Public Affairs Pamphlet* No. 372. New York, 1965. A physician writes practical hints in popular terms.

Mann, Marty. *New Primer on Alcoholism.* New York: Rinehart & Co., 1958. A competent and popular discussion written by the executive director of the National Council on Alcoholism.

Ogg, Elizabeth, "When a Family Faces Cancer." *Public Affairs Pamphlet* No. 286. New York, 1959. A summary of new experiences with the treatment of cancer. How the family can help.

Ogg, Elizabeth, "When a Family Faces Stress." *Public Affairs Pamphlet* No. 341. New York, 1963. The services of family agencies described and discussed.

Richman, T. Lefoy, "Venereal Disease: Old Plague—New Challenge." *Public Affairs Pamphlet* No. 292. New York, 1960. Never simple, the VD challenge is now complicated by changes in public attitudes and sex behavior in spite of more effective cures.

Waller, Willard. *The Veteran Comes Back.* New York: Dryden Press, 1944. Pp. 83–86, 130–142, 284–291. A war veteran sociologist examines the war veteran's special family problems.

XXI: *Separation, Annulment, Desertion, Divorce, Bereavement*

Bossard, James H. S., and Eleanor S. Boll. *Why Marriages Go Wrong.* New York: Ronald Press, 1958. A sociological study of the hazards of marriage and how to overcome them.

Bowman, LeRoy. *The American Funeral: A Study in Guilt, Extravagance, and Sublimity.* Washington, D. C.: Public Affairs Press, 1959. An objective study of an experience for which few American· families are prepared.

Duvall, Evelyn and Sylvanus, "Saving Your Marriage." *Public Affairs Pamphlet* No. 213. New York, 1959. A discussion for the use of those to whom a troubled husband or wife may turn for advice.

Feifel, Herman, ed. *The Meaning of Death.* New York: McGraw-Hill Book Co., 1960. A symposium by specialists in medicine, psychiatry, psychology, physiology, psychoanalysis, philosophy, anthropology, religion, art, and literature.

Goode, William Josiah. *After Divorce*. Glencoe, Ill.: Free Press, 1956. A survey of the consequences of divorce to the couple, their children, their friends and relatives, and their next mates.

Gorer, Geoffrey. *Death, Grief and Mourning*. New York: Doubleday & Co., 1965. A well-written sociological analysis.

Ogg, Elizabeth, "Divorce." *Public Affairs Pamphlet* No. 380. New York, 1965. Helpful advice to any concerned with any stage of a marital break-up.

Osborne, Ernest G., "When You Lose a Loved One." *Public Affairs Pamphlet* No. 269. New York, 1958. Comfort and aid to families faced by the death of a loved one.

Part Six: Conclusion

XXII: *Scientific Research*

Goode, William Josiah, "The Sociology of the Family." In: R. K. Merton, Leonard Broom, and Leonard S. Cottrell, Jr., eds. *Sociology Today, Problems and Prospects*. New York: Basic Books, 1959. Pp. 178–196. An essay on "horizons in family theory."

Himelhoch, Jerome, and Sylvia Fleis Fava, eds. *Sexual Behavior in American Society*. New York: W. W. Norton & Co., 1955. Chapters 7–11 reconsider the research design and statistical methods used in the two Kinsey reports.

Winch, Robert F., "Marriage and the Family." In: J. B. Gittler, ed. *Review of Sociology: Analysis of a Decade*. New York: John Wiley & Sons, 1957. Chapter 11. Critical summary of family research in the 1945–55 period.

XXIII: *The Happy Family*

Bossard, James H. S. *Parent and Child: Studies in Family Behavior*. Philadelphia: University of Pennsylvania Press, 1953. If behavior is learned and experience is the teacher, then "a major part of the study of personality formation is the study of the minutiae of living."

Farber, Seymour M., Piero Mustacchi, and Roger H. L. Wilson. *The Family's Search for Survival*. New York: McGraw-Hill Book Co., 1965. A symposium of specialists from many disciplines focused on today's family problems.

Josselyn, Irene M. *The Happy Child*. New York: Random House, 1955. A psychoanalytic discussion.

Levy, John, and Ruth Munroe. *The Happy Family*. New York: Alfred A. Knopf, 1938. A wise and popular book about the problems and satisfactions of family life.